Application of Anti-manipulation Law to EU Wholesale Energy Markets and Its Interplay with EU Competition Law

Energy and Environmental Law and Policy Series

VOLUME 35

Editor

General Editor: Professor Kurt Deketelaere, Professor of Law, University of Leuven, Belgium; Honorary Professor of Law, University of Dundee, UK; Honorary Chief of Staff, Flemish Government; Secretary-General, League of European Research Universities (LERU), Belgium. Kurt's CV – see www.kurtdeketelaere/en/kurt.

Introduction

Environmental protection and energy efficiency/security are important societal challenges. In order to tackle them, policy and legal frameworks are developed at national, regional and global level. Through study and best practices development, the challenges will prove to be solvable.

Contents/Subjects

Environment/Nature/Energy/Climate.

Objective

The aim of this series is to publish works of excellent quality that focus on the study of energy and environmental policy. Through this series the editors:

- contribute to the improvement of the quality of energy/environmental law and policy in general and environmental quality and energy efficiency in particular; increase the access to environmental and energy information for academics, non-governmental organizations, government institutions, and business; and
- facilitate cooperation between academic and non-academic communities in the field of energy and environmental law and policy throughout the world.

Readership

Academics and practitioners in environmental and energy matters.

The titles published in this series are listed at the end of this volume.

Application of Anti-manipulation Law to EU Wholesale Energy Markets and Its Interplay with EU Competition Law

Huseyin Cagri Corlu

Wolters Kluwer

Published by:
Kluwer Law International B.V.
PO Box 316
2400 AH Alphen aan den Rijn
The Netherlands
E-mail: international-sales@wolterskluwer.com
Website: lrus.wolterskluwer.com

Sold and distributed in North, Central and South America by:
Wolters Kluwer Legal & Regulatory U.S.
7201 McKinney Circle
Frederick, MD 21704
United States of America
Email: customer.service@wolterskluwer.com

Sold and distributed in all other countries by:
Air Business Subscriptions
Rockwood House
Haywards Heath
West Sussex
RH16 3DH
United Kingdom
Email: international-customerservice@wolterskluwer.com

ISBN 978-90-411-9603-3

e-Book: ISBN 978-90-411-9604-0
web-PDF: ISBN 978-90-411-9605-7

Table of Contents

Foreword

It is a great honour to have been given the chance to write this foreword after having supervised the PhD of Dr Huseyin Cagri Corlu on the topic of 'The Application of Anti-manipulation Law to EU Wholesale Energy Markets and Its Interplay with EU Competition Law'. Huseyin was a charismatic and exceptional student to supervise, and he proved this by defending the PhD in an excellent way which resulted in him being awarded it with no corrections, i.e., with distinction (equivalent to *summa cum laude*).

This book draws from the assertion of the European Commission that competition is a prerequisite for the establishment of an integrated community-wide energy market and security of supply. It shows that the Commission strived to achieve this via the adoption of a series of regulatory packages and via the extensive use of competition law (e.g., Article 9 of 1/2003 Regulation, Commitment Decisions procedure) as well as by undertaking initiatives such as an investigation in the EU energy sectors to identify the factors that hamper the establishment of a well-functioning, competitive, EU-wide energy market. However, as the author discusses, the 2007 Energy Sector Inquiry results led to adoption of several regulatory measures including, *inter alia,* the adoption of REMIT 2011. The book extensively discusses and analyses REMIT with a specific focus on the prohibition of market manipulation. As the adoption of REMIT does not preclude the jurisdiction of the European Commission under EU competition law, the book strives to analyse the factors and circumstances that determine when and what market conduct can be subject to REMIT or EU Competition Law and in case of an overlap, what course of action should be followed without giving effect to issues of double jeopardy. Not least, it analyses and discusses in detail the relevant US and EU case laws and provides proposals to mitigate the uncertainties posed by REMIT.

The analysis is thorough and the research conducted exhaustive. This book will be a valuable tool to various readership audiences, ranging from research students in energy law, to legal practitioners, academics and members of the judiciary who will find in it an invaluable tool to help them interpret various competition law aspects of wholesale energy markets and further understand and help the further shaping of the law in this fascinating yet complex field.

Dr Kyriaki Noussia
Senior Lecturer in Law, University of Exeter, Law School
Exeter, Devon, 27 March 2018

Preface

Of the findings, the European Commission established in its report on Energy Sector Inquiry, market manipulation constituted a major concern for the functioning and integrity of EU energy sectors. The Commission argued that the responsibility for high prices in wholesale energy markets could be attributed to manipulative practices of energy incumbents and the trust in the operation of operation of sector was largely compromised, due to these practices. Remedies, EU competition law provided, were considered as insufficient to resolve these shortcomings and thus should be supplemented with regulatory-based tools. The findings of the Energy Sector Inquiry and subsequent consultation documents by multiple EU institutions paved the way for the adoption of the Regulation on wholesale energy market integrity and transparency, REMIT, which incorporated into an anti-manipulation rule, specifically designed to prohibit and prosecute manipulative practices in EU wholesale energy markets. Nevertheless, as EU case law on market manipulation has yet to develop and there are uncertainties with respect to the concept of market manipulation. Furthermore REMIT does not preclude the jurisdiction of EU competition law, questions arise as to the scope and the extent of the application of this prohibition. Throughout its chapters, this book explores the scope of and the case law on market manipulation to determine what types of market practices are regarded as manipulative and thus prohibited under anti-manipulation rules. It also focuses on the interplay between REMIT and EU competition law and evaluates factors and circumstances that determine when and what market misconduct can be subject to enforcement proceedings under both anti-manipulation and antitrust rules. As the development of a single, coherent, rulebook that can be relied upon by market participant is fundamental for the functioning of EU wholesale energy markets, the book, finally, provides proposals and measures that can mitigate and resolve the legal uncertainties regarding the regulatory framework REMIT established.

List of Abbreviations

ACER	Agency for the Cooperation of Energy Regulators
AEP	Association of Energy Producers
BCA	Belgian Competition Authority
BCR	Bid Cost Recovery
BOM	Balance of Month
CAISO	California Independent System Operator
CBOT	Chicago Bureau of Trade
CCG	Constellation Energy Commodities Group
CCGT	Combined Cycle Gas Turbine
CCP	Central Clearing Part
CEA	Commodity Exchange Act
CES	Competitive Energy Services
CESR	Committee of European Securities Regulators
CFD	Contract for Difference
CFMA	Commodity Futures Modernisation Act
CFTC	Commodity Futures Trading Commission
CJEU	European Union Court of Justice
COB	California Oregon Border
CRRs	Congestion Revenue Rights
CWE	Central Western Europe
DAM	Day-Ahead Market
DALRP	Day-Ahead Load Response Program
DoJ	Department of Justice
DSO	Distribution System Operators

ECHR	European Convention for the Protection of Human Rights and Fundamental Freedoms
EEX	European Energy Exchange
ELCON	Electricity Consumers Resource Council
EMIR	European Market Infrastructure Regulation
EPAct	Energy Policy Act
ERGEG	European Regulators' Group for Electricity and Gas
ESMA	European Securities and Markets Authority
EU	European Union
EURIBOR	Euro Interbank Offered Rate
FERC	Federal Energy Regulatory Commission
FTC	Federal Trade Commission
FTR	Financial Transmission Rights
GC	European General Court
GT	Gas Turbine
HHI	Herfindahl-Hirschman Index
HPL	Houston Gas Pipeline
HSC	Houston Ship Channel
ICA	Italian Competition Authority
ICE	InterContinental Exchange
IFERC	Platts Inside FERC
IOSCO	International Organisation of Securities Commissions
ISO-NE	New England Independent System Operator
JPMVEC	J.P. Morgan Ventures Energy Corporation
LDES	Louis Dreyfus Energy Services L.P.
LIBOR	London Interbank Offered Rate
LMPs	Locational Marginal Prices
LNG	Liquefied Natural Gas
MAD 2003	Directive 2003/6/EC of the European Parliament and of the Council of 28 January 2003 on insider dealing and market manipulation
MAD 2014	Directive 2014/57/EU of the European Parliament and of the Council of 16 April 2014 on criminal sanctions for market abuse
MIDC	Mid-Columbia
MiFIR	Regulation (EU) No 600/2014 of the European Parliament and of the Council of 15 May 2014 on markets in financial instruments and amending Regulation

MiFID 2004	Directive 2004/39/EC of the European Parliament and of the Council of 21 April 2004 on markets in financial instruments amending Council Directives 85/611/EEC and 93/6/EEC and Directive 2000/12/EC of the European Parliament and of the Council and repealing Council Directive 93/22/EEC OJ L 145, (30 April 2004)
MiFID 2014	Directive 2014/65/EU of the European Parliament and of the Council of 15 May 2014 on markets in financial instruments and amending Directive 2002/92/EC and Directive 2011/61/EU (recast), [2014] OJ L173/348
MISO	Midcontinent Independent System Operator
MLSA	Marginal Loss Surplus Allocation
MMBTU	Million British Thermal Unit
MTF	Multilateral Trading Facilities
MOU	Memorandum of Understanding
NBP	National Balancing Point
NCG	NetConnect Germany
NGA	Natural Gas Act
NGI	Natural Gas Intelligence
NP	North Path
NYISO	New York Independent System Operator
NYMEX	New York Mercantile Exchange
OFGEM	Office of Gas and Electricity Markets
OMX	Nasdaq Commodities Exchange
OTC	Over-The-Counter
OTF	Organised Trading Facilities
PPATs	Persons Professionally Arranging Transactions
PSI	Pivotal Supplier Index
PV	Palo Vere
REMIT	Regulation on Wholesale Energy Market Integrity and Transparency
RSI	Residual Supplier Index
RTM	Real Time Market
SCA	Spanish Competition Authority
SEC	Security Exchange Commission
SEA	Securities Exchange Act
SIs	Systemic Internalisers
SoCAL	Southern California
SP	South Path

SPDCs	Significant Price Discovery Contracts
SPPC	Sierra Pacific Power Company
TGPNA	Total Gas & Power North America, Inc.
TFEU	Treaty on the Functioning of the European Union
TSO	Transmission System Operator
TTF	Title Transfer Facility
UTC	Up-To-Congestion transactions
WTI	West Texas Intermediate Crude Oil

List of Figures

Acknowledgements

This book is derived from my PhD thesis that I completed in University of Exeter, Law School.

Thinking of people to whom I would like to express my gratitude in getting this work done provides a perfect opportunity for me to recall memories, both enjoyable and stressful, which I have accumulated throughout my studies. Doing PhD was not an easy task, even for a person who suffers an intellectual hunger. The feeling of satisfaction acquired from a new knowledge had often been supressed by upcoming deadlines and extent of work that needs to be done. Knowing that there was no one but you who can pull your research together, continuously, yet still unexpectedly, hit you with feelings of loneliness. Every motivation you derive from your environment was fundamental, in finding a push during the darkest hours of this loneliness.

Fortunately, I am blessed with plenty of people who are very generous in sharing their friendship, guidance and love. I would like to express my special gratitude to Dr Kyriaki Noussia, Senior Lecturer in Law at the Law School of the University of Exeter, for all the help and motivation she has provided in getting this study together. I feel very lucky to have her as my supervisor. Without her, I would have had more sleepless nights. I would also like to extend my thanks to my second supervisor, Professor Radek Stech and Professor Matthew Cole for their valuable comments and recommendations.

I am grateful to my previous supervisors Professors Mel Kenny and Robert Lee for their guidance. Even though change of supervisors is considered as the worst nightmare, a PhD student would have in his/her studies, my experience with my previous supervisors proved otherwise. I benefitted deeply from each of them and their contribution to the content and the structure of my research topics was immense.

Many thanks go to my landlady, Janettja Longyear, who assisted me considerably with her proofreading and valuable feedback and helped me mould this work in a more coherent way.

I would like to express my sincerest gratitude to the Turkish Republic which, since its very founding, has been the best at financing students coming from lower and middle classes of the society.

I am also honoured to mention the following people who, in pursuing my studies, provided me invaluable assistance for which I am deeply grateful; Professor Melda Sur, Professor Muhammed Ozekes, Professor Christiana Ochoa, Professor Joseph L. Hoffmann, Mr Nevzat Corlu, Mr Halil Corlu, Mr Abdullah Calis, Mr Bulent Kilinc, Mr Muhittin Ertugrul Erturk, Muhterem Dilbirliği and Mehmet Ali Bulut.

My life in Exeter was filled with joy, laughter and unforgettable moments that will warm my heart for the rest of my life. I have been accompanied with people whose friendship were priceless and will always be remembered. I thank everybody I know without any reservation.

Of all the things that have motivated me, nothing is as more effective as the compliment: 'We are proud of you', I heard from my parents, Ali and Havva Corlu. Their everlasting trust and unconditional love mean the world to me. I have no words eloquent enough to express my gratitude for all they have done for me and thus I dedicate this book to them. Mom and dad, thank you very much.

Last, but not least, I would like to thank my beautiful wife, Zeynep Busra, whose love gave me strength and determination in pursuing my goals. She is my dearest and my eternal love.

Introduction

I GENERAL

Energy has always been one of the main instruments driving the political environment of the European continent. It was at the centre of the negotiations after World War II, and the organisation founded thereafter was named 'the European Community of Steel and Coal'[1] explicitly signifying the importance of the management of European energy resources. The political and economic integration objectives later expanded to cover other fields and markets, and the importance of energy in European integration started decreasing, due to the importation of new energy resources such as oil and natural gas which operated closely in relation to geopolitical dimensions. There were several factors that gave rise to concerns about the sustainability, security and reliability of these products. Europe lacked the domestic energy resources to meet its energy demands and had been relying heavily on external suppliers. The distances between resource-endowed countries and demand centres as well as the political volatility in some of the supplier and transit countries put energy trade issues into a more political context that was outside the Community's integration competences. This resulted in national energy markets being managed through state-owned, vertically integrated companies which were active in all areas of energy business with exclusive rights related to production, supply, transmission and distribution of energy products.

After the discovery of new energy reserves which alleviated the prospect that scarce energy resources as well as the 1987 Single European Act[2] which embraced the policy of creating a single European market and required the abolishment of state-owned monopolies, the structure of European energy markets started to change. Ever since 1990, when the first directive[3] that set forth rules on transparency in electricity

1. Treaty establishing the European Coal and Steel Community (Paris, 18 Apr. 1951).
2. Single European Act (Luxembourg, 1986).
3. Council Directive 1990/377/EEC of 29 Jun. 1990 concerning a Community procedure to improve the transparency of gas and electricity prices charged to industrial end-users, OJ L 185, 17 Jul. 1990.

and natural gas prices was adopted, EU energy markets have been subject to continuous sets of directives and regulations that aim at, *inter alia*, ensuring sustainability, security and competitiveness in energy supplies in and to the EU.[4] Competitive energy markets, in which prices for energy products are determined on the basis of market forces, were considered fundamental for a secure and sustainable supply of energy products.

Several regulatory and competition mechanisms were employed to pursue these energy policy objectives.[5] Vertically integrated companies, which had been designated as national monopolies and dominated national energy markets, were dismantled through different sets of unbundling measures[6] that separated network activities and transmission business from energy production and supply. The regime for the use of energy transmission networks was determined on the basis of third-party access rights requiring transmission system operators to provide non-discriminatory transmission service to all market participants who wish to transport their supplies through relevant transmission networks.[7] The European Commission also actively enforced its authority under Articles 101 and 102 and the Merger Regulation.[8]

4. Throughout the EU's liberalisation agenda, three sets of regulatory packages, establishing rules for natural gas and electricity, were adopted. The first package, in 1996, consisted of two directives: Directive 96/92/EC of the European Parliament and of the Council of 19 Dec. 1996 concerning common rules for the internal market in electricity OJ L 27, 30 Jan. 1997; Directive 98/30/EC of the European Parliament and of the Council of 22 Jun. 1998 concerning common rules for the internal market in natural gas OJ L 204, 21 Jul. 1998. The second package involved: Directive 2003/54/EC of the European Parliament and of the Council of 26 Jun. 2003 concerning common rules for the internal market in electricity and repealing Directive 96/92/EC, OJ L 176, 15 Jul. 2003; Directive 2003/55/EC of the European Parliament and of the Council of 26 Jun. 2003 concerning common rules for the internal market in natural gas and repealing Directive 98/30/EC OJ L 176, 15 Jul. 2003; Regulation (EC) No 1228/2003 of the European Parliament and of the Council of 26 Jun. 2003 on conditions for access to the network for cross-border exchanges in electricity, OJ L 176, 15 Jul. 2003; Regulation (EC) No 1775/2005 of the European Parliament and of the Council of 28 Sept. 2005 on conditions for access to the natural gas transmission networks OJ L 289 3 Nov. 2005. Finally, the third package, which repealed the second package and is currently in force, was introduced in 2009, comprising: Directive 2009/73/EC of the European Parliament and of the Council of 13 Jul. 2009 concerning common rules for the internal market in natural gas; Directive 2009/72/EC of the European Parliament and of the Council of 13 Jul. 2009 concerning common rules for the internal market in electricity; Regulation (EC) 2009/715 on conditions for access to natural gas transmission networks; Regulation (EC) 2009/714 on conditions for access to the network for cross-border exchanges in electricity.
5. For the development of regulatory and competition mechanisms applied to EU energy markets, *see* Peter D. Cameron, *Competition in Energy Market: Law and Regulation in the European Union* (2nd ed., OUP 2007); Jonathan Faull & Ali Nikpay (eds), *The EC Law of Competition*, 1361–1473 (OUP 2007); Bram Delvauz et al., (eds), *EU Energy Law and Policy Issues* (Intersentia 2013); Angus Johnston & Guy Block, *EU Energy Law* (OUP 2012); Francois Leveque, *Antitrust Enforcement in the Electricity and Gas Industries: Problems and Solutions for the EU* 19/5 The Electricity Journal 27 (2006).
6. The Third Energy Package provides three models for the structure and management of transmission system operators: Ownership Unbundling, Independent System Operator, Independent Transmission Operator. *See* Directives 2009/72/EC and 2009/73/EC. *See* Christopher Jones (ed.), *The Internal Energy Market: The Third Liberalisation Package* (3rd ed., Claeys & Casteels 2014).
7. Transmission business is a natural monopoly and the duplication of transmission networks is not economically feasible. Therefore, the undistorted third-party access to the existing

Continuous liberalisation of energy markets resulted in alterations in market designs. In electricity, the effective enforcement of EU regulations and third-party access regimes across the EU under liberalisation packages and electricity network codes such as capacity allocation and congestion management (CACM) mechanisms[9] and requirements for grid connection of generators,[10] led to a convergence of market structures among Member States.[11] The majority of electricity markets in the EU have been designed as energy-only markets where electricity supply has been carried out in day-ahead and intraday markets and the balancing of network systems has been secured through balancing markets.[12] Day-ahead and intraday markets are spot markets, in which market participants bid and offer their electricity supply and demand with respective prices connected to them. In balancing markets, transmission system operators increase or decrease electricity supply and/or demand to ensure system reliability and security, through market-based mechanisms.

In natural gas, the liberalisation packages sought to introduce entry-exit zones and hub-based trading.[13] Accordingly, several zones and hubs were established on the basis of energy consumption and the availability of transmission networks. The functioning and operability of these zones were later regulated under gas network codes.[14] Trading of natural gas was projected to take place in these hubs with the introduction and increased use of standardised short-term contracts such as 'Within-day', 'Day-Ahead', 'Balance of Week', 'Weekend' and 'Working Days Next Week'.[15]

---

transmission infrastructure is a prerequisite for the introduction of competition into energy markets. *See also* Alexander Schaub, *Competition Policy and Liberalisation of Energy Markets*, 4 (Speech At European Utilities Circle 2000) http://ec.europa.eu/competition/speeches/text/sp2000_023_en.pdf (accessed 29 Jun. 2017); Philip Lowe, *Effective Unbundling of Energy Transmission Networks: Lessons Learned from the Energy Sector Inquiry* 1 Competition Policy Newsletter 23 (2007); Adrien de Hauteclocque & Kim Talus, *Third Party Access: A Comparative Study on Access Regimes in EU Electricity Grids and Natural Gas Pipelines* 9/3 OGEL 1 (2011).

8. Council Regulation (EC) No 139/2004 of 20 Jan. 2004 on the control of concentrations between undertakings (the EC Merger Regulation) [2004] OJ L24/1.
9. Commission Regulation (EU) 2015/1222 of 24 Jul. 2015 establishing a guideline on capacity allocation and congestion management [2015] OJ L197/24.
10. Commission Regulation (EU) 2016/631 of 14 Apr. 2016 establishing a network code on requirements for grid connection of generators [2016] OJ L112/1.
11. Francisco Enrique Gonzales-Diaz, *EU Policy on Capacity Mechanisms*, in Leigh Hancher, Adrien De Hauteclocque & Malgorzata Sadowska (eds), *Capacity Mechanisms in the EU Energy Market: Law, Policy, and Economics* 3 (OUP 2015).
12. Petri Mantysaari, *EU Electricity Trade Law: The Legal Tools of Electricity Producers in the Internal Electricity Market* 13 (Springer 2015).
13. Regulation (EC) 2009/715. *See also* Katja Yafimava, *The EU Third Package for Gas and the Gas Target Model: Major Contentious Issues Inside and Outside the EU* OIES Paper: NG 75 3 (2013).
14. *See* Commission Regulation (EU) No 984/2013 of 14 Oct. 2013 establishing a Network Code on Capacity Allocation Mechanisms in Gas Transmission Systems and supplementing Regulation (EC) No 715/2009 of the European Parliament and of the Council [2013] OJ L273/5; Commission Regulation (EU) No 312/2014 of 26 Mar. 2014 establishing a Network Code on Gas Balancing of Transmission Networks [2014] OJ L91/15; Commission Regulation (EU) 2015/703 of 30 Apr. 2015 establishing a network code on interoperability and data exchange rules [2015] OJ L113/13.
15. Patrick Heather, *The Evolution and Functioning of the Traded Gas Market in Britain* OIES Paper: NG 44 7 (2010).

Within-day and day-ahead markets (DAMs) were regarded as balancing mechanisms through which the transmission system operators ensure system security.[16]

The advent of financial energy derivatives also introduced major ramifications to the functioning of EU energy markets. Trading of futures,[17] options,[18] swaps[19] and other contracts provided several risk management mechanisms through which energy market participants can hedge their financial risks. The availability of financial instruments related to the fundamentals of energy markets also resulted in new actors engaging in speculative trading, deriving profits from price arbitrage. These contracts are traded in several multilateral and organised trading platforms either through exchanges in which market operators take responsibility for counterparty risks or through brokers who only contribute the conclusion of agreements without being involved in the financial risks inherent to them.

After the publication of the Energy Sector Inquiry in 2007[20] and several consultation documents from the Committee of European Securities Regulators (CESR) and the European Regulators' Group for Electricity and Gas (ERGEG)[21] and the European Commission,[22] which recommended the adoption of a tailor-made legal framework to govern and ensure competitive trading in EU wholesale energy products, in 2011, the EU adopted the 'Regulation on Wholesale Energy Market Integrity and Transparency' (hereinafter REMIT).[23] REMIT applies to both electricity and natural gas wholesale markets and does not provide a distinction based on hub-based, spot market or

16. Article 7, Commission Regulation (EU) No 312/2014 of 26 Mar. 2014 establishing a Network Code on Gas Balancing of Transmission Networks [2014] OJ L91/15.
17. Futures are standardised contracts whose delivery date, location, quality, and quantity are determined by market places, such as exchanges. For example a NYMEX NG Futures Contract means a sale or buy of 10,000 million British thermal unit (mmBtu) to be delivered at Henry Hub in Louisiana. NYMEX Exchange Rulebook 220 Henry Hub Natural Gas Futures http://www.cmegroup.com/rulebook/NYMEX/2/220.pdf (accessed 29 Jun. 2017).
18. Options are agreements, according to which paying a fixed price, called a 'premium', the buyer of the agreement receives rights but not obligations to receive or make delivery of a certain product at certain time period at a certain price. For example, in an option, trader A, the buyer of an option contract, pays a premium, P, to trader B, the seller, in return for a right, but not an obligation, to deliver a certain amount of product X at price Y, at a certain expiration day. When the expiration day comes, if the market price for product X is lower than Y, trader A profits from this option contract.
19. Swaps are agreements between two parties who exchange price risks in relation to certain products over a determined time period. For example, in a swap agreement, trader A and trader B enter into an agreement, according to which A pays to B, the market price for product X, while trader B pays to A the market price for product Y for a certain period of time. The trader who receives more than it pays profits from this swap agreement.
20. Communication from the European Commission (COM(2006) 851 Final), 'the Inquiry pursuant to Article 17 of Regulation (EC) No 1/2003 into the European gas and electricity sectors' (hereinafter 'the Inquiry').
21. Committee of European Securities Regulators and the European Regulators' Group for Electricity and Gas, 'CESR and ERGEG advice to the European Commission in the context of the Third Energy Package; Response to Question F.20' (Market Abuse, October 2008) (hereinafter CESR and ERGEG).
22. European Commission Staff Working Document Impact Assessment Accompanying Document to the Proposal for a Regulation of the European Parliament and of the Council on energy market integrity and transparency COM(2010) (REMIT Impact Assessment).
23. Regulation (EU) No 1227/2011 of the European Parliament and of the Council of 25 Oct. 2011 on wholesale energy market integrity and transparency.

bilateral trading. Its prohibitions on market manipulation and insider trading are applicable to national markets, irrespective of the level of market liberalisation. Nevertheless, in practice, these types of practices often take place in established trading platforms in which market participants simultaneously engage in buying and selling orders to earn profit from either their output or price arbitrage. Prices in these markets are set through the aggregation of bids and offers by market participants, and each transaction has a direct impact on these market prices. Therefore REMIT's rules on market manipulation and insider trading are particularly relevant for trading in spot markets for electricity and hubs for natural gas.

This does not mean that REMIT is inapplicable to bilateral wholesale electricity and natural gas transactions. These trades can also be subject to anti-manipulation and insider trading proceedings, if they are connected to trades in electricity spot markets and natural gas hubs and are part of a scheme that aims at deriving profits from cross-market price relations. This is increasingly relevant with the use of prices that are set in electricity spot markets or natural gas hubs as benchmarks in bilateral transactions are growing.

The convergence of national natural gas markets fell behind that of EU electricity markets. Even though several trading hubs were established, only the northwestern hubs have been relatively active in natural gas trading. The majority of hub-based trading takes place in two national hubs, National Balancing Point (NBP) in the United Kingdom (UK) and Title Transfer Facility (TTF) in the Netherlands.[24] The share of exchange-traded natural gas contracts in these hubs reaches respectively 49% and 25% of overall traded natural gas volumes and the rest is carried out through Over-The-Counter (OTC) trading.[25] The NBP and the TTF have been followed by other active hubs, such as the NetConnect Germany (NCG) and Gaspool in Germany, Zeebrugge in Belgium, PEG Nord in France.[26] Other hubs, such as those AOC in Spain, VPGS in Poland, and GTF in Denmark have been inactive.[27]

The reasons that led to different levels of liquidity at hub-based trading vary across the EU. In hubs, where the liquidity in trading of natural gas products is high, liberalisation of national natural gas markets predates the EU's liberalisation packages. For example, in the UK, despite several sectoral and financial upheavals,[28] the NBP has been active in natural gas trading since the 1990s, long before hub-based trading was introduced into EU directives and regulations, while in other Member States, such as in the Baltic regions, Ireland, Portugal and Romania, natural gas hubs have yet to be developed.[29] Furthermore, it is not possible to discuss a homogenous natural gas market across the Member States. EU natural gas markets are mostly import-based,

24. European Commission, *Quarterly Report on European Gas Markets* 9/1 Market Observatory for Energy 24 (2015).
25. *Ibid.*
26. Dr Albrecht Wagner, *Functioning of European Gas Wholesale Markets* 5 (Wagner, Elbling & Company Management Advisors, Quantitative Study, Brussels 15 May 2014).
27. Patrick Heather, *The Evolution of European Traded Gas Hubs* OIES Paper: NG 104 18 (2015).
28. Such as the collapse of Enron in 2001 and the near collapse of Eastern Gas Markets in 2002 which caused the withdrawal of several US-based market participants from trading in the NBP. *See* Patrick Heather, 35 (2010).
29. Patrick Heather, 18 (2015).

supplying a major part of their natural gas demand from external resources[30] and the market for imported natural gas is far from competitive.[31] National priorities as to natural gas supply also reflect to security of supply concerns rather than Union-wide policies. While some Member States enjoy competition in energy supply with balanced energy mix,[32] abundant market players[33] and diversified energy supplies from multiple resources,[34] others are greatly vulnerable to energy shortages due to their insufficient fixed infrastructure and dependency on a single energy supplier.[35] It is very difficult to introduce efficient competitive hub-based trading in a national natural gas market with insufficient network capacity, limited market participants who are dependent on limited external suppliers. Dimensions in market conditions between Member States result in differences in the functioning of national natural gas markets.

Since spot market trading in electricity markets is more prevalent via the development of energy-only markets across the EU and hub-based trading is generally concentrated in Northwestern Europe in the NBP and the TTF, REMIT and its anti-manipulation and insider trading prohibitions will initially be more effective in electricity markets. The extent that REMIT applies to natural gas markets depends on the functioning and the development of hub-based trading in the EU. It is not possible to discuss an established hub-based market mechanism across the EU and case law on market manipulation in EU natural gas markets has yet to develop. Therefore, in the EU context, the main focus of this book is on electricity markets and practices that perpetrators employ to manipulate these markets. The book also discusses market

30. In 2015, indigenous natural gas production accounted for only 27% of gas supply in the EU. BP Statistical Review of World Energy (65th edn, June 2016).
31. The share of the two biggest natural gas suppliers, Russia and Norway, exceeds 76% of overall imported natural gas in the EU. *Ibid.*, *see also* David A. Wood, *Natural Gas Imports to Europe: The Frontline of Competition between LNG and Pipeline Supplies* 36 Journal of Natural Gas Science and Engineering A1–A4 (2016).
32. In the United Kingdom, the share of natural gas in domestic electricity generation is less than 30% used in domestic electricity generation. The other energy resources in the UK's energy mix include, solid fuels with 39%, nuclear with 19%, renewables with 13% and others with 1%. In Lithuania, the share of natural gas in electricity generation is 58%, followed by renewables with 32% and others with 5%. It is important to note that Lithuania's dependency on Russian natural gas is 100%. *See* European Commission, *EU Energy Markets in 2014* (Luxembourg 2014).
33. In the UK, the share of the biggest six upstream producers of natural gas is limited to the field in the UK and Norwegian continental shelfs and only Centrica can be regarded as having an appreciable market power, holding 12% market share in the UK and 2% in the Norwegian continental shelf. OFGEM, 'State of the Market Assessment' 88 (2014). In Lithuania, on the other hand, the two biggest natural gas suppliers, *AB Lietuvos dujos* and *UAB Dujotekana*, serve 99% of natural gas sold to Lithuanian wholesale gas market and gas consumers, the National Commission for Energy Control and Prices (NCC), *Annual Report on Electricity and Natural Gas Markets of the Republic of Lithuania to the European Commission* 44 (2014).
34. For example, the UK natural gas markets are mostly competitive with diversified energy supplies, and high levels of liquidity. Natural gas is supplied from several resources including field on the UK and Norwegian continental shelf, LNGs from global gas fields as well as via interconnectors lining the UK with Belgium and Netherlands.
35. Some Baltic states and Bulgaria to which Russia is the sole natural gas supplier, appeared to be greatly vulnerable, during 2009 gas crisis, and longer cut offs resulted in deep economic depression and even humanitarian concerns as many people could not afford to heat their households in these countries. *See* Edward Christie, *Energy Vulnerability and EU-Russia Energy Relations* 5/2 Journal of Contemporary European Research 225 (2009). *See also* European Commission, *EU Energy Markets in 2014* (Luxembourg 2014).

manipulation in the natural gas sector. The relation between anti-manipulation rules and natural gas markets is evident in the United States (US) which had liberalised its natural gas markets long before the EU's liberalisation packages.[36] In its analysis on US case law on energy market manipulation, the book discusses manipulative practices in natural gas hubs in greater detail. However, in the EU context, the book does not address natural gas markets in the same way as it deals with electricity markets.

II REMIT AS A TAILOR-MADE LEGAL FRAMEWORK

Even though the EU's liberalisation of energy markets has not provided the same results in all Member States, the share of short-term energy products traded in organised trading platforms is increasing,[37] leading to new market entries and more market liquidity.[38] Hub-based pricing in energy contracts has become dominant across the EU,[39] while oil-price indexation has been in decrease for over ten years, available in remaining long-term supply contracts.[40] In electricity, convergence of market designs across the EU is more successful with the introduction of energy-only markets and market coupling.[41] The volume of electricity supplied through spot electricity markets and exchanges increases and prices set on the basis of merit orders in spot markets also determine those in OTC bilateral electricity contracts.[42]

The regulatory framework, before the adoption of REMIT, as shown in Figure I.1, had included only structural remedies including unbundling measures, transparency

36. Henry Hub has been an active natural gas market since the early 1980s. *See* Shi Xunpeng, *Development of Europe's Gas Hubs: Implications for East Asia* 357 (Natural Gas Industry 2016).
37. *Supra* note 24.
38. Dr Albrecht Wagner (2014). For example, 'churn rate', which is the number of trades taking place between the date that energy contract are issued and the date they are settled or delivered, is used to calculate the liquidity in energy markets. Accordingly, in markets where hub-based trading is developed, such as in the UK and the Netherlands, the churn rates are significantly higher than less-liberalised markets. *See* Patrick Heather, 35 (2010).
39. Patrick Heather, 12 (2015).
40. Even though oil-price indexation did not reflect demand and supply and market fundamentals in natural gas, long-term supply contracts often included such clauses for pricing due to the lack of efficient natural gas-based pricing mechanisms. *See ibid.*, 2; *see also* Jonathan P. Stern, *Continental European Long-Term Gas Contracts: Is a Transition Away from Oil Product-Linked Pricing Inevitable and Imminent? Oxford Institute for Energy Studies* (2009); Jonathan P. Stern & Howard V. Rogers, *The Transition to Hub-Based Gas Pricing in Continental Europe* (2011) *Citeseer.*
41. Market coupling is a process designed by the EU for the convergence of exchange-traded electricity prices on a regional basis. Accordingly, several regional electricity exchanges are integrated through an implicit cross-border allocation mechanism, allowing market participants from different regional markets to participate in coupled electricity markets. In these coupled markets, undertakings in a specific coupled market can bid in each day-ahead and intraday markets. The process resulted in the emergence of several coupled markets, such as: Central Western Europe (CWE), encompassing Austria, Belgium, Germany, the Netherlands, Switzerland; British Isles, the UK and Ireland; Northern Europe, Denmark, Estonia, Finland, Latvia, Lithuania, Norway, Sweden. For the full account about the market coupling process *see* http://www.acer.europa.eu/Electricity/Regional_initiatives/Cross_Regional_Roadmaps/Pages/1.-Market-Coupling.aspx (accessed 29 Jun. 2017).
42. European Commission, *Quarterly Report on European Electricity Markets* 9/4 Market Observatory for Energy 14 (2016).

rules and third-party access rights to ensure the competitiveness of EU energy markets. Market practices that distort functioning of these markets had been prosecuted under national network codes or general antitrust law if they also constituted violation of national and/or EU competition law. In their advice document,[43] CESR and ERGEG concluded that certain types of market misconduct were neither regulated nor prohibited under energy market regulation and the scope of financial market regulation, 2003 Market Abuse Directive[44] (MAD 2003 hereinafter), was also limited, as it applies only to financial instruments and derivatives traded in regulated markets.[45] Market misconduct such as capacity withholding practices and cross-market manipulative practices that exploit price relations between different wholesale energy markets was not prosecutable under the financial regulatory framework. CESR and ERGEG proposed a tailor-made regulatory framework applicable to all types of wholesale energy products including physical wholesale energy contracts and also financial wholesale energy contracts traded in OTC markets, which were outside the scope of MAD 2003.[46]

Figure I.1 The Regulation of EU Energy Markets Before REMIT

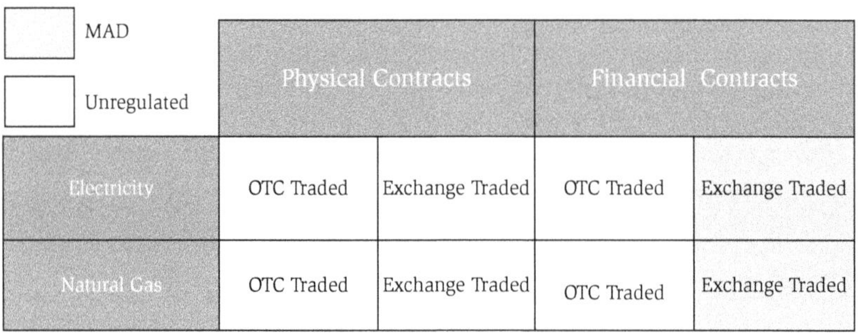

BEFORE REMIT

Market participants raised several concerns about the adoption of a new tailor-made regulatory framework.[47] They stressed that the proposed rules would cause over-regulation which could hamper new investments and market entries and introduce

43. CESR and ERGEG, 26 (2008).
44. Directive 2003/6/EC of the European Parliament and of the Council of 28 Jan. 2003 on insider dealing and market manipulation (market abuse) [2003] OJ L96/16.
45. Regulated market is described by the EU as '*a multilateral system operated and/or managed by a market operator, which brings together or facilitates the bringing together of multiple third-party buying and selling interests in financial instruments* (...) *with its non-discretionary rules*'. Directive 2014/65/EU of the European Parliament and of the Council of 15 May 2014 on markets in financial instruments and amending Directive 2002/92/EC and Directive 2011/61/EU (recast), [2014] OJ L173/348. Exchanges are the prominent examples of regulated markets, in which several financial and physical energy products are also traded. European Energy Exchange (EEX) and Nasdaq Commodities (OMX) are of the major European exchanges where financial and physical electricity and natural gas products are traded.
46. *Supra* note 43.
47. *Ibid.*, 3.

additional regulatory costs to be incurred by energy consumers.[48] Market practices that, according to CESR and ERGEG, necessitated the adoption of the proposed framework were already proscribed under national market rules and network codes governing the operation of trading activities and transmission networks.[49] Furthermore, market participants pointed out that EU competition law was still applicable to wholesale energy markets and there were substantial economic and regulatory risks in applying competition law with an overlapping sector-specific regime.[50] The proposed framework would result in potential problems such as conflict of laws, questions of the designation of competent authorities, costs attached to additional requirements and new regulatory barriers to entry.[51] It was also asserted that the relevant provisions and prohibitions such as insider trading and market manipulation were traditionally designed to address concerns about financial markets and thus not appropriate for the regulation of electricity and natural gas which have been predominantly physical markets.[52]

In evaluating whether a particular market is susceptible to regulation, the Commission applies an analysis involving three criteria.[53] First the Commission assesses if high and permanent barriers to entry, whether of legal, regulatory or structural nature, are present. Second, the analysis explores whether the structure of markets is such that they do not result in effective competition without a regulatory intervention. Finally, the Commission identifies whether competition law, alone, would constitute a sufficient remedy in ensuring competitiveness of these markets. The market participants' assertion that relevant market practices identified in CESR-ERGEG's advice document were already prosecutable under competition law was thus important in assessing whether a tailor-made regulation was necessary to ensure competitiveness of markets.[54] In its impact assessment, the Commission concluded that rules that govern the operation of wholesale energy markets did not suffice to ensure their effective functioning.[55] The findings of CESR and ERGEG in their advice

48. Association of Energy Producers, *AEP Response to CESR/ERGEG Consultation on Market Abuse* (2008), http://www.ceer.eu/portal/page/portal/EER_HOME/EER_CONSULT/CLOSED%20PUBLIC%20CONSULTATIONS/CROSSSECTORAL/Financial%20Services/Market%20abuse%20framework/RR/AEP.pdf (accessed 29 Jun. 2017).
49. British Energy, *CESR / ERGEG consultation paper on draft advice to the European Commission proposing an EU market abuse framework for energy markets* (2008), http://www.ceer.eu/portal/page/portal/EER_HOME/EER_CONSULT/CLOSED%20PUBLIC%20CONSULTATIONS/CROSSSECTORAL/Financial%20Services/Market%20abuse%20framework/RR/E08-PC-30%20-%2004 (accessed 29 Jun. 2017).
50. Association of Energy Producers (2008).
51. EnBW, *Response by EnBW on the CESR and ERGEG advice to the European Commission in the context of the Third Energy Package* (2008), http://www.ceer.eu/portal/page/portal/EER_HOME/EER_CONSULT/CLOSED%20PUBLIC%20CONSULTATIONS/CROSSSECTORAL/Financial%20Services/Market%20abuse%20framework/RR/EnBW%20Consultation%20on%20Market%20Abuse%20Response.2008.08.22.pdf (accessed 29 Jun. 2017).
52. *Ibid.*
53. Section 9, Commission Recommendation of 11 Feb. 2003 on relevant product and service markets within the electronic communications sector susceptible to ex ante regulation in accordance with Directive 2002/21/EC of the European Parliament and of the Council on a common regulatory framework for electronic networks and services, OJ 2003, L 114/45.
54. Association of Energy Producers (2008); EnBW (2008); British Energy (2008).
55. *Supra* note 22.

document and the Commission in its impact assessment later paved the way for the adoption of REMIT.

The scope of REMIT encompassed wholesale energy products that were not regulated under MAD 2003.[56] The Regulation did not provide any differentiation between OTC and Exchange trading as to physical wholesale energy products. All contracts that involve physical delivery of electricity or natural gas in relation with a sell and purchase activity were in scope of REMIT. As to financial wholesale energy products, the differentiation between OTC and Exchange trading determined the applicable regulatory framework. While exchange-traded financial wholesale energy contracts were under the jurisdiction of MAD 2003, OTC-traded financial contracts were regulated under REMIT as shown in Figure I.2.

Figure I.2 The Regulation of EU Energy Markets after REMIT

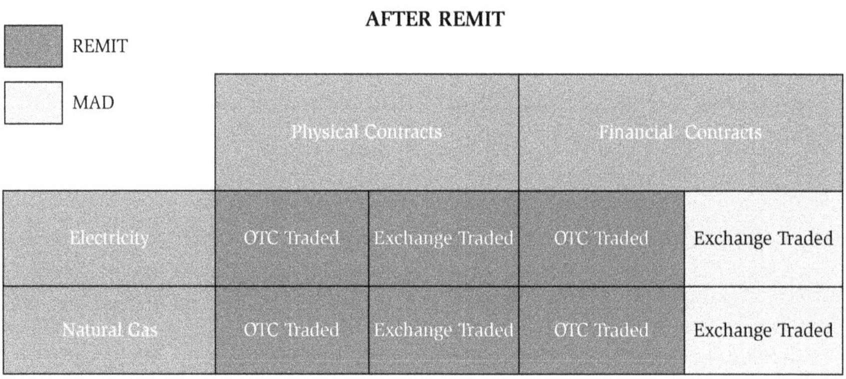

In 2014, the EU put forward a new set of financial regulatory instruments, including, *inter alia,* Market in Financial Instruments Regulation (MiFIR),[57] Market in Financial Instrument Directive,[58] Market Abuse Regulation[59] (MAR) and Market Abuse Directive 2014[60] (MAD 2014), which together repealed and replaced MAD 2003. This new regulatory framework brought about significant recalibrations to the scope of REMIT. First, the new regulation adopted a new trading venue classification significantly

56. Article 1(2), Regulation 1227/2011.
57. Regulation (EU) No 600/2014 of the European Parliament and of the Council of 15 May 2014 on markets in financial instruments and amending Regulation (EU) No 648/2012 OJ L173/84.
58. Directive 2014/65/EU of the European Parliament and of the Council of 15 May 2014 on markets in financial instruments and amending Directive 2002/92/EC and Directive 2011/61/EU (recast), [2014] OJ L173/348.
59. Regulation (EU) No 596/2014 of the European Parliament and of the Council of 16 Apr. 2014 on market abuse (market abuse regulation) and repealing Directive 2003/6/EC of the European Parliament and of the Council and Commission Directives 2003/124/EC, 2003/125/EC and 2004/72/EC, [2014] OJ L173/1.
60. Directive 2014/57/EU of the European Parliament and of the Council of 16 Apr. 2014 on criminal sanctions for market abuse (market abuse directive), [2014] OJ L173/179.

limiting the scope of OTC trading.[61] Several transactions that take place outside of the regulated markets and exchanges were included in the regulatory oversight through the concepts of 'Multilateral Trading Facilities' (MTFs)[62] and 'Organised Trading Facilities' (OTFs).[63] In addition, MAR introduced an exclusive authority over financial instruments, irrespective of the platforms through which they are traded.[64] All financial instruments including financial wholesale energy products traded in exchanges, MTFs, OTFs and OTC markets, were in scope of MAR's rules on insider trading and market manipulation.[65] This recalibration significantly limited the jurisdiction of REMIT with respect to the prohibitions of insider trading and market manipulation in financial wholesale energy markets as shown in Figure I.3.

Figure I.3 The Regulation of EU Energy Markets after MAR

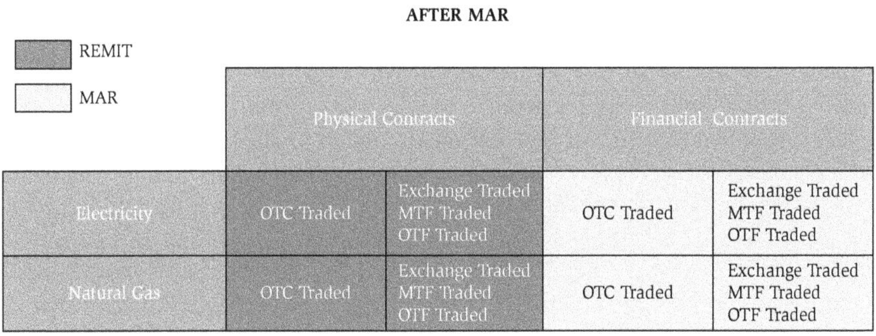

As of 2017, REMIT and MAR are the two fundamental regulatory instruments that proscribe market manipulation in wholesale energy markets at EU level. While the anti-manipulation prohibition of REMIT applies to practices that involve physical wholesale energy contracts, that of MAR has jurisdiction over financial wholesale energy contracts, such as energy futures, swaps and options contracts. Spot commodity products such as contracts that lead to the physical delivery of a certain product can also be in scope for MAR, if it is established that trading in these products has an impact on related financial instruments over which MAR has exclusive jurisdiction. However, this jurisdiction is not applicable to wholesale physical energy products, as there is a carve-out provision that exempts these products from MAR's jurisdiction.[66] As a sector-specific, tailor-made framework for wholesale energy markets, the book focuses

---

61. Article 4(1) Directive 2014/57/EU.
62. '"(M)ultilateral trading facility" or "MTF" means a multilateral system, operated by an investment firm or a market operator, which brings together multiple third-party buying and selling interests in financial instruments (...) with non-discretionary rules (...).'* Article 4(1)(22), Directive 2014/57/EU.
63. *'"(O)rganised trading facility" or "OTF" means a multilateral system which is not a regulated market or an MTF and in which multiple third-party buying and selling interests (...) are able to interact in the system (...).'* Article 4(1)(23), Directive 2014/57/EU.
64. Article 2(1), Regulation (EU) No 596/2014.
65. Article 2(2), Regulation (EU) No 596/2014.
66. Article 2(2)(a), Regulation (EU) No 596/2014.

on REMIT's anti-manipulation regime. Nevertheless, the legal regime established under MAR is also discussed in detail as it has important implications with respect to the prosecution of manipulative practices in wholesale energy markets.

The extent of market practices addressed by REMIT is broad. The Regulation introduced several prohibitions and obligations with which market participants in EU energy markets are required to comply. This book discusses these obligations and prohibitions briefly but critically, asserting that the way they are described and incorporated in the Regulation leads to uncertainties with respect to their implementation in EU wholesale energy markets. Lack of clarifications about the concepts of market manipulation, insider trading and inside information renders their application problematic. Undertakings operating in wholesale energy markets may find themselves subject to investigations without knowing that their conduct could constitute a breach of provisions under REMIT. Liquidity levels may further reduce and prices for energy may increase as a result. Providing a general discussion on these obligations and prohibitions helps the book demarcates the objectives that REMIT seeks to accomplish with respect to energy market liberalisation. However, particular focus is given to REMIT's anti-manipulation rules and the concept of market manipulation.

There are two significant reasons for this book to follow this path. First, the arguments about the concept of market manipulation raised during the consultation period clearly showed that there were significant uncertainties with which, market participants were concerned.[67] Even though it has been prohibited and prosecuted under US law for over a century,[68] the concept is rather new in the EU context, as the first provision that prohibited market manipulation at EU level was adopted in financial market regulation and no longer than fifteen years ago.[69] Furthermore, in contrast to the US, the case law on market manipulation in the EU is very limited, involving only a few disputes where competent authorities found a violation in accordance with relevant anti-manipulation rules. There are two cases in relation with the obligations and prohibitions adopted under REMIT: *Ellering* and *Iberdrola.* While the former involves a claim by Estonian Competition Authority that the defendant failed to comply with REMIT's data disclosure obligations, the latter relates to a market manipulation claim by Spanish Competition Authority (SCA) which asserted that the defendant violated REMIT's anti-manipulation rules.[70] There are significant questions as to the type of market practices that constitutes market manipulation and the legal methodologies adopted for the prosecution of these practices. The complexity of these questions is further elevated with increasing level of market monitoring by sector-specific regulators which would give effect to more enforcement proceedings under

67. *Supra* note 54.
68. Cotton Futures Act of 1914 was one of the early attempts to proscribe manipulative practices. Pub. L. No 174, 38 Stat. 693 (18 Aug. 1914). *See* Jerry Markham, *Law Enforcement and the History of Financial Market Manipulation* 36 (M.E. Sharpe Inc., 2015).
69. Market Abuse Directive of 2003 was the first EU level regulatory instrument that incorporated a prohibition of market manipulation. The prosecution of insider trading, on the other hand, is older, dating back the 1989 Insider Dealing Directive 89/592/EEC [1989] OJ L334/30.
70. *See First Economic Sanctions for REMIT Breaches in Europe* (Lexology 16 Feb. 2016), http://www.lexology.com/library/detail.aspx?g=66b554d0-514c-40b3-b4fb-67374a43b111 (accessed 29 Jun. 2017).

REMIT's prohibition of market manipulation. Therefore an extensive legal analysis that the book incorporates is fundamental in exploring the implications of anti-manipulation rules in EU wholesale energy markets.

Second, the interplay between EU competition law and REMIT with respect to the prosecution of anti-manipulation practice is more direct than those as to the enforcement of data disclosure obligations and insider trading prohibitions. The majority of market practices that are considered manipulative under REMIT and MAR can also give effect to antitrust proceedings as violations of Articles 101 and 102. This results in overlaps between the jurisdictions of sector-specific regulators and competition authorities. To what extent anti-manipulation rules and EU competition law are applied concurrently without giving effect to the *ne bis in idem* principle is a major concern that was raised during the consultation period, prior to the adoption of REMIT and discussed in greater detail in this book. Again, the increasing number of investigations of possible breaches of anti-manipulation rules, in parallel with the growth in monitoring activities by regulators, deems it necessary to conduct an extensive legal analysis that evaluates the dimensions of such concurrency. In this respect, it is the objective of this book to provide this extensive legal analysis and help market participants and other interested parties conceive the risks inherent in this new regulatory framework.

III OUTLINE OF THIS BOOK

The first chapter discusses REMIT, in general. It addresses the legal regime through exploring data disclosure obligations, insider trading and market manipulation prohibitions, which serve as the 'three pillars' of the new regulatory framework, applicable to EU wholesale energy markets. The chapter incorporates a textual analysis, evaluating the details of the definitions and explanations provided by the Regulation and identifying that legal uncertainties with respect to the definitions and the scope of REMIT are not limited only to the concept of market manipulation but, in fact, apply to the whole regulatory framework. It also addresses financial regulatory and competition jurisdictions applicable to EU wholesale energy markets. This chapter concludes that sector-specific regulators and competition authorities can open proceedings concurrently for the same market practices and explores the approach taken by the EU court to the concurrency to evaluate the concurrent application of REMIT and EU competition law.

The second chapter examines market manipulation prohibition, establishing an extensive literature review, along with discussions in case law. The majority of the academic literature and case law analysis is from the US, due to its long history of market manipulation prosecution. Therefore, the chapter also discusses how anti-manipulation rules have been formed and applied in the US. It also finds that establishing a definition of manipulation that applies to all types of manipulative activities for commentators and US courts has proved to be very difficult. This has resulted in ramifications in the approaches and definitions adopted by different regulatory authorities.

Finding that US case law has continuously prosecuted manipulative practices under relevant anti-manipulation rules, the book, in the third chapter, explores how anti-manipulation rules have been enforced in US energy markets. This chapter includes an extensive case law analysis encompassing different types of manipulative practices with a detailed discussion of legal methodologies that regulatory authorities have adopted. It also gives an insight into the types of physical and financial instruments that market participants have employed in devising their manipulative schemes. The case law analysis and the legal discussions provided in this chapter offer fundamental implications as to the types of manipulative practices that can be perpetrated in EU wholesale energy markets.

The fourth chapter discusses the enforcement and the prosecution of manipulative practices in the EU. The chapter looks at EU case law on manipulative practices in comparison with the approach taken by US authorities in prosecuting similar practices. Despite the differences between the two legal systems, this chapter identifies that US case law on energy market manipulation offers important legal implications as to the prosecution of manipulative practices in EU wholesale energy markets. Several scenarios are discussed and evaluated in relation to the definitions provided in REMIT and Agency for the Cooperation of Energy Regulators (ACER) guidance document. The legal analysis put forward in this chapter shows that the majority of practices that can constitute a violation of REMIT's anti-manipulation rules may also give effect to proceedings under antitrust rules which result in concerns about duplicative jurisdictions and double jeopardy/*ne bis in idem* principle.

The final chapter involves conclusions, policy recommendations to mitigate legal uncertainties arising from REMIT and related legal topics that can be subject to further research projects. In this chapter, the book highlights that there are significant problems and ambiguities related to the regulatory framework established by REMIT, and the effective functioning of this framework requires prompt mitigation measures that can be adopted and exercised in harmony at both national and EU level. This chapter proposes that while certain types of market practices should be dealt with under REMIT's anti-manipulation rules, others can be prosecuted more efficiently by competition authorities.

CHAPTER 1

The Legal Framework Applicable to EU Wholesale Energy Markets

§1.01 INTRODUCTION

The energy liberalisation process resulted in the dematerialisation of energy markets,[71] leading to the separation of electricity and natural gas contracts from physical delivery. These contracts started to be traded as commodities, separately from the physical underlying products, in MTFs, designed to render energy trading standardised and efficient. Continuous convergence of national energy markets through liberalisation resulted in the designation of common market models such as mandatory pools, called 'Energy-Only' markets, for electricity and 'Gas Target Model' for natural gas. The aim of these regulatory instruments has been to establish a market structure, which provides a level playing field for electricity and natural gas trading.

Energy regulatory packages[72] have not constituted the only instruments for the liberalisation of energy markets. Competition law rules have also played a major role in ensuring that market players act in a competitive manner within European energy markets. Competences that the European Commission have held as to the functioning of competition in the EU are diverse. It can initiate proceedings against market participants and Member States as well as adopt measures to design national or regional markets through its authorities under merger regulation,[73] state aid provisions,[74] and antitrust rules.[75] After the publication of the 'Energy Sector Inquiry' in 2007[76] (the Sector Inquiry), the Commission increased its intervention in national

71. CESR and ERGEG 7 (2008).
72. *Supra* note 4.
73. *Supra* note 8.
74. Consolidated Version of the Treaty on the Functioning of the European Union, Articles 107, 108 and 109, [2012] OJ C326/47.
75. *Ibid.*, Articles 101, 102 and 106, [2012] OJ C326/47.
76. *Supra* note 20.

energy markets through merger controls,[77] commitment[78] and infringement decisions.[79] Nevertheless these decisions constituted only *ex-post* remedies and did not establish a specific legal framework to deal with anti-competitive practices in European energy markets.

The evolution of energy markets has led to concerns as to whether the existing regulatory and antitrust provisions are sufficient to address the integrity of newly established energy markets and market abuses that cause inefficiencies and imbalances in the functioning of demand and supply. Noting the information asymmetry inherent in the market due to a high degree of vertical integration, which enables energy undertakings to share fundamental information as to capacity of production and transmission infrastructures with affiliates under the same energy undertakings,[80] the Sector Inquiry[81] found that the then-existing legal framework, which applied to energy markets did not suffice to prevent incumbent undertakings from exercising their market power and thus influencing electricity and natural gas prices.[82] Consequently, in 2008, the Commission sought consultation with the CESR and the ERGEG as to the applicability and effectiveness of the then-existing legal framework in ensuring the competitiveness of European energy markets. The advice[83] given by CESR and ERGEG to the Commission proposed the adoption of a tailor-made legal framework to specifically address inefficiencies in the European wholesale energy markets, which later paved the way for the adoption of the REMIT in 2011.

This chapter aims to identify the framework by the REMIT which was designed under the guidance of the consultation process between the Commission, CESR and ERGEG. In so doing, it first circumscribes the scope of the regulation identifying what type of products, markets and market behaviours are included and addressed within the new framework. Noting that REMIT has three important pillars in regulating the wholesale energy markets, the chapter focuses on the first pillar, disclosure obligations, including the types of information, which market participants have a duty to make public. The second pillar of the framework established by REMIT, the prohibition of insider trading, identifies the features needed for information to qualify as inside information, along with the concerns raised by market participants on legal ambiguity

77. *Sydkraft/Graninge* (Case COMP/M.3268) Commission Decision 2003/297/EC OJ C 297/22; EDP/ENI/GDP (Case COMP/M.3440) Commission Decision 2005/801/EC, [2005] OJ L302/69; *E.ON/MOL* (Case COMP/M.3696) Commission Decision 2006/622/EC OJ L253/20; *RWE/Essent* (Case COMP/M.5467) Commission Decision 23/06/2009 OJ C222/1; *EDF/British Energy* (Case COMP/M.5225) Commission Decision 22/12/2008 OJ C38/8.
78. *German Electricity Wholesale Market* (COMP/39.388) Commission Decision [2008] OJ C36/8; *Distigaz* (COMP/37.966) Commission Decision [2008] OJ C9/8; *Swedish Interconnectors* (Case COMP/39.351) Commission Decision [2010] OJ C 239/4.
79. *E.ON/GDF* (COMP/39.401) Commission Decision [2009] OJ C248/5; *Greek lignite* (COMP/38.700) Commission Decision [2009] OJ C243/5.
80. The Inquiry, 188.
81. Published in 2007, the Inquiry was an energy sector-specific document addressing the reasons why consumers are not reaping the full benefits of liberalisation in the energy markets. The Inquiry focused on areas, in which competition is not functioning effectively and the barriers that prevent effective competition in the energy markets. *Ibid.*, 4.
82. *Ibid.*, 124–125.
83. CESR and ERGEG (2008).

with respect to the definitions given by REMIT and the guidance[84] published by the ACER.

Next, the chapter addresses the prohibition of market manipulation, providing a legal analysis on the market behaviours classified under REMIT. Examples are also given by ACER in its guidance document shedding light upon how the National Regulatory Agencies should interpret market behaviours in the enforcement of REMIT at the national level. After discussing REMIT and its scope, this chapter explores other regulatory instruments applicable to EU wholesale energy markets. Certain definitions and rules under financial market regulation constitute great importance to comprehend the legal regime REMIT established. The chapter also provides details about the pertinence of EU competition law rules as to their application in regulated markets. The adoption of REMIT does not preclude the possibility that the market practices may also give effect to proceedings under antitrust rules. The multiplicity of applicable jurisdictions often leads to concerns about duplicative proceedings and double jeopardy/*ne bis in idem* principle. In this regard, the chapter discusses the concurrent application of EU competition law and sector-specific regulation and the approach adopted by EU courts in addressing *ne bis in idem* principle. Finally the analysis provides the basis for some conclusions on the effectiveness of the regulatory framework.

§1.02 REMIT

[A] General

REMIT is a regulatory framework, specifically tailored for the European wholesale electricity and natural gas markets. As the majority of its legal context and definitions are based on MAD 2003,[85] which also provided a legal framework for information disclosure, and the prohibition of insider trading and market manipulation, REMIT was structured to specifically address the transparency and integrity of the European energy markets. According to the 'Advice Document', prepared by the CESR and the ERGEG for the European Commission, MAD was not sufficient to deal with information asymmetries, insider dealing and market manipulation in the electricity and gas markets, as it only addresses trading in financial markets and has a limited disclosure obligation to market participants.[86] Additionally the position of issuer, who is responsible for information disclosure within this context is not present in energy markets. Identifying that only a small proportion of energy transactions is covered by the existing regulatory framework, CESR and ERGEG, in their advice document recommended the adoption of a tailor-made legal framework to address transparency and

84. ACER has published four editions of Guidance on the application of REMIT. As non-binding and drafted using non-legal terminology, Guidance is referred to National Regulatory Agencies to promote coordination and consistency. *See Supra* note 72.
85. Directive 2003/6/EC of the European Parliament and of the Council of 28 Jan. 2003 on insider dealing and market manipulation (market abuse) [2003] OJ L96/16. This directive was later repealed by Regulation (EU) No 596/2014.
86. CESR and ERGEG, 15 (2008).

market integrity in energy markets, which may be attributed to the rationale behind the adoption of REMIT.

[B] Scope of REMIT

According to Article 1(2) of REMIT, the regulation applies to trading in *'wholesale energy products'*, while the provisions on insider trading, Article 3 of REMIT, and market manipulation, Article 5 of REMIT, are not applicable to the wholesale energy products to which Article 9 of MAD applies, the obligation to publish inside information, Article 4 of REMIT, applies to all trading in energy markets including the transactions within the context of Article 9 of MAD, which states that the directive applies to *'any financial instrument admitted to trading on a regulated market in at least one Member State, or for which a request for admission to trading on such a market has been made, irrespective of whether or not the transaction itself actually takes place on that market'*. (Italics added) The transactions that are deemed to be financial instruments within the context of Article 9 of MAD were listed under Article 1(3) of MAD, including derivatives on commodities, options, swaps and other instruments traded in a regulated market. Article 1(4) of MAD referred to Article 4(1) of Directive 2004/39/EC (Markets in Financial Instruments Directive - called MiFID 2004 hereinafter), which identified the concept of a *'regulated market'* as '(...) *a multilateral system operated and/or managed by a market operator, which brings together or facilitates the bringing together of multiple third-party buying and selling interests in financial instruments* (...)'.[87] Accordingly, Articles 3 and 5 of REMIT were not applicable to financial energy products such as derivatives, options and swaps if the trading in these products took place in regulated markets, e.g. power exchanges, while information disclosure obligation was not subject to such restriction.

The financial energy derivatives, options and swaps that were not traded in regulated markets remained within the scope of REMIT. Several financial energy products that were traded bilaterally or in MTFs that did not fulfil the requirements of regulated markets were still subject to Articles 3 and 5 of REMIT. The Commission's impact assessment found that only 16% of trading in energy products were regulated under MAD 2003, and the remaining 84% of trading in energy products were out-scope of then-existing financial market regulation which, according to the Commission, necessitated the adoption of REMIT as a tailor-made regulatory framework for energy markets.[88] MAD 2003 was later repealed by Regulation (EU) No 596/2014, MAR[89] and Directive 2014/57/EU, MAD 2014[90] which together expanded the scope of market manipulation prohibition under new financial market regulation and started to extensively regulate all financial energy products, irrespective of venues they are traded in.

87. Article 4(1) of Directive 2004/39/EC of the European Parliament and of the Council of 21 Apr. 2004 on markets in financial instruments amending Council Directives 85/611/EEC and 93/6/EEC and Directive 2000/12/EC of the European Parliament and of the Council and repealing Council Directive 93/22/EEC OJ L 145 (30 Apr. 2004).
88. REMIT Impact Assessment, 13 (2010).
89. Regulation (EU) No 596/2014.
90. Directive 2014/57/EU.

This recalibration considerably limited the scope of REMIT's insider trading and market manipulation prohibitions.[91]

[1] Wholesale Energy Products

In order to circumscribe the scope of REMIT, identifying the concept of '*wholesale energy products*' within the meaning of Article 1(2) of REMIT is crucial. In Article 2(4), REMIT lists the following instruments irrespective of how and where they are traded:

(a) contracts for the supply of electricity or natural gas where delivery is in the Union;
(b) derivatives relating to electricity or natural gas produced, traded or delivered in the Union;
(c) contracts relating to the transportation of electricity or natural gas in the Union;
(d) derivatives relating to the transportation of electricity or natural gas in the Union.[92]

As the supply of electricity and natural gas to final users, including industrial, commercial and household energy consumers, is understood within the retail section of the energy supply chain, the contracts or derivatives with respect to the supply of energy to these consumers are not wholesale energy products and therefore remain outside the scope of REMIT. However, in line with the Commission's practice of relevant market analysis in energy cases,[93] attributing certain industrial customers, annual energy consumption of which exceeds 600 GW/h, to the wholesale markets, REMIT states that supply and distribution of energy to final consumers, whose energy consumption is greater than 600 GW/h are also within the scope of wholesale energy products.[94]

The definition given in Article 2(4) raises several questions with respect to the scope of the provisions in practice. From a legal perspective, derivatives are also a type of contract. The grounds on which Article 2(4) differentiates between contracts and derivatives is important for the application of the regulation. The reading of the Article suggests that what distinguishes contracts from derivatives is whether the energy subject to contracts or derivatives is physically delivered. Such an interpretation is problematic in practice as derivatives, despite being financial instruments, may also lead to physical deliveries in the energy transactions.[95] Furthermore, market manipulation and insider trading prohibitions under MAR do not provide a differentiation between financial energy products on the basis of physical settlement. All derivatives,

91. *See* section 1.03.
92. Article 2(4) of Regulation (EU) No 1227/2011.
93. Accordingly, the Commission focuses on whether the large industrial customers are supplied by the traders or companies at the wholesale level, or by the distribution companies in the retail markets. *See EDF/British Energy* (Case COMP/M.5224) Commission Decision 22/12/2008, OJ C38/8.
94. Article 2(5), Regulation No 1227/2011.
95. Regine Feltkamp & Cecile Musialski, *Integrity and Transparency in the EU Wholesale Electricity Market: New Rules for a Better Functioning Market?* 7 Oil, Gas & Energy Law 1 (2013).

swaps and options contracts that are physically delivered are also in scope for MAR. Demarcating derivatives and contracts on the basis of physical delivery, gives rise to questions as to the applicable regulatory jurisdictions and the scope of REMIT. Neither REMIT nor the ACER's guidance provides clear guidance on how the concepts of contracts and derivatives are to be determined within the wholesale energy markets.

The subparagraph of Article 2(5) stipulates that *'contracts for the supply and distribution'* of energy products to end users whose consumption levels are greater than 600 GW are regarded as wholesale energy products. In its document, Questions and Answers on REMIT, ACER concludes that this article means that both electricity and natural gas distribution networks and distribution system operators (DSOs) are considered final users and therefore remain outside the scope of REMIT, unless their capacity exceeds the relevant threshold.[96] However, in practice, the DSOs often participate in the wholesale energy markets to buy the energy products to supply their final users and fulfil their contractual obligations.[97] Excluding the contracts that the DSOs enter into to supply their customers will result in a very limited scope for the application of REMIT. Such an interpretation is also not in compliance with the relevant definition of final consumers as articulated under Directives 2009/72/EC and 2009/73/EC, which identify the final consumer as *'a customer purchasing electricity or natural gas for his own use'*.[98] Therefore, the ACER's consideration of DSOs as final consumers causes further uncertainties as to the application of REMIT.

In practice, certain electricity generation units or natural gas suppliers may also enter into transactions in the wholesale market for their own use, such as to cover their production losses or to carry out their operations. To what extent these market participants can be considered final users or such contracts can be regarded as wholesale energy products, is an open question. Again, neither REMIT nor ACER's guidance provides enough advice for the national regulatory authorities to interpret how the relevant REMIT provisions will be applied in such circumstances.

[2] Wholesale Energy Markets

In order to evaluate how different wholesale energy products are interlinked and certain behaviours affect the relevant prices of these products, defining wholesale energy markets where the competition between these products take place is crucial for the legal analysis of market manipulation and insider trading carried out under REMIT. According to Article 2(6), *'wholesale energy market means any market within the Union on which wholesale energy products are traded'*. Such a definition is very broad, encompassing both commodity and financial markets. In its guidance, ACER lists examples for the identification of the relevant markets:

96. Questions & Answers on REMIT, 12 (20th Edition) *see* https://www.acer-remit.eu/portal/custom-category/remit_questions (accessed 29 Jun. 2017).
97. *See* Petri Mantysaari, 535–539 (2015).
98. Article 2(9), Directive 2009/72/EC; Article 2(27), Directive 2009/73/EC.

- Balancing markets for the trading of electricity or natural gas with delivery in the Union;
- Intraday or within-day markets for the trading of electricity or natural gas with delivery in the Union;
- Day-ahead or two-day-ahead markets for the trading of electricity or natural gas with delivery in the Union, including week-end products;
- Physical markets for the trading of electricity or natural gas with delivery in the Union, including markets for physical forward contracts and non-standardised long-term contracts;
- Markets for the transportation capacities of electricity or natural gas in the Union;
- Derivatives markets relating to electricity or natural gas produced, traded or delivered in the Union, including financial OTC markets;
- Derivatives markets relating to the transportation of electricity or natural gas in the Union.[99]

The ACER's list is not exhaustive[100] and does not provide a comprehensive analysis of wholesale energy markets. First, it does not discuss the geographic aspects of energy markets. The demarcation of wholesale energy markets largely depends on the availability of transmission networks. While some wholesale energy products are limited to only subnational markets, others may be supplied in national or even regional wholesale energy markets. Second, ACER does not address how wholesale energy markets may differentiate or converge on the basis of a time period when wholesale energy products are supplied. Generally, during hours when demand for energy products is not high, wholesale energy markets may encompass wider geographic regions. For example, in Nordic countries, wholesale electricity market may include multiple national energy markets, as capacity in cross-border interconnectors is not congested as a result of electricity flow.[101] This is changed during peak hours when demand for electricity is at its highest. In these hours, the cross-borders interconnectors do not suffice to transmit enough volumes of electricity to supply demand and wholesale energy markets become national or even subnational on the basis of congestion levels at national transmission grids.

One can argue that ACER only sheds light upon what constitutes wholesale energy markets and is not expected to provide a detailed analysis of factors that determine the scope of wholesale energy markets, which differ on a case-by-case basis across the EU. It is true that it is not reasonable for ACER to establish a common framework for wholesale energy markets whose scopes differ considerably based on market structures and conditions. However, identifying the factors that affect the interplay and demarcation of wholesale energy markets is fundamental for the evaluation of market manipulation and other market abuse prohibitions. REMIT and ACER's guidance provides little understanding on the approach that should be taken by the national regulatory agencies in applying REMIT. It is hardly possible to derive from

99. ACER's Guidance, 16 (2016).
100. *'The Agency's understanding is that the definition of wholesale energy markets furthermore includes, among others, but is not limited to: (...).' Ibid.*, 15.
101. *Sydkraft/Graninge*, para. 12.

the wording of the definition an approach on how the national regulatory agencies can develop a common understanding for identifying the relevant wholesale energy markets. Given the lack of a common understanding on how REMIT will be applied in identifying the relevant wholesale energy markets, it is futile to expect that there will be a consistent legal approach adhered to by the national regulatory agencies. The importance of the establishment of a common methodology in identifying wholesale energy markets is discussed in greater detail in the following sections.

Articles and descriptions included in ACER's guidance, such as the concepts of trading, wholesale energy products and energy markets, are designed in very broad terms. While REMIT provides only limited guidance in explaining these concepts, the descriptions and examples given by ACER in its guidance paper, whose purpose is to assist national regulatory authorities in carrying out their duties established under REMIT, are far from illuminating such controversies. Even though it stresses that providing a legal interpretation of REMIT is not its intention in developing the guidance paper, ACER should provide a more detailed legal approach to assist national regulatory authorities in the application of REMIT at the national level.

[C] Data Disclosure

[1] General

In the final report of the Energy Sector Inquiry, the Commission found that '(t)*here is a general perception that generation data of vertically integrated incumbents is first shared with affiliates and not necessarily at all with other market participants, which undermines confidence in the wholesale markets*'.[102] Vertically integrated companies, which own assets in generation and transmission as well as distribution of energy products, hold a favourable position with respect to market information fundamental for the functioning of the market. Holding a better position in accessing information valuable for anticipating price movements leaves other market participants making poor trading decisions and making the European energy markets less competitive. Referring to the findings of the Energy Sector Inquiry, CESR and ERGEG, in their advice document, considered information asymmetry within the energy sector as a market failure, noting that such asymmetry, linked to poor levels of transparency, would facilitate the exercise of insider trading and market manipulation.[103] Furthermore, the lack of information and an efficient market monitoring practice needed by the national regulatory authorities would result in market abuse and the exercise of market power in the European energy markets would remain undetected and unprosecuted.[104] Identifying that then-existing legal provisions and guidelines on the obligations of transparency do not suffice to provide a level playing field for the market participants, CESR and ERGEG proposed the inclusion of new transparency obligations into the new tailor-made legal framework, specifically designed for the energy markets, involving

102. The Inquiry, 188.
103. CESR and ERGEG, 9 (2008).
104. *Ibid.*, 10.

the disclosure of information on fundamental data such as the availability of generation, transmission and storage capacities.[105] The legal framework proposed in the advice document was later adopted under REMIT.

[2] The Obligation

Article 4(1) of REMIT requires that '(m)*arket participants shall publicly disclose in an effective and timely manner inside information which they possess in respect of business or facilities which the market participant concerned, or its parent undertaking or related undertaking, owns or controls or for whose operational matters that market participant or undertaking is responsible, either in whole or in part. Such disclosure shall include information relevant to the capacity and use of facilities for production, storage, consumption or transmission of electricity or natural gas or related to the capacity and use of LNG facilities, including planned or unplanned unavailability of these facilities.*' Accordingly, a market participant which is in possession of and under obligation to disclose inside information is obliged to do so in an effective and timely manner. REMIT does not give further guidance on when and how a disclosure activity may constitute effective and in time.

Stressing that the disclosure should be as wide as possible, ACER, in its guidance notes that disclosure of information via reporting platforms, such as trade repositories, may constitute effective within the meaning of Article 4(1).[106] ACER introduces a dual approach for market participants to follow in fulfilling their disclosure obligations. Accordingly, a market participant should use transparency platforms that are operated by transmission system operators, power exchanges or third parties, to meet disclosure requirements. If such transparency platforms do not exist, market participants can publish inside information on their websites. Again market participants should take necessary measures to make sure that the disclosure of inside information through their websites is as wide as possible.[107]

[3] Inside Information

[a] Definition

The definition of inside information is fundamental to comprehend the scope of the obligation. REMIT gives the meaning of inside information as:

105. *Ibid.*, 16.
106. The disclosure practice is also required to meet criteria of minimum quality requirements. *See* Guidance on the application of Regulation (EU) No 1227/2011 of the European Parliament and of the Council of 25 Oct. 2011 on wholesale energy market integrity and transparency (4th ed., 17 Jun. 2016), 42–43 https://www.acer.europa.eu/Official_documents/Other%20documents/4th%20Edition%20ACER%20Guidance%20REMIT.pdf (accessed 29 Jun. 2017).
107. *Ibid.*

(a) information, which is required to be made public in accordance with Regulations (EC) No 714/2009 and (EC) No 715/2009, including guidelines and network codes adopted pursuant to those Regulations;
(b) information relating to the capacity and use of facilities for production, storage, consumption or transmission of electricity or natural gas or related to the capacity and use of LNG facilities, including planned or unplanned unavailability of these facilities;
(c) information which is required to be disclosed in accordance with legal or regulatory provisions at Union or national level, market rules, and contracts or customs on the relevant wholesale energy market, in so far as this information is likely to have a significant effect on the prices of wholesale energy products; and
(d) other information that a reasonable market participant would be likely to use as part of the basis of its decision to enter into a transaction relating to, or to issue an order to trade in, a wholesale energy product.[108]

The disclosure obligation for the information listed in *(a)* and *(c)* stems from existing transparency regulations as adopted under the Third Energy Package and network codes, such as congestion management and capacity allocation mechanisms.[109] Including such information within the scope of inside information, REMIT aims at disclosure of this transparency information in coherence with the disclosure of other information deemed to be fundamental for the functioning of energy markets. The scope of information listed in *(b)* and *(d)*, on the other hand, is broadly defined and may involve any information that has price effects within the wholesale energy markets.

[b] Examples of Inside Information

REMIT's definition of inside information gave rise to concerns about the categorisation of confidential information that is fundamental for practising business in wholesale energy markets as inside information within the meaning of reporting obligations. Noting that the relevant definition does not apply to confidential information that should not be public for the purpose of market participants' trading strategy, ACER provided a list of information, which has a significant effect on prices in the wholesale energy markets:

- Information relating to the capacity and use of facilities for production of electricity or natural gas, including planned and unplanned unavailability of these facilities;
- Information relating to the capacity and use of facilities for storage of electricity or natural gas, including planned and unplanned availability of these facilities;
- Information relating to the capacity and use of facilities for consumption of electricity or natural gas, including planned and unplanned unavailability of these facilities;

108. Article 2(1), Regulation (EU) No 1227/2011.
109. Commission Regulation (EU) 2015/1222 of 24 Jul. 2015 establishing a guideline on capacity allocation and congestion management, OJ L197/24.

- Information relating to the capacity and use of facilities for transmission, including planned or unplanned unavailability of these facilities;
- Information relating to the capacity and use of LNG facilities, including planned and unplanned unavailability of these facilities;
- Information required to be issued in accordance with legal or regulatory provisions at Union, or National level;
- Information required to be issued in accordance with Market Rules;
- Information required to be issued in accordance with Contracts;
- Information required to be issued in accordance with Customs on the market;
- other information that a reasonable market participant would be likely to use as part of the basis of its decision to enter into a transaction relating to, or to issue an order to trade in, a wholesale energy product.[110]

[c] Concerns About the Concept of Inside Information

The extent of information required to be made public in accordance with REMIT causes some concerns from the energy sector, especially from the producers. As can be seen from ACER's guidance, the main focus was directed to the question of availability with respect to the existing capacity of certain infrastructure, such as generation, transmission and storage. During the negotiations, prior to the development of the advice document, CESR and ERGEG received reports of serious concerns from market participants as to the disclosure of information on planned and unplanned outages in generation facilities.[111] It is asserted that the generator should not be deprived of the right to manage the risks arising from the operation of their assets. Disclosing the information on planned or unplanned outages in power generation without having the opportunity to secure their contractual and economic positions would place the energy producers in the position of distressed buyers of energy.[112] Accordingly such a requirement would further deter competition and distort the operation and prices of the market.

In order to address such concerns expressed by the market participants, Article 4(2) of REMIT submits that:

> a market participant may under its own responsibility exceptionally delay the public disclosure of inside information so as not to prejudice its legitimate interests provided that such omission is not likely to mislead the public and provided that the market participant is able to ensure the confidentiality of that information and does not make decisions relating to trading in wholesale energy products based upon that information.

---

110. ACER's Guidance, 28 (2016).
111. For all the responses from invited market participants, *see* https://www.esma.europa.eu/press-news/consultations/joint-consultation-cesr-and-ergeg-advice-european-commission-in-context (accessed 29 Jun. 2017).
112. *See*, in particular; Association of Electricity Producers' Response to CESR and ERGEG Consultation on Market Abuse; British Energy, CESR and ERGEG consultation paper on draft advice to the European Commission proposing an EU market abuse framework for energy markets; EDF Trading, CESR and ERGEG advice to the European Commission in the context of the Third Energy Package: Market Abuse. *See* https://www.esma.europa.eu/press-news/consultations/joint-consultation-cesr-and-ergeg-advice-european-commission-in-context (accessed 29 Jun. 2017).

The decision of when and how the submission of relevant information to the national regulatory agencies and ACER is delayed is under the discretion of market participants. In its guidance, ACER notes that market participants must ensure that the relevant information is made public after the legitimate positions are taken and secured.[113] Whether or not Article 4(2) should be or is applied in a legitimate way can be determined *ex-post*.[114]

ACER's role in collecting all the relevant information from market participants and monitoring the market with respect to abusive practices is important for the well-functioning of European energy markets. It is ACER's duty to collect and screen the information acquired from the market and ensure that national regulatory authorities carry out their monitoring and enforcement activities in coordination with each other. Stressing that the wholesale energy markets across the EU are increasingly integrated in a manner that a market abuse exercised in a market affects the price of energy in other markets, ACER is of the view that a holistic approach with respect to monitoring market conduct is essential. According to Article 4 of Commission Implementing Regulation (EU) No 1348/2014, ACER can also request certain contracts and details of transactions to be reported on an ad-hoc basis.[115] However, ACER lacks competence in investigating market abuse and prosecuting market participants under REMIT. According to Article 18 of REMIT, it is national regulatory authorities' duty to establish rules on the enforcement and penalties levied on market participants for any infringement of REMIT. How market abuse is prosecuted and what sanctions as well as remedies are available for the prohibited conduct will be dealt with and are open to interpretation by the national regulatory authorities.

[D] Insider Trading

[1] General

The perpetration of insider trading practices constitutes a major way for market participants to exploit information asymmetry, which predominantly exists in EU energy markets due to pre-liberalisation market structures and directly threatens the policy of liberalised, integrated and harmonised wholesale energy markets in the EU.[116] The concept of insider trading is described as a situation in which perpetrators who detect differences between the value and the price of wholesale energy products on the basis of undisclosed information, and engage in transactions to derive profits from this

113. ACER's Guidance, 18 (2016).
114. *Ibid.*, 44.
115. The details of reportable wholesale energy products and fundamental data are defined by the Commission Implementing Regulation (EU) No 1348/2014 of 17 Dec. 2014 on data reporting implementing Article 8(2) and Article 8(6) of Regulation (EU) No 1227/2011 of the European Parliament and of the Council on wholesale energy market integrity and transparency, OJ L 363/121.
116. CESR and ERGEG, 28 (2008).

information.[117] Providing a detailed legal and economic analysis on insider trading practices is not among the purposes of this book as, despite being closely related, the law of insider trading prohibitions is distinct from that of market manipulation and cannot be dealt with in a book with this extent. However, identifying the legal framework under REMIT, with respect to obligations and prohibitions that market participants are required to adhere to in energy markets, is fundamental in understanding the rationale behind the adoption of market manipulation rules.

[2] The Prohibition

Article 3(1) of REMIT prohibits three types of behaviour carried out by persons who have inside information on wholesale energy products:

(a) using that information by acquiring or disposing of, or by trying to acquire or dispose of, for their own account or for the account of a third party, either directly or indirectly, wholesale energy products to which that information relates;
(b) disclosing that information to any other person unless such disclosure is made in the normal course of the exercise of their employment, profession or duties;
(c) recommending or inducing another person, on the basis of inside information, to acquire or dispose of wholesale energy products to which that information relates.

The main prohibition in Article 3(1) is the use of inside information. The term '*use*', in a broader context may cover a wide range of commercial activity extending to corporate behaviour, which is not necessarily regarded as abusive within the context of REMIT. In order to understand the extent of the prohibition of insider trading, it is important to determine whether the wording of '*by acquiring or disposing of, or by trying to acquire or dispose of,*' is included in an illustrative or exclusive manner. The interpretation of the article in an exclusive manner results in an exclusion of negative acts such as a failure to acquire or dispose of wholesale energy products.[118] A person within the context of Article 3 of REMIT may decide not to acquire or dispose of wholesale energy products in accordance with the implications derived from the use of inside information. A strict reading of Article 3(1)(a) will not apply to such market practices, even though the person acting in the wholesale energy markets used inside information. In its guidance, ACER interprets the article in the strict sense, stating that '(a)*rticle 3(1)(a) of REMIT not only prohibits using inside information by acquiring or disposing of wholesale energy products* (...), *but also prohibits using inside information by trying to acquire or dispose of wholesale energy products* (...)'.[119] Accordingly, the

117. Emilios E. Avgouleas, *The Mechanics and Regulation of Market Abuse: A Legal and Economic Analysis* 79 (OUP 2005).
118. Regine Feltkamp & Cecile Musialski, 23 (2013).
119. Guidance on the application of Regulation (EU) No 1227/2011 of the European Parliament and of the Council of 25 Oct. 2011 on wholesale energy market integrity and transparency (4th ed., 17 Jun. 2016), 48. https://www.acer.europa.eu/Official_documents/Other%20documents/4th%20Edition%20ACER%20Guidance%20REMIT.pdf (accessed 29 Jun. 2017).

prohibition included in Article 3(1)(a) only applies to the use of inside information while acquiring or disposing of or trying to acquire of dispose of the wholesale energy markets. Other types of using inside information in transactions with respect to the wholesale energy products, such as refraining from engaging in certain transactions with using inside information remain outside the scope of REMIT.[120]

Whether or not the use of inside information causes a price impact or an economic profit is irrelevant with respect to the prohibition included in Article 3 of REMIT. It is even irrelevant whether the person entered into transactions concerning wholesale energy products due to reasons acquired through the use of inside information.[121] The article only prohibits the use of inside information by certain persons, while entering into specified transactions. The evaluation of whether a person who has inside information on a specific wholesale energy product actually uses this inside information, while acquiring or disposing of or trying to acquire or dispose of that wholesale energy product is fundamental for the application of the prohibition of insider trading. The lack of clarification brings further legal questions as to who has the burden to prove that a person used inside information when acquiring or disposing of wholesale energy products or whether there is a presumption that a person who possesses inside information is regarded as in violation of Article 3 of REMIT when acquiring or disposing of or trying to acquire or dispose of wholesale energy products to which the information is related. Neither REMIT nor the guidance document published by ACER provides an assessment on when insider trading has taken place and how the legal responsibility for its violation can arise.

The prohibition of insider trading does not require that persons as listed under Article 3(2) of REMIT intentionally committed one or more of the behaviours addressed in Article 3(1). A specific intent element that refers to a person's consciousness in violation of the prohibition is absent. Accordingly, the national regulator has no obligation to prove that the person in question used the relevant inside information intentionally in, for example, acquiring or disposing of wholesale energy products.[122] This is in line with the approach taken in MAD 2003 and preserved in MAR to the prohibition of insider trading.[123]

[3] Information Concerned

According to subparagraph of Article 2(1) of REMIT, the information listed is regarded as inside information, if it is:

- of a precise nature;
- not made public;
- related directly or indirectly to one or more wholesale energy products;

120. Regine Feltkamp & Cecile Musialski, 28 (2013).
121. *Ibid.*, 23.
122. *Ibid.*
123. Article 2, Directive 2003/6/EC; Articles 7, 8, Regulation No 596/2014. *See also* Emilios E. Avgouleas, 252 (2005).

- made public, would be likely to significantly affect the prices of those wholesale energy products.

REMIT, in the third subparagraph of Article 2(1), further provides an explanation on how and when the information is deemed to be of a precise nature: Accordingly, '*(i)nformation shall be deemed to be of a precise nature if it indicates a set of circumstances which exists or may reasonably be expected to come into existence, or an event which has occurred or may reasonably be expected to do so, and if it is specific enough to enable a conclusion to be drawn as to the possible effect of that set of circumstances or event on the prices of wholesale energy products*'. Statements or claims with questionable accuracy and sources, vague indications and rumours that are not distinct and specific enough to direct market participants to have a particular opinion on its effect on the prices of wholesale energy products will not be considered as inside information.[124] REMIT does not provide details with respect as to when the information is of a precise nature and how it is regarded as having been made public or having a significant impact on prices of energy products. In its guidance document, ACER elaborates the definitions given in REMIT and provides further explanations as to the characteristics of inside information.

ACER provides that the information will be regarded as public if it is available to the 'broad trading public'. Accordingly, the information, which is known by a relatively small number of market participants or is open to a specific group of traders, such as publishing the information through exchanges, which is available only to exchange members, will not be deemed public within the context of REMIT.[125] Whether or not the information is made public by the market participant, who is responsible for publishing the information or by a third party is irrelevant for the determination of inside information.[126] However, the partial disclosure of relevant information does not relieve the market participant of infringing the prohibition of insider trading, if it uses the information not made public during the partial disclosure.[127]

In order to be inside information within the context of Article 2(1) REMIT, information would also be likely to have a significant effect on the prices of wholesale energy products, if it were made public.[128] Whether or not the disclosure did result in a price effect on wholesale energy products is irrelevant for the determination of this requirement.[129] As information listed under the subparagraph of Article 2(1) is open to interpretation, what type of information can be deemed to be or under what circumstances information can qualify as inside information are the questions that need to be answered to have an insight into the legal implications of REMIT. In its guidance document, ACER provides that it perceives the requirement of a significant price effect

124. Niamh Moloney, *EU Securities and Financial Markets Regulation* 720 (3rd ed., OUP 2014).
125. ACER's Guidance, 29 (2016).
126. *Ibid.*
127. *Ibid.*, 30.
128. *Ibid.*
129. C-45/08 *Spector Photo Group NV, Chris Van Raemdonck v. Commissie voor het Bank-, Financie- en Assurantiewezen (CBFA)* [2009], ECR I-12073, para. 69.

as an instrument to limit the scope of information with respect to wholesale energy markets. Accordingly only important information, which has or will potentially have a significant impact on the prices of wholesale energy products, will be regarded as inside information, while the information, which has no or only a negligible price effect will be outside the scope of the prohibition included in Article 3 of REMIT.

Ex ante determination of information that is likely to or potentially affects the prices of wholesale energy products requires a legal assessment of the relationship between information and the economic effects of using that information within the relevant wholesale energy market. In the guidance document, noting that experience will provide clear implications as to which kind of information would be likely to cause significant price effects, ACER states that the following data can be used as indications as to the effects likely to take place as a result of the use of inside information:

- the type of information is the same as information which has, in the past, had a significant effect on prices;
- pre-existing analysts research reports, price reporter publications and opinions indicate that the type of information in question has effects on prices;
- the market participant itself has already treated similar events as inside information;
- another reasonable market participant has already treated similar events as inside information.[130]

Accordingly ex-post considerations derived from previous experiences may be regarded as indications of inside information likely to affect the prices of wholesale energy products. However, such an approach, while constituting a part of the legal analysis to be carried out, may mislead the regulators and market participants. The consequences under which a use of information causes price differentials may differ on a case-by-case basis. While any historical comparison might show that a use of information had once had a price impact in certain demand and supply conditions, a similar use of information may have no price impact under different market conditions. There is not enough guidance as to how a direct relationship between the use of information and the price impact on wholesale energy products is established and to what extent a price differential can be regarded as significant within the context of Article 2(1). As the definitions provided are subjective and provide no effective criteria, the application of REMIT in the energy sector may result in unnecessary disclosure of strategic data or a failure to detect use of information which has significant price effects, both of which further distort competition in wholesale energy markets.

[4] Persons Concerned

It is important to note that the prohibition of insider trading is not only applicable to market participants active in the wholesale energy markets. Article 3(2) specifically

130. ACER's Guidance, 32 (2016).

provides that the prohibition identified in Article 3(1) applies to the following persons when they have inside information to which the wholesale energy products relates:

(a) members of the administrative, management or supervisory bodies of an undertaking;
(b) persons with holdings in the capital of an undertaking;
(c) persons with access to the information through the exercise of their employment, profession or duties;
(d) persons who have acquired such information through criminal activity;
(e) persons who know, or ought to know, that it is inside information.[131]

The list of persons who may be deemed to be responsible for insider trading is formulated in a way that encompasses a broader range of legal and natural people, who are directly or indirectly concerned with trading in wholesale energy markets, such as external consultants and legal advisors.[132] Accordingly, the mere possession of inside information by persons listed in *(a), (b), (c), (d)* is sufficient to prove that such persons violated the prohibition of insider trading when they committed behaviours included in Article 3(1). With respect to '*persons who know, or ought to know, that it is inside information*', there is a legal uncertainty as to how the possession of such knowledge is determined and when such a person is regarded as one who ought to know that it is inside information. Whether the legal analysis carried out to identify whether the person knows or ought to know that the relevant data is inside information stipulates an intent element that is also important for the application of Article 3 of REMIT. Again in its guidance document, ACER provides no further explanation or clarification with respect to the approach to be taken by the national regulators in developing their respective legal analyses.

[E] Market Manipulation

[1] General

The prohibition of market manipulation is an important aspect of the new legal framework established by REMIT. In CESR-ERGEG's advice document and the impact assessment by the Commission, manipulative practices are regarded as a major problem within wholesale energy markets, distorting prices and hedging mechanisms as well as lowering trust and liquidity in energy markets.[133] Such market practices would be left undetected and/or unprosecuted without a legal framework tailored to detect and prosecute them.[134] The conclusions of CESR-ERGEG and the Commission in their respective advice documents paved the way for the adoption of REMIT in 2011. The prohibition is included in Article 5 of REMIT, according to which '*(a)ny engagement in, or attempt to engage in, market manipulation on wholesale energy markets*

131. Article 3(2), Regulation No 1227/2011.
132. Regine Feltkamp & Cecile Musialski, 26 (2013).
133. REMIT Impact Assessment, 29 (2010); CESR and ERGEG, paras 26-44 (2008).
134. CESR and ERGEG, 37 (2008).

shall be prohibited'. It is the objective of this book to discover the legal implications that new anti-manipulation rules under REMIT would have in dealing with anti-competitive practices in EU wholesale markets. Therefore, it is important to understand how the prohibition of market manipulation is defined and designed under REMIT.

[2] Definition of Market Manipulation

Even though the concept of market manipulation is a contentious subject that has been heavily discussed by the legal and economic literature,[135] which are provided in detail in the following section, REMIT provides definitions and examples of market manipulation that give insight into what type of actions are deemed to be manipulative in relation to wholesale energy markets. Article 2(2) gives the meaning of manipulation as:

> (a) entering into any transaction or issuing any order to trade in wholesale energy products which:
> (i) gives, or is likely to give, false or misleading signals as to the supply of, demand for, or price of wholesale energy products;
> (ii) secures or attempts to secure, by a person, or persons acting in collaboration, the price of one or several wholesale energy products at an artificial level, unless the person who entered into the transaction or issued the order to trade establishes that his reasons for doing so are legitimate and that that transaction or order to trade conforms to accepted market practices on the wholesale energy market concerned; or
> (iii) employs or attempts to employ a fictitious device or any other form of deception or contrivance which gives, or is likely to give, false or misleading signals regarding the supply of, demand for, or price of wholesale energy products;
> or
> (b) disseminating information through the media, including the internet, or by any other means, which gives, or is likely to give, false or misleading signals as to the supply of, demand for, or price of wholesale energy products, including the dissemination of rumours and false or misleading news, where the disseminating person knew, or ought to have known, that the information was false or misleading.

135. *See* Craig Pirrong, *Commodity Market Manipulation Law: A (Very) Critical Analysis and a Proposed Alternative* 51/3 Washington and Lee Law Review 945 (1994); Albert S. Kyle & S. Viswanathan, *How to Define Illegal Price Manipulation* 98/2 American Economic Review: Papers & Proceedings 278 (2008); Shaun D. Ledgerwood & Paul R. Carpenter, *A Framework for the Analysis of Market Manipulation* 8/1 Review of Law & Economics 253 (2012); Frank A. Wolak and Robert H. Patrick, *The Impact of Market Rules and Market Structure on the Price Determination Process in the England and Wales Electricity Market* (1997); Severin Borenstein & James Bushnell, *An Empirical Analysis of the Potential for Market Power in California's Electricity Industry* 47 Journal of Industrial Economics (1999); Scott M. Harvey & William W. Hogan, *Further Analysis of the Exercise of Market Power in the California Electricity Market* (2001).

This article provides two categories for market manipulation; transaction-based market manipulation and information-based market manipulation.[136] In the former, perpetrators engage in transactions, either deceptive or not, to manipulate wholesale energy markets through giving false or misleading signals to the market as to levels of supply and demand as well as the availability of production, storage or transportation capacity. The latter, on the other hand, does not require the existence of a transaction for the perpetration of market manipulation. Instead, market participants manipulate wholesale energy markets via dissemination of false or misleading information, which could result in erroneous implications as to the fundamentals of the respective wholesale markets for other market participants.

As mentioned above, serious concerns were raised by market participants during the consultation period prior to the formulation of REMIT.[137] The majority of responses submitted by market participants to the CESR and ERGEG, stressed that since the very term, manipulation, suggests the concealment of important misconceptions and ambiguities with respect to market behaviours, a new tailor-made legal framework should clearly define what types of market conduct can be deemed manipulative and what really separates a legitimate trading activity from market manipulation within the boundaries of wholesale energy markets.[138] The question of how to identify strategic withholding of production capacity and energy supply in the wholesale markets to move the price of relevant products to the desired levels was heavily discussed in the consultation process. It is important to note that outages in production or supply have important implications as to market fundamentals, which leads to price movements. Determining when the energy producers and suppliers withhold their supply capacity to sustain their maintenance or to benefit from the lack of efficient supply and illiquidity of markets is fundamental to designating behaviour as market abuse. According to the Commission's Energy Sector Inquiry, there are two ways that market participants in the wholesale energy markets can drive energy prices to levels which benefit positions held by themselves:

i. either by withdrawing capacity (which may force recourse to more expensive sources of supply); or
ii. by imposing high prices when they know their production is indispensable to meet demand.[139]

---

136. The structure of Article 2(2) of REMIT was different from market manipulation prohibition under Article 1(2) of MAD 2003, which used also a fraud-based formulation of market manipulation in addition to transaction-based, information-based definitions. This formulation was also preserved in Article 9 of MAR with one significant recalibration, which is the introduction of benchmark manipulation. For detailed discussion, *see* section 1.03[F][2][b].
137. *Supra* note 111.
138. Such a concern is analogous to the rationale behind the formulation of competition law rules, which are designed to prevent on the one hand punishing market participants involved on legitimate market activities (*Type 1 Error, False Positive*), on the other acquitting traders acting, in fact, in an anti-competitive manner distorting the market (*Type 2 Error, False Negative*). Alison Jones & Brenda Sufrin, *EU Competition Law; Text, Cases, and Materials* (Oxford 5th ed., 2014).
139. The Inquiry, 132–133.

In competitive markets, the market power of incumbents is constrained by potential competition as high prices above competitive levels would attract new investors and entries into the markets.[140] This is not the case for the energy markets as they are capital intensive industries requiring high investment costs for potential entries.[141] Undertakings with market power or even monopoly power can freely exercise monopoly pricing behaviour without restraints from would-be competitors.[142] The ability of energy producers and suppliers to move prices based on their will is further elevated by the fact that the demand for energy is inelastic with respect to price increases, which provides a vertical feature as to the demand and supply curve, different from other markets.[143] Benefiting from the lack of competitive restraints available in the market, incumbent generators and suppliers are able to manipulate prices easily in the wholesale energy markets.

[3] Examples of Market Manipulation

Even though the main issue discussed heavily within the consultation process was how to identify whether withholding of generation capacities was based on legitimate foundations, the concept of market manipulation involves a wider reach within REMIT. Dividing manipulative behaviours into transaction-based and information-based, Article 2(2) gives a broad definition of market manipulation involving any market behaviour that either provides *false or misleading signals* as to the fundamentals of the market or secures the prices at *an artificial level*. In order to provide further details on what type of behaviours may constitute market manipulation, REMIT itself gives examples in its Recitals 13 and 14. Accordingly the types of market manipulation are:

> placing and withdrawal of false orders; spreading of false or misleading information or rumours through the media, including the internet, or by any other means; deliberately providing false information to undertakings which provide price assessments or market reports with the effect of misleading market participants acting on the basis of those price assessments or market reports; and deliberately making it appear that the availability of electricity generation capacity or natural gas availability, or the availability of transmission capacity is other than the capacity which is actually technically available where such information affects or is likely to affect the price of wholesale energy products.[144]

Furthermore, examples of market manipulation include market behaviours that secure '*a decisive position over the supply of, or demand for, a wholesale energy product which has, or could have, the effect of fixing, directly or indirectly, prices or creating other unfair trading conditions; and the offering, buying or selling of wholesale energy*

140. There are three main competitive contracts to which firms are subject; demand substitutability, supply substitutability, potential competition. *See* Commission Notice on the definition of the relevant market for the purpose of Community competition law [1997] OJ C372/5, para. 13.
141. CESR and ERGEG, 43 (2008).
142. Alison Jones & Brenda Sufrin, 87 (2014).
143. Petri Mantysaari, 62 (2015).
144. Recital 13, Regulation No 1227/2011.

products with the purpose, intention or effect of misleading market participants acting on the basis of reference prices'.[145] The guidance given by REMIT as to the concept of market manipulation is more about the *ex-post* analysis that sheds light upon market conditions succeeding market manipulation. It also provides no detail as to what type of implications can be interpreted as '*false or misleading signals*' or when and how the price of a wholesale energy product is deemed to be at '*an artificial level*'.[146] In its guidance document, ACER submits further examples of market manipulation derived from the National Regulatory Agencies' experience in the energy industry and the experience of financial authorities in financial markets.[147] Based on the classification of manipulative conduct given in Article 2(2), ACER provides these examples under four sub-headings:[148]

(1) False/misleading transactions.
(2) Price positioning.
(3) Transactions involving fictitious devices/deception.
(4) Dissemination of false and misleading information.

[a] False/Misleading Transactions

ACER gives three market manipulation schemes as examples of false or misleading transactions.[149] These are:

- wash trades;
- improper matched orders; and
- placing orders with no intention of executing them.

Wash trades occur when a market player enters into transactions with no material effects, such as no changes in financial interests, or risks or the interest and risks take place only between the colluding parties of the transactions to affect the price of the relevant wholesale energy product.[150] Such transactions involve no economic exchange yet mislead other market participants into thinking that the trading volume of the relevant wholesale energy product has increased and greater trading activity is taking place, which results in price movements within the wholesale energy markets as to the relevant product. Improper matched orders can also be included in wash trades, since this also involves no material effects, financial interests, risks and economic exchange between the colluding parties. In such transactions, in fact, some actual

145. Recital 14, Regulation No 1227/2011.
146. The requirement of an artificial price for the determination of market manipulation has been heavily discussed in US case law and is often construed as problematic as relevant economic analysis carried out in the legal proceedings would result in further methodological problems as to what type of data should be considered as an indicator of manipulative conduct. For details *see* Craig Pirrong, 960–968 (1994).
147. ACER's Guidance, 39 (2016).
148. *Ibid.*, 37–39.
149. *Ibid.*, 37.
150. *Ibid.*

trading does take place in the market, yet the order is succeeded by an offsetting trade for the same price and volume in a way that no change in financial benefits occurs between the parties of the transaction. According to US case law,[151] ACER's classification of wash trades, improper matched orders and placing orders with no intention of executing them as false/misleading transactions under Article 2(2)(a)(i) is erroneous. Since they do not involve material effects and price risks that are inherent in other transactions, these types of trades are generally considered closed market transactions which are dealt with in Article 2(2)(a)(iii) rather than Article 9(2)(a)(i).[152]

ACER's identification of 'placing orders with no intention of executing them' as false or misleading transactions, gives rise to legal questions as to when and how such orders can be deemed manipulative. As will be seen in the following chapters,[153] placing orders with no intention of executing them is, in fact, a common practice in both physical and financial markets as such transactions allow their parties to hedge financial risks arising from vulnerabilities in the market prices as the result of inefficiencies, e.g. shortages or illiquidity. The majority of the transactions taking place in futures markets as well as the practice of virtual bidding[154] for the purpose of converging prices to interrelated markets are examples of placing orders with no intention of executing them. Assuming such practices constitute manipulation would result in great discontent from the market as they are fundamental instruments used by market participants to hedge their financial risks and future positions. Whether ACER's explanation, that is *'(t)he intention is not to execute the order but to give a misleading impression that there is demand for supply of the wholesale energy product at that price'*,[155] is in compliance with Article 2(2) of REMIT is also questionable as is the intent element, which will be discussed in greater detail in later chapters, is irrelevant with respect to identifying a market conduct as manipulative under the legal framework established by REMIT. ACER's identification of intent as a requirement to conclude that market participants, placing orders and not executing them, violate Article 5 is not in compliance with REMIT.

[b] Price Positioning

ACER gives the following market behaviours as examples for price positioning:

- Marking the close.
- The abusive squeeze.
- Cross-market manipulation.
- Actions undertaken by persons that artificially cause prices to be at a level not justified by market forces of supply and demand, including actual availability

151. *See Sundheimer v. CFTC*, 688 F.2d 150 (2d Cir. 1982), *cert. denied*, 460 U.S. 112 (1983); *United States v. Radley*, 659 F. Supp. 2d 803 (S.D. Tex. 2009).
152. *See* sections 3.02[C] and 4.03[D][1].
153. *See* section 3.03[B][3][f].
154. *See* Shaun D. Ledgerwood & Johannes P. Pfeifenberger, *Using Virtual Bids to Manipulate the Value of Financial Transmission Rights, Brattle Group* (2012).
155. ACER's Guidance, 37 (2016).

of production, storage or transportation capacity, and demand (physical withholding).[156]

Marking the close is a type of manipulation where a market participant engages in a number of transactions near the close of the market to affect the closing or settlement price of the relevant wholesale energy product. As discussed in greater detail in the following chapter,[157] this type of market manipulation was historically considered as a clear example of trade-based market manipulation and was a feature of securities markets.[158] The effect of excessive bids and offers made at the close of market is further elevated by other market fundamentals such as the market power held by the executing party, the level of concentration in the relevant market or the degree of liquidity existing in trading activities with respect to the relevant wholesale energy product. Even though such manipulation may take place in a heavily traded market, the ability of a market participant to move prices requires holding substantial market power as other market participants, not knowing the motivation of the relevant bids and offers made by the manipulator, will develop assumptions from prices at the close of the market.

The abusive squeeze, also known as the corner, involves a market participant who takes a large long position as to the relevant wholesale energy product, accumulating large futures contracts with certain delivery dates, which forces other market participants who hold short positions to physically deliver the energy products.[159] The short positions, unable to deliver the relevant energy product within the relevant geographic market due to illiquidity or market tightness, are required to buy back their short contracts at higher costs from the market participant with the large long position. In order to squeeze the market, the cornering market player must hold substantial market power as benefitting from the squeeze requires that the market players, other than the cornering player lack the relevant energy product to supply and cannot bring additional supplies from the markets other than the relevant markets without incurring an exceptional financial burden.[160]

Cross-market manipulation requires an action by a trader in a primary market, which affects prices of an energy product in a linked market, in which the trader also holds positions, whose value benefits from the action in the primary market.

156. *Ibid.*, 38–39.
157. *See* section 2.03[C][4][b][i].
158. Emilios E. Avgouleas, 133 (2005). For the economics of trade-based manipulation, *see* Franklin Allen & Douglas Gale, *Stock-Price Manipulation* 5/3 The Review of Financial Studies 503, 515–520 (1992).
159. The concepts of short and long positions are used in financial terminology to indicate liabilities that market participants are required to fulfil in accordance with their financial contracts. A market participant with a short position undertakes to sell certain financial contracts at a certain delivery date. A market participant with a long position on the other hand, undertakes to buy certain financial contracts at a certain delivery date.
160. Craig Pirrong, *Energy Market Manipulation: Definition, Diagnosis, and Deterrence* 31/1 Energy Law Journal 1, 3 (2010).

Accordingly the manipulator enters into a transaction at a loss in the primary market. This is not problematic, because in most competitive markets, nearly half the transactions are closed at a financial loss. An undertaking can also incur losses due to legitimate reasons such as the need for liquidation. What makes such a transaction suspicious is that perpetrators engage in such loss-making transactions on a continuous basis and yet they profit from a financial positions in linked markets whose values are derived from these loss-making transactions in primary markets.[161] However, it is not enough to hold the party responsible whose behaviour in a market at a loss derives profits from the positions held in a linked market. This is also a common practice in the wholesale energy markets where the market players legitimately enter into such transactions at a loss to hedge their financial risks. The intent of a market participant entering into transaction is determinative in identifying the relevant market behaviour is manipulative or not. However, the prohibition of market manipulation as articulated in REMIT does not require national competent authorities to prove that the market participant intentionally or at least recklessly entered into manipulative conduct. Therefore on what basis market behaviour is evaluated as to whether it constitutes market manipulation is missing within the current legal framework.

The last example for price positioning ACER gives is the practice of physical withholding, where the generator of electricity or wholesale supplier of natural gas or an owner of transmission or storage infrastructure does not offer its capacity to the market in order to drive the price of the relevant wholesale energy product higher so that it can optimise its benefits from the market in exchange for creating imbalances between demand and supply fundamentals. Capacity withholding practices were considered a change in the market fundamentals, affecting generation availability and thus a major factor in the determination of price levels at energy markets.[162] In its guidance document, ACER states that such withholding accounts to market manipulation only if it is carried out without justification and '*with the intention*' of increasing prices.[163] The intent element is very important in evaluating market manipulation to determine whether withholding occurred due to maintenance concerns or it is practised as a means to maximise profits in exchange for distorting demand and supply in the market. Even though ACER's mention of the intent element is crucial for the legal approach taken by the national regulatory agencies in enforcing market manipulation rules, its compliance with the framework established by REMIT is open to discussion, since the latter does not provide a requirement that market participants have specific intent in manipulating wholesale energy markets.[164]

161. Shaun D. Ledgerwood & Paul R. Carpenter, 255 (2012).
162. CESR and ERGEG, 32 (2008).
163. ACER's Guidance, 38 (2016).
164. Office of Gas and Electricity Markets (OFGEM), British energy regulator, warned market participants to be careful when they are trading in energy markets since the REMIT does not require intent to hold market participants liable for market manipulation. *See* REMIT Open Letter September 2015, https://www.ofgem.gov.uk/ofgempublications/96553/20150814 remitopenletterseptember2015-pdf (accessed 29 Jun. 2017).

[c] *Transactions Involving Fictitious Devices*

The following behaviours are given by ACER as examples of market manipulation:

- Scalping.
- Pump and Dump.
- Circular Trading.
- Pre-arranged trading.

Scalping involves dissemination of false and misleading information, in order to move prices in a direction that is favourable to the position held or a transaction planned by the disseminating market participant.[165] Such manipulation occurs, for example, when a market participant who has a position in the futures market disseminates false information about its production or supply volumes to move prices in the futures market, which is determined on the basis of implications from the production or available supply levels. Pump and dump, a scheme similar to scalping, is a market manipulation in which the market participant buys a large volume of wholesale energy product and then disseminates false information, which increases the price of the relevant wholesale energy product.[166] Accordingly, the manipulator buys a large volume of wholesale energy products, (such as collecting futures contracts, or entering into long-term supply contracts as a buyer of energy products at lower prices), and disseminates false information, (such as its demand for energy increased considerably for a certain period of time), which misleads the other market players into believing that the actual value of the given energy product is higher. The manipulator then sells the product at the higher price.

In circular trading, the manipulator knowing that an offsetting long position is ready to be held takes a short position with respect to a wholesale energy product.[167] Similar to the wash trades and improper matched orders in circular trading, there are no financial risks for either party and transactions are carried out to influence market prices with the impression that a trading takes place as to the relevant wholesale energy product. Pre-arranged trading consists of two market participants, who agree to trade which each other at pre-arranged prices to exclude other competitors from the market where the pre-arranged trading takes place or is linked to it.[168] ACER also provides that if it is carried out according to the rules of the relevant market place, the pre-arranged trading can be considered as an accepted market practice and legitimate.[169]

[d] *Dissemination of False and Misleading Information*

The manipulation schemes given so far by ACER in its guidance document represent transaction-based manipulation, which involve a transaction undertaken by one or

165. *Supra* note 163.
166. *Ibid.*
167. *Ibid.*
168. ACER's Guidance, 38–39 (2016).
169. *Ibid.*

multiple market participants to distort the market fundamentals. In the dissemination of false and misleading information, market participants do not necessarily need to carry out a transaction to manipulate the market.[170] A mere spreading of false or misleading information through the media, failing to disclose price sensitive information, or a market behaviour which does not correspond to the concept of transaction, e.g. the movement of physical commodity stock having implications for commodity future markets, can be manipulation in the category of the dissemination of false and misleading information.

[4] Attempt to Manipulate

REMIT also prohibits the attempt by market participants to manipulate the wholesale energy markets. According to the definition in Article 2(3), an attempt to manipulate the wholesale energy markets involves:

> (a) entering into any transaction, issuing any order to trade or taking any other action relating to a wholesale energy product with the intention of:
>
> (i) giving false or misleading signals as to the supply of, demand for or price of wholesale energy products;
>
> (ii) securing the price of one or several wholesale energy products at an artificial level, unless the person who entered in to the transaction or issued the order to trade establishes that his reasons for doing so are legitimate and that that transaction or order to trade conforms to accepted market practices on the wholesale energy market concerned; or
>
> (iii) employing a fictitious device or any other form of deception or contrivance which gives, or is likely to give, false or misleading signals regarding the supply of, demand for, or price of wholesale energy products
>
> or
>
> (b) disseminating information through the media, including the internet, or by any other means with the intention of giving false or misleading signals as to the supply of, demand for, or price of wholesale energy products.

The main distinction between the prohibitions of market manipulation and an attempt to manipulate is REMIT's inclusion of the '*intent*' element in the definition of the latter concept. Article 2(3) specifically notes that market participants would be liable for the prohibition of attempting to manipulate only if they enter into false or misleading transactions or disseminate false or misleading information '*intentionally*'. It is reasonable to assume that the prohibition of an attempt to manipulate intrinsically involves an intent element, yet a clear inclusion of the intent element under Article 2(3) has implications as to why such an inclusion is not present under Article 2(2), the prohibition of market manipulation. ACER in its guidance document mentions intent elements with respect to the perpetration of market manipulation.[171] This position is

170. *Ibid.*, 39.
171. *Ibid.*, 37.

also supported by some commentators[172] who argued that the reading of the Article implies an intent element to prove that a market manipulation has taken place. Nevertheless such a conclusion can also apply to Article 2(3) of REMIT. The notion of making an attempt intrinsically includes an intent element to prove that the manipulator tried to execute the prohibited behaviour. This did not prevent REMIT from including the intent element under Article 2(3). Accordingly, while requiring the presence of intent with respect to the prohibition of an attempt to manipulate, REMIT does not include such a requirement under the prohibition of market manipulation. The importance of the intent element in defining and dealing with market manipulation will be discussed in greater detail in the following chapters.[173] However, REMIT's omission of the intent element in market manipulation raises several problems in establishing a common legal approach that national competent authorities could adopt in dealing with market abuse in the wholesale energy markets.

§1.03 FINANCIAL MARKET REGULATION

[A] General

The rules that prohibit manipulative activities in European wholesale energy markets are not limited to those adopted under REMIT. The prohibitions on market manipulation and insider trading which are called market abuse, have been included in several pieces of EU-wide legislation which, to a certain extent, were also applicable to wholesale energy markets before the adoption of REMIT. Early attempts to prevent market manipulation were generally made under the regulation of financial markets[174] seeking to establish a level playing field for the trading of equities, such as stocks and shares and non-equity products, bonds, structured finance products, and derivatives. The majority of energy traded across the EU has remained outside the scope of financial regulation, as it has mostly taken place at OTC level rather than in regulated multilateral trading venues. Nevertheless, certain wholesale energy contracts traded as commodity products in early European power exchanges, such as Nord Pool, in scope to these financial regulatory instruments.[175]

[B] Background

The EU's regulation of financial markets dates back to the 1966 Segre Report,[176] proposed by a group of experts appointed by the European Commission (the

172. Leigh Hancher, *Energy Markets: A legal Perspective on Market Abuse (REMIT)*, (Florence April 2013), https://www.youtube.com/watch?v = 3tSmdPtTG1k (accessed 29 Jun. 2017).
173. *See* section 2.03[C][4][a][ii].
174. Directive 2003/6/EC.
175. In identifying its scope, MAD 2003 referred to Annex 1, Section C of Directive 2004/39/EC (MiFID 2004).
176. Report by a Group of Experts Appointed by the EEC Commission, the Development of a European Capital Market (1966) (Segre Report).

Commission) finding that progress in the development of a European capital market fell far behind the EU's economic union agenda, and a closer cooperation in national economic policies was a prerequisite for the establishment of a monetary union.[177] The succeeding development in financial markets had not come before the CJEU's 1985 decision in *Casis De Dijon*,[178] in which the court held that products produced and traded in one Member State should be admitted to other Member States without additional regulatory requirement creating a thrust on the side of Member States for more coordination in the development of harmonised regulatory frameworks. In 1989, the Commission adopted its first EU-wide legislation on financial markets, the Insider Dealing Directive[179] which aimed at deterring market participants from the use of inside information in a manner arbitraging information asymmetry in European financial markets. Leaving vast areas of financial regulation unharmonised, the directive was later regarded as inadequate in promoting the integration of financial markets.[180]

The major changes in the EU's financial landscape during the late 1990s and early 2000s, such as the adoption of the euro as a single currency for Member States and developments in technical capacity for cross-border investment services promoting pan-European trading of financial products, led to the introduction of the first European rulebook for EU financial markets[181] which incorporated MAD 2003,[182] and MiFID 2004.[183] While the former provided a market abuse regime that would play a central role in the development and the harmonisation of national laws on the prohibition of insider trading and market manipulation, the latter addressed the provision of cross-border investment services and the regulation of trading venues. Adopted in the form of directives,[184] this first regulatory framework conferred discretion on Member States in designing their financial markets regulation, ensuring that national priorities should not hamper the harmonisation of national financial frameworks and efficient functioning of cross-border investment services. In order to oversee the harmonisation process, Article 65 of MiFID 2004 required the Commission to provide reviews assessing the application of the directive's rules in European financial markets.

177. *Ibid.*, 15.
178. Case 120/78 *Rewe-Zentral AG v. Bundesmonopolverwaltung fur Branntwein* (Casis de Dijon) [1979] ECR 649.
179. Council Directive of 13 Nov. 1989 coordinating regulations on insider dealing 89/592/EEC [1989] OJ L334/30, (Insider Dealing Directive).
180. Niamh Moloney, 707 (2014).
181. *Ibid.*, 24.
182. Directive 2003/6/EC.
183. Directive 2004/39/EC.
184. According to Article 288 of TFEU, both regulations and directives are binding instruments that EU institutions adopt in the development of EU policies in particular areas. While regulations are directly applicable in all Member States, directives set out policy purposes, leaving the choice of form and methods to the national authorities.

[C] Regulatory Reform

In its 2010 consultation on the MiFID 2004 Review,[185] and subsequent proposals[186] and impact assessments for the MiFIR and MiFID 2014,[187] findings of which paved the way to the corresponding regulatory framework of financial markets, the Commission concluded that despite the evidence that there had been significant developments with respect to lower transaction costs and greater competition in financial transactions, the MiFID 2004 needed to be revised and updated to ensure that the majority of transactions and financial instruments traded in financial markets remained within the scope of market regulation and divergences in the application of the regulatory provisions at national level would be kept to a minimum.[188] The reform agenda was based on the regulatory atmosphere during the aftermath of the global financial crisis of 2007–2008 and the subsequent 2009 G20 summit in Pittsburgh which discussed the underlying reasons for the financial breakdown in global markets and proposed a series of measures for members to take, in dealing with the recession and reforming financial markets regulation.[189]

The findings of the G20 Summit and the Commission's subsequent MiFID 2004 review identified that the current regulatory structure of financial markets was susceptible to market abuse practices.[190] Only the financial instruments that were traded in regulated markets such as stock and commodity exchanges and MTFs which were operated by investment firms on a non-discriminatory basis, were under regulatory oversight, leaving a vast amount of financial instruments traded in market platforms in other regulated and multilateral market venues outside the scope of MiFID 2004, which gave rise to concerns about information asymmetry and market abuse in financial markets.[191] Furthermore, the divergence in the application of financial markets regulation at national level and the lack of coordination between cross-border regulatory authorities allowed market participants to engage in regulatory arbitrage and to exploit the differences between national approaches to financial regulation.[192]

185. European Commission, Public Consultation. Review of the Markets in Financial Instruments Directive (2010).
186. European Commission Proposal for a Regulation of the European Parliament and of the Council on markets in financial instruments and amending Regulation [EMIR] on OTC derivatives, central counterparties and trade repositories, COM (2011) 652/4 (2011 MiFIR Proposal); European Commission Proposal for a Regulation of the European Parliament and of the Council on markets in financial instruments repealing Directive 2004/39/EC of the European Parliament and of the Council, COM (2011) 656/4 (2011 MiFID 2014 Proposal).
187. European Commission Staff Working Paper Impact Assessment Accompanying the document Proposal for a Directive of the European Parliament and of the Council on Markets in financial instruments [Recast] and the Proposal for a Regulation of the European Parliament and of the Council on Markets in financial instruments COM (2011) 656/4 (2011 MiFID 2014/MiFIR Impact Assessment).
188. 2011 MiFID 2014/MiFIR Impact Assessment, 5.
189. Pittsburgh G20 Summit, September 2009, Leaders' Statement, Strengthening the International Financial Regulatory System, https://www.oecd.org/g20/summits/pittsburgh/G20-Pittsburgh-Leaders-Declaration.pdf (accessed 29 Jun. 2017).
190. 2011 MiFID 2014 Proposal, 6; Pittsburgh G20 Summit, para. 13 (2009).
191. Article 1, Directive 2004/39/EC, MiFID 2004.
192. Niamh Moloney, 20–21 (2014).

The policy recommendations proposed by the G20 reform agenda plus the subsequent proposals and impact assessments, resulted in the adoption of a series of regulatory measures, including the MAR 2014[193] and the MAD 2014[194] which together replaced MAD 2003. MAD/MAR 2014 brought new types of market abuse as well as financial instruments within their scope with the MiFIR[195] and MiFID 2014[196] providing a new type of trading venue classification that encompasses a wider scope for financial instruments including those that were not regulated under MiFID 2004. Furthermore, the EU adopted a new regulation for derivatives contracts, Regulation No 648/2012, (EMIR), which provided a data reporting regime to enhance market transparency with respect to all derivatives transactions traded in the EU.[197] Accordingly, all market participants who trade derivatives contracts in either trading venues identified under MiFID/MiFIR 2014 or OTC markets through bilateral trading, are under an obligation to report the details of their transactions to competent trade repositories. The data reporting obligation is designed to extend the regulatory oversight over financial instruments and markets which are outside the scope of MiFID/MiFIR 2014, yet still have an impact on the competitiveness and functioning of in-scope financial markets. At the institutional level, the European Securities and Markets Authority, (ESMA), designated as the new EU-wide market authority overseeing the functioning and competitiveness of financial markets as well as ensuring close cooperation between national regulatory agencies, is in place with respect to enhancing Pan-European transparency levels and detecting market abuse.[198]

It is important to note that the reforms of financial market regulation came after the adoption of REMIT which also covered market abuse provisions and data reporting obligations with respect to wholesale energy products including physical and financial energy supply contracts. In their advice document of 2008,[199] CESR and ERGEG found that the majority of wholesale energy products had been traded in OTC markets and thus was outside the scope of MAD 2003, as the latter was not applicable to OTC-traded contracts.[200] MAD 2003 followed MiFID 2004's classification of trading venues which was applied only to regulated markets and MTFs.[201] The MiFID/MiFIR 2014 developed a new trading venues classification, called 'Organised Trading Venues', which covered all transactions and contracts traded in a trading platform other than regulated markets or MTFs.[202] The transactions and contracts which were regarded in OTC markets in the

193. Regulation (EU) No 596/2014.
194. Directive 2014/57/EU.
195. Regulation (EU) No 600/2014.
196. Directive 2014/65/EU.
197. Regulation (EU) No 648/2012.
198. Regulation (EU) No 1095/2010 of the European Parliament and of the Council of 24 Nov. 2010 establishing a European Supervisory Authority (European Securities and Markets Authority), amending Decision No 716/2009/EC and repealing Commission Decision 2009/77/EC OJ L331/84.
199. CESR and ERGEG (2008).
200. CESR and ERGEG, 14 (2008).
201. Article 1(3), Directive 2003/6/EC.
202. Article 4(1)(23), Directive 2014/65/EU.

previous regime have become in scope for financial regulation under a different trading venue classification. MAR 2014 also followed this new classification.[203]

REMIT's scope was limited to products which were not regulated by MAD 2003.[204] After the adoption of MAR 2014, the new regulatory reforms broadened the scope of the market abuse regime, which affected and further limited the scope of REMIT. Certain financial wholesale energy products that were regarded as OTC under MAD 2003 and MiFID 2004 under the jurisdiction of REMIT, are now included in the new financial regulation and thus are within the scope of MAR 2014. Certain data reporting obligations and market abuse practices which were under REMIT's regulatory authority prior to the adoption of MAR 2014, are now in scope under the new financial regulation.

In this section, the chapter does not delve into the details of obligations that each of these new regulatory instruments might present with respect to financial market regulation, as evaluating financial markets as a whole is not one of this book' objectives. Rather, the chapter addresses the legal implications that the new financial regime provides within the context of REMIT and European wholesale energy markets. In so doing, the chapter briefly discusses the data reporting obligations that form the part of each regulatory instrument with respect to the financial markets to show that the problem of overlapping jurisdictions is not limited to the context of market abuse regimes and is, in fact, endemic within the regulation of financial markets as a whole. Particular focus is given to the market abuse regime adopted under MAR 2014 as it directly affects and recalibrates REMIT's jurisdictional dimension. The demarcation of market abuse regimes applicable to wholesale energy markets will provide greater clarity on the scope of REMIT and the types of market manipulation that would be enforceable under the REMIT framework.

[D] MiFID/MiFIR 2014

[1] General

Replacing MiFID 2004, MiFID/MiFIR 2014 brought significant changes to financial markets regulation providing a broader regulatory framework, governing trading in financial markets with more interventionist features.[205] The new regime consists of two sets of legislation. MiFID 2014 provides rules on the authorisation and operation of investment firms, market operators and data reporting service providers as well as supervision, cooperation and enforcement by competent authorities.[206] These rules are included in the form of a directive as some degree of discretion was deemed to be appropriate with respect to their implementation at national level. MiFIR establishes a framework with respect to disclosure obligations and non-discriminatory access to

203. Article 3(6), (7), (8), Regulation No 596/2014.
204. Article 1(2), Regulation No 1227/2011.
205. Niamh Moloney, 21 (2014).
206. Article 1, Directive 2014/65/EU.

clearing services and to trading in benchmarks,[207] which will be applicable directly at the national level as uniformity in the implementation of these rules is regarded as essential.

[2] Recalibrations

Of the changes that MiFID/MiFIR 2014 has brought with respect to financial market regulation, the new trading venue classification is the major one which recalibrates the extent and the scope of other legislation and regulatory authorities at both national and union level. There are three different regulatory regimes designated for the trading venues included in the framework. The first regime applies to trading in multilateral markets which are:

(i) Regulated Markets.
(ii) MTFs.
(iii) OTFs.[208]

According to Article 4(1)(21) of MiFID 2014, a regulated market is '(...) *a multilateral system operated and/or managed by a market operator, which brings together or facilitates the bringing together of multiple third-party buying and selling interests in financial instruments* (...)' in a non-discretionary manner. The feature that distinguishes regulated markets from the MTFs is that the regulated markets can also operate as primary markets in which new equities and/or non-equity products are first introduced. The MTFs also function as regulated markets operated by a market operator or investment firms bringing together multiple third parties in the trading of financial instruments in a non-discretionary manner, but they can only operate as secondary markets where financial instruments are traded from their first issuance at the primary market until their expiration or maturity date.

One of the striking features of the new regulatory regime under MiFID/MiFIR 2014 is the introduction of the OTFs, a new venue classification designated to bring all OTC transactions traded in organised trading platforms under regulatory oversight, corresponding to the objectives laid down in the G20 Summit.[209] Article 4(1)(23) defines OTF as '(...) *a multilateral system which is not a regulated market or an MTF and in which multiple third-party buying and selling interests in bonds, structured finance products, emission allowances or derivatives are able to interact* (...)' OTFs are regulated as MTFs and regulated markets with two distinguishing features. First, OTFs can operate on a discretionary basis[210] meaning that they enjoy a limited degree of discretion in matching bids and orders in their trading data. Second, OTFs cannot offer

207. Article 1, Regulation (EU) No 600/2014.
208. Article 1(7), Directive 2014/65/EU.
209. Pittsburgh G20 Summit, para. 11 (2009).
210. Article 20(6), Directive 2014/65/EU.

trading of equity or equity-like products such as depositary receipts, exchange-traded funds and certificates.[211] This limitation was accepted after long negotiations between the European Council and Parliament on the grounds that due to their discretionary nature, which would create deficiencies in the quality of transparency data, price formation of equity and equity-like products which can be distorted under OTF markets.[212]

The other two regulatory regimes set forth under MiFID/MiFIR 2014 are designed to capture, to a certain extent, the OTC transactions that are not traded in multilateral, organised trading platform as in OTFs. The first regime applies to Systematic Internalisers (SIs), which are investment firms who on a systematic basis, deal with their clients' bids and orders through their own portfolio without operating a multilateral system.[213] The second regime relates to bilateral OTC trading which is outside the scope of operational and trading venue obligations under MiFID/MiFIR 2014. The new financial market regulation seriously restricts the extent of the bilateral OTC market, stipulating that only financial instruments other than equity and equity-like products can be traded bilaterally in OTC markets.[214] If an investment firm who wishes to trade equity and equity-like products through OTC markets, can do so only through the SI, under which they are obliged to follow regulatory obligations with respect to authorisation and transparency provision under MiFID/MiFIR 2014. For non-equity instruments, such obligations do not apply to market participants in bilateral OTC trading. However, it is important to note that these market participants are required to follow data reporting obligations for derivatives under EMIR.[215]

[3] Financial Instruments

The scope of the new financial market regulation is governed by financial instruments enumerated under MiFID 2014 Annex I, Section C. Accordingly, financial instruments under the new regime are:

1) Transferable securities;
2) Money-market instruments;
3) Units in collective investment undertakings;
4) Options, futures, swaps, forward rate agreements and any other derivative contracts relating to securities, currencies, interest rates or yields, emission allowances or other derivatives instruments, financial indices or financial measures which may be settled physically or in cash;
5) Options, futures, swaps, forwards and any other derivative contracts relating to commodities that must be settled in cash or may be settled in cash at the option of one of the parties other than by reason of default or other termination event;

211. Article 4(23), Directive 2014/65/EU.
212. Niamh Moloney, 466 (2014).
213. Article 1(20), Directive 2014/65/EU.
214. Article 23, Regulation (EU) No 600/2014.
215. Regulation No 648/2012.

6) Options, futures, swaps, and any other derivative contract relating to commodities that can be physically settled provided that they are traded on a regulated market, a MTF, or an OTF, except for wholesale energy products traded on an OTF that must be physically settled;
7) Options, futures, swaps, forwards and any other derivative contracts relating to commodities, that can be physically settled not otherwise mentioned in point 6 of this Section and not being for commercial purposes, which have the characteristics of other derivative financial instruments;
8) Derivative instruments for the transfer of credit risk;
9) Financial contracts for differences;
10) Options, futures, swaps, forward rate agreements and any other derivative contracts relating to climatic variables, freight rates or inflation rates or other official economic statistics that must be settled in cash or may be settled in cash at the option of one of the parties other than by reason of default or other termination event, as well as any other derivative contracts relating to assets, rights, obligations, indices and measures not otherwise mentioned in this Section, which have the characteristics of other derivative financial instruments, having regard to whether, *inter alia*, they are traded on a regulated market, OTF, or an MTF;
11) Emission allowances consisting of any units recognised for compliance with the requirements of Directive 2003/87/EC (Emissions Trading Scheme).[216]

In point '6', the list includes a specific carve-out provision for wholesale energy derivatives which excludes wholesale energy derivatives that *must be settled physically*. Accordingly, wholesale energy derivatives that can be settled financially are in scope for the new financial markets regulation. Whether or not a contract must be settled physically is determined by criteria established by ESMA, according to which an energy derivative contract must be settled physically if:

(I) it contains provisions which ensure that parties to the contract have proportionate arrangements in place to be able to make or take delivery of the underlying commodity;
(II) it establishes unconditional, unrestricted and enforceable obligations of the parties to the contract to deliver and take delivery of the underlying commodity;
(III) it is not possible for either party to replace physical delivery with cash settlement; and
(IV) the obligations under the contract cannot be offset against obligations from other contracts between the parties concerned, without prejudice to the rights of the parties to the contract, to net their cash payment obligations.[217]

Such a formulation confers on MiFID/MiFIR 2014 a considerable authority over wholesale energy derivatives, such as swaps, options and futures which are often settled financially and traded in regulated markets, MTFs, OTFs and SIs. What types of derivative contracts will be considered outside the scope of financial markets regulation remains to be seen.

216. Annex I, Section C, Directive 2014/65/EU.
217. Final Report ESMA's Technical Advice to the Commission on MiFID II and MiFIR of 19 Dec. 2014, ESMA/2014/1569 406.

[E] EMIR

EMIR was adopted as a result of the commitments made at the 2009 G20 Summit in Pittsburgh in which the countries agreed that '(a)*ll OTC derivative contracts should be traded on exchanges or electronic trading platforms, where appropriate, and cleared through central counter-parties by end-2012 at the latest*'.[218] EMIR introduced a regulatory framework in European financial markets which stipulates clearing and reporting requirements with respect to derivatives aimed at assessing and reducing counterparty and systemic risk in OTC trading. Accordingly, the regulation imposes two major obligations on market participants. First, all market participants, including both financial or non-financial counterparties using derivatives as hedging mechanisms rather than profit maximisation purposes, are required to report all of their transactions in which they traded derivatives.[219] The reporting is made to trade repositories which are legal persons that centrally gather and keep the details of derivatives transactions.[220] The reporting obligation is not limited to OTC derivatives and applies to all derivative contracts referring to the list of financial instruments set out in points (4)–(10) of MiFID 2004 Annex I Section C.[221] Second, EMIR provides a clearing obligation for all OTC derivatives[222] traded between financial counterparties and non-financial counterparties with a clearing threshold to be cleared at a central clearing part (CCP).

EMIR's reporting obligations are far-reaching to the extent that they overlap not only with those set out under REMIT but also the reporting obligations that MiFID/MiFIR 2014 imposes on investment firms and trading venues. The reporting regime under MiFID/MiFIR 2014[223] requires all financial instruments listed under Annex I Section C and which are traded in a trading venue, e.g. regulated markets, MTFs or OTFs, to be reported to public or national competent authorities through a 'Approved Reporting Mechanism' meaning that the reporting of transactions is carried out by an authorised reporting service supplier on behalf of investment firms.[224] How this 'Approved Reporting Mechanism' interplays with reporting to trade repositories under EMIR remains to be seen. Moreover, market operators and investment firms that operate a trading venue are also obliged to make public, on a weekly basis, the aggregated positions with respect to the current bid and offers for equities and non-equities including derivatives traded in the financial markets.[225] One distinctive

218. Pittsburgh G20 Summit, September 2009, Leaders' Statement, Strengthening the International Financial Regulatory System, para. 13.
219. Article 9, Regulation (EU) No 648/2012.
220. Article 2(2), Regulation (EU) No 648/2012.
221. Article 2(5), Regulation (EU) No 648/2012.
222. Article 5(1), Regulation (EU) No 648/2012. Certain OTC derivatives may not be suitable for central clearing. EMIR lays down other risk mitigation measures for non-centrally clearing OTC derivatives, such as timely confirmation of terms, dispute resolution processes, marking to market, margin requirements, etc., to make sure that such contracts may not constitute systemic risks to financial markets. Article 11, Regulation (EU) No 648/2012.
223. Article 26, Regulation (EU) No 600/2014.
224. Article 4(54), Directive 2014/65/EU.
225. Recital 129, Directive 2014/65/EU.

feature of reporting obligations under MiFID/MiFIR 2014 is that these obligations are imposed solely on financial counterparties which are evaluated on the basis of their commercial activity. Such a differentiation between financial and non-financial entities is not present in EMIR under which the reporting requirement is relevant for all derivatives, irrespective of the characteristic of reporting entities. EMIR's jurisdiction authority over derivatives extends beyond MiFID/MiFIR 2014's authority, as the latter only regulates derivatives traded in trading venues, while the former also oversees derivatives traded through bilateral OTC markets.

Article 4 of REMIT provides a general obligation to disclose inside information. The concept of inside information is defined as information of a precise nature relating to wholesale energy products that has not been made public, and would be likely to significantly impact prices in wholesale energy markets.[226] REMIT's disclosure obligation stipulates that the information to be disclosed should include details as to the capacity and use of facilities for output, storage, consumption and transmission of energy products as well as expected and unexpected outages during the operation of these facilities.[227] Whether or not the wholesale energy product is a financial instrument is irrelevant for the application of reporting obligations.

Further clarification on the reportable contracts under REMIT is given under Article 3(1)(a) and(b) of the REMIT Implementing Regulation[228] providing a list that includes:

- options, futures, swaps and any other derivatives of contracts relating to electricity or natural gas traded or delivered in the European Union (EU);
- options, futures, swaps and any other derivatives of contracts relating to the transportation of electricity or natural gas in the EU.

REMIT's disclosure obligation with respect to these derivatives contracts overlaps with the disclosure obligations under both EMIR and MiFID/MiFIR 2014. While MiFID/MiFIR 2014 is not applicable to wholesale energy products that are traded in OTC and wholesale energy derivatives that must be settled physically, it applies to all wholesale energy derivatives that can be settled financially, as long as they are traded in a regulated market, MTF, OTF or an SI.[229] The disclosure obligation under REMIT, on the other hand, applies to all wholesale energy derivatives including those traded in OTC markets. ACER notes that reporting of these derivative contracts under MiFID/MiFIR 2014 also satisfies the disclosure obligation under REMIT.[230] However, the latter requires the reporting to be made to national competent authorities or to ACER, while the former is carried out through 'Approved Reporting Mechanisms'. How

226. Article 2(1), Regulation No 1227/2011.
227. Article 4(1), Regulation No 1227/2011.
228. Commission Implementing Regulation No 1348/2014 of 17 Dec. 2014 on data reporting implementing Article 8(2) and Article 8(6) of Regulation (EU) No 1227/2011 of the European Parliament and of the Council on wholesale energy market integrity and transparency OJ L 363, 18.12.2014.
229. Article 26, Regulation (EU) No 600/2014.
230. ACER, Annex III – Reporting of REMIT derivatives contracts under EMIR, Transaction Reporting User Manual (TRUM), of 7 Jan. 2015.

ACER is notified as to the wholesale energy products reported through Approved Reporting Mechanism remains to be seen.

Given the reference to Annex I Section C of MiFID 2004,[231] EMIR's disclosure requirements for derivative contracts do not encompass wholesale energy products that are traded in OTC and must be settled physically. The wholesale energy derivatives that can be settled financially in regulated markets MTFs, OTFs and OTC markets are in scope for EMIR disclosure obligations. REMIT Implementing Regulation notes that reporting of these derivative contracts to the trade repositories under EMIR is accepted.[232] However, the market participants who reported their wholesale energy derivative contracts through the trade repositories under EMIR should make sure that the relevant trade repositories notify relevant national competent authorities or ACER as to the reported products.[233] According to REMIT, the reporting requirement is not regarded as fulfilled unless wholesale energy derivatives are referred to the national competent authorities or ACER.

ACER provides some scenarios in which market participants engage in transactions with respect to wholesale energy derivatives while the same transactions do not give rise to a disclosure obligation under EMIR.[234] These scenarios often relate to transactions that are engaged in by foreign nationals and market participants in EU financial markets. EMIR disclosure obligations do not apply to non-EU counterparties, even though these counterparties have branches operating in the EU.[235] The disclosure obligations under REMIT, on the other hand, applies to any person engaging in transactions in wholesale energy derivatives across the EU, or outside the EU, if that person also enters into other transactions in one or more wholesale energy markets within the EU.[236] This is in line with the approach taken by MiFID/MiFIR 2014 in exercising its jurisdiction over third-country firms providing investment services in the EU, as the disclosure obligations of both REMIT and MiFID/MiFIR 2014 aim at detecting market abuses, insider trading and market manipulation.[237] Nevertheless, the reporting of derivatives to trade repositories under EMIR is carried out to assess systemic risks and to allow a comprehensive overview of markets.[238]

[F] MAR/MAD 2014

[1] General

The MAR is the cornerstone in regulating market abuse in European financial markets. Providing prohibitions on market manipulation and insider trading along with

231. Article 2(5), Regulation (EU) No 648/2012.
232. Article 6(4), Regulation No 1348/2014.
233. Article 8(1), Regulation No 1227/2011.
234. ACER, Transaction Reporting User Manual of 7 Jan. 2015, (TRUM), 28.
235. Article 9, Regulation (EU) No 648/2012.
236. Article 8, Regulation No 1227/2011.
237. Recital 32, Regulation (EU) No 600/2014; Recital 17, Regulation No 1227/2011.
238. Recital 43, Regulation (EU) No 648/2012.

disclosure obligations with respect to inside information that are directly applicable at national level, MAR replaced MAD 2003 on the ground, that the latter as a directive, led to divergences in the interpretation and the implementation of national market abuse regimes. The necessity for the revision of MAD 2003 was stressed in the Commission's consultation document in 2010 which identified that the regulatory gaps in the market abuse regime with respect to trading venues and financial instruments along with limited and diverging enforcement powers at the national level posed great challenges for the functioning and the integrity of EU financial markets.[239] The scope of MAD 2003 was limited to financial instruments admitted or who had requested for admission to trading on a regulated market, leaving financial markets under certain trading venues, such as MTFs and OTC trading, and certain types of financial instruments, such as contracts for differences, credit default swaps, climatic derivatives and emission allowances, unregulated.[240] MAR is accompanied by the MAD of 2014 which introduced criminal sanctions for perpetrators of market manipulation and insider trading.[241] MAD 2014 provides some degree of flexibility for Member States in their implementation of criminal sanctions. Accordingly, national regulators are obliged to impose criminal sanctions against market abuse when it is established that the effects of such misconduct are severe to the extent that they threaten the integrity and functioning of financial markets as a whole.

[2] The Scope of the New Market Abuse Regime

MAR provides significant reforms to the scope of market abuse regimes for financial markets regulation. MAR does not expressly list in-scope products, enabling national regulators to exercise their authority over a wide range of products including credit default swaps, contracts for difference and emission allowances.[242] Products traded on MTFs and OTFs, which were left unregulated by MAD 2003 are now in-scope. In principle, the market abuse regime does not directly apply to commodity spot markets where commodities such as agricultural products are traded, settled and delivered physically. However, the new regime extends its regulatory grip over these markets when they affect the value of derivatives or other financial instruments traded in in-scope trading venues.[243] The prohibitions of market manipulation and insider trading are applicable to spot commodity products, if it is established that transactions in these products are likely to have an impact on the value of in-scope financial instruments.

239. European Commission, Public Consultation on A Revision of the Market Abuse Directive, [2010], 13.
240. Articles 1(3) and 9 of Directive 2003/6/EC.
241. Directive 2014/57/EU.
242. Niamh Moloney, 715 (2014).
243. Article 2(2)(a), Regulation No 596/2014.

[a] Carve-Out Provision

MAR includes a carve-out provision for non-financial wholesale energy markets. According to Article 2 of MAR, its prohibitions on insider trading and market manipulation do not apply to wholesale energy commodities, even if they have an effect on MAR's in-scope products. Article 2(4) of REMIT identifies wholesale energy commodities as contracts for the supply of electricity or natural gas where delivery is in the EU and contracts relating to the transportation of electricity and natural gas are also in the EU. Nevertheless, MAR's carve-out provision does not include wholesale energy derivative contracts. Options, futures, swaps and any other derivatives of contracts relating to electricity or natural gas traded or delivered in the EU or relating to the transportation of electricity or natural gas in the EU are in-scope financial instruments under the new market abuse regime.

Article 1(2) of REMIT exempts financial wholesale energy products from the prohibitions of market manipulation and insider trading and defines financial wholesale energy products as financial instruments to which Article 9 of MAD 2003 applies. The scope of Article 9 applies to all financial instruments traded in regulated markets, excluding those traded in MTFs and OTFs. This resulted in the application of REMIT to financial wholesale energy products which were not traded in regulated markets. The new market abuse regime has brought a significant recalibration in the scope of REMIT. Under MAR, financial instruments are identified as any financial contract traded in regulated markets, MTFs or OTFs.[244] The prohibitions on insider trading and market manipulation of MAR are applicable to all wholesale energy derivatives. Whether or not these derivatives must be settled physically is irrelevant to the application of MAR. This directly contradicts MiFID/MiFIR 2014 which considers wholesale energy derivatives that must be settled physically as not being financial products[245] and creates inconsistency and ambiguity for the establishment of a single rulebook for the financial market and wholesale energy market regulation in the EU.

[b] Benchmark Manipulation

The prohibition of market manipulation under MAR retains the previous formulation of MAD 2003 with a one significant calibration. Article 12 of MAR identifies market manipulation as:

(a) transactions that give or are likely to give false or misleading signals as to the supply of, demand for, or price of, or secure or are likely to secure the price of one or several in-scope financial or non-financial products, unless the reasons for engaging in such transactions are legitimate;

244. Article 2(1), Regulation No 596/2014.
245. Annex I, Section C, Directive 2014/65/EU.

(b) transactions or any other activities that affect or are likely to affect the price of one or more in-scope financial and non-financial products through the employment of fictitious device or any other deception or contrivance;
(c) dissemination of information through media, internet or other means of telecommunication that gives or is likely to give false or misleading signals as to the supply of, demand for, or price of, an in-scope financial or non-financial product where the person who disseminated the information knew, or ought to know, that the information was false or misleading.

In addition, Article 12(1)(d) introduces a new type of market manipulation, called 'Benchmark manipulation', defined as:

> transmitting false or misleading information or providing false or misleading inputs in relation to a benchmark where the person who made the transmission or provided the input knew or ought to have known that it was false or misleading, or any other behaviour which manipulates the calculation of a benchmark.

Benchmark manipulation involves perpetrators reporting transactions that do not represent true forces of demand and supply in markets to benchmark publishing indices which are used as reference prices with respect to relevant products and relevant markets. The rationale behind this type of manipulation is to move these benchmark prices at a level that is profitable for other positions whose value is determined by a reference to benchmark prices. The global rate fixing scandals with respect to Libor and Euribor interest rates[246] and significant growth in the use of indices and benchmarks experienced in recent years for pricing and risk management purposes in financial instruments[247] gave rise to concerns about the applicability of market manipulation prohibition under MAD 2003 to market practices that manipulate and distort indices and benchmark prices,[248] which provided a major impulse for the EU to introduce an anti-manipulation provision specific to this type of manipulative activity.

The adoption of a benchmark manipulation on the grounds that that MAD 2003 did not address this type of market manipulation, has two important legal implications for the prohibition of market manipulation under REMIT. First, the concept of benchmark manipulation constitutes a type of cross-market manipulation through which perpetrators seek to exploit price relations between different products and markets. The existing US case law on energy market manipulation shows that, in the majority of cross-market manipulation cases, perpetrators aim at distorting indices

246. The scandal involved, *inter alia,* submission of interest rates which were different from those used by the perpetrator banks in practice. The European Commission levied fines worth EUR 1.71 billion with respect to the alleged abusive practices. *See* Commission, Press Release 4 Dec. 2013 (IP/13/1208).
247. The estimated size of the benchmark industry is worth EUR 1,000 trillion. European Commission, Staff Working Document Impact Assessment, Accompanying the document Proposal for a Regulation of the European Parliament and of the Council on indices used as benchmarks in financial instruments and financial contracts (SWD (2013) 336/2), (Benchmark Proposal Impact Assessment), 6.
248. Benchmark Proposal Impact Assessment, 1 (2013). *See also* European Commission Proposal for a Regulation of the European Parliament and of the Council on indices used as benchmarks in financial instruments and financial contracts, COM(2013) 641 final, 2.

which operate as benchmark prices to seek further profits from their related financial and physical positions.[249] The introduction of benchmark manipulation, which is a clear example of cross-market manipulation, as a separate type of market manipulation on the grounds that this misconduct was not addressed under MAD 2003, gives rise to concerns about the prosecution of cross-market manipulation under REMIT which derived its anti-manipulation regime from MAD 2003. In its Recital 13, REMIT provides that '(...) (m)*anipulation and its effects may occur across borders, between electricity and gas markets and across financial and commodity markets* (...)'. ACER also considers cross-market manipulation as an example of price positioning and thus prosecutable under Article 2(2)(a)(ii).[250] Therefore it is reasonable to expect that REMIT is applicable to cross-market manipulation. Second, the introduction of benchmark manipulation under MAR distinguishes it from other types of cross-market manipulation, as MAR also includes the prohibition on price positioning.[251] Accordingly REMIT does not include benchmark manipulation, while specifically addressing price positioning.[252] This leads to the conclusion that while it prohibits cross-market manipulation as price positioning, REMIT does not apply to benchmark manipulation since it does not specifically include such a prohibition in its anti-manipulation rules.

One can argue that REMIT's lack of authority over benchmark manipulation does not constitute any practical importance for the prosecution of such manipulative schemes as they often involve wholesale energy derivatives and are therefore prosecutable under MAR. It is true that the manipulative activities aimed at distorting benchmark prices to profit from financial wholesale energy products are regulated under MAR and therefore prosecutable under its benchmark manipulation. However, changes in price benchmarks can result in profits from a greater range of portfolios also involving non-financial wholesale energy products. Article 2(2)(a) clearly stresses that non-financial wholesale energy products are excluded from the scope of MAR's prohibitions on market manipulation and insider trading, even if these products have an effect on the price or value of in-scope financial instruments. For example, a benchmark price with respect to a wholesale energy product can be used as a reference for a bilateral OTC wholesale energy contract where the parties of the contract have an incentive to change benchmark prices and which is outside the scope of MAR. In these transactions, REMIT is the only regulatory instrument to prevent exploitation of these price relations between non-financial contracts and benchmarks. If REMIT is considered as not applicable to these manipulative practices as it does not have a specific prohibition, a major type of market manipulation may go unpunished in the wholesale energy markets.

A positive answer for the applicability of REMIT to benchmark manipulation leads to concerns about a possible jurisdictional overlap between MAR and REMIT.

249. *Energy Transfer Partners, L.P. et. al.*, 120 FERC ¶ 61,086 (2007); *Amaranth Advisors L.L.C. et. al.*, 120 FERC ¶ 61,085 (2007); *Total Gas & Power North America Inc., et al.*, 155 FERC ¶61,105 (2016); *BP America Inc., BP Corporation North America et al.*, 144 FERC ¶ 61,100 (2013); *Barclays Bank PLC, Daniel Brin, Scott Connelly, et al.*, 141 FERC ¶ 61,084 (2012).
250. ACER's Guidance, 38 (2016).
251. Article 12(1)(a)(ii), Regulation No 596/2014.
252. Article 2(2)(a)(ii), Regulation No 1227/2011.

The profitability of a benchmark manipulation depends on, *inter alia,* the diversity of portfolios held by perpetrators. Such portfolios can include wholesale derivative contracts such as swaps, options, or futures, as well as physical contracts on supplying a certain amount of energy at a certain delivery period, such as intraday, day-ahead, weekly, monthly or yearly contracts. As long as these values are priced by reference to a specific benchmark, market participants who hold positions in these contracts will have an incentive to drive up or down the price of this specific benchmark. A market participant can have positions in both financial and non-financial contracts, which together derive their value from benchmark prices. When a market participant engages in conduct aimed at driving up or down a benchmark price to profit from the resultant financial and non-financial positions, the manipulative activity can fall under the jurisdictions of both MAR[253] and REMIT.[254] One can argue that, in such a case, MAR is applicable, as Article 1(2) of REMIT provides that the provisions under REMIT are without prejudice to MAD 2003 which is replaced by MAR. This will result in an extension in the regulatory authority of MAR in cases of benchmark manipulation.

[c] A Hypothetical Scenario

Consider a market participant who engages in physical transactions in wholesale energy products and reports these transactions to indices which provide benchmark prices for the relevant wholesale energy products. The same market participant also holds financial positions such as swaps and physical positions such as forward contracts which are together priced with reference to the benchmark price. In order to derive profit from its physical (forward contracts) and financial (swaps) positions, the market participant engages in loss-making physical transactions and reports them to indices to move the benchmark prices up or down. The only ground for the applicability of MAR to these transactions is the existence of financial positions from which the market participant derives profits, as the loss-making physical transactions are not in-scope for MAR. If it is established that the aim of the manipulation was to derive profits only from physical positions rather than financial positions or the market participant does not hold any financial position related to physical transactions, the prosecution depends on the applicability of REMIT's jurisdiction to benchmark manipulation. The application of MAR to this scenario results in an extension of the MAR's jurisdiction within the context of benchmark manipulation, as neither the transactions reported by the market participant nor the positions from which profits are derived are an in-scope instrument for MAR. The application of MAR to this case contradicts MAR itself as Article 2(2)(a) directly provides that its anti-manipulation rule, Article 12, does not apply to non-financial wholesale energy products even if they affect the price or value of in-scope financial products. If it is found that the market participant also held and derived profit from financial positions as a result of the loss-making transactions, the question still remains as to whether the prohibition of benchmark manipulation

253. Article 12(1)(d), Regulation No 596/2014.
254. Article 2(2)(a)(ii), Regulation No 1227/2011.

under MAR is applicable as a whole or rather to the profits derived from financial instruments. If the latter is correct, the applicability of anti-manipulation rules under REMIT and cooperation between ACER and the ESMA and national competent authorities responsible for the enforcement of these jurisdictions are key issues for the effective application of anti-manipulation rules in wholesale energy markets.

[d] Competent Authorities

Article 22 of MAR requires each Member State to designate an administrative competent authority which will monitor market behaviours and enforce anti-manipulation and insider trading provisions when a market abuse is detected. These authorities are monitored by the ESMA, the financial competent authority at EU-wide level which supervises national authorities and governs cooperation among multiple competent authorities in multiple Member States to ensure that market monitoring duties and enforcement of market abuse provisions are integrated at EU level without giving effect to regulatory arbitrage.[255] In wholesale energy markets, the involvement of ACER in this cooperation process is fundamental, as these markets are subject to market abuse provisions under both REMIT and MAR. As discussed above, the existing financial market regime suffers a lack of clarity and overlapping jurisdictions and it is difficult to mention a single rulebook that governs European financial market regulation. European wholesale energy markets are not exempt from this regulatory complexity. The integrated approach with respect to the application of anti-manipulation to wholesale energy markets at both national and EU-wide levels largely depends on effective and consistent coordination between ACER and the ESMA. These two institutions entered into a 'Memorandum of Understanding' (MOU) on 18 July 2013 concerning consultation and cooperation with respect to their regulatory responsibilities in EU wholesale energy markets. The extent that this cooperation succeeds remains to be seen.

§1.04 EU COMPETITION LAW

[A] General

Even though the application of EU competition law to practices in EU energy markets is not a new phenomenon as it dates back to *Costa v. Enel*[256] in 1964 in which the defendant objected to the nationalisation of electricity markets in Italy, the Commission's first intervention to regulate energy markets came three decades later.[257] Regulatory practices were followed by antitrust intervention through which the Commission sought to support its liberalisation agenda and oversee the functioning of

255. Recital 11, Regulation (EU) No 1095/2010.
256. Case 6/64 *Costa v. ENEL* [1964] ECR 585. It is a landmark case in EU law, as the CJEU established the supremacy of EU rules over domestic law.
257. Council Directive 1990/377/EEC; Council Directive 1990/547/EEC of 29 Oct. 1990 on the transit of electricity through transmission grids, OJ L313, 13.11.1990; Council Directive 1991/296/EEC of 31 May 1991 on the transit of natural gas through grids OJ L147, 12.6.1991.

energy markets.[258] Especially after the adoption of Regulation 1/2003,[259] which granted the Commission the powers to issue sector inquiries, commitment decisions and structural remedies, energy markets and practices have increasingly become subject to the antitrust proceedings under EU competition law. The Commission's authority over the structure of EU energy markets was also approved in the 2007 Lisbon Treaty,[260] which included a new chapter on energy conferring competences on the Commission to:

(a) ensure the functioning of the energy market;
(b) ensure security of energy supply in the Union; and
(c) promote energy efficiency and energy saving and the development of new and renewable forms of energy; and
(d) promote the interconnection of energy networks.[261]

[B] The Application of Competition Law

In order to pursue such objectives the Commission opened several proceedings to prosecute cartels[262] and abuses of dominance,[263] to control mergers[264] and to supervise state aids.[265] Regulation 1/2003 provides two separate enforcement procedures for the enforcement of competition law. First, Article 7 allows the Commission or national competent authorities to issue infringement decisions establishing that defendants violated relevant provisions under EU competition law. As a result of infringement decisions, defendants can be sanctioned behavioural remedies and if these remedies are not effective, structural remedies.[266] Article 9, on the other hand, enables the Commission or national competent authorities to conclude 'Commitment Decisions', according to which the Commission and national competent authorities can accept commitments offered by defendants. Once they are accepted, the commitments become binding on defendants.[267] It is important to note that commitment decisions do

---

258. Ulrich Scholz & Stephan Purps, *Application of EU Competition Law in the Energy Sector* 6/3 Journal of European Competition Law & Practice 200, 209 (2015).
259. Council Regulation (EC) No 1/2003 of 16.12.2002 on the implementation of the rules on competition laid down in Articles 81 and 82 of the Treaty [2003] OJ L1/1.
260. Treaty of Lisbon, Amending the Treaty on European Union and the Treaty Establishing the European Community [2007] OJ C306/1.
261. Article 194, TFEU.
262. *E.ON/GDF* (Case COMP/39.401) Commission Decision [2009] OJ C248/5; *Power Exchanges* (Case AT/39.952) Commission Decision [2014] OJ C334/5.
263. *German Electricity Wholesale Market* (COMP/39.388) Commission Decision [2008] OJ C36/8; *German Electricity Balancing Market* (COMP/39.389) Commission Decision [2008] OJ C36/8.
264. *Sydkraft/Graninge* (Case COMP/M.3268) Commission Decision 2003/297/EC [2003] OJ C297/22; *EDP/ENI/GDP* (Case COMP/M.3440) Commission Decision 2005/801/EC [2005] OJ L302/69.
265. *AB Klaipedos nafta* (Case S.A. 36740) Commission Decision [2013] 2013/N; *Investment Contract (early Contract for Difference) for the Hinkley Point C New Nuclear Power Station* (Case S.A. 3497) Commission Decision 2013/C (ex 2013/N) [2014] OJ C69/60.
266. Article 7(1), Regulation 1/2003.
267. Article 9(1), Regulation 1/2003.

not include the conclusion of an infringement by the defendants and unless a certain set of circumstances are present, they cannot be reopened.[268]

EU competition law is generally applied by national competition authorities at national level and the European Commission at EU level. While the jurisdictions that national competition authorities can exercise are limited to national or regional scope, the Commission investigates cases in which anti-competitive practices affect trade between more than three Member States[269] or EU-wide enforcement is required for efficient prosecution.[270] Competences that competition authorities hold, under Regulation 1/2003, in enforcing EU competition law are parallel.[271] One important distinction is that national competition authorities do not have the legal authority to conclude non-infringement decisions.[272] A national competition authority can find that there are no grounds for an infringement decision about a given market conduct. However, only the Commission can conclude that a certain market practice does not constitute a violation and infringement of EU competition law.

In addition to national competition authorities and the Commission, national regulatory authorities, such as the 'Office of Gas and Electricity Markets' in the UK, can also be conferred on enforcement powers to prosecute practices within their relevant regulatory jurisdictions.[273] A national regulator which encompasses powers to enforce EU competition law can prosecute anti-competitive practices within their jurisdictional scope without the need for referring the conduct to the national competition authority and they are considered a national competent authority with respect to EU competition law analysis. This is not the case for all Member States. In Germany and France, for example, competition law enforcement is under the jurisdiction of national competition authorities, while the authority of sector-specific regulators is limited to the enforcement of relevant regulations.[274] There are also other domestic regimes such as those adopted in Spain and the Netherlands in which national competition authorities also incorporate regulatory enforcement authorities and responsibilities.[275] According

268. According to Article 9(2) of Regulation 1/2003; (t)*he Commission may, upon request or on its own initiative, reopen the proceedings:*
   (a) *where there has been a material change in any of the facts on which the decision was based;*
   (b) *where the undertakings concerned act contrary to their commitments; or*
   (c) *where the decision was based on incomplete, incorrect or misleading information provided by the parties.*
269. Commission Notice on cooperation within the Network of Competition Authorities [2004] OJ C101/43, para. 14.
270. *Ibid.*, para. 15.
271. Alison Jones & Brenda Sufrin, 1051 (2014).
272. Case C-375/09, *Prezes Urzedu Ochrony Konkurencji i Konsumentow v. Tele2 Polska sp. Z o.o., now Netia SA* [2011] ECR I-3055.
273. Renato Nazzini, *Concurrent Proceedings in Competition Law: Procedure, Evidence and Remedies*, 57 (OUP 2004).
274. Cosmo Graham, *UK: The Concurrent Enforcement by Regulators of Competition Law and Sector-Specific Regulation* 7/6 Journal of European Competition Law & Practice 407, 407 (2016).
275. *Ibid.*, 407.

to Regulation 1/2003, Member States are allowed to determine which authority will enforce EU competition law and what mechanisms will be applied for the investigation and the prosecution of anti-competitive practices.[276] Therefore, in referring to the authorities that enforce competition law, the book uses the term 'national competent authorities' rather than directly addressing national competition or regulatory authorities.

[C] The Multiplicity of Jurisdictions

As discussed, there are multiple jurisdictions applicable to wholesale energy markets. In addition to those articulated under REMIT, MiFID/MiFIR 2014, MAR and EMIR also put forward data foreclosure obligations and market manipulation and insider trading prohibitions that apply to wholesale energy products, along with financial instruments. Therefore, market misconduct in a wholesale energy market can be in scope for both energy and financial market regulations and also subject to proceedings under EU competition law, if it constitutes a violation of one or both antitrust rules, Articles 101 and 102. This results in parallel enforcement proceedings in which regulatory frameworks and competition law are applied to the same market misconduct by different competent authorities. For example, in some Member States, where national regulatory authorities also possess authority to enforce competition law, such as the UK, misconduct can be prosecuted under either competition law or the regulatory framework, while in others, where the enforcement authority is under sector-specific regulation and is also incorporated in national competition authorities, such as Spain, the decision to determine the applicable framework is bestowed upon national competition authorities.

Even though in its Recital 29, REMIT provides that: *'(n)ational regulatory authorities, competent financial authorities of the Member States and, where appropriate, national competition authorities should cooperate to ensure a coordinated approach to tackling market abuse on wholesale energy markets which encompasses both commodity markets and derivatives markets'*,[277] it does not provide guidance on how a coordinated approach can be developed within competent authorities. The absence of a coherent framework that specifically establishes competences in wholesale energy markets results in concerns about the concurrent application of competition rules and sector-specific regulation and double jeopardy or the principle of *ne bis in idem*. In this respect, a legal analysis of the concurrency of competition and sector-specific rules is of great importance in evaluating to what extent the legal approach developed in EU law suffices to tackle market manipulation in wholesale energy markets.

276. Alison Jones & Brenda Sufrin, 1051 (2014).
277. Recital 29, Regulation 1227/2011.

[D] Concurrency of the Applicable Jurisdictions

[1] Parameters of Concurrency

The multiplicity of available jurisdictions results in legal and regulatory uncertainties with respect to the development of a single rulebook that can be followed by market participants. The same market conduct that is prohibited under REMIT can also be subject to proceedings by financial regulators under financial regulation (MiFID/MiFIR 2014, MAR and EMIR) and by competition authorities at EU and national level under EU Competition Law. Certain market practices may even lead to conflicting decisions by different jurisdictional authorities. This is particularly relevant for data disclosure obligations, as the disclosure of certain market information that is required under REMIT and financial market regulation can result in the Commission's or national competition authorities' intervention under EU competition law.[278] Since the focus of this book is mainly the prohibition of market manipulation and its enforcement and prosecution in wholesale energy markets, the interplay between competition law and data disclosure obligations as well as insider trading is not discussed in detail. Nevertheless, it is important to note that overlapping jurisdictions with respect to data disclosure obligations under REMIT, financial regulation and EU Competition Law clearly illustrate how the uncertainties with respect to the legal framework applicable to wholesale energy markets are pervasive and not limited solely to the prohibition of market manipulation.

Concurrency has many facets. Several authorities can claim jurisdiction over the same market practices by the same market participants on several grounds. First, concurrency can take place when multiple regulators exercise their authority. This was particularly the case in the US, as both the Commodity Futures Trading Commission (CFTC) and Federal Energy Regulatory Commission (FERC) considered themselves competent in prosecuting manipulative practices in wholesale energy markets. Second, two different national competition authorities can assert jurisdiction over a manipulative conduct. Such concurrency can occur in two ways; horizontally and vertically.[279] Horizontal concurrency involves two competition authorities from different national jurisdictions. For example a manipulative conduct may affect two different national markets and give rise to proceedings by the national competition authorities in these markets. Vertical concurrency, on the other hand, involves manipulative conduct that is prosecuted by both national competition authorities at national level and the Commission at EU level. Finally, concurrency can also occur between competition and regulatory authorities. Accordingly market misconduct can become subject to proceedings by regulatory and competition authorities under relevant regulation and/or EU competition law.

278. For detailed discussion, *see* John Ratliff, *Transparency under REMIT and EU Competition Law* 1/2 Competition Law and Policy Debate 82 (2015).
279. *See* D. Geradin & R. O'Donoghue, *The Concurrent Application of Competition Law and Regulation: The Case of Margin Squeeze Abuses in the Telecommunications Sector* 1/2 Journal of Competition Law & Economics 355, 410 (2005).

The chapter does not provide detailed analysis on the concurrent application of competition law by different competition authorities. This type of concurrency was addressed in the Commission's notices on the cooperation between the Commission and the courts[280] and on cooperation within the network of competition authorities,[281] which together stipulate the case allocation between competition authorities. Accordingly cases brought into notice are prosecuted by the *'well-placed'* competition authority which would be designated on the basis of facts. Again the chapter provides very limited analysis on the concurrency between regulators. As discussed above, there are several issues where jurisdictions of financial and energy markets regulators overlap and the development of the case law on how case allocation should be determined depends on the functioning of memoranda of understanding,[282] published by ACER, ESMA and national regulatory authorities. This chapter focuses on the concurrency between EU competition law and market regulation. The question of what types of manipulative practices can lead to proceedings under REMIT, MAR and EU Competition Law is delved into in the following sections.[283] The analysis of the concurrent application of competition law and sector-specific regulation and its legal implications as to the prosecution of market manipulation in wholesale energy markets are fundamental to understanding the interplay between antitrust rules and energy market regulation.

[2] Concurrent Application of Competition Law and Sector-Specific Regulation

Concurrency is not limited to energy markets and can occur in any market, subject to sector-specific regulation. This is especially the case when state authorities engage in liberalisation policies to introduce competition in sectors which were previously dominated by legal monopolies with exclusive rights in buying and/or selling in energy products. Market practices which were allowed under monopolistic market conditions have been no longer considered legal and are thus prohibited under liberalising regulations. Nevertheless, opening of these ex-monopolistic markets also results in intervention by competition authorities which are no longer bound by exemptions provided for ex-monopolies allowing them to operate without being subject to antitrust rules. This results in double-regulation of these newly liberalised markets. A market

280. Commission Notice on the co-operation between the Commission and the courts of the EU Member States in the application of Articles 81 and 82 EC [2004] OJ C101/54.
281. Commission Notice on cooperation within the Network of Competition Authorities [2004] OJ C101/43.
282. Memorandum of Understanding between ESMA and ACER concerning the consultation and cooperation regarding their regulatory responsibilities in relation to EU wholesale energy markets, 18 Jul. 2013; Multilateral Memorandum of Understanding between the Agency for the Cooperation of Energy Regulators and National Regulatory Authorities and market monitoring bodies concerning cooperation and coordination of market monitoring under Regulation (EU) No 1227/2011 of the European Parliament and of the Council on wholesale energy market integrity and transparency (REMIT), 23 Aug. 2013.
283. *See* Ch. 4.

practice that is prohibited under regulation may also lead to opening of proceedings under competition law.

In the US, concurrency is not allowed when the court established that a given market conduct is under strict scrutiny by sector-specific regulation. There are two cases in which the US courts were asked to apply competition law to a conduct which was already prohibited and remedied under regulation. In *Trinko*, the US Supreme Court refused to uphold a complaint alleging that the defendant violated Section 2 of the Sherman Act by failing to provide third-party access to its fixed telecommunication infrastructure.[284] The court held that the relevant telecommunications market was under a strict regulatory regime under the Telecommunications Act of 1996[285] and the misconduct at issue had already been remedied in according with the regulatory obligations.[286] The court suggested that '(a)*ntitrust analysis must always be attuned to the particular structure of the industry at issue*'.[287] The availability of a regulatory framework established to deter and remedy anti-competitive harm rendered the additional protection from antitrust enforcement negligible.[288] Accordingly, the court deemed it unnecessary to apply antitrust rules to an anti-competitive conduct which had already been prohibited and remedied under the sector-specific regulation.[289]

In *Credit Suisse,*[290] the Supreme Court followed the same approach and further stressed that the existence of a sector-specific regulation and the availability of a sector-specific regulator that continuously supervised and enforced its authority over the regulated market resulted in an 'implied immunity' from the application of antitrust rules.[291] The case involved allegations of anticompetitive practices in securities markets which were strictly regulated by the Security Exchange Commission (SEC) under the Securities Exchange Act (SEA) of 1934.[292] The court required four conditions to be met to conclude the implied immunity from antitrust rules. First, the availability of a sector-specific regulator supervising market activity was necessary. Second, it must be shown that the regulatory authority enforced its authority over the given market misconduct. Third, a potential conflict between the regulatory framework and antitrust rules must affect the regulator's jurisdictional authority. Finally, the Court required that there must be a serious risk of conflict the antitrust and regulatory regimes.[293] Applying a very lenient approach to the evaluation of the third and fourth elements, the Court concluded that all of these requirements were present in the current case and

284. *Verizon Communications Inc v. Law Offices of Curtis V Trinko LLP*, 3540 US 398 (2004).
285. Telecommunications Act of 1996, Pub L No 104-104, 110 Stat 56.
286. The defendant was required to pay more than $10 million to other market participants under state and federal regulation. *Verizon Communications Inc v. Law Offices of Curtis V Trinko LLP*, 3540 US 398, 403–404 (2004).
287. *Ibid.*
288. *Ibid.*
289. *Ibid.*
290. *Credit Suisse Securities (USA), LLC, et al. v. Billing et al.*, 127 S.Ct. 2383 (2007), *Credit Suisse Securities (USA) LLC v. Billing* 551 U.S. 264 (2007).
291. *Credit Suisse Securities (USA), LLC, et al. v. Billing et al.*, 127 S.Ct. 2383, 2389 (2007).
292. The Securities Act of 1934, 17 C.F.R. § 240.10b-5 (2011).
293. *Credit Suisse Securities (USA), LLC, et al. v. Billing et al.*, 127 S.Ct. 2383, 2397 (2007).

thus antitrust rules could not be applicable to the relevant market misconduct under implied immunity.[294]

The CJEU's approach to concurrency is different from that of the US Supreme Court. EU case law identifies three situations in which EU courts are barred from applying EU competition law and sector-specific regulation concurrently to a particular market misconduct. First, EU competition law cannot be applied to regulated markets, if the regulatory framework includes an explicit derogation for that purpose.[295] Second, EU competition law is not applicable to a regulated market which is not open to competition.[296] This is particularly the case in markets which are dominated by de jure or de facto monopolies.[297] Third, EU competition law cannot be applied to a market conduct which is required under sector-specific regulation.[298] This type of exception is called 'State Action Defence'[299] and can be invoked only when it is established that market participants engage in an anti-competitive conduct to comply with their obligations required under the regulatory framework. In other words, the regulatory framework must deprive market participants of the ability to act independently in the market with respect to the contested misconduct.[300]

In conflicts where any of these exceptions are not present, both EU competition law and sector-specific regulation can be applied to the same market misconduct and market participants. The telecommunications sector is illustrative of the approach taken by EU courts to concurrency. In *Deutsche Telekom*,[301] the CJEU identified that the defendant could autonomously act to refrain from breaching EU competition law rules without violating their obligations under the relevant regulatory framework for the telecommunications sector and thus could not invoke State Action Defence to avoid paying penalties.[302] The ability of market participants to act autonomously was interpreted very broadly. Even if the extent to which market participants could act autonomously was small under relevant regulatory frameworks, they can still be refused the right to invoke State Action Defence.[303] Whether or not contested market behaviour has been remedied under the regulatory framework is also irrelevant for the concurrent application.[304] Accordingly the defendants could still be fined for a breach of competition law, even if a remedy for the misconduct has been provided under the regulatory framework.

294. *Ibid.*
295. Case T-398/07 *Spain v. Commission* [2012] EU:T:2012:173, para. 55.
296. Case T-360/09 *E.ON Ruhrgas AG and E.ON AG v. Commission* [2012] EU:T:2012:332, para. 84.
297. Niamh Dune, *Competition Law and Economic Regulation: Making and Managing Markets* 216 (CUP 2015).
298. Joined Cases C-359/95 & C-379/95 P *Commission v. Ladbroke Racing Ltd.*, ECR I-6265 para. 33.
299. *See* Fernando Castillo De La Torre, *State Action Defence in EC Competition Law* 28/4 World Competition 407 (2005).
300. Niamh Dune, *Competition Law and Economic Regulation: Making and Managing Markets*, 217 (CUP 2015).
301. C-280/08 P *Deutsche Telekom AG v. Commission* (2010) ECR I-9555.
302. *Ibid.*, paras 84–89.
303. Niamh Dune, 218 (2015).
304. *Telekomunikacja Polska* (Case COMP/39.525) Commission Decision [2011] OJ C327/7 paras 131, 138.

The difference between US and EU case law on concurrency is strongly related to the difference between legal approaches to the question as to whether there is a hierarchy between competition law and sector-specific regulation. US case law does not discuss a hierarchy between these two legal instruments.[305] The Sherman Act does not have any supremacy over the Telecommunications Act of 1996, EP Act 2005 or other sector-specific regulatory frameworks. This is not the case in EU law. While the majority of sector-specific regulatory frameworks have been adopted in secondary legislation such as directives and regulations which require further legislative actions for their implementation at national law, competition rules are based on primary legislation in the EU Treaty.[306] EU courts acknowledge that the treaty rules prevail over domestic rules.[307] This is also supported by several directives and regulations which specifically provide that their rules and provisions are applied without prejudice to the application of EU competition law.[308] The lack of a deference mechanism in EU case law, and the courts' insistence on the concurrency results in the duplication of proceedings and thus gives rise to concerns about double jeopardy/*ne bis in idem* principle.

[3] **Ne Bis In Idem *Principle***

Originating in criminal law, the principle of *ne bis in idem* or double jeopardy is related to the right of a person not to be subject to multiple investigations or prosecutions for the same offence.[309] The principle was also included in Article 4(1) of Protocol No 7 to the European Convention for the Protection of Human Rights and Fundamental Freedoms (ECHR),[310] and also in Article 50 of European Charter of Fundamental Rights.[311] In *PVC (No 2)* the CJEU adopted a very limited approach to the application of this principle in EU competition law.[312] The Court defined the principle as it '*merely prohibits a fresh assessment in depth of the alleged commission of an offence which would result in the imposition of either a second penalty, in addition to the first, in the event that liability is established a second time, or a first penalty in the event that liability not established by the first decision is established by the second*'.[313] Accordingly if the courts find that a decision of the Commission must be rejected due to procedural flaws without further evaluation of legal liability attributed to defendants, the *ne bis in idem* principle does not apply and new proceedings can be opened.

305. D. Geradin & R. O'Donoghue, 418 (2005).
306. *Ibid.*
307. Case 6/64 *Costa v. ENEL* [1964] ECR 585, 593; Case 14/68 *Walt Wilhelm and Others v. Bundeskartellamt* [1969] ECR 1, 13–15.
308. Article 1(2), Regulation 1227/2011.
309. Renato Nazzini, 115 (2004).
310. Convention for the Protection of Human Rights and Fundamental Freedoms (the European Human Rights Convention) (Rome, 4 Nov. 1950), Protocol No 7.
311. Charter of Fundamental Rights of the European Union [2000] OJ C364/1.
312. Joined Cases C-238/99 P, C-244/99 P, C-247/99 P, C-250/99 P, C-251/99 P, C-252/99 P and C-254/99 P *Limburgse Vinyl Maatschappij NV (LVM) v. Commission of the European Communities (PVC No 2)* [2002] ECR I-8375. *See also* Renato Nazzini, 55 (2004).
313. *PVC No 2*, para. 61.

The CJEU's decision in *PVC (No 2)* is related to multiple antitrust proceedings and does not directly address the concurrent application of competition law and sector-specific regulation. It is *Aalborg Portland,*[314] in which the CJEU elaborated on concurrency and established a threefold criteria to evaluate whether the principle of *ne bis in idem* was violated as a result of multiple proceedings under competition law and sector-specific regulation. In order to invoke the double jeopardy defence, defendants must show that three elements present in concurrent proceedings are the same: (i) persons; (ii) facts; and (iii) the legal interests protected. In *Telekomunikacja Polska,*[315] the Commission applied these threefold criteria to the defendant, the incumbent telecommunications operator in Poland which had been previously investigated and remedied under national regulations due to its continuing failure to provide third-party access to its fixed broadband infrastructure.

Evaluating whether the defendant's failure constituted a refusal to supply in violation of Article 102 of TFEU, the Commission concluded that even though the defendant's conduct had been previously prosecuted under national regulations, fulfilling the first and the second elements of the criteria, the legal interests protected by the regulation and competition law were different and thus *ne bis in idem* principle could not hinder the proceedings brought under EU competition law.[316] According to the Commission, the aim of EU competition law was '*to preserve undistorted competition within the European Union*', while that of Polish telecommunications regulation was to include '*other objectives*' *such as* '*development and use of modern telecommunications infrastructure, maximum benefits for users in terms of choice, price and quality of telecommunications services and net neutrality*'.[317] To what extent the available rules on the prohibition of market manipulation give rise to concerns about the principle of *ne bis in idem* is addressed in greater detail in the following sections.[318]

§1.05 CONCLUSION

This chapter has discussed the legal framework established by REMIT, which consists of three important pillars addressing the transparency and integrity of wholesale energy markets across the EU. The main objective of the regulation is to provide a common regulatory approach taken by the National Regulatory Agencies to ensure confidence and a fair as well as competitive interplay between demand and supply in the wholesale energy markets.[319] This is important as national energy markets across the EU are increasingly integrated with each other and market conditions and inefficiencies in one jurisdiction influence market conditions and prices in others.[320]

314. Case C-204/00 P *Aalborg Portland A/S et al. v. Commission* [2004] ECR I-123.
315. *Telekomunikacja Polska* (Case COMP/39.525) Commission Decision [2011] OJ C327/7.
316. *Ibid.*, paras 138–139.
317. *Ibid.*, para. 138.
318. *See* section 4.03[E].
319. Recital 1, Regulation No 1227/2011.
320. The trade of energy through exchanges provides an effective means for price convergence. For example, in the electricity markets, market coupling, which designates the volumes and the prices based on the marginal pricing principle, is performed under two procedures; the Central

Accordingly, disclosure obligations and prohibitions of insider trading and market manipulation are adopted to ensure that wholesale energy trading across the EU is carried out via a common, well-established legal approach, which clearly identifies and proscribes market behaviours that are regarded as market abuse. However this chapter argues that the concepts and definitions introduced under REMIT are far from being precise and thus fulfilling the designated objectives.

As to information disclosure and the prohibition of insider trading, REMIT set very broad obligations and definitions leading to further ambiguities and concerns of potential collusion among market participants benefitting from higher levels of transparency. Even though REMIT provides a list of inside information and therefore should be made public, the obligations and definitions are designed very broadly and cause greater uncertainties as to what type of information might qualify as inside information and as to what sanctions and remedies should be provided in the case of non-compliance. As the guidance document published by ACER also fails to clarify the concepts presented or provide further explanation as to the definitions given under REMIT, it is not reasonable to expect the development of a common approach across national jurisdictions in addressing information asymmetry and insider trading in the wholesale energy markets.

REMIT provided a definition for the prohibition of market manipulation and ACER also gave further details as to what types of activities can be deemed to be manipulative under these definitions. The concept was first included in the EU context with the adoption of the MAD in 2004, from which REMIT derived its definitions of market abuse. The scope of MAD was limited to financial markets and did not apply to wholesale energy products.[321] The chapter shows that the examples and classifications provided under REMIT and ACER are far from establishing a legal methodology to be followed by competent authorities in prosecuting market manipulation. The necessary guidance in EU case law with respect to identifying what type of market behaviours can constitute manipulation, how to detect them and what makes existing market designs and structures practical for market manipulation is missing.

The regulatory and legal frameworks applicable to EU wholesale energy markets are not limited to REMIT. Several rules under financial regulation and EU competition law constitute great importance in establishing the legal regime that govern the energy sector. Nevertheless, the chapter shows that uncertainties remain, as to the scope of the existing legal framework that applies to wholesale energy. Several wholesale energy products are under the jurisdiction of multiple regulatory and competition authorities. While energy market regulators are entitled to monitor and ensure the functioning of wholesale energy markets, financial regulators also exercise close market oversight in wholesale financial contracts such as options, swaps and futures. Finally, competition

West Europe (CWE) including Germany, France and Benelux countries and the European Market Coupling (EMCC), encompassing CWE and Scandinavia. For the full account of the market coupling process, *see* http://www.acer.europa.eu/Electricity/Regional_initiatives/Cross_Regional_Roadmaps/Pages/1.-Market-Coupling.aspx (accessed 29 Jun. 2017).

321. As mentioned, according to Article 9 of MAD 2003, wholesale energy products that are traded in regulated markets are within the jurisdiction of Directive's market manipulation rules.

authorities at both national and EU levels oversee both financial and energy markets and intervene when a violation of competition law rules is alleged.

Energy market participants are obliged to follow several requirements and obligations provided under MiFID/MiFIR 2014, MAR/MAD 2014, EMIR, REMIT and competition law. EU courts' approach to the concurrent application of competition law and sector-specific regulation further elevates the uncertainties with respect to establishing the applicable legal regimes. The availability of these multiple jurisdictions renders a uniform and transparent single rulebook that an energy market participant can rely on when operating in energy markets a still distant dream.

Addressing certain examples of market manipulation derived from the experience of the national regulatory agencies, the guidance document published by ACER also fails to provide a common understanding of a legal approach in dealing with market manipulation across the EU. Many of the examples given as market manipulation can also be part of legitimate trading activity and the document does not provide any explanation on how a market behaviour is deemed to be manipulative and on what basis a market conduct can be separated from legitimate trading. As REMIT does not include an intent element in its legal analysis, a demarcation of market behaviours with respect to their economic effects on the wholesale energy markets is needed to determine whether they are manipulative or not. However, to what extent the existing legal tools are sufficient to deliver such demarcation is questionable.

The existing case law on market manipulation in EU wholesale energy markets involves only one case, *Iberdrola*, in which the defendant was found liable for violating Article 5 of REMIT through perpetrating capacity withholding practices in Spanish wholesale energy markets.[322] Given the growing level of transparency through data disclosure obligations and market oversight, the number of proceedings brought against market participants for possible breaches of anti-manipulation rules is envisaged to increase.[323] Nevertheless, questions as to what types of market practices can be considered manipulative under REMIT remain unanswered. Since EU case law on market manipulation has yet to be developed, the need for an extensive legal analysis on market manipulation beyond the EU is blatantly obvious to understand how market manipulation can be a concern in energy markets.

In this regard, US case law on market manipulation in energy markets provides an insight into how energy markets can become subject to market manipulation and what types of market misconduct can result in proceedings under anti-manipulation rules. In the following chapter, the book first discusses the rules that prohibit market manipulation under US statutes and attempts to define and clarify the concept in academic literature. The findings of the next chapter clearly show that defining a single common definition of market manipulation has been also problematic in the US where

322. Peter Willis & Hermenegildo Altozano, *Spanish Authority Fines Iberdrola €25m in First REMIT Market Manipulation Infringement Decision*, (Bird&Bird 4 Feb. 2014). https://www.twobirds.com/en/news/articles/2016/spain/spanish-authority-fines-iberdrola-25m-in-first-remit-infringement-decision (accessed 29 Jun. 2017).
323. John Ratliff & Roberto Grasso, *REMIT – Implementing Measures Clarifying Data Reporting Obligations* (Wilmerhale 2015). https://www.wilmerhale.com/pages/publicationsandnewsdetail.aspx?NewsPubId=17179876224 (accessed 29 Jun. 2017).

the prosecution of market manipulation took place before anywhere else in the world and the concept is historically known to be rife with uncertainties and ambiguities.[324] In the following chapter, the book delves into the application and formulation of these anti-manipulation rules under US case law. Even though there are significant differences between REMIT's formulation of market manipulation as transaction-based and information-based and the evolution of the concept in US case law, the analysis and arguments provided in the following chapters are of great importance in understanding how the legal framework established by REMIT will be applied to EU wholesale energy markets and what types of market practices may result in proceedings by competent authorities under the prohibition of market manipulation.

324. In *Cargill v. Hardin*, the Eighth Circuit noted that, '*The methods and techniques of manipulation are limited only by the ingenuity of man.*' *Cargill v. Hardin*, 452 F.2d 1154 (8th Cir. 1971), *cert. denied*, 406 U.S. 932 (1972). *See* Shaun Ledgerwood & Dan Harris (2012).

CHAPTER 2

Anti-manipulation Law: Its Strengths and Weaknesses

§2.01 INTRODUCTION

Even though it has been generally considered the main culprit for crashes and dysfunction in financial markets,[325] the regulation of financial markets has been historically rife with confusion about what constitutes market manipulation. In *Cargill*, the US Court of Appeals, Eighth Circuit, stated that '(t)*he methods and techniques of manipulation are limited only by the ingenuity of man*'.[326] The inefficiencies in legal standards categorising manipulative behaviours have caused case law and legal literature to develop an abstract '*I know it when I see it*' [327] approach that provides very limited guidance to market participants on how to operate in the market without breaching anti-manipulation laws.[328] Since legal and economic theories have failed to remove the uncertainties in the application of anti-manipulation rules to market behaviour, many commentators have taken it upon themselves to develop frameworks to define and identify market manipulation.

In order to analyse the practice of market manipulation and functioning of REMIT more efficiently, this book provides a detailed analysis of the identification and classification of market manipulation as developed in case law as well as legal

325. During the tumultuous times of the 'Great Depression' and 'Wall Street Crash' in the 1920s and the 1930s, President Franklin D. Roosevelt, in his speech to US Congress, stated that '(t)*he people of this country are, in an overwhelming majority, fully aware of the fact that unregulated speculation in securities and in commodities was one of the most important contributing factors in the artificial and unwarranted boom which had so much to do with the terrible conditions of the years following 1929*'. *See* Jerry Markham, 66 (2015).
326. *Cargill v. Hardin*, 452 F.2d 1154 (8th Cir. 1971), *cert. denied*, 406 U.S. 932 (1972).
327. '*Sophisticated economic justification for the distinctions made in this area of law may at times seem questionable. Sometimes the know it when you see it test appears most useful*' *Frey v. CFTC*, 931 F.2d 1171, 1175 (7th Cir. 1991).
328. Jerry Markham, 211 (2015).

discussions introduced by many commentators as to the problems and uncertainties with respect to the application of the concept. In the second section, this chapter covers the development of anti-manipulation law in the US. The third section introduces a traditional understanding of and legal discussion on the categorisation of market manipulation in US case law providing the classification of fraud-based and artificial price-based manipulation. The fourth section discusses the reconceptualisation attempts of market manipulation by legal commentators proposing alternative definitions and frameworks for the functioning of markets. The fifth section comprises of the conclusions.

§2.02 THE CONCEPT OF MARKET MANIPULATION

The concept of market manipulation, though at the centre of current legal discussion, is not a new phenomenon. In the US, where the early attempts to prosecute market manipulation date back to the Revolution,[329] the perpetration of market manipulation has been subject to regulatory and judicial oversight since the operation of pools, earlier in the nineteenth century, where issuers and speculators traded physical and financial products heavily.[330] It was believed that the price fluctuations in these pools caused by the manipulative behaviour of market participants in the early decades of the twentieth century led to the stock market crash in 1929 and eventually, the 'Great Depression' of the 1930s.[331] This was followed by the prohibition of market manipulation by the SEA[332] in 1934 and the Commodity Exchange Act[333] (CEA) in 1936. The formulation of these two statutes was different. While the former proscribed fraud-based market manipulation, the latter prohibited behaviours that make market prices artificial, which was called artificial price-based manipulation.

The majority of the examples introduced within the ACER's guidance document,[334] such as wash trades, improper matched orders, pump and dump schemes etc., are derived from the experience of US Courts in prosecuting under the SEA's fraud-based market manipulation Rule of 10(b)-5.[335] The development of judicial practice in US courts for over a hundred years[336] has led to a belief that market manipulation is a

329. George Washington pointed at '*monopolisers, forestallers and engrossers*' as culprits of inflated commodity prices during the Revolution and asserted individuals responsible should be '*hung in gibbets*'. *See ibid.*, 14.
330. In 1817, the New York Stock Exchanges adopted the prohibition of fictitious sales. *Ibid.*, 14.
331. Daniel R. Fischel & David J. Ross, *Should the Law Prohibit Manipulation in Financial Markets?* 105 Harvard Law Review 503 (1991). For further details on pools, *see* Steve Thel, '*The Original Conception of Section 10(b) of the Securities Exchange Act*' 42/2 Stanford Law Review 385 (1990).
332. 17 C.F.R. § 240.10b-5 (2011).
333. The Commodity Exchange Act of 1936, 7 U.S.C. § 13b (2010), *see* https://www.law.cornell.edu/uscode/pdf/lii_usc_TI_07_CH_1.pdf (accessed 29 Jun. 2017).
334. ACER's Guidance, 36–40 (2016).
335. *See* Jerry Markham (2015).
336. For further information on the history of market manipulation, *see* Jerry Markham (2015).

type of fraud as it involves covert and disguised positions and intentions.[337] Such a conclusion was reasonable, since judicial history with respect to market behaviour that resulted in artificial prices in relevant products has been silent and the majority of the prosecutions carried out in US law involved certain types of deceitful and fraudulent behaviour.

The approach taken in SEA's fraud-based manipulation rule was also adopted by other US sector-specific regulators. Particularly in the energy sector, with the rapid increase in the trading of derivatives markets in the 2000s providing liquidity and means for market participants not only to hedge their positions in the energy markets but also to invest in financial instruments, the US Congress enacted the Energy Policy Act in 2005[338] (EPAct), which introduced fraud-based manipulation provisions into the Federal Power Act (FPA)[339] and the Natural Gas Act (NGA).[340] Accordingly, the anti-manipulation rule adopted by the FERC following the reading of the SEA Rule 10b-5, prohibits fraudulent behaviour in the US energy markets by traders, who have acted with a requisite intent. This formulation does not require FERC to prove price artificiality. Neither does it have to carry out extensive economic analysis on price levels. Nevertheless, prosecuting manipulative behaviour solely on the basis of a fraud-based definition caused certain complexities in practice. In the *Radley*[341] case, the US court found it problematic to construe a market behaviour, which intrinsically does not involve any fraudulent or deceptive device or scheme, as a fraud-based market manipulation.

The CFTC also pursued cases against traders on the basis of manipulation of energy derivatives[342] as its jurisdiction covers trading in physical and financial energy commodity exchange. This resulted in an overlap of its jurisdiction with the FERC's. In *Amaranth Advisors,*[343] both the FERC and CFTC exercised their jurisdiction and initiated enforcement proceedings against market behaviours based on the manipulation of future contracts. The CFTC also declared that it will apply its provisions to certain energy products that had been within the scope of the FERC's jurisdiction. As the FERC's ability to prosecute market manipulation is limited due to its fraud-based formulation, the CFTC's enforcement of anti-manipulation rules on the basis of price artificiality is of greater importance. However, in order to comprehend the relationship between fraud-based and artificial price-based manipulation in the energy markets, it is necessary to demarcate the legal borderlines between these two types of market manipulations along with the ways they converge with or diverge from each other.

---

337. Frank H. Easterbrook, *Monopoly, Manipulation, and the Regulation of Futures Markets* 59/2 The Journal of Business 103 (1986).
338. Energy Policy Act of 2005 (Public Law 109–58).
339. The Federal Power Act. 16 U.S.C. §§ 791-828c (2006).
340. The Natural Gas Act. 15 U.S.C. §§ 717-717z (2006).
341. *United States v. Radley*, 659 F. Supp. 2d 803 (S.D. Tex. 2009). For greater detail, *see* section 3.02[C].
342. Shaun Ledgerwood & Dan Harris, 1, 4 (2012), note 37.
343. *Amaranth Advisors L.L.C. et. al.*, 120 FERC ¶ 61,085 (2007).

§2.03 DEMARCATING FRAUD-BASED AND ARTIFICIAL PRICE-BASED FORMULATIONS

[A] General

The distinction between fraud-based and artificial price-based manipulation is not clear-cut. This is partly due to varying definitions of market manipulation in the legal and academic literature. Even though both early legal statutes and US case law applied and enforced anti-manipulation rules, there is not any common definition which clearly demarcates the extent and characteristics of market manipulation.[344] Identifying manipulation is a difficult task for a regulator. Almost every movement and strategy carried out by firms and traders have consequences on market prices and determining whether or not such price differences are based on legitimate trading activities or manipulative schemes is, in certain conditions impossible, without clear indications about the perpetrators' true intentions. This has resulted in some commentators, such as Jerry Markham, considering market manipulation an unprosecutable crime.[345] Daniel R. Fischel and David J. Ross, went further and argue that existing market manipulation law must be repealed as it poses a serious threat to the well-functioning of markets.[346] Others have proposed various market manipulation definitions. Forging an appropriate definition that clearly sheds light upon the nature of market manipulation and identifies characteristics that separate its functioning from other types of market abuses as well as from legitimate trading activities is an issue long discussed intensively in the academic literature. There have been various attempts by several commentators to define market manipulation which will be analysed in greater detail in the following sections.[347] The aim of this paper is not to provide an alternative market manipulation definition. Neither does it undertake to provide an evaluation of the effectiveness or the functionality of these definitions in addressing manipulative conduct. Instead, it focuses on the borderlines that separate fraud-based and artificial price-based manipulations and evaluates how these two legal concepts interact with each other in practice.

In order to comprehend the extent and application of these two concepts, it is necessary to address the conceptual problems that the academic literature seeks to answer in developing alternative definitions for market manipulation. It can be noted that the definitions of market manipulation refrain from establishing two separate prohibitions with respect to fraud and price artificiality. The fact that proving price artificiality has been traditionally problematic results in the perception that adoption of a definition integrating both artificial price-based and fraud-based manipulation would alleviate evidentiary burdens. Such a formulation would also be consistent with the idea that artificial price-based manipulation intrinsically features the characteristics of

344. Jerry Markham, 211 (2015); *see also* Wendy C. Purdue, *Manipulation of Futures Markets: Redefining the Offense* 56 Fordham Law Review 345, 346 (1987).
345. Jerry W. Markham, *Manipulation of Commodity Futures Prices-The Unprosecutable Crime* 8/2 Yale Journal on Regulation 281 (1991).
346. *See* Daniel R. Fischel & David J. Ross (1991).
347. *See* section 2.04.

fraud and therefore should be considered as a part of fraud-based market manipulation.[348] To what extent these two concepts can be prohibited under a common formulation requires a legal analysis involving the identification of the market behaviour each prohibition undertakes to deal with and the legal elements that they seek to establish for the enforcement of the prohibitions.

[B] Fraud-Based Manipulation

[1] General

This type of manipulation involves any deceptive behaviour that is designed to mislead other market participants into believing that the value of a certain product is lower or higher than its true level or that supply and demand conditions in the market are different than actual existing conditions. Such market behaviour has no legitimate purpose other than to create a false impression, which causes other market participants to act in a manner desired by the manipulator. Even though the legal analysis required in US case law to determine whether a fraud-based manipulation has taken place may differ from that of EU,[349] whether or not the manipulator accrues any benefit from the fraudulent behaviour is irrelevant in both jurisdictions. Moreover, whether or not the prices change in relation to the products or markets that the fraudulent behaviour is related to is also irrelevant.

[2] The Formulation

The main focus of the prohibition of fraud-based market manipulation is the reliability of the information present in the market.[350] Therefore, the formulation of its legal analysis differs from that of artificial price-based market manipulation, which focuses on price effects in the markets. Accordingly, SEA, Section 10(b)-5 provides that:

> *(i)t shall be unlawful for any person, directly or indirectly, by the use of any means or instrumentality of interstate commerce or of the mails, or of any facility of any national securities exchange, (a) to employ any device, scheme, or artifice to defraud, (b) to make any untrue statement of a material fact or to omit to state a material fact necessary in order to make the statements made, in the light of the circumstances under which they were made, not misleading, or (c) to engage in any act, practice, or course of business which operates or would operate as a fraud or deceit upon any person, in connection with the purchase or sale of any security.*[351] (italics and parenthesis added)

348. Frank H. Easterbrook, 118 (1986); Shaun D. Ledgerwood & Paul Carpenter, 258 (2012).
349. For example, the intent requirement, which is an important component of anti-manipulation rules in the US, is not required in the EU's formulation of market manipulation.
350. Craig Pirrong, 6 (2010).
351. 17 C.F.R. § 240.10b-5 (2011).

SEA's jurisdiction covers security trading, such as the purchase and sale of equities in stock exchanges. In order to apply Article 10(b)-5 to manipulative behaviour, it must be proved that:

(1) a fraudulent or deceptive device, scheme or statement must be utilized;
(2) such a device, scheme, or statement must be in relation to sale or purchase of a product in the stock market; and
(3) the perpetrator of the device, scheme or statement must act with a requisite intent.

[3] *Examples of Fraud-Based Manipulation*

This fraud-based definition of market manipulation has been successful in prosecuting deceptive and fraudulent practices in the securities markets.[352] Traditionally, the nature of a fraudulent device is irrelevant for the determination of fraud-based manipulation. Manipulation via fraudulent transactions which do not involve real risks and material effects has also been considered fraud.[353] In other words whether market manipulation is transaction-based or information-based is irrelevant for the finding of fraud under the SEA's formulation.

As SEA's Rule 10b-5 provides, the use of any fraudulent device, scheme, or statement in relation to the sale or purchase of a relevant product with a requisite intent is prohibited. Such fraudulent devices may involve dissemination of false information to the market or entering into transactions that create a false impression regarding the relevant products or the conditions of the markets. For example in pump and dump schemes, the perpetrator, who buys a large long position with respect to a product, disseminates false information, which moves the prices to a level favourable to the perpetrator's position and sells its position at this inflated price. Wash trades, on the other hand, involve the perpetrator both buying and selling the same product at the same price to create a false impression that there is a lot of activity in the market with respect to the relevant product.

Another example of a fraudulent transaction is matched orders, in which the perpetrator places a sale or purchase order, with the knowledge that another party is placing an identical order, which matches the size and price of the first order. Both wash trades and matched orders are transactions used to create a churn in market activity. The only difference between them is that while in wash trades it is the same person who places both the purchase and sale order, in a matched order, this practice is done with a party in a coordinated way.

352. Shaun D. Ledgerwood, *Market Manipulation Without Market Power* (*Law360* 23 Jun. 2011) http://www.law360.com/articles/252314/market-manipulation-without-market-power accessed 10 May 2016.
353. Emilios E. Avgouleas, 114 (2005).

As discussed, both MAR[354] and REMIT[355] provide a classification as information-based manipulation and transaction-based manipulation. While the former concept consists of dissemination of false information as well as a failure to make inside information public, transaction-based market manipulation involves fraudulent transactions and artificial price-based manipulation, a classification, totally at odds with the evolution of the concept in practice. The question of whether a false impression is created by the dissemination of false information or a fictitious transaction directly affects the applicable rules and the legal analysis required to determine the behaviour as manipulative. Of the definitions given in Article 2(2), only Article 2(a)(ii) mentions price artificiality as a factor in establishing market manipulation. Nevertheless, this article does not require that prices are artificially moved as a result of given market conduct. Therefore the legal and economic logic that underlies the formulation of EU law is not in harmony with the traditional concept of market manipulation. The example-driven approach taken in the ACER's guidance document also fails to provide a pertinent manipulation theory.

[4] Intent Element

As discussed earlier, EU law does not provide an intent requirement to determine whether market behaviour is deemed to be manipulative. In contrast, in US law, the intent element constitutes an important part of the legal analysis for market manipulation. Even for some commentators, the intention of the perpetrator is the only instrument that separates manipulative conduct from legitimate trading.[356] In both fraud-based and artificial price-based manipulation, the regulator is required to prove that the perpetrators were intentionally involved in or carried out the relevant manipulative schemes. Yet the legal and economic analysis developed by the courts for the intent element in fraud-based and artificial price-based manipulations is distinct. Compared to that of artificial price-based manipulation, the intent element of fraud-based manipulation is less problematic with respect to the evidentiary burden. The US courts developed the *'but for'* test, which evaluates *but for* the manipulative intent, whether the perpetrator would have devised the fraudulent scheme.[357] Accordingly, unless the perpetrator provides an alternative economically feasible explanation for the transaction, order, or scheme in question, its behaviour will be held manipulative. On what grounds an explanation can be regarded as legally and economically feasible is decided on a case-by-case basis. Such a standard of proof is also problematic, since in almost every transaction or market behaviour, a perpetrator may provide a legitimate explanation to hide its manipulative intent. The fact that the case law has not provided any sufficient criteria for the standards of proof, results in difficulties in distinguishing manipulative behaviour from legitimate trading.[358]

354. Article 12, Regulation (EU) No 596/2014.
355. Article 2(2), Regulation (EU) No 1227/2011.
356. Daniel R. Fischel & David J. Ross, 510 (1991).
357. *SEC v. Masri*, 523 F. Supp. 2d 361, 372-372 (S.D.N.Y. 2007).
358. Albert S. Kyle & S. Viswanathan, 278 (2008).

Even though the concept of fraud-based market manipulation is not devoid of legal uncertainties, the case law developed under the SEA' Rule 10b-5, has been relatively successful, when compared to the legal difficulties in identifying price levels under CEA's artificial price-based market manipulation. FERC and later the CFTC itself adopted fraud-based market manipulation formulations in their context to benefit from the legal precedent of Rule 10b-5. Nevertheless, it must be noted that the concept of fraud-based manipulation is far from addressing market manipulation in general, due to the fact that the markets can be manipulated through several behaviours, which cannot be construed as fraud.[359] Whether or not the concept of market manipulation can be regulated by a single catch-all prohibition is not the subject of this paper. However, it can be derived from legal practice that while a price effect is not required under fraud-based manipulation, a market participant can manipulate prices without being involved in fraudulent behaviour.

[C] Artificial Price-Based Manipulation

[1] The Formulation

The CEA's formulation of market manipulation is different from that of the SEA. The CEA applies to trading in physical and financial commodity products in commodity exchanges. Prior to the 'Wall Street Dodd-Frank Reform' (Dodd-Frank hereinafter),[360] in order to prove market manipulation, the CFTC, the US regulatory body overseeing trading in commodity exchanges, had to prove that:

(1) the perpetrator had the ability to influence market prices;
(2) the perpetrator specifically intended to create or effect a price or price trend that does not reflect legitimate forces of supply and demand;
(3) artificial prices existed; and
(4) the perpetrator caused the artificial prices.[361]

The judicial burden to prove these elements of manipulative conduct under the CEA and to provide evidence as to the price levels deemed to be artificial and therefore manipulative, has proved to be problematic.[362] Recognising that proving price artificiality is a *sine qua non* for the establishment of the manipulative conduct, US case law has failed to provide a firm criterion to identify price artificiality. Early case law[363] employed historical price comparisons as benchmarks for identifying appropriate price

359. This view is criticised by other scholars. *See* Frank H. Easterbrook (1986).
360. The Dodd–Frank Wall Street Reform and Consumer Protection Act, Pub. L. No 111-203, 124 Stat. 1376 (2010).
361. *In re Indiana Farm Bureau Cooperative Association*, [1982–1984 Transfer Binder] Commodity Futures Law Reporter (CCH) ¶ 21,796, 27,287 (CFTC 1982); *In re Cox*, [1986–1987 Transfer Binder] Comm. Fut. L. Rep. (CCH) ¶ 23,786 (CFTC 1987).
362. Shaun D. Ledgerwood & Paul R. Carpenter, 257 (2012).
363. *Cargill v. Hardin*, 452 F.2d 1154 (8th Cir. 1971), *cert. denied*, 406 U.S. 932 (1972); *Great Western Food Distributors Inc, v. Brennan*, 201 F.2d 476 (7th Cir. 1953), *cert denied*, 345 U.S. 997 (1953).

levels. In *Great Western Distributors, Inc v. Brennan*[364] the US court defined the concept of artificial price as '*the price deviated notably from the level reflecting the basic forces of supply and demand*' (emphasis added). Such a price level is identified, in economic language, as a '*non-equilibrium price*'. Accordingly the equilibrium price will be determined through monitoring historical price correlations and the regulators will identify manipulation when there is a price differentiation that cannot be explained through the analysis of market forces.

[2] Determination of an Artificial Price

The analysis of historical price comparisons as a test of price artificiality has been subject to strong criticism in the legal literature. How large a deviation from the historical price levels is regarded as enough for a finding of artificiality of the relevant prices is an open question. As prices can deviate from historical price levels due to factors, which are not related to manipulation, the courts, in these cases, provide no legal standards on how to determine the extent of price deviations.[365] In addition, it is hard to identify the existing size of supply and demand on the basis of historical analysis of supply and demand, because the historical prices only provide a reflection of an historical level of supply and demand.[366] The test also provides no comment on whether or not historical price levels themselves are artificial.[367] The test's failure in providing answers to the questions raised by critics led to its omission in the CFTC's later decisions.[368]

Another test used by the CFTC for the determination of price artificiality is called the 'unusual' price test.[369] Accordingly, the artificiality of price levels is determined with the severance of the usual pricing mechanisms with no apparent reason other than the reference to supply and demand conditions. The unusual price differentials between the underlying asset and forward contracts, or the price inconsistencies between the prices of similar products on different market zones can be regarded as strong evidence for the existence of artificial prices.[370] The determination of an artificial price through the unusual price has also proved to be problematic. The test does not involve a substantial analysis of the conditions that reflect prices of relevant products or markets. It is not clear how certain market conditions may affect the prices of similar products in different ways. The test also provides no answer as to whether the prices with which comparisons are drawn are themselves subject to manipulation. The

364. *Great Western Food Distributors Inc, v. Brennan*, 201 F.2d 476, 480-81 (7th Cir. 1953), *cert denied*, 345 U.S. 997 (1953).
365. Craig Pirrong, 960 (1994).
366. Emilios E. Avgouleas, 109 (2005).
367. Wendy C. Perdue, *Manipulation of Futures Markets: Redefining the Offense* 56 Fordham L. Rev 345, 365 (1987).
368. *Supra* note 361.
369. For a detailed analysis on these tests, *see* Benjamin E. Kozinn, *The Great Copper Caper: Is Market Manipulation Really a Problem in the Wake of the Sumitomo Debacle* 69 Fordham Law Review 243, 261–262 (2000).
370. Emilios E. Avgouleas, 110 (2005).

uncertainty in the normality of the prices used as reference in price comparisons results in concerns about the reliability of finding the relevant price levels artificial or not.[371]

In *Indiana Farm Bureau*, members of the CFTC were of the view that divergence in price levels was a common phenomenon, due to varying levels of demand and supply conditions noting that *'all market prices are equilibrium responses to the various forces operating on them'*.[372] If all the factors that reflect the forces of supply and demand are held to be legitimate under the concept of an equilibrium price, the result is that there is no such a thing as an artificial price[373] The historical analysis of demand and supply does not provide the necessary price correlations in identifying the existing conditions of demand and supply for a commodity. Instead, in *Indiana Farm Bureau,* the CFTC adopted that:

> to determine whether an artificial price has occurred, one must look at the aggregate forces of supply and demand and search for those factors which are extraneous to the pricing system, are not a legitimate part of the economic pricing of the commodity, or are extrinsic to that commodity market. When the aggregate forces of supply and demand bearing on a particular market are all legitimate, it follows that the price will not be artificial. On the other hand, when a price is effected by a factor which is not legitimate, the resulting price is necessarily artificial.[374]

Even though there has been an extensive discussion in the academic literature as to the type of economic methodology to effectively determine price levels,[375] prosecution of market manipulations under the CEA's artificial price standard has remained contentious, due to the difficulty of identifying competitive and non-competitive price levels, which is also noted by the CFTC Commissioner Bart Chilton who conceded in 2010 that *'in 35 years, there has been only one successful prosecution from manipulation'*.[376] Problems in practice as to the prosecution of artificial price-based market manipulation resulted in academic and legal discussions as to what type of market behaviour can be deemed manipulative and how market players can move prices to an artificial level. Apart from corners and squeezes, which require exercise of market power by the perpetrators and will be discussed in detail later, judicial history is silent about the extent of manipulative behaviours that move the prices of relevant products to an artificial level. Lacking practical certainty, legal and academic literature developed the *'I know it when I see it'* approach, which presupposes that it is impossible to detect market manipulations, prior to its effects felt in the market. The only feasible approach to the identification of market manipulations intrinsically involves *ex-post* legal and economic analysis, which have also proven to be complicated in practice.

---

371. *Ibid.*, 111.
372. *In re Indiana Farm Bureau Cooperative Association*, [1982–1984 Transfer Binder] Comm. Fut. L. Rep. (CCH) ¶ 21,796 (CFTC 1982).
373. Emilios E. Avgouleas, 109 (2005).
374. *In re Indiana Farm Bureau Cooperative Association*, [1982–1984 Transfer Binder] Comm. Fut. L. Rep. (CCH) ¶ 21,796 (CFTC 1982).
375. Craig Pirrong, 964 (1994). *See also* Wendy C. Perdue (1987); Daniel R. Fischel & David J. Ross (1991).
376. Shaun Ledgerwood & Dan Harris, 4 (2012), *see* note 6.

[3] Reforming the Prohibition

The difficulty in bringing manipulation actions under the CEA's artificial price standard was later addressed in 2010, in the *'Dodd-Frank Wall Street Reform'*[377] (Dodd-Frank), which amended the previous artificial price standard and introduced a market manipulation definition encompassing also the SEA's definition of fraud-based market manipulation, expanding the CFTC's regulatory authority. Accordingly, the CEA provides that:

> (i)t shall be a felony ... for ... (a)ny person to manipulation or attempt to manipulate the price of any commodity in interstate, commerce, or for future delivery on or subject to the rules of any registered entity, or to corner or attempt to corner any such commodity or knowingly to deliver or cause to be delivered for transmission through the mails or interstate commerce by telegraph, telephone, wireless, or other means of communication false or misleading or knowingly inaccurate reports concerning crop or market information or conditions that affect or tend to affect the price of any commodity in interstate commerce, or knowingly to violate the provisions of section 6, section 6b, subsections (a) through (e) of subsection 6c, section 6h, section 6.[378]

Prohibiting the delivery of *'false or misleading or knowingly inaccurate reports'*, the current formulation of the anti-manipulation rule of CEA after Dodd-Frank, encompasses both fraud-based and artificial price-based manipulation definitions. It is agreed that the inclusion of the SEA's Rule 10b-(5) definition of market manipulation provides access to the judicial precedent of fraud-based case law aligning with the anti-manipulation authority of the SEC and the FERC as well as efficiency in identifying and prosecuting market manipulation easing the burden required to prove price artificiality. However, the need for a new approach to the identification of artificial price-based manipulation remains, since the CFTC, for manipulation other than fraud, is still required to prove that the market prices are artificially moved, and in order to measure the appropriate remedy for the losses induced by the manipulation.

Given the foregoing analysis, the legal literature on anti-manipulation laws is mostly sceptical about the requirement of price artificiality as *sine qua non* in deciding manipulation cases. Obliging the courts to employ a very complex analysis of markets and economic conditions has made the prohibition of market manipulation inapplicable and the tests and approaches developed for the determination of price artificiality have been ineffective.[379] The bottleneck in the enforcement of anti-manipulation rules, has led some commentators to argue that the law should either tolerate certain

---

377. *Supra* note 360.
378. 7 U.S.C. § 13a (2009).
379. '(T)*the law governing manipulations has become an embarrassment –confusing, contradictory, complex and unsophisticated'*, Edward T. McDermott, *Defining Manipulation in Commodity Futures Trading: The Futures Squeeze* 74/2 Northwestern University Law Review 202, 205 (1979). *See also* Wendy C. Perdue, *Manipulation of Futures Markets: Redefining the Offense* 56 Fordham Law Review 345, 373 (1987).

manipulative practices to the extent that they cause no harm[380] or should not prohibit manipulation at all, due to the complexities in identifying artificial prices.[381]

[4] Examples of Artificial Price-Based Manipulation

As the literature and case law struggle to define the concept of artificiality, the focus of the legal analysis turns on the ability of market participants and the schemes they can conduct to move prices, which are not considered as fraudulent under the meaning of the SEC Rule 10b-5. The economic theory first provides the concept of market power through which the perpetrators move the prices to levels favourable to the positions held by themselves and manipulate the markets. Therefore, the oldest and the best known example of price manipulation is market power manipulation. Whether or not other types of price distortion, such as trade-based manipulation and cross-market manipulation are considered under market power manipulation is contentious. While some commentators identify them separately from market power manipulation, others suggest that the perpetrators of trade-based and cross-market manipulation also need to have substantial market power in these types of manipulations to move prices. The next section discusses market power manipulation and provides a legal analysis of its interplay with other types of price manipulation.

[a] Market Power Manipulation

[i] Market Manipulation Versus Market Power

Though considered as market inefficiency, the holding of market power by a market participant is not prohibited by antitrust rules per se.[382] Antitrust rules are applicable only when it is established that a market participant, with a dominant position in the market, uses its market power to increase prices of relevant products[383] or exclude existing or potential competitors in the relevant markets. In order to determine if the perpetrator has a dominant position, competition authorities conduct certain economic analyses demarcating the relevant geographic and product markets. When it is held that the market share held by the market participant accounts for market power, the

380. Thomas A. Hieronymus, *Manipulation in Commodity Futures Trading: Toward A Definition* 6/1 Hofstra Law Review 41, 53 (1977).
381. Daniel R. Fischel & David J. Ross (1991).
382. The concept of market power relates to the capacity of market participants by undercutting their production to increase prices, which is fundamental in economic theory providing incentives to trade. *See* Damien Geradin, Anne Layne-Farrar, Nicolas Petit, *EU Competition Law and Economics* (OUP 2012).
383. In the US, mere exercise of market power to increase prices is not considered as an abuse of Section 2 of the Sherman Act, unless it is accompanied with exclusionary practices, such as tying and bundling, refusal to supply, margin squeeze. William J. Baer & Edith Ramirez, *Antitrust Tools for Challenging Capacity Withholding in Wholesale Electricity Markets* 3 (AAI The American Antitrust Institute 2014).

competition authorities, then turn to the question of whether the market participant exploited its market power through abusive practices.[384]

The general logic with respect to the concept of market power in anti-manipulation laws is similar. Market power manipulation involves a market distortion, in which a market participant and its associates acquire a substantial share of the demand or supply of physical commodities, futures contracts or any other financial instruments and use their market power to move prices to a level favourable to them. According to the case law, in order to establish that a market participant's behaviour accounts for market power manipulation, the following elements must be present:

(a) a dominant position in deliverable supplies;
(b) a dominant position in the futures market for a certain delivery period;
(c) existence of manipulative intent in gaining dominant positions in futures markets and deliverable supplies; and
(d) prices are distorted by the use of these dominant positions.[385]

The fact that the concept of market power is an important element in both antitrust and manipulation rules leads to misinterpretation by the majority of commentators in the legal and economic literature as to the determining factor of these types of manipulation. It is argued that the determining factor of market power manipulation is whether the dominant position is used to move the price of relevant products such as futures or other financial instruments.[386] The interplay between antitrust rules and anti-manipulation laws will be examined in detail.[387] However, it is important to note that the determining factors of market abuse in antitrust and market power in anti-manipulation rules are different.

The use of market power to dictate prices, which is prohibited under antitrust laws, and acquiring market power to dictate prices, which is the logic underlying the prohibition of market power manipulation should not be confused. Section 2 of the Sherman Act and Article 102 of TFEU involve prohibition of the use of market power and dominant position for the purposes of distorting competition in the markets. The market players, who hold dominant positions in the markets, are subject to antitrust laws only if they use their dominance to affect market prices[388] or eliminate the competition in the markets. In market power manipulation, the perpetrator accumulates market power to dictate the prices. Therefore, the accumulation of market power and dictating market prices are the market behaviours that are subject to market power

384. In antitrust law, market players abuse their dominant positions through two types of practices. Accordingly, they can conduct either exclusionary abuses such as predatory pricing, margin squeeze and refusal to supply, which are designed to use market power for the elimination of competition in the relevant market or exploitative abuses such as imposing unfair purchase or selling prices or other unfair trading conditions, where a monopolist can exploit its position. *See* Alison Jones & Brenda Sufrin, 396 (2014).
385. Emilios E. Avgouleas, 148 (2005).
386. *Ibid.*
387. *See* Ch. 4.
388. *Supra* note 383.

manipulation. The legal analysis carried out by the market regulators must demonstrate that the market power and dominant position was created to affect the price of relevant market products and that the market prices were, in fact, affected. If the perpetrator establishes that the accumulation of market power is not part of a manipulative scheme, that is it has accumulated market power or a dominant position as a legitimate trading strategy, the price effects resulted from the use of this dominant position cannot constitute market power manipulation and is not punishable under anti-manipulation rules.[389]

This interpretation is also in compliance with the concept of attempts at market manipulation. As discussed before, both the EU[390] and the US[391] anti-manipulation rules require the intent element with respect to prohibition of attempts to manipulate markets. As the existence of the intent element is a *sine qua non* in establishing such violations, the accumulation of market power with the intent to manipulate market prices is important in understanding the determining factor of market power manipulation. Once it is established that market power has been accumulated for the purpose of affecting market prices, the prohibition of attempting market manipulation is applicable, irrelevant as to whether the market prices were affected by underlying market behaviour. If it is also established that price levels have changed due to the accumulation of market power, then the prohibition of market power manipulation applies. Therefore reading these two different prohibitions, the prohibition of market manipulation and the attempt to manipulate markets, leads to the conclusion that the determining factor in regarding a trading activity as manipulation is the perpetrators' requisite intent during its accumulation of market power.

[ii] The Importance of Intent

US courts acknowledge that the market players that accumulate market power in the relevant markets and use this dominant position to move prices at artificial levels can only be held liable for market power manipulation, if it is established that the perpetrator's intention in the accumulation of market power was to distort market prices rather than a legitimate trading or hedging activity.[392] This ruling has been subject to criticism in the legal literature. Underlining the difficulty of identifying the perpetrator's intent in the accumulation of market power, some commentators argue that the intent requirement in market power manipulation should be recalibrated and applied to the perpetrator's reasoning in using its market power to dictate market prices.[393] It is true that the identification of manipulative intent in US case law, especially for artificial price-based manipulations, has proved to be difficult for market

389. However, antitrust rules may still be applicable to these types of market behaviours.
390. According to Article 2(3) of REMIT; '"*attempt to manipulate the market" means: (a) entering into any transaction, issuing any order to trade or taking any other action relating to a wholesale energy product with the intention of:* (...)'.
391. The Dodd–Frank Wall Street Reform and Consumer Protection Act, Pub. L. No 111-203, 124 Stat. 1376 (2010) (2010), § 753.
392. *Supra* note 372.
393. Craig Pirrong, 10 (2010).

regulators. However the market behaviour that the perpetrator carried out for the purpose of moving prices at artificial levels is important for the difference between the jurisdictions of antitrust and anti-manipulation laws. The application of the intent requirement, contrary to this approach, results in further overlaps and complexities for the regulation and functioning of markets. This is a challenge that the national regulatory authorities have to deal with in the context of EU law.[394]

Implications of Intent Element under REMIT

There is no legal uncertainty in the reading of prohibitions under MAR and REMIT that both provisions are intended to apply to market power manipulation. Article 12(2) of MAR provides that it will be considered as market manipulation if:

> the conduct by a person, or persons acting in collaboration, to secure a dominant position over the supply of or demand for a financial instrument, related spot commodity contracts or auctioned products based on emission allowances which has, or is likely to have, the effect of fixing, directly or indirectly, purchase or sale prices or creates, or is likely to create, other unfair trading conditions.[395]

According to the Recital 14 of REMIT:

> (e)xamples of market manipulation and attempts to manipulate the market include conduct by a person, or persons acting in collaboration, to secure a decisive position over the supply of, or demand for, a wholesale energy product which has, or could have, the effect of fixing, directly or indirectly, prices or creating other unfair trading conditions; and the offering, buying or selling of wholesale energy products with the purpose, intention or effect of misleading market participants acting on the basis of reference prices.[396]

However, as the requirement of a requisite intent is not present in EU law for market manipulation, the application of these prohibitions to the use of market power becomes problematic. It is possible that a market player could accumulate market power through legitimate trading and then decide to use this market power to dictate prices. According to the determining factor under anti-manipulation laws, this trading activity cannot account for market manipulation and thus is not prohibited as the trader does not have a requisite intent during its accumulation of market power. However, since the intent element is not part of EU law, how the regulators or courts distinguish the manipulative accumulation of market power from legitimate trading is an open question. The lack of distinction between legitimate trading and manipulative intent with respect to market power manipulation causes concerns on false positive market behaviours.[397] This legal uncertainty is further elevated with the application of Article 102, the prohibition on abuse of market power. Since the anti-manipulation rules in EU law do not involve an intent requirement and may be applied to the market

394. *Supra* note 164.
395. Article 12(2), Regulation (EU) No 596/2014.
396. Recital 14, Regulation (EU) No 1227/2011.
397. *Supra* note 138.

power accumulated as a result of a legitimate trading, both Article 102 and anti-manipulation laws may apply and this will result in overlap between jurisdictions and regulatory inefficiencies.

[iii] Examples of Market Power Manipulation

The most well-known examples of market power manipulation are corners and squeezes, whose perpetrators acquire a large portion of the buy or sell position in the markets.[398] These types of market practices involve futures markets where exercise of their market power distorts the market prices of the relevant products. In corners, a market player accumulates a large amount of futures contracts with a certain delivery period regarding a deliverable product. The market player also acquires a large portion of the underlying product, holding a dominant position in supply of the relevant product market. At the delivery date, when the dominant market participant forces other parties of the futures contracts to fulfil their contractual obligations, the market participants in the sale positions, unable to access the supplies held by the dominant market participant, are compelled to settle their contracts at inflated prices. The settlement of these contracts at inflated prices moves the market prices to higher levels and thus constitutes market manipulation. The rationale behind the practice of squeezes represents the opposite side of the logic behind corners. In squeezes, the market participant accumulates a large portion of the sell position in the futures markets and fulfils the delivery obligations, which drives the prices of relevant products down at lower levels. In each scheme, prices are changed artificially.

The majority of the case law with respect to artificial-based market manipulation involves the market participants cornering the markets to dictate the prices to the levels most favourable to them.[399] This is reflected in the reading of the CEA's artificial price-based definition, which uses manipulation and corner as synonyms in the commodity markets.[400] Even though they can also be practised in the securities market, the commodities markets are more vulnerable to corners, as the market participants are able to require physical deliveries and demand and supply side substitutions are limited to the characteristics of the underlying products, which allow the market participants to easily exploit the illiquidity of relevant markets.

[iv] Irrelevance of Fraud-Based Formulation

Market participants, noticing that a trader is trying to acquire a dominant position in a certain product, will economically take necessary measures such as liquidating its

398. Craig Pirrong, 950 (1994).
399. *Cargill v. Hardin*, 452 F.2d 1154 (8th Cir. 1971), *cert. denied*, 406 U.S. 932 (1972); *Great Western Food Distributors Inc, v. Brennan*, 201 F.2d 476 (7th Cir. 1953), *cert denied*, 345 U.S. 997 (1953); *In re Indiana Farm Bureau Cooperative Association*, [1982–1984 Transfer Binder] Commodity Futures Law Reporter (CCH) ¶ 21,796, 27,287 (CFTC 1982); *In re Sumitomo Corp.*, [1996-1998 Transfer Binder] Comm. Fut. L Rep. (CCH) ¶ 27,327 (CFTC 1998).
400. 7 U.S.C. s 13(a) (2009).

position before the delivery date to escape the corner or squeeze. Therefore the cornering party will try to acquire large positions without the notice of other market participants. The characteristic of accumulation of large buy or sell positions in the commodity markets as a covert activity caused some commentators to argue market power manipulation as a type of fraud, within the context of SEA's Rule 10b-5.[401] This argument was rejected by the US courts in *Radley*.[402] Accordingly, the court found that although the perpetrators concealed their accumulation of market power from other market participants, this did not constitute fraudulent behaviour as they never engaged in a conduct, such as false statements or transactions that created false or misleading impressions. Accordingly, it is true that in the majority of manipulative schemes, the perpetrators enter into a variety of market behaviours, which involve different types of manipulation including fraud-based and artificial price-based manipulation. However, market power manipulation features certain types of market behaviour, which cannot be dealt with under a fraud-based manipulation formulation.

[v] Concerns About Limited Case Law

Since the CEA's artificial price-based definition is short in providing further guidance on manipulative schemes and how market participants can manipulate prices, and market power manipulation is the best known example of this type of distortion, it is contentious in the legal literature whether or not holding market power in a relevant market is the only way to move prices at artificial level. Some commentators suggest that market participants without market power can also impact prices by making strategic trading activities at certain time periods.[403] Accordingly, the products in physical and financial markets are linked and trading activities or price changes in one market affect the prices of the products in the linked markets. It is argued that these types of market manipulation are different from market power manipulation and therefore their prohibition requires a different legal analysis involving price relations between different products and markets without necessarily establishing that that market power or dominant position is used for manipulative schemes. Professor Pirrong objected to this type of classification arguing that the market participants that enter into such practices can succeed in their schemes only if they have market power with respect to the linked products and employ this market power in their trading activities.[404]

Given the lack of efficient economic analysis, the legal discussion in this context is mostly related to how products in different markets are interrelated and to what extent this interrelation between physical and financial market affects prices in respective markets. Providing the arguments in the legal literature, the next section discusses the types of market manipulation regarded by some as different from market power manipulation. It also introduces recent studies on the legal and economic

401. *See* Frank H. Easterbrook (1986); Shaun D. Ledgerwood & Paul R. Carpenter (2012).
402. *Supra* note 341.
403. Emilios E. Avgouleas, 148 (2005).
404. Craig Pirrong, 4–5 (2010).

analysis of market manipulation, which significantly diverge from the traditional understanding of market manipulation.

[b] Market Manipulation Without Market Power

The discussion as to whether or not the holding of market power is fundamental to manipulating prices in the relevant markets has led to the adoption of different classifications of market manipulation. Professor Pirrong's view that the undertakings must have market power to move prices artificially is criticised by many commentators.[405] The idea that only the use of market power can move prices artificially can result in a wide range of corporate behaviours moving prices artificially without resorting to market power allowing those behaviours to remain outside the scope of the prohibition of market manipulation. It is argued that an undertaking without market power can also manipulate prices by strategically structured trading activities.[406] Accordingly, there are two types of market manipulation that move prices artificially without necessarily requiring a market power position. Trade-based market manipulation is perpetrated through strategic purchasing or selling of relevant products at certain time periods to influence the price levels of traded products. Contract-based market manipulation, on the other hand, involves cross-market price relations that the perpetrators exploit by trading in one market, which has price effects on a position held by the perpetrators in a different but linked market. A detailed legal analysis is required to demarcate these two types of manipulation.

[i] Trade-Based Market Manipulation

Every trading activity in a market, more or less affects prices, since they directly reflect demand and supply levels in the relevant markets. For example, a purchase agreement for a product, while increasing the demand levels, will also result in a decrease in supply levels available for sale, which indicates further price increases for the relevant product. Trading for the purpose of profit maximisation is the essence of legitimate trading, that is, every market player acts in a manner to maximise profits from their trading activities. A purchaser of a product will continue to buy as long as the price of the relevant product is less than the amount it is willing to pay. Equally, a seller will continue to sell as long as the price of the relevant product is more than its average marginal cost. Price relations between demand and supply levels constitute the core aspect of legitimate trading strategies in the markets.

In trade-based manipulation, the perpetrator does not act on the basis of price relations between demand and supply levels. Instead, trading activities are designed to move prices to a level more favourable for the perpetrator.[407] Early examples of

405. Emilios E. Avgouleas, 131–132 (2005); Shaun D. Ledgerwood & Paul R. Carpenter, 254 (2012).
406. Fischel provides four types of hypothesis demonstrating how trading can cause changes in prices. These are: substitution hypothesis; information hypothesis; liquidity hypothesis and; price pressure hypothesis. *See* Daniel R. Fischel & David J. Ross, 514–517 (1991).
407. Franklin Allen & Douglas Gale (1992).

trade-based manipulations emerged during the operation of 'the Wall Street Pools',[408] where traders entered into large-scale trading activities to move prices artificially. In order for this type of manipulation to affect market prices, the perpetrator must engage in strategic and large-scale trading, which induce other traders to act in the same manner, assuming that the perpetrator has private information as to the true value of the relevant products. Consequently the price that the perpetrator traded at in its manipulative scheme is perceived as the market price for the relevant product and thus prices are changed artificially without the need to hold market power. It is also possible for the manipulators to affect prices through trading activities in illiquid markets. In these markets, due to imbalances between demand and supply levels and mismatches between purchasing and selling interests, the perpetrators have incentives to move prices through strategic trading, exploiting market illiquidity.

'Marking the close' and 'Successive bidding' practices are the major examples of trade-based market manipulation. In 'marking the close', traders concentrate their trading activity at the time when the closing of the relevant markets approaches.[409] This allows the perpetrators to issue excessive bids without being subject to offsetting transactions, which moves the closing price of the relevant product in a more favourable direction for the perpetrators. The effectiveness of this strategy is questioned by some commentators. It is argued that in the majority of market places, traders generally concentrate their trading activities during the market closing, due to the common policy of monitoring the developments and price movements in the markets before taking a position. Given the high concentration of trading activity at the closing of markets, any manipulative trading activity has less ability to move prices at artificial level, unless the activity is so large that it constitutes a major part of the overall trading activity.[410] It is argued that since 'marking the close' practices are too risky to employ and are intrinsically self-deterring, the perpetrators only engage in these practices if they hold cross-market positions or related contracts whose value is influenced by the closing price.[411] However, even if such perpetrators hold cross-market or contractual positions that benefit from the closing price, it is still very difficult to affect the closing price through marking the close during the concentrated trading activities, which decreases the likelihood of reaping profits from cross-market or contractual positions.

'Successive bidding' is a strategy involving successive purchases by the perpetrator bidding at prices higher than the prevailing price so as to increase the price of the relevant product and sell it at inflated prices, making a significant profit.[412] The forcing

408. These pools are usually divided into two types of traders: bulls and bears. While the former refers to traders who intentionally pay higher prices to increase the prices in the relevant markets and sell these products at these inflated prices, reaping the profits derived from price differentiations, the latter involves traders selling certain products at lower prices to purchase them in the future at depressed prices. *See* Emilios E. Avgouleas, 132–133 (2005).

409. Technical Committee of the International Organisation of Securities Commissions (IOSCO), 'Investigating and Prosecuting Market Manipulation', (May 2000), 87. *See also* Praveen Kumar & Duane J. Seppi, *Futures Manipulation with Cash Settlement* 47/4 The Journal of Finance 1485, 1486 (1992).

410. Daniel R. Fischel & David J. Ross, 520 (1991).

411. *Ibid.*

412. Emilios E. Avgouleas, 141 (2005).

of price increases through the 'successive bidding' strategy is also questioned by many commentators. It is argued that increasing prices through successive bidding at high prices is a capital intensive strategy and very expensive without a subsidisation from other markets or positions whose value is linked to the manipulated prices.[413] The perpetrator needs prices to increase after its successive bidding practices to gain profit from its later sales. Since it is not evident that prices will react to the successive bids as desired, the employment of this strategy is also self-deterring and unlikely to succeed.

Due to their self-deterring character as well as the improbability of achieving the desired outcomes, the effectiveness of prohibiting trade-based market manipulation has been questioned by many commentators.[414] For example, Fischel argues that along with the difficulty of manipulating prices successfully through large-scale trading strategies, the prohibition of trade-based market manipulation is inefficient, since detecting such practices is a difficult task involving regulatory bodies addressing social and economic costs as well as concerns about separating legitimate trading activities from the manipulation.[415] Acknowledging the need for detecting and enforcing anti-manipulation laws against trade-based manipulation, the majority of commentators are critical of this view. Ledgerwood asserts that as they are too risky and self-deterring due to their capital intensive character, this type of market manipulation needs subsidies from cross-market or contractual positions, thus they need to be considered along with contracts-based market manipulation.[416] Pirrong notes that as the perpetration of trade-based manipulation requires large-scale trading and it is not economically feasible to affect prices for a market player who has a small market share in the relevant market, such manipulation also constitute market power manipulation and can also be prohibited under anti-manipulation rules.[417] The reconceptualisation attempts of these commentators will be addressed in later sections, yet it is important to note that there is little consensus in the legal and economic literature on the definition, and classification of trade-based manipulation.

[ii] Cross-Market Manipulations

As we have seen, trade-based manipulation is economically feasible only if subsidised through cross-market positions whose value is linked to prevailing market prices. In cross-market market manipulation, perpetrators who have positions in two distinct but interrelated markets, undertake a trading strategy to influence prices in one market, which further leads to price changes in the other, from which the perpetrators reap benefits. In these schemes, the profits do not come from manipulative trading. The perpetrators are aware that there is a price relation between two different products so use their contractual position to exploit it to earn profits, even if they make loss-incurring transactions in the prevailing market. Whether or not the perpetrators

413. *Ibid.*, 142.
414. Albert S. Kyle & S. Viswanathan, 282 (2008).
415. Daniel R. Fischel & David J. Ross, 521 (1991); Albert S. Kyle & S. Viswanathan, 282 (2008).
416. Shaun D. Ledgerwood & Paul R. Carpenter, 255 (2012).
417. Craig Pirrong, 6 (2010).

undertake further transactions in the prevailing market at inflated or depressed prices is irrelevant.

The identification of cross-market manipulation plays an important role, especially in the derivative markets. The value of the products in the derivative markets, such as future contracts, is mostly dependant on the value of the underlying products in the physical, or security markets. Any price change occurring in these markets influences the prices in the derivatives markets. With the growth of derivative markets during the 2000s, the incentives to manipulate prices in these markets increased.[418] Perpetrators buying contracts in the derivatives markets, such as future positions for an underlying asset, can enter into purchases at inflated prices enabling them to exploit inflated returns from their future positions. The profits from future positions surpass the losses incurred in the physical or security markets.

The traders in derivatives markets use the derivative products as either an investment tool to seek profits from demand and supply levels or as a hedging strategy to reduce the risks arising from their transactions in the prevailing markets. The use of derivatives as a hedging strategy renders the separation of manipulative acts from legitimate trading activities complicated. The majority of commentators sought to evaluate relevant trading activity along with the nature of the perpetrators' activities in the linked markets. According to Ledgerwood, cross-market profits derived from positions in the derivative markets should be considered as manipulative, if it is held that the perpetrators' transaction for the underlying asset is uneconomic.[419] Whether a trading activity is regarded as uneconomic is decided according to its opportunity costs. To what extent traders are capable of making their decisions on the basis of their opportunity costs is an open question. Pirrong construes that the existence of cross-market positions held by perpetrators is an illustration of the perpetrator's manipulative intent in entering into large-scale trading in order to create price impacts in the prevailing markets.[420] Identifying a separate type of market manipulation for cross-market positions is not necessary to prohibit these types of market manipulation representing an important aspect of evaluating trade-based manipulation. Pirrong asserts that moving prices artificially through large-scale trading requires market power, thus cross-market manipulation as an aspect of trade-based manipulation can be dealt with effectively under the prohibitions of market power manipulation.[421]

Pirrong's assertion that market prices can be moved at artificial levels only through the use of market power is not true for all sectors. Especially in markets with imperfect liquidity, small trading activities can also result in price changes leading other market players to believe that the settlement price in the underlying market represents the true value of the relevant products. *Great Western Energy Crisis* and *the Enron crash*[422] in the early 2000s are clear examples of how energy market prices can

418. IOSCO, 2 (2000).
419. Shaun D. Ledgerwood, *Screens for the Detection of Manipulative Intent* 41 (2010), http://papers.ssrn.com/sol3/papers.cfm?abstract_id = 1728473 (accessed at 10 May 2016).
420. Craig Pirrong, 5 (2010).
421. *Ibid.*, 14–15.
422. *In Re Enron Corp. Securities*, 586 F. Supp. 2d 732 (S.D. Tex. 2008) *See* Paul L. Joskow, *California's Electricity Crisis* 17/3 Oxford Review of Economic Policy 365 (2001); Paul Joskow

be manipulated by market players who have neither market power nor a dominant position in the sense of antitrust rules.[423] The strategies employed to manipulate prices and nature of the markets the anti-manipulation rules are directed across different sectors.[424] Therefore, a general statement that all artificial price-based manipulation can be regarded as market power manipulation is problematic. Criticising Pirrong's argument, some commentators note that as the uncertainty in the concept of market manipulation remains, a reconceptualisation of market manipulations is needed to deal with market inefficiencies more efficiently.

§2.04 THE RECONCEPTUALISATION OF MARKET MANIPULATION

[A] General

The majority of commentators agree that the traditional formulation of anti-manipulation law is problematic and inefficient in identifying and preventing manipulative market practices. Especially in the US, the CFTC's policy of combining both fraud-based and artificial price-based manipulation to deal with price manipulation more effectively with Dodd-Frank caused further complications as US case law has developed different prima facie cases for these areas. Furthermore the new formulation of the CEA does not provide any guidance as to how a fraud-based formulation of the anti-manipulation rule can help the prosecution of artificial price-based manipulation. The uncertainty in defining market manipulation and identifying the manipulative intent needed to show that the perpetrators carried out trading activity to move prices at artificial levels and manipulate the markets, results in concerns as to the separation of legitimate trading from manipulative acts. In order to address the inefficiencies in the traditional formulation of anti-manipulation rules, several commentators have sought to reconceptualise the concept of market manipulation.

[B] Attempts to Define Market Manipulation

As mentioned, several definitions for the detection and prosecution of market manipulation have been proposed in the academic literature. While some commentators, such as Judge Easterbrook, Perdue, Avgouleas, and Ledgerwood, have provided single

---

& Edward Kahn, *A Quantitative Analysis of Pricing Behavior in California's Wholesale Electricity Market During Summer 2000* 23/4 Energy Journal 1 (2002); Severin Borenstein, *The Trouble with Electricity Markets: Understanding California's Restructuring Disaster* 16/1 Journal of Economic Perspectives 191 (2002).

423. During the crisis, it is noted that none of the market players operating in the California energy market held market shares of more than 20%. The market is also regarded as competitive, involving more than ten competitors. *See* J-M Glachant, *Understanding the REMIT: Aims and Limits*' (GME Annual Conference 11 Jul. 2012) https://www.mercatoelettrico.org/en/MenuBiblioteca/Documenti/20120711RelazioneAnnuale2011Glachant.pdf (accessed on 22 Nov. 2015).

424. According to the advice document proposed by CESR and ERGEG; '(a) *sector specific regulatory framework could address (...) abusive practises, taking into account the specifics of the energy markets*'. CESR and ERGEG, 25 (2008).

catch-all definitions that apply to all types of manipulation, others, such as Pirrong, assert that such an approach would result in inconsistencies and inefficiencies in the prosecution of different types of market manipulation.[425] According to Judge Easterbrook, market manipulation should be defined as '*conduct in which the profit flows solely from the trader's ability to conceal his position from other traders and the trades do not move price more quickly in the direction that reflects long-run conditions of supply and demand*'.[426] Judge Easterbrook formulated his definition on the grounds that all types of market manipulation were, in fact, a species of fraud and market prices did not reflect long-term market fundamentals. This definition was later criticised by Fischel asking that '(w)*hat if the trades do not move prices at all or move prices in the direction that reflects short-run conditions of supply and demand? Most importantly, what happens if the trades move prices in one direction because the trader genuinely believes that prices will move in this direction, but trader turns out to be wrong and prices ultimately move in the opposite direction.*'[427] According to Fischel, Judge Easterbrook's formulation did not distinguish market manipulation from legitimate trading activities.

Perdue adopted a different approach to defining market manipulation. Instead of focusing on the artificiality or reasonableness of prices, Perdue focused on the nature of market practice and asks '*whether the conduct of the people involves is reasonable*'.[428] Accordingly, market manipulation was defined as uneconomical or irrational market conduct, absent an impact on market prices.[429] Avgouleas introduced a more detailed definition which considers that market manipulation is a:

> (b)ehaviour effected through any one, or a combination of any of the following: misrepresentations and other false statements or concealments, artificial transactions, and trading schemes, which are made or structured in such a way as to induce market participants to engage in the trading of financial investments or the exercise of rights in financial investments. Relevant trading must be in such a direction or the exercise of rights must be effected in such a way, as to either lead the price of these investments to an artificial level, and/or enable the perpetrators of the behaviour to materialize, from interests held in the specific or related investments, financial gains that would not be possible, in the absence of such behaviour.[430]

This definition encompasses both fraud-based and artificial price-based manipulation. It also recalibrates the intent element, providing that the nature of the behaviours, misrepresentations, false statements or transactions aimed at moving prices at artificial level, in relation to the direction of market participants' trades, thus following the behaviour in question would reveal the intentions of the perpetrator. Markham

425. Craig Pirrong, 11 (2010).
426. Frank H. Easterbrook, 118 (1986).
427. Daniel R. Fischel & David J. Ross, 509 (1991).
428. Wendy C. Perdue, 348 (1987).
429. *Ibid.*, 348.
430. Emilios E. Avgouleas, 116 (2005).

criticised this definition, stating that the definition did not touch upon when prices were considered artificial and how the relationship between market misconduct and artificial prices was established.[431] The CFTC's experience on the prosecution of artificial price-based market manipulation has shown that price artificiality and causation elements were very difficult to establish. Avgouleas discussed the gains that perpetrators derived from their positions.[432] Nevertheless further clarification on what types of benefits were considered as these financial gains was missing.

The formulation of single catch-all definitions was criticised by Pirrong who asserts that the prosecution of different types of market manipulation require different definitions that specifically address and proscribe relevant market practices.[433] According to Pirrong, fraud-based and artificial price-based manipulation should be prosecuted under different legal frameworks.[434] In identifying intent, Pirrong argues that market manipulation is an economic offence[435] and regulators should focus on economic analysis, rather than market participants' subjective state of mind.[436] As to price artificiality, Pirrong concludes that the only way that market participants can move prices at artificial level, other than distorting information through fraud, is through the use of market power.[437] Ledgerwood argues that the legislative background of market manipulation proved otherwise as there are certain examples in the case law that market players manipulate prices without the existence of market power or dominant position.[438]

Ledgerwood further proposes a different type of formulation to define market manipulation. Mirroring the arguments raised by Perdue,[439] Ledgerwood's formulation includes a third type of market manipulation called 'uneconomic trading'.[440] Accordingly there are three types of market behaviour that trigger market manipulation; the use of market power, outright fraud and uneconomic trading. Ledgerwood establishes a legal framework that involves a single catch-all definition to prosecute all types of market manipulation.[441] Adopting a combination of taxonomy-based and effects-based approach to the formulation of anti-manipulation law, the framework provides an insight into the methods and incentives that market participants can have in perpetrating manipulative practices. Therefore, this chapter deems it necessary to include a specific legal analysis to discuss the proposed framework.

431. Jerry Markham, 211 (2015).
432. Emilios E. Avgouleas, 116 (2005).
433. Craig Pirrong, 14 (2010).
434. *Ibid.*, 12–13.
435. Craig Pirrong, 947 (1994).
436. Craig Pirrong, 14 (2010).
437. *Ibid.*, 5.
438. Shaun Ledgerwood & Dan Harris, 30 (2012).
439. *Supra* note 428.
440. Shaun D. Ledgerwood & Paul R. Carpenter, 271 (2012).
441. *Ibid.*, 256.

[C] The Ledgerwood Framework

Professor Ledgerwood defines manipulation as:

> intentionally losing money on transactions that (or make) a price to benefit the value of related positions that tie to (or take) that price.[442]

Providing no indication as to whether the behaviours relate to the instruments of fraud or they move prices in the relevant positions artificially, this definition features a functional approach involving an economic analysis of price relations between the market where the conduct has taken place and the market where its effects are felt. The nature of the profits reaped by the perpetrator in relation to its conduct reveals whether the perpetrator has actually intended to accrue profits and therefore manipulated markets.

Ledgerwood argues that the perpetration of market manipulation requires two separate markets, a primary market and a secondary market.[443] In order for market trading to be uneconomic, it is necessary to show that the behaviour in the primary market is of a loss-making character on a stand-alone basis. The perpetrator's true profits come from its position in secondary markets whose value is linked to price changes in the primary markets. The market regulators must prove that the transactions entered into by the perpetrator in the primary market are designed to affect prices in the secondary markets. The perpetrator's manipulative intent is important because the loss-incurring character of the behaviour is deemed to be manipulation only if it is shown the perpetrator traded with manipulative intent. In establishing an intent requirement, the framework mirrors the economic analysis approach adopted by Pirrong.[444] Ledgerwood suggests that in order to prove the perpetrator's manipulative intent, the loss-incurring character of uneconomic trading should be assessed along with its opportunity cost on a case-by-case basis.[445] The transactions in the primary market should be of such a nature that the perpetrator would have not undertaken such a loss-incurring trade, '*but for*' the economic benefits from positions held in secondary markets.

The framework lists three elements which are designed to identify manipulation conduct and its effects.[446] The first element is the '*trigger*', a market behaviour that corresponds to either market power manipulation, outright fraud or uneconomic trading. This element examines whether the price-making trades by the perpetrators distort the market participants' perception as to the value of a particular product and thus cause price changes. The second element, the '*target*', is price-taking positions, in which the perpetrators hold assets and derive profits from price changes caused by the trigger. Such target positions generally consist of contracts in the derivative markets such as futures contracts, options, swaps, etc. The third element the framework

442. Gary Taylor, et al., *Market Power and Market Manipulation in Energy Markets; From the California Crisis to the Present,* 16 (Public Utilities Report Inc. 2015).
443. *Ibid.*, 19.
444. Craig Pirrong, 14 (2010).
445. Shaun D. Ledgerwood & Paul R. Carpenter, 289 (2012).
446. Shaun Ledgerwood & Dan Harris, 25 (2012).

introduces is the *'nexus'*, which is the market mechanism that provides the linkage between the price-making trigger and the price-taking target positions. Accordingly, in order to hold a trader liable for market manipulation, the framework requires that the price movements in trigger and target are interrelated and that the trader's behaviour in the trigger, in fact, caused the price changes in the targeted positions. Ledgerwood states that the nexus element is fundamental not only for the causal link between market behaviour and price change but also for the assessment of manipulative intent, providing economic evidence needed to establish that the perpetrator designed its trading scheme based on price relations between different products in the different markets.[447]

Ledgerwood's concept of uneconomic trading represents a legal reformulation of cross-market manipulation. The legal literature on this concept treats the contract-based and trade-based market manipulations differently, albeit the existence of the former is sometimes considered as evidence that the trader perpetrated the latter with a manipulative intent, knowing that its losses will be subsidised. According to Ledgerwood, trade-based market manipulation can be better dealt with through antitrust laws as in this type of manipulation, all three elements of the legal framework occur in the primary markets.[448] If it is established that the effects of market behaviour occur in markets other than the primary market, Ledgerwood concludes that anti-manipulation laws should apply, arguing that the traditional antitrust methodology, such as identifying market power, is less useful.

Ledgerwood's framework applies to all types of market manipulation.[449] It is irrelevant whether the perpetrator used market power, fraudulent information or uneconomic trading to trigger the manipulation. It must be shown that the effects of triggering market behaviour occur in a secondary market and it is the market behaviour that caused the targeted market outcome. The framework incorporates the intent requirement in US case law into the nexus element noting that once it is established that the market participant trading activity in the primary market resulted in price movements in the secondary market and if it is unreasonable for the market participant to act in this manner but for the financial benefits derived from the financial positions in the secondary market, the market participant should be deemed to have intended to manipulate the market prices. Ledgerwood asserts that this approach will solve the problem of proving manipulative intent, which has been one of the main problems faced by the courts and legal commentators in the enforcement of anti-manipulation laws.[450]

[D] Comments on Ledgerwood's Framework

Constructing his legal framework, Ledgerwood does not distinguish between different types of market manipulation, based on a single market manipulation definition. The

447. *Ibid.*, 32.
448. Gary Taylor, et al., 19 (2015).
449. Shaun Ledgerwood & Dan Harris, 36 (2012).
450. Shaun D. Ledgerwood & Paul R. Carpenter, 286 (2012).

framework is practical providing a legal standard and, especially for the uneconomic trading or contract-based market manipulations, a prima facie case that the legal practitioners ought to look for to identify manipulative behaviour, price effects and any causal link between them. The trigger and the target are useful for clarifying financial positions and incentives held by the perpetrators in devising their manipulative schemes. The nexus element requiring cross-market economic analyses is also helpful for understanding market fundamentals, providing further guidance on the enforcement of market manipulation. Nevertheless the framework's functioning when dealing with market manipulation other than uneconomic trading or contract-based distortions is an open question.

In his analysis, Ledgerwood generally focuses on cross-market relations and applies the framework to uneconomic trading. Asserting that only market behaviours that have cross-market price effects should be deemed as manipulation, Ledgerwood also addresses market power and fraud-based manipulation to the extent that their effects are felt in markets other than those the manipulative schemes are devised in. This interpretation leaves a considerable amount of manipulative behaviour outside the scope of the framework. Fraud-based manipulation and market power manipulation, such as corners, which are the most well-known examples of market manipulation and can be perpetrated in one defined market, cannot be dealt with by the framework. The omission of these types of practices from the concept of market manipulation on the grounds that they are perpetrated in a single market is problematic.

Antitrust rules also do not support a distinction between manipulation and market power based on the markets affected. A market participant, possessing market power in a relevant market can be held liable for abuse of dominance, due to its activities in different but related markets in which it is not dominant. In *Akzo,*[451] the CJEU adopted a wider relevant market encompassing two different yet related sectors, the flour additives and plastic sectors. While the defendant was dominant market player in the latter, its share in the former was extremely small.[452] The court found that the defendant engaged in predatory pricing practices in the additives sectors. Even though these sales were loss incurring on a stand-alone basis, the profits from the plastic sector which had a higher financial turn over were more than enough to compensate for the losses incurred in the additives sector. The court concluded that the defendant violated Article 102, (then Article 86), through its pricing practices, even though they were aimed at a market in which the defendant was not dominant.[453] In *Tetra Pak,* the General Court clearly stressed that the defendant's '(...) *practices on the non-aseptic markets are liable to be caught by Article 86 of the Treaty (now 102 of TFEU) without its being necessary to establish the existence of a dominant position on those markets taken in isolation, since that undertaking's leading position on the non-aseptic markets, combined with the close associative links between those markets and the*

451. Case C-62/86 *AKZO Chemie BV v. Commission of the European Communities* [1991] ECR I-03359, 286.
452. *Ibid.*, para. 40.
453. *Ibid.*, para. 45.

aseptic markets, gave Tetra Pak freedom of conduct compared with the other economic operators on the non-aseptic markets, such as to impose on it a special responsibility under Article 86 to maintain genuine undistorted competition on those markets'.[454] Accordingly the demarcation of market manipulation and the use of market power as a violation of abuse of dominant position is not compatible with the approach taken by antitrust law.

As mentioned above, many commentators have sought to define and clarify the concept based on the nature of market behaviours and their effects. Ledgerwood's definition does not provide a specific distinction among the types of market manipulation. However its formulation, along with the legal framework, is designed to address cross-market manipulation. Certain characteristics, such as the loss-incurring character of market behaviours, which the framework deems to be fundamental for identifying cross-market manipulation, are irrelevant for other types of manipulation such as outright fraud, in which the perpetrator manipulates the market by dissemination of false information, or wash or matched trades where the perpetrators apparently enter into transactions while taking no financial risks in manipulating prices.

§2.05 CONCLUSION

The historical precedents set by manipulation cases in the early twentieth century divided the concept into types of manipulations. While the SEA's fraud-based definition proscribes fraudulent activities that deceive other traders with respect to the value of securities or the fundamentals of demand and supply levels,[455] the CEA's artificial price-based definition undertakes to prohibit market behaviours that are designed to influence price levels and move prices at artificial levels.[456] The prohibition of fraudulent behaviour does not involve any burden on the claimant's part to demonstrate that market prices are affected due to the prohibited act. It is enough to show that a reasonable market participant can be induced by the fraudulent device, or scheme to act in a certain direction. Whether or not a market is distorted under the CEA's artificial price-based definition, on the other hand, requires an evaluation of price levels for the relevant products and the relevant markets to establish if prices are moved at artificial levels by the manipulative behaviours.

The concept of artificial price-based manipulation and its interplay with fraud-based manipulation has been intensely debated in the legal literature. The case law on price artificiality has been less than successful in providing guidance on how to identify and prevent price manipulation, and the legal discussions of several commentators on this subject are confused and contradictory. Several commentators, such as Easterbrook,[457] assert that the basis of market manipulation is fraud, arguing that all manipulative behaviours in practice are of a fraudulent nature, since they hide their

454. Case T-83/91 *Tetra Pak International SA v. Commission of the European Communities* [1994] ECR II-00755 246, para. 122.
455. 17 C.F.R. § 240.10b-5 (2011).
456. *Supra* note 361.
457. Frank H. Easterbrook (1986).

manipulative intent from the market during the trading activities or make loss-making transactions in order to deceive market participants as to market conditions. This is criticised by Professor Pirrong who asserts that fraud-based definitions are not suitable in dealing with artificial price-based manipulations.[458]

Identifying price levels has proved to be very difficult in case law. The courts even struggled to define the meaning of price artificiality and have developed different approaches as to when price levels in the markets are considered artificial. According to Pirrong, since prices can be moved artificially only through the use of market power, the determining factor to determine whether prices have changed artificially is whether the perpetrators held market power with respect to the relevant commodity and used this power to influence prices. Other types of artificial price-based manipulation, such as trade-based and cross-market manipulation also involve holding market power, as the perpetration of these schemes requires large-scale trading, which is not possible for small market players. Pirrong's assertion on the requirement of market power is partly true. In the majority of commodity markets, where the option of a physical delivery of a relevant commodity and friction can arise from transportation costs, play an important role in trading activities, market power is important to dictate prices. However, in certain sectors with peculiar characteristics, such as energy markets, the imbalances between demand and supply levels and illiquidity in the markets may allow small market participants to influence prices through strategically placed orders. Therefore, limiting artificial price-based definition only to the concept of market power manipulation is problematic.

Given the uncertainties of the case law on market manipulation, several commentators have developed alternative definitions. While Easterbrook,[459] Perdue,[460] Avgouleas,[461] and Ledgerwood[462] propose a single catch-all definition encompassing all types of market manipulation, Pirrong rejects this formulation, arguing that regulation of fraud-based and market power manipulation under a single anti-manipulation rule requires '*logical connotations to fit the square market power peg in the round fraud and deceit hole*'.[463] Since the legal elements required to prove fraud-based and artificial price-based manipulation are different, adoption of a single catch-all definition may result in certain market manipulation schemes remaining outside the scope of the anti-manipulation provisions.

Professor Ledgerwood also proposes a framework analysing market manipulation under a three-part test, *trigger*, *nexus*, and *target*.[464] Accordingly, the framework establishes three types of triggers for market manipulation, market power, outright fraud and uneconomic trading. Providing very little evaluation of market power and

458. Craig Pirrong (2010).
459. Frank H. Easterbrook (1986).
460. Wendy C. Perdue (1987).
461. Emilios E. Avgouleas (2005).
462. Shaun D. Ledgerwood & Paul R. Carpenter (2012); Shaun Ledgerwood & Dan Harris (2012); Gary Taylor et al. (2015).
463. Craig Pirrong, 17 (2010).
464. *Supra* note 446.

fraud-based manipulation, the framework focuses on uneconomic trading. Ledgerwood constructed his market manipulation definition on the basis of loss-making trades, where traders intentionally lose money in primary markets to profit from positions held in secondary markets. The framework proposed by Ledgerwood has important implications for manipulation in energy markets. As will be discussed later in greater detail, energy markets are particularly vulnerable to manipulation due to periodic constraints in demand and supply, their reliance on indices for pricing. The case law on energy markets, such as *Amaranth Advisors,*[465] *DiPlacido,*[466] *Constellation Energy,*[467] clearly illustrate cross-market activities providing incentives for traders to exploit price correlations and manipulate the markets without the presence of traditional market power.

According to Ledgerwood, other types of manipulation where the trigger, nexus and target take place in the same market are outside the scope of his market manipulation definition and should be dealt with under antitrust rules.[468] It is important to note that the legal theory developed so far has not provided guidance on the interplay between anti-manipulation and antitrust rules and distinguishing the jurisdictions on the basis of markets affected may cause overlapping regulatory jurisdictions of certain types of market manipulation escaping the manipulation prohibitions. Such a demarcation is particularly problematic in energy markets, since some market behaviour, such as capacity withholding which are generally perpetrated in a single market. As discussed, according to the advice document published by CESR and ERGEG on dealing with market abuse in energy markets,[469] the practice of withholding the energy supply, which involves generation operators reducing their supply capacity to exploit supply-demand imbalances, especially during peak-demand periods, to inflate energy prices is regarded as a major rationale behind the adoption of the anti-manipulation rules under REMIT.

US law and the academic literature have been rife with confusion over the definition of market manipulation. Establishing a legal framework that applies to both fraud-based and artificial price-based market manipulation has proved to be very difficult. This has resulted in the application of different standards and prima facie rules to different types of market manipulation. The rules and academic discussions have not sufficed to derive legal conclusions as to what type of legal standards should be applied in prosecuting market manipulation in energy markets. Therefore a detailed case law analysis on energy market manipulation is important to understand how wholesale energy markets can fall victim to manipulative practices and the legal standards that are adopted for the prosecution. In Chapters 3 and 4, this book provides a detailed analysis of US and EU case law on market manipulation in energy markets.

---

465. *Amaranth Advisors L.L.C. et. al.*, 120 FERC ¶ 61,085 (2007); *CFTC v. Amaranth Advisors, L.L.C., et. al.*, 523 F. Supp. 2d 328 (S.D.N.Y. 2007).
466. *In re DiPlacido*, [2007-2009 Transfer Binder] Comm. Fut. L. Rep. (CCH) ¶ 30,970 (CFTC 2008); *In re Avista Energy, Inc. and Michael T. Griswold*, CFTC Docket No.: 01-21, 2001 WL 951736 (CFTC 2001).
467. *Constellation Energy Commodities Group Inc.*, 138 FERC ¶ 61,168 (2012).
468. *Supra* note 448.
469. CESR and ERGEG (2008).

While in the former, this book discovers the extent of manipulative practices that can be relevant in energy markets, in the latter particular attention is given to certain market practices that EU institutions such as CESR and ERGEG, and ACER consider fundamental to cope with and prosecute under a tailor-made legal framework, REMIT. Given the particular importance placed upon the prosecution of capacity withholding under EU law, this book addresses these types of practices separately from other types of market manipulation. Thus, despite being a US case, *KeySpan,* in which the defendants engaged in capacity withholding practices is discussed in chapter four. The cases involving other types of market manipulation, such as *Amaranth Advisors, DiPlacido,* and *Constellation*, on the other hand, are addressed in Chapter 3.

CHAPTER 3

Manipulative Practices in Energy Markets in US Case Law

§3.01 INTRODUCTION

During the 1970s, the oil crisis led the US government to adopt certain measures on pricing control of oil products such as gasoline and heating oil. These measures proved to be ineffective and resulted in US energy price spikes in the late 1970s, which caused serious energy shortages and economic losses across the country. In order to mitigate the economic damage, the US government started lifting price controls and adopted a market-based approach involving the trading of energy products in organised market places such as the New York Mercantile Exchange (NYMEX) and the Chicago Bureau of Trade (CBOT). Energy trading in these markets at market rates gave birth to the trading of energy derivatives and futures contracts by energy suppliers seeking to manage and hedge pricing risks which arose out of the high volatility and oil price increases.

Trading in derivatives with respect to securities and commodities markets was not a new phenomenon. These products had been regulated by the SEC[470] and the CFTC[471] for over forty years before the birth of energy derivatives. While the SEC regulates trading in securities, the CFTC's main focus is the trade of commodities, for example in the agriculture sector and especially in the energy sector, with the growth of trading in energy products. The CFTC has been active in providing regulatory oversight over pricing mechanisms and enforcing the CEA[472] rules, when market distortions occur. Effective functioning and reliability of these markets have developed through substantive case law on the legality and efficiency of market practices. Market

470. 17 C.F.R. § 240.10b-5 (2012).
471. Before the CFTC, the Commodity Exchange Authority, a small bureau operating under the State Department of Agriculture administered commodity trading and prosecuted market manipulation. *See* Jerry Markham, xiii–xiv (2015).
472. 7 U.S.C. § 13b (2010).

distortions in the energy sector, especially at the wholesale level, became visible immediately after the trading in energy futures started in NYMEX and CBOT.[473] Yet the effective application of the CEA rules to the wholesale energy markets by the CFTC was not substantial, as trading in energy futures and derivatives remained thin until the enactment of the Commodity Futures Modernisation Act (CFMA) in 2000.

After the adoption of CFMA 2000 which exempted energy derivatives, such as futures, swaps and options traded in OTC markets from the CFTC's regulatory oversight, the US energy markets witnessed a huge growth in the size of derivatives trading.[474] The absence of regulation with respect to these products made the energy derivatives major trading instruments involving not only energy suppliers who sought risk management and hedging purposes but also speculators who traded on price arbitrage between different products and markets. However, the lack of regulatory oversight monitoring the trading practices of suppliers and traders was fundamental in the eruption of the 2001 *'Great Western Energy Crisis'* or *'California Energy Crisis'*, a major collapse of California energy markets involving electricity prices in California at unprecedented levels, supply shortages, continuous blackouts and extensive government intervention. Several factors have been identified with respect to the collapse, such as poor market design and deregulation in electricity markets.[475] However, along with the collusion of other market participants, the manipulative schemes[476] developed by Enron, then the world's leading energy giant, owner of pipelines, generation facilities and EnronOnline, an OTC trading platform involving trade of USD 880 billion in energy contracts, were fundamental in first giving effect to price spikes between 2000–2001 and then the collapse of California energy markets.[477]

After the failure of the California wholesale energy supply mechanism, both the CFTC,[478] having jurisdiction over commodity futures, and the FERC, having jurisdiction over the physical supply and transmission of natural gas and electricity products, commenced investigations into what market fundamentals were present in the markets and how practices by traders changed market conditions and prices during the crisis. The investigations revealed that the lack of regulatory authority overseeing market activities and price levels was influential in the extent of the energy crisis and

473. Certain market behaviours involved use of energy futures contracts as a way of creating fictitious economic losses for tax purposes The gaming of oil markets by infamous commodity speculator Marc Rich, who employed a so-called daisy chain transactions scheme for tax evasion purposes as well as to exploit the dual pricing system adopted by the US government against increasing prices during the oil crises, is illustrative of the early manipulative practices in energy futures contracts. *See* http://www.forbes.com/sites/shahgilani/2013/06/28/marc-rich-the-legend-behind-the-legend/#7e544b495feb (accessed 29 Jun. 2017).
474. Allan Horwich, *Warnings to the Unwary: Multi-Jurisdictional Federal Enforcement of Manipulation and Deception in the Energy Markets after the Energy Policy Act of 2005* 27/2 Energy Law Journal 364, 376 (2006).
475. *See* Christopher Weare, *The California Electricity Crisis Causes and Policy Options* (Public Policy Institute of California 2003); Paul L. Joskow (2001); Paul Joskow & Edward Kahn (2002); Severin Borenstein (2002).
476. Traders in Enron provided iconic names in developing manipulative schemes, such as *'Ricochet'* (megawatt laundering), *'Fat Boy'* (false reporting), and *'Death Star'* (circular scheduling). *See* Gary Taylor, et al. (2015).
477. Jerry Markham, 275 (2015).
478. *CFTC v. Enron Corp., & Hunter Shively*, H-03-909, 2004 WL 594752 (S.D.Tex. 2004).

availability of effective legal tools in the prevention of market manipulation is crucial for the effective functioning of energy markets.[479] Consequently, both FERC and the CFTC developed market rules and legal frameworks that were specifically aimed at prohibiting and prosecuting manipulative practices in energy markets.

In the second section, the chapter discusses jurisdictional issues arising from the enforcement of anti-manipulation rules by multiple agencies in the US, such as the SEC, the CFTC and FERC. Focusing specifically on the regulatory authority exercised by the CFTC and FERC on energy markets, the chapter also addresses the interpretation of anti-manipulation rules by the SEC, important for understanding the prosecution of market manipulation by the CFTC and FERC. The third section examines case law on market manipulation in energy markets. Analysing the traditional approach developed in case law, the chapter provides further demarcations based on the characteristics of manipulative practices and energy markets. The section first discusses cases involving market power manipulation in energy markets. This type of manipulation is prevalent in commodity markets in which market participants engage in cornering by accumulating market power. In this part, the chapter provides examples of this type of market manipulation as exercised in energy markets. The section then discusses trade-based market manipulation which is a relatively newly defined concept involving manipulative practices that do not involve the use of market power within the meaning of market power manipulation and fraud. The chapter provides a further demarcation for these types of market manipulation noting that market participants can devise several trading strategies that are not identical yet constitute trade-based manipulation. The final type of market manipulation which the chapter explores in the third section is outright fraud providing a case in which market participants manipulate energy markets via fictitious activities. The fourth section comprises the conclusion.

§3.02 AVAILABLE JURISDICTIONS IN US ENERGY REGULATION

After the 2001 California energy crisis, trading practices in energy markets across the US, including the trading of electricity, natural gas and oil supply contracts, were put under regulatory scrutiny by multiple jurisdictions. The majority of case law with respect to the determination of manipulative market behaviours has been developed through investigations initiated by these regulatory agencies. Therefore, an overall analysis of the relevant jurisdictions is fundamental to understanding the approaches taken by the US regulatory agencies in the enforcement of anti-manipulation rules in relation to trading practices in the wholesale energy markets.

479. FERC Staff Report, Final Report on Price Manipulation in Western Markets Fact-Finding Investigation of Potential Manipulation of Electric and Natural Gas Prices, (FERC Staff Report) Docket No PA02-2-000 (March 2003), http://www.ferc.gov/legal/maj-ord-reg/land-docs/PART-I-3-26-03.pdf (accessed 29 Jun. 2017).

[A] General

Regulation of wholesale energy markets in the US is carried out by three different agencies: the CFTC; FERC; and the Federal Trade Commission (the FTC). While the CFTC regulates commodity exchanges and futures contracts traded in exchanges or OTC markets, FERC has a subject matter jurisdiction over electricity and natural gas markets monitoring competition, trading, transmission, and price rates in energy products. Both FERC and the CFTC apply anti-manipulation rules to prevent and prosecute abusive trading behaviours in these markets. The last regulatory agency that regulates energy-related products is the FTC. For the purpose of addressing manipulative practices, especially in natural gas and electricity markets, the chapter does not delve into the extent of the FTC's jurisdiction in regulating energy markets, as their main focus is on the markets of crude oil, gasoline and petroleum distillates,[480] which are outside the scope of this chapter. Therefore only FERC's and the CFTC's jurisdictions will be addressed in detail.

[B] FERC's Jurisdiction

FERC has regulatory jurisdiction in both electricity and natural gas markets. The jurisdiction of FERC in electricity markets is defined under the FPA.[481] Accordingly, FERC regulates '*the transmission of electric energy in interstate commerce and to the sale of electric energy at wholesale in interstate commerce* (...)' and has authority and responsibility '(...) *over all facilities for such transmission or sale of electric energy* (...)'.[482] Section 205 of the FPA states that it is also FERC's responsibility to ensure that rates for jurisdictional power sales and transmission services are reasonable so any market practices that directly or indirectly affect those rates will be subject to FERC's jurisdiction.[483]

In natural gas, FERC's regulatory authority is determined in the NGA of 1938[484]. FERC's jurisdiction in the NGA encompasses:

> the transportation of natural gas in interstate commerce, to the sale in interstate commerce of natural gas for resale for ultimate public consumption for domestic, commercial, industrial, or any other use, and to natural-gas companies engaged in such transportation or sale, and to the importation or exportation of natural gas in foreign commerce and to persons engaged in such importation or exportation (...).[485]

480. The Energy Independence and Security Act of 2007, Pub. L. 110–140, title VIII, § 811, 19 Dec. 2007, 121 Stat. 1723, 42 U.S. Code § 17301.
481. The Federal Power Act, 16 U.S.C. (2006).
482. 16 U.S.C § 824(b)(1) (2006).
483. 16 U.S.C § 824d (2006).
484. Natural Gas Act of 1938 (15 U.S.C., Chapter 15B).
485. Section 1(b) of the NGA (15 U.S.C. § 717b).

The 'first sales' of natural gas products are excluded from the application of this provision. What constitute the 'first sale' of natural gas is identified in the Natural Gas Policy Act of 1978,[486] which describes as:

> any volume of natural gas—
>
> (i) to any interstate pipeline or intrastate pipeline;
> (ii) to any local distribution company;
> (iii) to any person for use by such person;
> (iv) which precedes any sale described in clauses (i), (ii), or (iii); and
> (v) which precedes or follows any sale described in clauses (i), (ii), (iii), or (iv) and is defined by the Commission as a first sale (...).[487]

After the California energy crisis in 2001, FERC adopted Order 644 in November 2003 which establishes a code of conduct to prevent and prosecute market behaviours that are without legitimate business purpose and affect market conditions with respect to sales and transmission of energy products.[488] Accordingly FERC's code of conduct prohibits:

> (a)ny person making natural gas sales for resale in interstate commerce (...) from engaging in actions or transactions that are without a legitimate business purpose and that are intended to or foreseeably could manipulate market prices, market conditions or market rules for natural gas. Prohibited actions and transactions include but are not limited to: (1) Pre-arranged offsetting trades of the same product among the same parties, which involve no economic risk and net change in beneficial ownership (sometimes called wash trades); and (2) Collusion with another party for the purpose of manipulating market prices, market conditions, or market rules for natural gas.[489]

The prohibition requires that market behaviour has no legitimate business objective other than a manipulative intent and it foreseeably affects prices, conditions and rules of natural gas markets. In the second part of the rule, FERC also provides examples of behaviour that will be regarded as manipulative within the meaning of illegitimate business practice. In Order 644, FERC defines wash trades, involving transactions prearranged to cancel each out with no actual economic risk.[490] Such trades are designed to create a fictitious liquidity in the trading of products which affects price levels that are generally measured based on volume average calculation of sale and purchase orders with respect to relevant products.

FERC's adoption of anti-manipulation raised some concerns about jurisdictional conflict with the CFTC, which has a long history of enforcing anti-manipulation rules for commodities markets and also exercises its jurisdiction over trading in energy products in regulated markets, e.g., commodity exchanges. FERC's entrance into the prosecution of manipulative practices, part of which is regulated under the CFTC's

486. Natural Gas Policy Act of 1978 (15 U.S.C. Ch. 60).
487. 15 U.S.C § 3301(21).
488. Federal Energy Regulatory Commission, '18 CFR Part 284' (17 Nov. 2003) Docket No RM03-10-000; Order No 644 (hereinafter FERC, Order No 644).
489. *Ibid.*, 403, 61.
490. *Ibid.*, 22.

authority, resulted in concurrent application of multiple jurisdictions and double jeopardy questions.[491] This was the case in *Energy Transfer Partners*[492] in which FERC and the CFTC filed a simultaneous action alleging that the same conduct done by the defendants violated the anti-manipulation provisions of both jurisdictions. The defendants later settled with both regulatory agencies and the case did not lead to a serious conflict of jurisdictions as investigation by both regulators proceeded in coordination. However, after the enactment of the Energy Policy Act of 2005[493] (EP Act 2005), the regulatory interests of the two agencies collapsed each other.

As a reaction to the California energy crisis, the US Congress enacted new legislation that changed the regulatory structure of the US energy markets. The EP Act 2005 did not extend FERC's jurisdiction by including new transactions and markets that were previously outside the scope of FERC's authority. Instead, it amended both the NGA and FPA by providing an anti-manipulation mandate based on SEC's Section 10b-5[494] fraud-based definition of market manipulation. Sections 315 and 1283 of the EP Act 2005 provide that:

> (i)t shall be unlawful for any entity, directly or indirectly, to use or employ, in connection with the purchase or sale of natural gas and electric energy or the purchase or sale of transportation and transmission services subject to the jurisdiction of the Commission, any manipulative or deceptive device or contrivance (...).[495]

The EPAct 2005 empowered FERC to prosecute manipulative practices not only by direct participants in physical electricity and natural gas markets, but also by any entity directly or indirectly committing manipulation in relation to the jurisdictional transactions. The legislation also provided additional legal tools and remedies to punish and deter violations, including civil penalties up to USD 1 million per violation, per day.[496]

In order to implement the EP Act 2005, FERC adopted Order No 670,[497] which establishes FERC's legal jurisdiction over manipulative practices and identifies the elements of market manipulation within the meaning of FERC's anti-manipulation mandate. While Section 1c.1 addresses practices in natural gas markets, Section 1c.2 prohibits market manipulation in electricity markets. Accordingly:

> (a) (i)t shall be unlawful for any entity, directly or indirectly, in connection with the purchase or sale of natural gas and electric energy or the purchase or sale of transportation or transmission services subject to the jurisdiction of the Commission,
> (1) To use or employ any device, scheme, or artifice to defraud,

491. Allan Horwich, 397–398 (2006).
492. *Energy Transfer Partners, L.P. et. al.*, 120 FERC ¶ 61,086 (2007); *CFTC v. Energy Transfer Partners L.P.*, Civil Action No 3-07-Cv. 1301 (N.D. Tex. 2007).
493. *Supra* note 338.
494. 17 C.F.R. § 240.10b-5 (2011).
495. Energy Policy Act of 2005 §§ 315, 1283.
496. 15 U.S.C § 717t-1.
497. Federal Energy Regulatory Commission, '18 CFR Part 1c' (19 Jan. 2006) Docket No RM06-3-000; Order No 670 (hereinafter FERC Order No 670).

(2) To make any untrue statement of a material fact or to omit to state a material fact necessary in order to make the statements made, in the light of the circumstances under which they were made, not misleading, or
(3) To engage in any act, practice, or course of business that operates or would operate as a fraud or deceit upon any entity (...).[498]

Even though the prohibition deliberately adopts the fraud-based definition of market manipulation, FERC interprets it in such a way as to monitor all forms of abuse, including fraudulent and artificial price-based manipulation that affect markets over which FERC has jurisdiction. The broad interpretation and application of the EPAct's anti-manipulation provisions to certain transactions and markets on the basis of their effects on natural gas and electricity markets has resulted in jurisdictional conflict between FERC and the CFTC.

[C] The CFTC's Jurisdiction

Given the complexities which arose in the CFTC's regulatory practice with respect to proving artificial prices, the application of the CEA anti-manipulation rules to wholesale energy trading has also proved to be far from easy. Initially, the CFTC used Section 4(c) of the CEA to deal with early manipulative practices involving the trading of energy contracts for tax evasion purposes.[499] Section 4(c) of the CEA prohibits any transaction involving the purchase or sale of any commodity for future delivery and of a character of wash sale, accommodation trade or fictitious sale.[500] This provision provided an efficient way, for a while, for the CFTC to prohibit and prosecute manipulative practices as it does not require the CFTC to establish that prices with respect to the relevant wholesale energy trading are artificial as a result of manipulative conduct. However, the application of Section 4(c) to practices which are not of the character of a wash sale, or fictitious trade was contested in case law.

In the *Sundheimer*[501] case, Section 4(c) did not provide appropriate tools to prosecute a rigged trading practice as manipulative. The trades at issue were not of a fictitious character and in fact, caused actual change in market positions. They were real trades rather than wash trades and therefore outside the scope of the manipulation prohibition under Section 4(c). These trades are generally called open trade transactions, which are bona fide transactions entered into with a manipulative intent and involve actual parties and actual economic risks.[502] The practices that Section 4(c) prohibits are closed market trades, e.g., wash trades and fictitious trades, which are non-bona fide transactions, without any engagement in an actual trade or economic risks within the market. Such differentiation is also supported in *US v. Radley, et al.*, finding that the defendants involved actual bids and offers and thus their trading activities cannot be regarded as misleading or fraudulent, irrespective of the parties'

498. 18 C.F.R. § 1c.1, 1c.2.
499. *The CFTC v. Savage*, 611 F.2d 270,284 (9th Cir. 1979); *United States v. Turkish*, 623 F.2d 769 (2d Cir. 1980), *cert. denied*, 449 U.S. 1077 (1981).
500. 7 U.S.C. § 6c.
501. *Sundheimer v. CFTC*, 688 F.2d 150 (2d Cir. 1982), *cert. denied*, 460 U.S. 112 (1983).
502. *Energy Transfer Partners, L.P. et. al.*, 120 FERC ¶ 61,086 (2007), 27.

motivation.[503] The court further asserted that '*(a)cting in a manner that shifts the price of a commodity in a favourable direction is the business of profit-making enterprises, and if it is done without fraud or misrepresentation, it does not clearly violate the CEA*'.[504] Some commentators said that the ruling in *US v. Radley, et al.*, would render unfeasible the prosecution of manipulation in commodity products.[505]

In order to prosecute manipulative practices which are not of a fraudulent character, and also alleviate the complexities with respect to proving artificial prices, the CFTC adopted another strategy. In reaction to the differentiation between open and closed market trading, the CFTC started enforcing the prohibition against attempting to manipulate, which does not involve an artificial price standard element. The prohibition against such an attempt is included under Sections 6(c), 6(d) and 9(a)(2) of the CEA, which authorises the CFTC to decide whether one or multiple market participants directly or indirectly manipulated or attempted to manipulate the market price of any swap, or of any commodity, in interstate trading, or for future delivery.[506] In order to hold defendants liable for the attempted manipulation, the CFTC has to prove:

(1) that the defendants intended to manipulate prices; and
(2) that there should be some overt act committed in furtherance of that intent.[507]

Whether the defendants have the ability to affect prices artificially, or whether price artificiality as a result of a manipulative practice exists is irrelevant in the finding of attempted manipulation. The adoption of this new strategy proved to be very beneficial for the CFTC which prosecuted forty-two energy undertakings and thirty-one individuals on the basis of false reports and attempted manipulation between 2002 and 2009.[508]

A turning point in the CFTC's enforcement of anti-manipulation rules was *DiPlacido* in 2009, in which the CFTC won its first victory, finding a defendant liable for market manipulation by successfully establishing that the defendant was able to affect prices artificially and in fact artificial prices existed as a consequence of the defendant's conduct.[509] As will be discussed in greater detail later, in this case the CFTC applied the four-part test[510] to a market behaviour which involved actual bids and offers. Basing its

503. *Supra* note 341.
504. *Ibid.*, 816.
505. Jerry Markham, 285 (2015).
506. 7 U.S.C. §§ 9, 13b, 13(a)(2).
507. *In re Hohenberg Brothers*, [1975-1977 Transfer Binder] Comm. Fut. L. Rep. (CCH) ~ 20,271 at 21,477 (CFTC 18 Feb. 1977).
508. For cases prosecuted under false reporting and attempted manipulation provisions, *see* Jerry Markham, *Law Enforcement and the History of Financial Market Manipulation* 276, footnote 88 (M.E. Sharpe Inc. 2015).
509. *In re DiPlacido*, [2007-2009 Transfer Binder] Comm. Fut. L. Rep. (CCH) ¶ 30,970 (CFTC 2008).
510. According to the traditional four-part test for artificial price-based market manipulations, the CFTC must establish by a preponderance of the evidence that:

(1) the respondent had the ability to influence market prices;
(2) the respondent specifically intended to influence market prices;
(3) an artificial price existed; and

justification on the ruling of *Henner,*[511] the CFTC stated that artificial prices had been created by DiPlacido, who in his bids and offers, which accounted for a large portion of the trading activity for the relevant periods, paid more or less than what was required without legitimate factors and thereby moved prices at an artificial level.[512]

DiPlacido was the only successful prosecution of market manipulation by the CFTC under the traditional four-part test in more than forty years of commodity markets regulation.[513] In order to overcome the historical shortcomings of the CFTC's anti-manipulation authority, 'the Dodd–Frank Wall Street Reform and Consumer Protection Act'[514] (Dodd-Frank) gave the CFTC additional market manipulation authority. Similar to the prohibition adopted under Sections 315 and 1283 of the EP Act 2005 which are based on SEC Rule 10(b), Section 753 of Dodd-Frank provides that:

> (i)t shall be unlawful for any person, directly or indirectly, to use or employ, or attempt to use or employ, (...), any manipulative or deceptive device or contrivance (...).[515]

Accordingly, the CFTC is not required to decide on whether the practices at issues were intended to move or did move market prices at artificial level. This new authority aligned the CFTC with FERC and the SEC in the enforcement of anti-manipulation rules. The broad, catch-all formulation allows the regulatory authority to reach all forms of manipulative practices that deceive or defraud market participants. Furthermore, the new authority also provides the CFTC access to case law developed under SEC Rule 10(b) which results in increased certainty in enforcement practice.

The CFTC stated that '*to account for the differences between the securities markets and the derivatives markets, the Commission will be guided, but not controlled, by the substantial body of judicial precedent applying the comparable language*'.[516] Implementing the new manipulation authority, the CFTC adopted 'Final Rule'[517] 180.1. Accordingly, the CFTC is required to establish that the respondents, either intentionally or recklessly:

(1) use or employ, or attempt to use or employ any manipulative device, scheme or artifice to defraud,

---

(4) the respondent caused the artificial price. *In re Cox,* [1986-1987 Transfer Binder] Comm. Fut. L. Rep. (CCH) ¶ 23,786 (CFTC 1987).

511. *In re David G. Henner,* 30 Agric. Dec. 1157, CEA Docket No. 161. (CFTC 15 Sept. 1971).
512. *In re DiPlacido,* [2007-2009 Transfer Binder] Comm. Fut. L. Rep. (CCH) ¶ 30,970 (CFTC 2008), 18.
513. Shaun D. Ledgerwood (2010), *quoting* remarks by Bart Chilton a member of the CFTC who stated that '(...) 35 years, there has been only one successful prosecution for manipulation'.
514. The Dodd–Frank Wall Street Reform and Consumer Protection Act, Pub. L. No 111-203, 124 Stat. 1376 (2010).
515. *Ibid.,* § 753.
516. *In re Total Gas & Power North America, Inc., and Therese Tran,* CFTC Docket No. 16 -03 (7 Dec. 2015).
517. Commodity Futures Trading Commission, 76 Final Rule 41398, (17 C.F.R. Part 180) Prohibition on the Employment, or Attempted Employment, of Manipulative and Deceptive Devices – Prohibition on Price Manipulation.

(2) make or attempt to make any untrue or misleading statement of a material fact or to omit to state a material fact necessary in order to make the statements made not untrue or misleading,
(3) engage, or attempt to engage in any act, practice, or course of business, which operates as a fraud or deceit upon any person, (...).[518]

In Rule 180.2, the CFTC also retains the old manipulation definition providing that '*(i)t shall be unlawful for any person, directly or indirectly, to manipulate or attempt to manipulate the price of any swap, or of any commodity in interstate commerce, or for future delivery on or subject to the rules of any registered entity*'.[519] Therefore the adoption of the new fraud-based definition does not deprive the CFTC of its authority over artificial price-based manipulation and the traditional four-part test can still be relied on in cases where the manipulative practices are not considered to be of a fraudulent character. Even though, it is noted that the structure of fraud-based anti-manipulation rules is formulated to reach all forms of manipulative conduct, the CFTC, persuaded by its failure in *Sundheimer* and *US v. Radley*, chose to differentiate two separate anti-manipulation rules and keep both authorities under its legal framework.

After Dodd-Frank, both FERC and the CFTC have similar anti-manipulation provisions based on SEC's Section 10(b). While the CFTC keeps two different prohibitions and interprets the fraud-based and artificial price-based definition as different types of market manipulation, FERC applies its fraud-based authority reaching all types of manipulative practice. Both FERC and the CFTC regulate trading in wholesale energy markets and the agencies' jurisdictions have overlapped in prosecuting manipulative practices on several occasions. However, uncoordinated and even contradictory interpretations on the regulatory side can give rise to uncertainty with respect to the application of anti-manipulation rules.

[D] The Collision of Jurisdictions in the Energy Trading

In the wake of the California crisis, both FERC and the CFTC, under their jurisdictions, initiated investigations into reasons for the price spikes which had occurred throughout the collapse of the energy markets. Actions were brought against market participants who had engaged in manipulative practices exploiting the wholesale energy markets during the crisis. While the CFTC brought an action against the defendants' manipulative bidding activities in the EnronOnline which was settled later,[520] FERC, publishing a final report on price manipulation during the crisis,[521] issued orders for gaming practices that violated regional market rules and tariffs under its jurisdiction.[522] The concurrent exercise of regulatory authorities did not cause jurisdictional conflict

518. 17 C.F.R. Part 180, § 180.1.
519. *Ibid.*, § 180.2.
520. According to the terms of settlement, one of the traders in the EnronOnline, Hunter Shively, was required to pay USD 300,000 to the CFTC to settle the case on contested bidding practices. *See CFTC v. Enron Corp., & Hunter Shively*, H-03-909, 2004 WL 594752 (S.D.Tex. 2004).
521. FERC Staff Report (2003).
522. *Ibid.*, ES-15.

between FERC and the CFTC during the crisis. However, the variety and complexity of manipulative schemes[523] employed by perpetrators in exploiting price relations and market rules affected the approach taken by the agencies in the regulation of energy markets.

After the California crisis, FERC as a federal energy regulator, overseeing inter-state market conduct of energy undertakings, adopted market rules specifically aimed at prohibiting market manipulation in energy markets.[524] The application of these anti-manipulation rules is not limited to the physical trading of wholesale energy markets. After the enactment of the EPAct in 2005 which gave FERC the ability to exercise its jurisdiction over practices in regulated markets that are under the jurisdiction of the CFTC, FERC can also bring actions against trading activities in exchanges that affect prices and conditions in FERC-jurisdictional markets.[525] The bidding activities in exchanges involving, for example, future contracts over which the CFTC has exclusive jurisdiction can be subject to regulatory proceedings brought by FERC against market participants on the basis of their effect on prices in the physical trading of wholesale energy products.

The extent of the jurisdictional complexity was further elevated with the number of critics increasing after the California energy crisis as to the ineffectiveness of the CFTC's regulatory oversight over OTC trading.[526] In reaction to its lack of authority over the regulation of OTC trading, the CFTC started to monitor energy trading in exchanges and other regulated markets more closely, bringing proceedings against attempts to manipulate using the false reporting prohibitions.[527] The regime, which had been created by CFMA 2000, that exempted trading in energy products in the OTC markets from the CFTC's authority[528] was later repealed by the CFTC Reauthorization Act of 2008,[529] which expanded the CFTC's jurisdiction over OTC trading activities and created a new regulatory authority, called 'Significant Price Discovery Contracts' (SPDCs),[530] including OTC energy contracts previously exempted under CFMA 2000.

The first case that both FERC and the CFTC brought manipulation claims against a market practice was *Energy Transfer Partners*,[531] in which the defendant was accused

---

523. *Supra* note 476.
524. Investigation of Terms and Conditions of Public Utility Market-Based Rate Authorisations, 105 F.E.R.C ¶ 61,218 (2003), *reh'g denied*, 107 FERC ¶ 61,175 (2004) at Appendix A (Market Behaviour Rules Order).
525. Federal Energy Regulatory Commission, '18 C.F.R. Part 1c' (19 Jan. 2006) Docket No RM06-3-000; Order No 670, 16.
526. Jerry Markham, 340 (2015).
527. *See supra* note 506.
528. The exemption regime created after the CFMA 2000 was called 'Enron Loophole', as it was the direct result of Enron's lobbying activities, in which it had a particular interest with respect to its trading platform, EnronOnline that provided market participants the OTC trading services. *See* Mark Jickling, *The Enron Loophole* CRS Report for Congress (7 Jul. 2008).
529. Title XIII of the Food, Conservation, and Energy Act of 2008, H.R. 2419, Pub. L. No 110-234 (2008).
530. Jerry Markham, 310 (2015).
531. *Energy Transfer Partners, L.P. et. al.*, 120 FERC ¶ 61,086 (2007); *CFTC v. Energy Transfer Partners L.P.*, Civil Action No 3-07-Cv. 1301 (N.D. Tex. 2007).

of manipulating index prices by employing uneconomic trades in physical wholesale natural gas markets in favour of its financial positions and concealing its market position as a net buyer of natural gas. The action brought in *Energy Transfer Partners* was coordinated between FERC and CFTC, as the defendants settled with them paying respectively USD 30 million and USD 10 million. It was *Amaranth*,[532] which first gave rise to concerns on conflicting jurisdictions.

In *Amaranth* the defendants were alleged to have manipulated the prices of natural gas products traded in an exchange, which is under the CFTC's authority, yet affected the value of financial positions in the OTC market, over which FERC exercises jurisdiction. Both the CFTC and FERC, in compliance with their jurisdictions, filed an action against the defendants on the basis of their trading activities. The defendants argued that FERC lacked jurisdiction on the grounds that the trading activity at issue was employed in a regulated market over which the CFTC had exclusive authority, which was also supported by the CFTC in a memorandum presented to the District Court of Appeals in 2013.[533] In response, FERC, citing *United States v. Reliant Energy*, argued that its jurisdiction did not pre-empt the CFTC's anti-manipulation jurisdictions.[534] As *Amaranth* later settled with FERC by agreeing to pay USD 7.5 million in addition to a civil penalty of USD 5.5 million, the district court rejected the claim that FERC lacked regulatory jurisdiction over the trading at issue on the basis of the CFTC's exclusive jurisdiction.

The jurisdictional conflict between the two agencies was further elevated after the adoption of the Dodd-Frank and Reauthorization Act of 2008. Its new anti-manipulation rule based on SEC's rule, Section 10(b), along with the grant of jurisdiction over OTC trading, expanded the CFTC's authority in the energy markets extensively. Furthermore, the dual formulation of its new anti-manipulation rules as including two separate prohibitions for fraud-based and artificial price-based manipulation differentiated from the formulation of anti-manipulation provisions in both FERC's Rule 1c and SEA, caused concern about conflicting anti-manipulation enforcement for a market practice to which multiple jurisdictions apply. Both the EPAct 2005 and Dodd-Frank instructed the two agencies to develop a MOU[535] to address the concerns on overlapping jurisdictions and to ensure that any conflicting or duplicative regulation was avoided. By January 2014 the agencies finally agreed on a memorandum that provided steps which the agencies could follow when they encounter

532. *Amaranth Advisors L.L.C. et. al.*, 120 FERC ¶ 61,085 (2007); *CFTC v. Amaranth Advisors, L.L.C., et. al.*, 523 F. Supp. 2d 328 (S.D.N.Y. 2007).
533. *Hunter v. FERC*, 711 F.3d 155 (D.C. Cir. 2013).
534. *United States v. Reliant Energy*, 420 F. Supp. 2d (N.D. Cal. 2006) 1043, 1045 (*quoting United States v. Borden Co.*, 308 U.S. 188, 198 (1939) (*'[I]t is a cardinal principle of construction that … when there are two acts upon the same subject, the rule is to give effect to both' and 'Congressional intent behind one federal statute should not be thwarted by the application of another federal statute if it is possible to give effect to both laws.'*)).
535. Energy Policy Act of 2005 (Public Law 109–58), § 26(4)(c)(1); The Dodd–Frank Wall Street Reform and Consumer Protection Act, Pub. L. No 111-203, 124 Stat. 1376 (2010), § 1034(d).

activities that may involve overlapping jurisdictions.[536] How this MOU will help the agencies overcome jurisdictional conflicts remains to be seen.

§3.03 MANIPULATIVE PRACTICES IN US CASE LAW

An extensive analysis of case law will provide an insight into how market participants can employ manipulative schemes with respect to wholesale energy trading exploiting price relations between different energy products. Traditionally, US case law distinguishes three types of market manipulation. Despite the intensive arguments in the academic literature as to their classification and characteristics,[537] they can be simply listed as: (1) market power manipulation; (2) trade-based manipulation (called open market transactions); and (3) outright fraud (called closed market transactions).[538] As the evaluation of these manipulative schemes under the traditional market manipulation classification will be useful in understanding how the application of anti-manipulation rules to wholesale energy trading differentiates from other markets and commodities, the chapter follows the traditional approach, listing the manipulative schemes under the concepts of market power, trade-based and fraud-based manipulation.

[A] Market Power Manipulation

[1] Overview

Manipulative market schemes in which the perpetrator uses its acquired market power to move prices artificially are generally called corners and squeezes. These types of practices involve the accumulation of large buy (long) or sell (short) positions in futures contracts for a particular deliverable product with a particular delivery period. They must also possess a large enough portion of the underlying product so that other parties cannot fulfil their obligations under the futures contracts unless they have access to the perpetrator's holding of underlying products. Unable to have access to enough supplies, the counterparties of the perpetrators are forced either to find and bring additional supplies from outside the market at extra cost, or to settle with the perpetrator on a cash basis at higher prices. In either case, the perpetrator is responsible for high price levels from which its large positions profits significantly.

In the energy markets, there are two cases that can be characterised as corners within the meaning of market power manipulation; *Apex Oil v. Di Mauro*[539] and *the*

536. Memorandum of Understanding Between The Federal Energy Regulatory Commission and The Commodity Futures Trading Commission Regarding Information Sharing and Treatment of Propriety Trading and Other Information, (2 Jan. 2014).
537. *See* Craig Pirrong (2010); Shaun Ledgerwood & Dan Harris (2012); Frank H. Easterbrook (1986); Daniel R. Fischel & David J. Ross (1991); Jerry Markham (2015), 204–212.
538. Craig Pirrong, 5 (2010).
539. *Apex Oil Co. v. Di Mauro*, 713 F. Supp. 587 (S.D.N.Y. 1989).

CFTC v. Parnon.[540] Both cases concern oil deliveries and involve the accumulation of a position in the futures market that exceeded the available deliverable supply. A detailed analysis on the market practices in these cases follows.

[2] Apex Oil v. Di Mauro[541]

This case involves a claim by Apex, an oil company selling heating oil to its customers through futures contracts traded on NYMEX, alleging that the defendants squeezed Apex's short position by collectively conspiring to force Apex to deliver heating oil for February 1982. Apex was a big seller of heating oil for that period, holding a short position on 4,378 out of 4,906 outstanding contracts and according to NYMEX rules, buyers of heating oil generally can make requests from the sellers as to date and method of the deliveries. If the shorts' deliveries do not match the conditions required by the longs, they may be obliged to pay for default penalties. Apex's efforts to change delivery dates and methods proved to be unsuccessful and the plaintiff had to purchase oil from other markets to fulfil its contractual obligations as determined by the buyers. Apex avoided default penalties at a considerable cost.

Apex brought both antitrust and manipulation claims, claiming that the defendants, by conspiring to squeeze the plaintiff's short positions in NYMEX heating oil futures contracts had violated the Sherman Act Sections 1 and 2 as well as Sections 9(b) and 13(a) of the CEA, the prohibition of manipulation or attempts to manipulate provisions. Apex alleged that the methods and date required by the buyers for the delivery obligations aimed at reducing the available supply that Apex could access to fulfil its contractual obligations. In order to supply the defendants, Apex was forced to seek additional supplies at extra cost, which moved market prices to higher artificial levels. Accordingly it is alleged that the defendant's squeeze of Apex's short positions was in violation of not just anti-manipulation provisions but also antitrust rules.

The US District Court for the Southern District of New York allowed antitrust claims based on Section 1 of the Sherman Act[542] to be taken forward but did not find that the defendants' activities were in violation of Section 2 of the Sherman Act[543] nor the anti-manipulation provisions under the CEA.[544] According to the District Court:

> (t)he acquisition of market dominance is the hallmark of a long manipulative squeeze. For without the ability to force shorts to deal with him either in the cash or futures market, the manipulator is not able to successfully dictate prices because a short may buy [the commodity] from other sources and deliver against his commitments.[545]

540. *CFTC v. Parnon Energy Inc.*, 11 Civ. 3543 (S.D.N.Y. 2014).
541. *Apex Oil Co. v. Di Mauro*, 713 F. Supp. 587 (S.D.N.Y. 1989).
542. *Ibid.*, 594.
543. *Ibid.*, 599.
544. *Ibid.*, 601.
545. *Ibid.*, 602, citing *In re Indiana Farm Bureau Cooperative Association*, [1982-1984 Transfer Binder] Comm. Fut. L. Rep. (CCH) ¶ 21,796 (CFTC 1982).

In Apex, the Court found that the defendants had not had enough physical oil to force Apex to settle with them at artificially high prices. The economic analysis demonstrated that the deliverable supply that Apex could have purchased for its contractual obligations exceeded their requirements by 2.5 times. Apex's ability to access 2,700,000 barrels of oil for the immediate supply of heating oil illustrated that the defendants lacked the dominance to dictate to Apex a cash settlement and thus move prices to artificially high prices.[546]

[3] The CFTC v. Parnon Energy Inc.[547]

In this case the US District Court for the Southern District of New York investigated a manipulation claim by the CFTC, alleging that the defendants, Parnon and other traders in 2008 manipulated the West Texas Intermediate crude oil (WTI) prices which is the cost of a thousand barrels of oil that is delivered to Cushing (an important delivery location for crude oil trading in the US). The manipulative scheme devised by the defendants consisted of three types of WTI contracts: (1) futures contracts; (2) physical contracts; (3) calendar spread contracts.[548] Futures contracts involve transactions for buying or selling of WTI for delivery at a fixed time in the future and can be traded on different markets, such as NYMEX and InterContinental Exchange, (the ICE, an OTC trading platform). The earliest delivery month for a futures contract is near month, which is the month for which the delivery of crude oil is traded and the trading of a futures contract for a near month is no longer tradeable after the fixed expiration day. For example, the expiration day for a NYMEX WTI futures contracts to be delivered in February 2008 is January 22. After that, March 2008 becomes the earliest delivery month, near month for WTI futures contract.[549]

Physical contracts involve the trading of WTI contracts for the following month. Market participants can trade physical contracts until three business days after the expiration day for the near month futures contracts. A near month futures contract becomes a physical contract after the expiration day. In this three-day period, which is called the 'cash window', parties try to balance their positions and make arrangements for the near months deliveries.[550] The price of physical trades is determined based on the average settlement price and total volume of contracts for crude oil to be delivered in the near month.

Calendar spread contracts are contracts priced at the difference between the average settlement price of oil to be delivered in the near month and the average settlement price of oil to be delivered in the followings months after the near month. Longer-term futures contracts are generally priced higher than near-term futures contracts due to additional costs, such as storage, insurance, financing and several other expenses that are all included in the calculation of settlement prices. This price

546. *Ibid.*
547. *CFTC v. Parnon Energy Inc.*, 11 Civ. 3543 (S.D.N.Y. 2014).
548. *Ibid.*, 1.
549. *Ibid.*, 2.
550. *Ibid.*, 2.

relation is termed '*contango*'.[551] If any tightness can occur in the immediate supply of oil in the overall market, the price of closer-term futures contracts can be higher than longer-term futures contracts. This price relation is called '*backwardation*'.[552] Market participants who purchase calendar spread contracts buy the WTI in the near month and sell the same amount of WTI in the following month, benefitting from the higher near-term supply prices.

Between 8 and 18 January, the defendants entered into transactions, purchasing 4.6 million barrels of WTI oil which accounted for 92% of the overall supply and kept their positions until 22 January, the last trading day for the near-month WTI futures contracts. Commercially the defendants had no need for this amount of oil and were expected sell the excessive amount at a considerable loss during the three-day cash window period in order to balance out their purchase transactions. However, the defendants also acquired large long positions of February/March calendar spreads equal to 13.6 million barrels of oil, profiting from higher near-term WTI futures prices. These calendar spreads are sensitive to end-of-month balances of oil supply.

The defendants' accumulation of large amounts of oil during the relevant time period in January resulted in tight supply during the cash window, and moved the price of oil for February at a level higher than that for following months causing a market outcome of backwardation. In order to balance their physical position, the defendants dumped all of their 4.6 million barrels on the market at a considerable loss, on 25 January, the last day of the cash window. Due to the scale of the sale of oil at low prices for balancing purposes, the market condition turned from backwardation to contango, which is called the 'burying the body effect'. However, the profits derived from backwardation in the February/March price spreads more than subsidised the defendants' losses incurred from the balancing of physical positions.

In 2011, the CFTC brought an action before the US District Court for the Southern District of New York alleging that the defendants had manipulated and attempted to manipulate both physical and futures markets for WTI contracts during the relevant periods between January and March 2008.[553] The Court noted that there are two different provisions for the prohibition of market manipulation and the underlying factor that the alleged scheme was based upon was the abuse of market power rather than fraud. Applying the artificial price-based prohibition, the Court approved the CFTC's finding that the defendants' activities during the cash window did not constitute fraud, and the scheme did not involve misstatements or material omissions. Instead, the defendants established market dominance over a deliverable supply of the WTI, and used this dominance to create tightness and affect prices for a relevant trading period, which increased the value of the positions the defendants held in calendar spread contracts. According to the court, the alteration of market conditions between backwardation and contango clearly illustrated the defendants' ability to

551. *Ibid.*, 4, *citing:* Kenneth M. Morris, *Standard & Poor's Dictionary of Financial Terms* 41 (McGraw-Hill Professional; Rev Ed. 2007).
552. *Ibid.*, *quoting:* Jerry M. Rosenberg, *Dictionary of Banking and Finance* 41 (John Wiley & Sons Inc 1982).
553. *CFTC v. Parnon Energy Inc., et al.*, 'Complaint for Injunctive and Other Equitable Relief and Civil Monetary Penalties Under the Commodity Exchange Act' (S.D.N.Y. 2011), para. 16.

affect prices and constituted evidence that the manipulative scheme, in fact, created artificial prices in the market.[554]

The manipulative scheme employed in the *CFTC v. Parnon Energy Inc* differed from the traditional corner and squeeze cases, such as *Apex Oil v. Di Mauro*. In corners and squeezes, the perpetrators devise their manipulative scheme in one single market rendering other market participants unable to fulfil their contractual obligation. However, in the *CFTC v. Parnon Energy Inc,* rather than forcing the other parties to settle for higher prices, the defendants sought to derive profits from their positions held in calendar spread contracts, which are different yet the value of which is still tied to conditions in the physical and futures markets for WTI. In order to analyse how the acquisition of market power played a role in the *CFTC v. Parnon Energy Inc.* different from traditional corner and squeeze cases, the characteristics of market conditions under which the manipulative schemes carried out in these cases should be evaluated in more detail.

[4] Evaluation

It is important to note that the underlying products that became subject to anti-manipulation investigations in both *Apex Oil v. Di Mauro* and the *CFTC v. Parnon Energy Inc* were crude oil and by-products of oil. Trading in oil markets differentiates from trading in natural gas and electricity in certain ways. Oil markets are not regarded as network-based markets as the capacity restraints with respect to transport and storage of oil products do not give rise to particular concerns in designing the markets.[555] In electricity and natural gas markets, building large positions in both futures and physical markets is not probable as electricity cannot be stored in large quantities and natural gas requires facilities that are specifically build for the storage of natural gas. The demand and supply mechanism for these products is carried out instantly with a balancing system to ensure the availability of supply whenever the demand for power arises and that demand and supply prospect are always matched to system requirements. As the perpetrators of market power manipulation cannot build large positions in electricity and natural gas due to lack of storability, these examples of market power manipulation in *Apex Oil v. Di Mauro* and *CFTC v. Parnon Energy Inc* involved oil products rather than electricity or natural gas.

Apex v. Di Mauro is a clear example of traditional market power manipulation involving corner and squeeze practices. It is an early case addressing a market practice that took place in 1982, well before the effective use of futures and derivatives for hedging and speculation purposes in energy markets started in the 2000s. The

554. *CFTC v. Parnon Energy Inc.*, 11 Civ. 3543 (S.D.N.Y. 2014), 18.
555. Pipelines still constitute an effective means of transporting crude oil over long distances yet having access to an external supply without the establishment of a fixed infrastructure exerts competitive pressure on suppliers. However, in electricity and natural gas, absence of transmission and storage facilities isolates a region from external suppliers. Therefore, natural gas and electricity markets are designed and operated on the basis of capacity restraints. *See* Thomas W. Walde & Andreas J. Gunst, *International Energy Trade and Access to Energy Networks* 36/2 Journal of World Trade 191 (2002).

defendants' scheme in *Apex v. Di Mauro* was related to the trading of a single product, heating oil, in a single market, the NYMEX. Estimating the availability of supply along with the large short positions held by *Apex Oil v. Di Mauro*, the defendants were able to dictate their delivery standards forcing the plaintiff to seek additional supplies at additional costs. After futures contracts and other derivatives in energy markets became subject to hedging mechanisms and speculative trading,[556] arbitraging price differences between two products or for the same product between two markets or with different delivery durations, traders discovered the prospects of new positions that can be valuable on the basis of market changes that can be affected by prices in different but linked markets. *CFTC v. Parnon Energy Inc.* is illustrative as to how these price relations can be exploited in manipulative schemes.

CFTC v. Parnon Energy Inc. is characterised as a type of market power manipulation, as the court directly noted that it was the use of market power that gave effect to market manipulation. However the conduct committed by the defendants did not account for a corner or squeeze.[557] Aware that the tightness of oil supply for a particular delivery month can affect positions held in calendar spread contracts, the defendants in *CFTC v. Parnon Energy Inc* sought to exploit price relations between these interlinked markets, by creating a temporary tightness that moved the value of positions in calendar spread contracts to a more favourable level. Even though the defendants used their market power to create the tightness in the supply, this market practice can be characterised as a type of trade-based or in particular cross-market manipulation as they derived their profits from cross-market positions.

CFTC v. Parnon Energy Inc. blurs the distinction between market power and trade-based manipulation. The defendants' manipulative scheme involved both the use of market power and cross-market price relations. It is established in case law that market power is not substantial in the determination of market manipulation.[558] However, as will be addressed in greater detail, the perpetrators' ability to affect prices was an important factor in identifying manipulative practices in trade-based market manipulation cases. The establishment of the ability to affect prices and the existence of artificial prices has proved to be difficult in case law. The CFTC's struggle in the enforcement of artificial price-based anti-manipulation provisions directed FERC towards adopting SEC's fraud-based rule, Section 10(b) in its anti-manipulation provisions.[559] However, in its investigations, in order to prove the perpetrators' manipulative intent, FERC also undertook a legal analysis of whether the perpetrators had the ability to move prices to artificial levels, which is very similar to the analysis committed

556. *See supra* note 475.
557. *CFTC v. Parnon Energy Inc.*, 11 Civ. 3543 (S.D.N.Y. 2014), 16.
558. *In re DiPlacido*, [2007-2009 Transfer Binder] Comm. Fut. L. Rep. (CCH) ¶ 30,970 (CFTC 2008), 43: '*A dominant or controlling position in the market is not a requisite element to either manipulation or attempted manipulation and is not essential to altering successfully the forces of supply and demand', quoting In re Hohenberg Brothers*, [1975-1977 Transfer Binder] Comm. Fut. L. Rep. (CCH) ¶ 20,271 (CFTC 1977).
559. FERC, Order No 670, 5–6.

to identify whether the perpetrators accumulated and used market power in manipulating prices.[560] *CFTC v. Parnon Energy Inc.* provides a good example illustrating the complexities between the concepts of market power and the ability to affect prices in anti-manipulation regulation.

[B] Trade-Based Market Manipulation

[1] Overview

The legal analysis carried out against manipulative practices differs based on regulatory agencies and anti-manipulation provisions. For a procedure by FERC under the SEC's Rule Section 10(b), whether the relevant market practices at issue are fraudulent is irrelevant for the determination of market manipulation.[561] This is not the case for the CFTC. After the adoption of the Dodd-Frank, the distinction of fraudulent and non-fraudulent market manipulation became important to identify anti-manipulation procedure to be followed under a regulatory investigation. Even though the legal analysis applied by both agencies in enforcing anti-manipulation rules looks similar, incoherence in respective anti-manipulation rules results in uncertainty for the classification of manipulative practices.

The underlying factor behind the characteristics of trade-based market manipulation is that these market practices often involve strategic and large-scale trading activities and the legal analysis necessary for the determination of this type of manipulation does not require the regulators to establish that the perpetrators hold market power with respect to the products at issue.[562] As it is also characterised under artificial price-based manipulation developed under the precedent of the CFTC, rather than SEC's fraud-based formulation, price artificiality as a result of trading activity is crucial for a finding of manipulation. 'Marking the close' and 'successive bidding'[563] practices are regarded as the prominent examples of trade-based manipulation.[564] However identifying these types of market practices as manipulative and therefore illegitimate on the basis of artificial prices without resorting to market power analysis gives rise to legal questions on factors that make a trading activity manipulative. The case law and academic literature have also failed so far, in providing an appropriate definition that demarcates the concept of trade-based market manipulation.[565]

560. *See Amaranth Advisors L.L.C. et. al.*, 120 FERC ¶ 61,085 (2007); *CFTC v. Amaranth Advisors, L.L.C., et. al.*, 523 F. Supp. 2d 328 (S.D.N.Y. 2007), para. 45, quoting the Supreme Court's decision in *Ernst & Ernst v. Hochfelder*, 425 U.S. 185, 199 (1976) that market manipulation is a market practice '*designed to deceive or defraud investors by controlling or artificially affecting the price of securities*'.
561. FERC, Order No 670, 50.
562. *Supra* note 558.
563. Emilios E. Avgouleas, 141 (2005).
564. IOSCO, 287 (2000).
565. Jerry Markham, 204 (2015).

Given the lack of clarity in the concept of trade-based market manipulation, the chapter provides an example of trade-based manipulation case law where the regulatory agencies did not include an assessment of market power in their anti-manipulation inquiry, and market practice did not directly involve outright fraud and fictitious trades without actual financial risks. The case law indicates several types of trading activities that traders and energy suppliers employ in manipulating markets and prices. Generally, these market participants commit gaming of market rules exploiting loopholes in energy market design to derive financial profits. The manipulative schemes may involve multiple positions in different but interlinked markets. In these schemes, the perpetrators seek to achieve a certain outcome in a market that affects prices in a different market according to which the perpetrators' positions profits. Finally, these manipulative practices can also exploit capacity restraints and congestion payment mechanisms developed by transmission system operators and system providers to mitigate congestion risks related to transmission of energy products. The term that the case law uses in defining such practices is 'open market transactions'.[566] Accordingly, the chapter identifies three types of trade-based market manipulation:

(1) gaming of market rules;
(2) cross-market manipulation; and
(3) congestion-related manipulation.

[2] Gaming of Market Rules

As a liberalised and network-based sector, energy markets require a set of market rules governing trading and an uninterrupted flow of energy products that are fundamental for the objectives of security of supply and functioning of competitive energy markets. However these market rules and designs are not free from flaws and loopholes, which, once spotted, have been exploited by market participants. This section involves energy markets cases in which perpetrators were found in violation of anti-manipulation provisions, by exploiting profits and payments from the gaming of market rules.

[a] Rumford Paper Company[567]

In this case, FERC alleged that the defendant, the Rumford Paper Company, which operates a lumber mill and also a generation facility for paper production, violated Section 1c.2 of FERC's Order 670, an anti-manipulation rule for the electricity markets, by engaging in fraudulent behaviour and exploiting ISO New England Inc.'s (ISO-NE) Day-Ahead Load Response Program (DALRP). ISO-NE, the regional transmission system operator for New England, consisting of a transmission network involving six

566. *Energy Transfer Partners, L.P. et. al.*, 120 FERC ¶ 61,086 (2007), para. 63.
567. 140 FERC ¶ 61,030 *Rumford Paper Company* Docket No IN12-11-000 (17 Jul. 2012).

states, *Connecticut, Maine, Massachusetts, New Hampshire, Rhode Island, and Vermont*,[568] designed the DALRP to introduce incentives for electricity consumers to reduce their load during peak-demand hours.[569] Demand for electricity is generally inelastic. Consumers are generally willing to pay more, rather than reduce their consumption levels. By designing the DALRP, the ISO-NE intended to provide an additional incentive for customers to reduce their demand levels during peak-demand hours in which the price of electricity is more expensive than other hours of the day.

In 2007, Rumford, in compliance with the instructions of the Competitive Energy Services (CES), an independent energy services company providing consulting services to suppliers and consumers with respect to energy-related issues, established a scheme to receive payments under the ISO-NE's DALRP, without reducing its energy consumption during peak hours of the day. During the initial load baseline period in which Rumford's energy demand was calculated by an average of hourly meter data from 7:00 am through 6:00 pm for five business days after the sign up for the system of DALRP, Rumford ceased the operation of its generation facility and bought its electricity need from external suppliers for which it paid USD 120,000.[570] Once its load baseline was calculated, Rumford started to generate electricity and use it again for production purposes. Even though Rumford did not reduce its electricity demand for the peak hours, it started to receive payments from DALRP, as the purchases of electricity from external suppliers reduced after the re-operation of its generation facilities. For over six months between 2007 and 2008, by gaming the ISO-NE's DALRP rules, Rumford was paid for a demand reduction response that, in fact, never happened.[571]

FERC alleged that Rumford had violated 18 C.F.R. Section 1c.2, which prohibits any market participant from:

(1) using a fraudulent device, scheme or artifice, or making a material misrepresentation or a material omission as to which there is a duty to speak under a Commission-filed tariff, Commission order, rule or regulation, or engaging in any act, practice, or course of business that operates or would operate as a fraud or deceit upon any entity;
(2) with the requisite scienter;
(3) in connection with a transaction subject to the jurisdiction of the Commission.[572]

According to FERC, Rumford's scheme to receive payments from DALRP constituted a fraudulent scheme or artifice on the basis of misrepresentations with respect to the defendant's true levels of demand and its willingness and ability to reduce that demand. By perpetrating the scheme, the defendant incurred financial losses by purchasing electricity needed as a result of the curtailment of the generation capacity for a certain period of time. However these losses were recouped with the payments received via DALRP.

568. *See* https://www.ferc.gov/market-oversight/mkt-electric/new-england.asp (accessed 18 Apr. 2018).
569. 140 FERC ¶ 61,030 *Rumford Paper Company* Docket No IN12-11-000 (17 Jul. 2012), 1.
570. *Ibid.*
571. *Ibid.*, 16.
572. 18 C.F.R. §1c.2.

[b] J.P. Morgan Ventures Energy Corporation[573]

The defendant, J.P. Morgan Ventures Energy Corporation (JPMVEC) operated several electricity generators with relatively high heat rates, that is, they were less efficient than newer and more modern generation facilities which produced more output at less expensive prices. Therefore the defendant's generation units were mostly out of money and not picked up by the transmission system operators that JPMVEC served.[574] In order to make its energy operations more profitable, JPMVEC developed a strategy that exploited the market rules to receive extra payments from its bidding activities.

The relevant markets in which the defendant carried out its bidding strategy were the California Independent System Operator (CAISO) and Midcontinent Independent System Operator (MISO), regional transmission and market operators in the Midwest and California regions. In these markets buyers (such as entities that serve electricity to end users and retail customers) and sellers (such as generators) of electricity submit their bids and offers involving prices at which they are willing to trade. These prices differ considerably based on the transmission route that power flows from the point (source) that suppliers inject the power that is delivered by the transmission operator to another point (sink) where buyers receive it. Each route in the transmission system is called a 'node', and these nodes have different congestion levels and capacities. The price of electricity is determined on the basis of each node in what is called 'locational marginal prices' (LMPs).[575]

Regional transmission system operators generally operate two markets for the electricity supply. These are DAMs and Real-Time markets (RTMs). In DAMs, suppliers and buyers of electricity are transacting for the delivery of electricity on the next day. In RTMs, electricity is transmitted on the day that trading takes place. While DAMs are the main markets in which the bulk of the energy needs are supplied in a given location, RTMs operate as a balancing mechanism, where suppliers and buyers resort to balancing their shortages or additional energy needs. As they serve different purposes, day-ahead and real-time prices of electricity are usually different, even if they are traded for the same hour. These price differences allow market participants to benefit between DAMs and RTMs. A generator whose generation is picked up by the transmission operators for electricity supply in the DAM can pay another generator to supply on the next day in the RTM, (called 'buying back the Day-Ahead Award'),[576] if the prices are lower than the ones in the DAM. In so doing, generators acquire profits from trading of electricity between RTMs and DAMs on the basis of price differences without even being obliged to deliver electricity to a transmission grid.

Transmission system operators usually make payments to suppliers at the market rate which is the average price of all bids in each node across the transmission grid. In certain instances transmission system operators can also provide 'make-whole' or 'uplift' payments, when they commit a generator whose bids on the DAM was higher

573. *In Re Make-Whole Payments and Related Bidding Strategies*, 144 FERC ¶ 61,068 (2013).
574. *Ibid.*, para. 17.
575. *Ibid.*, para. 12.
576. This trading activity is also called as being '*dec'ed down to Pmin*'. *See ibid.*, para. 37.

than these market rates in order to compensate the generator's 'bid cost'[577] that includes the cost of electricity that the generator produces at its minimum operational level and the cost of electricity that is produced at any level above the minimum operational level. Accordingly, when a transmission system operator commits a generator whose bid is higher than market prices, it will pay the generator its bids rather than market rates by making additional make-whole payments on the basis of the generator's operation level. This payment system is called 'Bid Cost Recovery' (BCR) adopted under market rules.[578]

In order to make its old and inefficient electricity generators more profitable, the JPMVEC designed a bidding strategy exploiting the market rules on the BCR system. Accordingly JPMVEC issued successive bids over market prices in DAMs to ensure that CAISO and MISO picked up its generation. Once its generation was picked up for DAM, it bought back its day-ahead award in the RTM, paying another supplier to produce the electricity. While CAISO and MISO made make-whole payments under the BCR system to JPMVEC in DAMs to compensate its bid cost, JPMVEC paid market prices to other generators to supply in RTMs. Through this bidding scheme and the gaming of market rules, JPMVEC extracted substantial profits from trading between DAMs and RTMs.

FERC alleged that JPMVEC's practices operated as a fraud in the electricity market and violated its anti-manipulation rule for electricity markets, Section 1c.2.[579] The defendant's bids were not made on the basis of the aggregate forces of demand and supply in the market and not aimed at profiting from market fundamentals. In fact, JPMVEC made loss-incurring trades in the DAMs and RTMs which were uneconomic but for the payments received from the BCR system. By exploiting the market rules on make-whole payment mechanism, the JPMVEC created artificial market conditions which led the CAISO and the MISO to make unnecessary uplifting payments to the defendant.[580]

[c] Coaltrain Energy L.P., et al.[581]

This case involves a financial firm, Coaltrain, which devised a trading strategy to receive certain payments from the PJM Interconnection LLC (PJM) under the Marginal Loss Surplus Allocation (MLSA) system.[582] The PJM is a regional transmission organisation in a thirteen state region, operating as wholesale day-ahead and real-time electricity markets and managing the flow of electricity through the transmission grid

577. Bid cost is the price that energy suppliers submit to the CAISO and should not be confused with a unit's actual operational costs. A bid usually involves a bundled price for a generation capacity running at its lowest operation level (Pmin) and price for each additional quantity of electricity above Pmin. *Ibid.*, para. 20.
578. *Ibid.*, para. 25.
579. *Supra* note 497.
580. *In Re Make-Whole Payments and Related Bidding Strategies*, 144 FERC ¶ 61,068 (2013), para. 76.
581. *Coaltrain Energy L.P., et al.*, 154 FERC ¶61,002 (2016).
582. *Ibid.*, 10.

under market rules.[583] Electricity prices in the PJM are dependent on the specific locations and nodes within the transmission grid. Each node has two points: (i) the source, where the power is injected to the grid; and (ii) the sink where the power is delivered to its final destination. When the congestion at a specific node occurs, price difference between the source and the sink will grow, as the price of electricity being lower at the source will increase at the sink.

The congestion levels in each node differ widely and LMPs also vary in the same grid. There are three elements used in the calculation of LMPs: (1) energy price, which is the same at each node; (2) congestion cost which varies on the basis of capacities available in the transmission system; and (3) line losses which represent the heat losses occurring at the grid during the flow of electricity.[584] The PJM adopted the MLSA system to provide compensation for the line losses the suppliers incurred during the flow of electricity in the grid. This system operates as a mechanism to distribute surplus revenues that the PJM collects for line losses to market participants.

The PJM also provides Up-To-Congestion (UTC) transactions, virtual products of purchase and sale contracts with no physical obligation.[585] First developed as a hedging strategy for risks arising out of price differences due to congestion, these products were later used by speculators to profit from price arbitrage between the congestion levels at both DAMs and RTMs. A market participant who buys the UTC product from the PJM pays the price difference between the sink and the source for a specific node in the DAM and receives the price difference between the sink and the source for the same node but in the RTM. The buyers of the UTC transactions monitoring the direction of transmission congestion and its effects on prices between the sources and the sinks on the transmission system profit or lose money on the basis of deviations in prices and congestion levels.

The trading scheme at issue involved the UTC transactions that are aimed at receiving MLSA payments rather than profiting from price differences. Despite being a virtual trading instrument with no obligation to make or receive delivery of electricity, the UTC transactions act in the transmission systems similar to physical trades. The PJM market rules dictate that each party to a UTC transaction is also required to reserve transmission capacity equivalent to the amount determined under the transaction and the parties to the transactions who have booked and paid for the transmission service in compliance with the PJM's market rules are also entitled to claim MLSA payments. Coaltrain paid fees for its reservation of transmission capacity devised its UTC trading strategy to collect these MLSA payments.[586]

In order to make its scheme profitable, Coaltrain had to engage in large trading of UTC transactions. Each transaction required an equivalent capacity reservation in the transmission grid and had the risk of increasing congestion causing differentiating prices between the source and the sink exposing Coaltrain to the risk of incurring losses

583. *See* http://www.pjm.com/about-pjm/who-we-are/territory-served.aspx (accessed 29 Jun. 2017).
584. *Coaltrain Energy, L.P., et al.*, 154 FERC ¶ 61,002 (2016), 7.
585. *Ibid.*, 8.
586. *Ibid.*, 15.

from its UTC transactions as a result of these price changes. For the profitability of its scheme, Coaltrain had to make sure that congestion levels at the transactional node were minimal and that price differences between the source and the sink remained stable.[587] Accordingly, Coaltrain's UTC transactions involved specific transmission nodes with relatively low congestion levels and insignificant price differences. Without the risk of increasing congestion, Coaltrain was able to engage in large trading in UTC transactions and collected significant revenues from MLSA payments.

FERC alleged that Coaltrain's trading of the UTC transactions to make profits on MLSA payments was fraudulent and violated its anti-manipulation rule for electricity, Section 1c.2.[588] According to FERC, a legitimate trading activity in the UTC transactions should involve seeking profits from price differences between the transactional sources and sinks on the basis of estimated congestion levels. Coaltrain, on the other hand, embraced a different strategy specifically looking for transmission paths that involve limited congestion and price differences to enter into the UTC transactions which provided very little or no profits to their holders. Furthermore, Coaltrain continuously lost money due the transmission fees it paid for the capacity reservations required by the PJM market rules for the UTC transactions. The main purpose of the relevant trading activity was not seeking profits from arbitraging price differential as it was loss incurring and uneconomic. Coaltrain lost more than USD 96,000 on the price spreads and USD 3.93 million total when transmission fees were included but these losses were surpassed by the profits of USD 8.05 million derived from MLSA payments.[589] FERC found that engaging in large uneconomic trading in the UTC transactions to collect MLSA payments constituted a fraudulent trading activity and was in violation of the Commission's anti-manipulation provisions.

[d] Evaluation

[i] General

The gaming of market rules by finding and exploiting loopholes in the design of energy markets constitutes a violation of anti-manipulation rules and therefore is prohibited.[590] In these types of practices, the perpetrators seek to establish a market position which will be paid or benefitted with the grant of certain rights on the basis of market rules. These payments and financial positions are generally designed by the transmission operators to provide a balancing and compensation mechanism for losses incurred in the transmission system. A trading strategy that specifically aims at receiving these payments and financial rights at the expense of financial risks associated with the fundamentals of demand for and supply of energy available in the market is considered

587. *Ibid.*, 85.
588. *Ibid.*, 74.
589. *Ibid.*, 75.
590. Comments of The Electricity Consumers Resource Council (ELCON), Fact-Finding Investigation Into Possible Manipulation of Electric and Natural Gas Prices, DOCKET NO. PA02-2-003 3. *See* http://www.elcon.org/Documents/FERCFilings/CAISOgamingcomments.pdf (accessed 29 Jun. 2017).

to be distorting the well-functioning of these markets and against the main purposes for which these market rules were adopted.[591]

[ii] Identifying Gaming

The nature of the trading activity is important in establishing the perpetrators' intent for the gaming of market rules. A legitimate trading activity which is carried out on the basis of market fundamentals may also claim such payments. The attainment of these financial benefits alone does not constitute market manipulation. For a trading activity to constitute a gaming of market rules, it should be demonstrated that in engaging in the trading activity, the perpetrators specifically aimed at reaping financial benefits granted by these financial rules applied in connection with the market conditions as a result of the relevant trading activity.[592] The legal analysis should identify that the relevant trading activity is uneconomic and not feasible to the extent that it would not be employed by the perpetrators without the financial benefits provided under the market rules.[593]

This assertion does not place a burden on the market participants always to act in an economic manner as each market participant can unintentionally engage in uneconomic activities on a stand-alone basis that is a fundamental part of a legitimate trading activity and for the well-functioning trading environment. The market participants' persistence in uneconomic trades and the continuous attainment of the related benefits are important in identifying the manipulative nature of the relevant market practices.[594] Therefore, each legal analysis investigating an allegation of market manipulation through gaming market rules should clearly demonstrate that the underlying factor that leads market participants to employ such practices is the availability of financial benefits that can be acquired in their connection.

[iii] Gaming as Fraudulent Behaviour

A market activity that constitutes the gaming of market rules can be fraudulent. The perpetrators can devise fraudulent schemes to deceive other market participants or transmission system operators or other market providers that conditions required by market rules for the application of a financial payment are met, while the necessary conditions are not present. This was the case in *Rumford Paper Company* in which the perpetrator deceived the market operator with respect to its load-reduction capacities by withholding its generation capacity for a certain period. It can be argued that the perpetrator's decommissioning of its own generation facility for the relevant period constitutes an outright fraud as it is a material misrepresentation and omission of the fact that it needed less energy for the operation of its lumber mill. However, the perpetrator did not just provide fraudulent reports as to its levels of energy

591. *Coaltrain Energy, L.P., et al.*, 154 FERC ¶ 61,002 (2016), 102.
592. *Ibid.*, 70.
593. *Ibid.*, 76.
594. *Ibid.*, 83.

consumption. It, in fact, created a real position by purchasing electricity from external suppliers, instead of producing it in its generation facility. On a stand-alone basis the perpetrator's activity was uneconomic, as it increased the perpetrator's energy costs.[595] The trading activity was only profitable when the benefits from ISO-NE's DALRP are included. Even though it can be regarded as fraudulent, deceiving other market participants and market operator as to the perpetrator's true load-reduction capacity, the practices of withholding generation capacity and resorting to external electricity supplies cannot be considered as fictitious trades and thus outright fraud.

[iv] Gaming as a Non-fraudulent Behaviour

Non-fraudulent activities can also give rise to concerns about market manipulation through gaming of market rules. In both *J.P. Morgan Ventures Energy Cooperation*[596] and *Coaltrain Energy L.P., et al.*,[597] the perpetrators engaged in trading activities that did not operate as a fraud on the side of other market participants and transmission service providers. The characteristics of the market practices did not involve a material misrepresentation or an omission of a fact in market fundamentals and the perpetrators manipulated the markets without distorting the information available in the market. The gaming of market rules in *J.P. Morgan Ventures Energy Cooperation* and *Coaltrain Energy L.P., et al.*, was not based on deceiving other market participants' and market operators' perception of market conditions. One can assert that the manipulative practices employed in *J.P. Morgan Ventures Energy Cooperation* and *Coaltrain Energy L.P. et al.*, should also be regarded fraudulent, as FERC found that these market practices violated its anti-manipulation rules which are based on SEC's Rule Section 10(b) fraud-based formulation. In applying its anti-manipulation jurisdiction, FERC defines the concept of fraud as encompassing '*any action, transaction, or conspiracy for the purpose of impairing, obstructing, or defeating a well-functioning market*'.[598] FERC's interpretation of fraud is designed to address all types of market manipulation including fraudulent and non-fraudulent market activities and therefore not enough to identify that the market practices investigated in *J.P. Morgan Ventures Energy Cooperation and Coaltrain Energy L.P., et al.*, are fraudulent by nature.

[3] Cross-Market Manipulation

Wholesale energy products can be traded in different markets under different conditions. They can be traded on the basis of contract duration such as long-term or short-term contracts. They can be traded in different trading venues such as exchanges or OTC facilities. They can also involve different contractual obligations as certain

595. *Rumford Paper Company*, 140 FERC ¶ 61,030 (2012), 1.
596. *In Re Make-Whole Payments and Related Bidding Strategies*, 144 FERC ¶ 61,068 (2013).
597. *Coaltrain Energy, L.P., et al.*, 154 FERC ¶ 61,002 (2016).
598. *Ibid.*, 100.

contracts require the parties to make and take physical delivery of energy products, others involve financial obligations on the basis of price movements related to the underlying products. Each energy product in the wholesale energy trading has a particular trading behaviour and is treated differently by market operators and traders. However, these market products also have significant price relations that a change or development in market fundamentals for one or multiple energy products can affect the trading of other energy products significantly. In cross-market manipulation, perpetrators try to reap financial benefits exploiting price relations between the trading of different energy products.[599]

Prices of wholesale energy products are generally interlinked with each other through benchmarking instruments. Benchmarks consist of prices which are determined via a formula involving pricing data accumulated from different market participants participating in multiple segments of wholesale energy markets.[600] These benchmarks can be determined in trading venues, such as exchanges which usually organise a settlement period in daily, weekly or monthly trading hours to demonstrate the price levels at which relevant wholesale energy products are traded. These types of benchmarks are called 'settlement prices'.[601] Several pricing benchmarks are also provided by independent reporting agencies collecting information from market participants on a voluntary basis and publishing pricing and market reports. The reports and magazines that provide pricing information with respect to wholesale energy products are called 'indexes'.[602]

These benchmarks are fundamental to the design of manipulative schemes. The pricing information determined and published in these benchmarks is again used in energy markets. The majority of energy trading taking place in either exchanges or OTC markets refers to these instruments in their pricing of wholesale energy products.[603] Therefore, in cross-market manipulation, the perpetrators who seek to exploit price relations between different markets often aim at affecting benchmark prices. This section provides examples of cross-market manipulation in US case law involving market participants by affecting settlement periods and indexes, seeking to move market prices to levels more favourable to their positions.

599. Daniel R. Fischel & David J. Ross, 523 (1991); Emilios E. Avgouleas, 144 (2005).
600. *See* Ofgem, Pricing Benchmarks in Gas and Electricity Markets – A Call for Evidence, (6 Jun. 2013) https://www.ofgem.gov.uk/ofgem-publications/40363/pricing-benchmarks-gas-and-electricity-markets.pdf (accessed 29 Jun. 2017).
601. For example, the settlement price of the Henry Hub Natural Gas Futures contract is an important benchmark for natural gas extensively used by market participants in their hedging and trading activities. *See* http://www.cmegroup.com/trading/energy/natural-gas/natural-gas.html (accessed 29 Jun. 2017).
602. Index prices are published by trade press entities such as Natural Gas Intelligence and Platts. The major index prices include *Gas Daily* and *Platts Inside FERC*. *See* https://www.platts.com/IM.Platts.Content/ProductsServices/Products/gasmarketreport.pdf (accessed 29 Jun. 2017).
603. Ofgem, Wholesale Energy Markets in 2015, (9 Sept. 2015) 35 https://www.ofgem.gov.uk/sites/default/files/docs/2015/09/wholesale_energy_markets_in_2015_final_0.pdf (accessed 29 Jun. 2017).

[a] In re Avista Energy Inc.[604]

This case involved a manipulation claim by the CFTC against the defendants, Avista Energy, Inc. et.al., who sought to manipulate the settlement price of two electricity products, the electricity futures contracts for delivery at Palo Verde (PV) and California Oregon Border (COB), (collectively Western) traded in NYMEX between April 1998 through August 1998 (the 'Relevant Period').[605] According to NYMEX rules, the last day for trading Western contracts was the fourth business day before the first calendar day of the delivery month. For example, for an electricity futures contract to be delivered to PV in August 1998, the last trading day was 28 July 1998. NYMEX rules also established an expiration day for trading in options contracts, which immediately precede the last futures trading day, that is 27 July 1998, according to the example given above. The settlement price of options contracts traded in NYMEX would be determined on the basis of the average price of transactions that take place during the last two minutes (the Close) of the expiration day for options contracts.[606]

Prior to the relevant period of April-August 1998, the defendants had also entered into options contracts in the OTC markets whose value is derived from the settlement price determined during the Close on NYMEX's expiration day for options trading. The defendants had financial incentives to exploit the price relations between the options contracts in NYMEX and the OTC markets. Any price fluctuations in NYMEX options contracts for electricity futures delivery to PV and COB would affect the value of the options contracts the defendants entered into in the OTC markets. Accordingly, options traded in the OTC markets would profit, when the increase or decrease in the settlement price for NYMEX Western options contracts exceeded certain price thresholds.

In order to move the settlement prices for the relevant periods in NYMEX, the defendants devised a scheme involving selling options at very short prices to move prices down or buying options at high prices to move prices up in relation to the positions held in the OTC options trading. The defendants' trading activity was concentrated on the close (last two minutes) of the options expiration day and as the market for Western electricity futures contracts was illiquid with a very low volume of trading, the defendants could increase and decrease the settlement prices with large buy and sell orders.[607] The defendants incurred substantial financial losses during their large trading as they sold at lower prices to decrease and bought at higher prices to increase the settlement prices. However, the larger positions held in the OTC options markets were more than enough to compensate for these losses.

The findings in *Avista* were important to a related case, *DiPlacido*,[608] which was brought against an employee of Avista Energy Inc., overseeing and operating the

604. *In re Avista Energy, Inc. and Michael T. Griswold*, CFTC Docket No.: 01-21, 2001 WL 951736 (CFTC 2001), 2.
605. *Ibid.*, 3.
606. *Ibid.*, 3–4.
607. *Ibid.*, 4.
608. *In re DiPlacido*, [2007-2009 Transfer Binder] Comm. Fut. L. Rep. (CCH) ¶ 30,970 (CFTC 2008).

company's business on the NYMEX trading floor. This was the CFTC's first victory in its history of anti-manipulation prosecution. In these cases, the CFTC alleged that the defendants' trading activity between NYMEX and the OTC options contracts constituted market manipulation and attempted manipulation under Section 9 of the CEA, the anti-manipulation provision. In *Avista*, the CFTC and the defendants settled with the latter paying more than USD 2 million in penalties.[609] In *DiPlacido*, on the other hand, the defendant refused the CFTC's settlement offer, and the case went to decision which found that the relevant trading activity employed by the defendants constituted a violation of the CEA's anti-manipulation rules.

[b] Energy Transfer Partners[610]

In this case, Energy Transfer Partners, L.P. et. al., the defendants, employed two distinct manipulative schemes involving wholesale trading of natural gas in multiple hubs on 23 and 28 December 2005. In their first scheme, the defendants manipulated the next month's fixed-price gas markets at Houston Ship Channel (HSC), a major trading hub, in which natural gas contracts are traded for daily, weekly, monthly and longer terms. The fixed-price gas markets at HSC are markets where the price for natural gas is determined on the basis of bilateral trades or agreements, similar to the OTC transactions. Market participants buying and selling in these markets use a price index, Platts Inside FERC (IFERC), which publishes monthly prices of natural gas for delivery at HSC. The defendants' scheme, manipulating the next month's fixed-price markets at HSC, involved a large selling activity of natural gas contracts at relatively low prices and reporting these transactions to indexes. As the defendants' share constituted more than 80% of total sales in the market, reporting the transactions moved down the average price for natural gas calculated by the index.[611]

Suppressed index prices benefited the defendants in two ways. First, the defendants, though engaging in high selling activity at HSC, were net buyers of natural gas, that is, the amount of natural gas the defendants purchased in the market exceeded the amount that they sold.[612] By suppressing the index prices through their selling activity, the defendants acquired price benefits in purchasing natural gas at depressed prices. Second, the defendants also entered into financially based swaps based on the price difference between the IFERC index price and the settlement price for natural gas contract traded in NYMEX.[613] The defendants, sellers of the swap agreement, received the settlement price of NYMEX and paid the IFERC index price. As they suppressed the IFERC index price by their short selling activity, the defendants acquired significant benefits from their swap agreements. The strategy proved to be useful for the defendants as they practised it eight more times.[614]

609. *Ibid.*, 14.
610. *Energy Transfer Partners, L.P. et. al.*, 120 FERC ¶ 61,086 (2007).
611. *Ibid.*, 3.
612. *Ibid.*, 4.
613. *Ibid.*, 5.
614. *Ibid.*

In their second scheme, the defendants also manipulated daily natural gas prices for delivery at Waha and Permian, two other natural gas hubs, where natural gas contracts are delivered and traded between market participants.[615] In these markets, defendants sold index swaps which benefitted on the basis of price differences between daily and monthly IFERC index prices, according to which, the defendants benefitted from low daily prices in comparison with monthly prices. In order to make their swap positions profitable, the defendants entered into a trading scheme involving selling fixed-price daily gas at Waha and Permian hubs on 23 December 2005 and 28 December 2005 and buying back a similar volume of natural gas on the same day. Selling at low prices, the defendants drove down the daily natural gas prices and increased the value of their index swap positions.

FERC alleged that the defendants' practice of depressing prices violated its Market Behaviour Rule 2, the anti-manipulation rule for natural gas before EPAct 2005 preceding Section 1c.1 constituted according to which '*any person making natural gas sales for resale in interstate commerce (…) is prohibited from engaging in actions or transactions that are without a legitimate business purpose and that are intended to or foreseeably could manipulate market prices, market conditions, or market rules for natural gas*'.[616] Citing the SEC's precedent on market manipulation creating a downward pressure on prices, FERC found that the defendants' short sales constituted manipulation as they created impressions that did not represent the actual conditions on demand and supply. Accordingly, it is noted that '*(t)he failure to disclose that market prices are being artificially depressed operates as a deceit on the market place and is an omission of a material fact*'.[617]

FERC also found that the trading activity the defendants engaged in was of an open market character in which the perpetrators manipulated the markets by placing buy and sell orders. FERC argued that these practices also operated as a deceit on the market as the defendants' concealment of their role as a net buyer of natural gas constituted fraud and was therefore manipulative. FERC's view in *Energy Transfer Partners* illustrated the opposite to that of the CFTC, as the latter distinguished fraud-based market manipulation from these trade-based open market practices and adopted two distinct anti-manipulation provisions for the prosecution of these practices separately after the Dodd-Frank. As discussed before, *Energy Transfer Partners* was the first case that both FERC and the CFTC brought concurrent enforcement of their anti-manipulation provisions on the basis of the same trading activities.[618] Even though the defendants later settled with both agencies, the case illustrates a good example of the differences between the regulatory approaches taken by the two agencies to the prohibition of market manipulation in energy markets.

615. *Ibid.*, 7.
616. *Supra* note 497.
617. *Energy Transfer Partners, L.P. et. al.*, 120 FERC ¶ 61,086 (2007), 12.
618. *CFTC v. Energy Transfer Partners L.P.*, Civil Action No. 3-07-Cv. 1301 (N.D. Tex. 2007).

[c] Amaranth Advisors L.L.C. et al.[619]

The CFTC and FERC initiated subsequent proceedings against the defendants, Amaranth Advisors and its main trader, Brian Hunter, finding that they manipulated and attempted to manipulate the settlement price for NYMEX Natural Gas Futures Contracts (NG Futures Contract) which operated as a fundamental benchmark for pricing in other financial and physical natural gas contracts.[620] If there was a difference between the approaches to the existence of price artificiality, the agencies' formulations of anti-manipulation charges were also different. As discussed above, the CEA's definition of market manipulation requires the CFTC to establish that existing market prices are artificial as a result of the perpetrators' practices, which has turned out to be difficult to prove. Therefore instead of applying the four-part test under its artificial price-based definition, the CFTC applied its attempted prohibition alleging that the defendants attempted to manipulate the NG futures contracts by intending to affect market prices and engaging in an overt act in furtherance of that intent.[621] FERC, on the other hand, under no obligation to establish the existence of artificial prices, identified that the defendants' activities deceived other market participants as to the existing forces of supply and demand in the market by artificially affecting the price of physical and financial contracts.[622]

The settlement price for the NG Futures Contracts that the defendants sought to affect was a fundamental component of the valuation and profitability of several financial and physical markets. The NG Futures Settlement Price is the volume-weighted average price of transactions carried out during the settlement period which is the last thirty minutes of the last trading day, the third-to-last business day of the month before the near month the delivery is to take place.[623] For example the last business day of August 2007 was August 31 and thus the last trading day for contracts for which delivery would take place in September was on August 29 between 2:00–2:30 pm, the last thirty minutes of the trading day. As the liquidity of trading activity during the settlement periods was reduced and the majority of the market participants sought to balance their positions for delivery obligations, the defendants concentrated their trading activity during these periods as they had a better opportunity to affect settlement prices by engaging in large-scale trading.[624] The trading activity was also designed to create price trends during the settlement periods signalling the other market participants about the price levels at which they were willing to trade.[625]

The defendants had several financial and physical positions, including swaps, options, physical basis and index transactions that profited from the affected NG futures settlement prices.[626] Swap agreements, by their nature, involve its parties

619. *Amaranth Advisors L.L.C. et. al.*, 120 FERC ¶ 61,085 (2007).
620. *Ibid.*, para. 2.
621. *CFTC v. Amaranth Advisors, L.L.C., et. al.*, 523 F. Supp. 2d 328 (S.D.N.Y. 2007), 16.
622. *Amaranth Advisors L.L.C. et. al.*, 120 FERC ¶ 61,085 (2007), para. 45.
623. *Ibid.*, para. 63.
624. *Ibid.*, para. 96.
625. *Ibid.*, para. 79.
626. *Ibid.*, 8.

betting as to levels of prices determined as benchmarks under the contracts. In their selling of natural gas futures swaps, the defendants paid the buyers the NG Futures settlement price and received a fixed price. Moving down the NG Futures settlement prices below the levels of fixed prices, the defendants acquired significant benefits from their swap positions. As the defendants were able to affect the NG Futures settlement price in pursuant to their will, the relevant swap agreement was not a bet at all. The defendants' scheme of exploiting the pricing relations between the NG Futures Contracts and its financial swap agreements is a clear example how a cross-market manipulation operates in wholesale energy markets.

The defendants also entered into options agreements whose value was based on the changes of price levels during the NG Futures Contracts settlement periods.[627] An Options contract gives its buyer a right but not the obligation to buy or sell a fixed number of futures contracts for a specified month at a particular, 'strike' price. There are two types of options contracts; call options and put options. While the former provides the right to buy, the latter gives the buyer the right to sell the futures contracts. In both agreements, the buyer of the options makes a payment, an option premium, to the seller for the duration of the options agreement. Affecting the NG Futures settlement prices through their trading activity, the defendants were able to benefit from their positions in the options markets.

The defendants were also aware that there was a strong relationship between the NG Futures settlement prices and transactions involving the physical delivery of natural gas.[628] Pricing of certain natural gas transactions between buyers and suppliers of natural gas referred to the NG Futures settlement prices as benchmark prices. Furthermore the natural gas indexes published by several trade press entities such as Platts or Natural Gas Intelligence (NGI)[629] and referred to by sellers and buyers of natural gas in pricing their contracts, also use the NG Futures settlement price as an important component in calculating their index prices. Any manipulative activity that changes the settlement prices for the NG Futures Contracts would affect physical delivery of natural gas directly through physical transactions or indirectly through index transactions.

FERC found that the defendants violated its Section 1c.1, anti-manipulation rule for natural gas by trading in NYMEX NG Futures Contracts to manipulate the settlement price, which operated as a benchmark for several FERC-jurisdictional physical and financial transactions. The trading scheme in NYMEX was uneconomic on a stand-alone basis. The defendants continuously lost profits or received payoffs that were less than that from a legitimate, price-taking trading activity.[630] The trading activity was only profitable when the defendants' profits derived from other financial and physical positions were taken into account. The value of these positions increased in correlation with a decline in the NG Futures settlement prices. As the defendants' physical and financial positions were in a scale larger than their sales in NYMEX, the

627. *Ibid.*, 10.
628. *Ibid.*, 64.
629. *Supra* note 602.
630. *Amaranth Advisors L.L.C. et. al.*, 120 FERC ¶ 61,085 (2007), 4.

profits from the former outweighed the losses incurred from the latter and therefore created enough of an incentive for the defendants to engage in the relevant scheme, though it was loss incurring. Citing the CFTC's decision in *Avista,* FERC concluded that such a trading strategy constituted a clear example of open market transactions, which involves real trades and real economic risks in contrast to fictitious, closed market transactions and was therefore prohibited.[631]

FERC's decision was later challenged by the CFTC alleging that it had exclusive jurisdiction over futures trading in regulated markets such as NYMEX and FERC did not have any regulatory authority over trading in the NG Futures Contracts.[632] The CFTC's authority over futures markets was not contested by FERC, acknowledging that mere trading activities that take place in NG Futures Contracts are in the province of the CFTC and outside its jurisdiction. However, the scope of the relevant trading activities was not limited to the NG Futures contracts as the defendants also engaged in activities in FERC-jurisdictional transactions, such as the physical basis and index transactions, and trading of swaps and options in the OTC markets, e.g., ICE. The defendants later settled with both the CFTC and FERC paying more than USD 30 million penalties. Yet FERC's ruling against the Amaranth trader, Brian Hunter, was later rejected by the federal court on the grounds that FERC was devoid of regulatory jurisdiction over a trader's activities limited to the trading floor of NYMEX.[633]

[d] Total Gas & Power North America Inc. Total et al.[634]

The defendants, Total Gas & Power North America, Inc. (TGPNA) and the company's employees working in the trading department, called 'the West Desk' were alleged to have manipulated the price of natural gas at four regional trading hubs; Southern California (SoCal), Permian, Waha, and San Juan, between June 2009 and June 2012 in order to move index prices at a level profiting their linked financial positions.[635] The defendants engaged in a scheme which consisted of trading in several monthly physical contracts involving monthly fixed price, physical basis and monthly index contracts. Monthly fixed-price contracts are transactions in which the price of the underlying product is fixed by the parties. In physical basis transactions, the parties use the settlement price of NYMEX futures contracts as a benchmark price for the delivery of natural gas in the upcoming month.[636] Finally, as the name indicates, in index transactions the parties agree to refer to index-published prices.

The defendants' financial position which benefitted from the monthly physical contracts, involved two swap contracts; financial basis swaps and financial index swaps.[637] Financial basis swaps profit from the price difference between the settlement price of NYMEX and a monthly index prices at a particular location. The buyers of these

631. *Ibid.*, para. 51.
632. Shaun Ledgerwood & Dan Harris, 7 (2012).
633. *Supra* note 533.
634. *Total Gas & Power North America Inc., et al.,* 155 FERC ¶61,105 (2016).
635. *Ibid.*, 2.
636. *Ibid.*, 15.
637. *Ibid.*, 16.

swap contracts benefit from higher locational index prices in comparison to the settlement price of NYMEX. In index swaps, the parties exchange price risks between the monthly index prices and the daily index price in relation to a particular location. The buyers of the index swaps pay the monthly index price in return for the daily index price and therefore benefit from lower monthly index and higher daily index prices.

Throughout their manipulative trading activity, the defendants entered into large buy orders to increase the monthly index prices when their related financial positions profited from higher prices and large sell orders to decrease the monthly index prices when their related positions profited from lower prices.[638] The trading activity was strategically concentrated on bidweeks, which are the last five business days of the month, in which the market participants report their transactions to trade press entities, Platts and NGI, for the calculation of index prices. The defendants also engaged in strategic early trading activities which created trends in the markets and signalled other market participants with respect to expected price movements throughout the trading period. The buy and sell orders submitted by the defendants were not motivated to pay lowest or be paid at highest prices. Instead, the defendants aggressively hit the bids by paying high prices and made sure that their sale offers were at prices low enough that other market participants immediately lifted them.

FERC identified several factors indicating the fraudulent nature of the trading strategy the defendants adopted.[639] For example, the relevant trading activities were of an uneconomic character. The transactions entered into were self-defeating on a stand-alone basis, involving large buy and sell orders at respectively high and low prices, which were the opposite of trading activity that a profit-seeking trader would choose. The defendants continued to engage in this uneconomic trading strategy in a consistent pattern and also failed to provide legitimate explanations as to their motives in developing the relevant trading strategy. FERC concluded that the defendants' market practices during the relevant periods at the relevant trading locations were fraudulent and therefore in violation of its anti-manipulation rule Section 1c.1 and Section 4A of the NGA.[640]

The relevant trading activity also became subject to the CFTC's anti-manipulation authority which enforced its jurisdiction over trading in commodity futures pursuant to Section 6(c) and 6(d) of the CEA.[641] The CFTC brought two manipulation claims against the defendants.[642] First, it asserted that the relevant trading activity constituted an attempt to manipulate the monthly index settlement prices of natural gas at four trading locations.[643] Second, the defendants also violated the CFTC's Regulation 180.1, a fraud-based anti-manipulation provision adopted after the Dodd-Frank. In its decision the CFTC cited the SEC's decision of *In re Donald L. Koch*[644] in which the SEC

638. *Ibid.*, 19.
639. *Ibid.*, 37.
640. *Ibid.*, 66.
641. 7 U.S.C. §§ 6c, 6d, 13b (2010).
642. *In the matter of Total Gas & Power North America, Inc., and Therese Tran*, CFTC Docket No 16 -03 (CFTC 2015).
643. *Ibid.*, 7.
644. *Ibid.*, 9, *citing; In re Donald L. Koch*, SEC Release No 3836, 2014 WL 1998524 (2014).

found that a conduct of 'marking the close' constituted a manipulation under its fraud-based Rule of 10b-5. The CFTC's finding of Regulation 180.1 violation in this case, in relation with the SEC's decision in *In re Donald L. Koch,* is important as the relevant trading activity was of a character of an open market transaction over which the CFTC traditionally applied its jurisdiction of artificial price based manipulation.[645] After the Dodd-Frank, the CFTC kept its traditional manipulation provision to apply to market behaviours which are not fraudulent or involve an artifice of fraud. However, in this case, the CFTC applied its attempt and fraud-based prohibitions rather than its traditional approach, which gives rise to concerns as to how the CFTC will demarcate these two types of market manipulation prohibition and under what conditions an open market activity will trigger an anti-manipulation enforcement on the basis of the CFTC's traditional artificial price-based market manipulation authority.

[e] BP America Inc., BP Corporation North America Inc. et al.[646]

This case involved a manipulation claim by FERC against the defendants, BP America Inc., BP Corporation North America Inc., et al. who had devised a scheme to profit from their financial positions related to differences between daily physical natural gas prices at the HSC and the Henry Hub. After Hurricane Ike, which caused the collapse of HSC gas prices, realising that their financial positions had a potential to gain millions of dollars, when the daily price spread at the Henry Hub and the HSC became wide, the defendants developed a trading strategy to make sure that that price spread between the two hubs remained wide and even grew wider.[647] The defendants had two financial index swap positions in the HSC and the Henry Hub. They were selling index swaps in the HSC meaning that they were paying the daily index price and receiving the monthly index price for natural gas.[648] In the Henry Hub, the defendants paid the monthly index price and received the daily index price for natural gas.[649] The profitability of these financial positions was later determined as a spread between the HSC and the Henry Hub meaning that the relevant financial positions profited more if the difference between daily physical natural gas prices in the HSC and the Henry Hub increased.

In order to suppress daily index prices in the HSC, the defendants entered into a number of trading activities on a large scale selling daily natural gas contracts at low prices and reporting these trades to trade press entities publishing indexes.[650] The defendants' trading activities also involved the purchase and transportation of physical natural gas from an external trading hub, the Katy, to sell in the HSC thus further suppressing the daily natural gas prices. In accessing external supplies, the defendants used the BP's, the parent company, underutilised Houston Gas Pipeline (HPL) to

645. Jerry Markham, 329 (2015).
646. *BP America Inc., BP Corporation North America et al.*, 144 FERC ¶ 61,100 (2013).
647. *Ibid.*, 48.
648. *Ibid.*, 17.
649. *Ibid.*, 18.
650. *Ibid.*, 25.

transport natural gas from the Katy to the HSC.[651] The new supplies brought with the HPL provided the defendants efficiency in suppressing natural gas prices further, as they exerted an additional competitive pressure on the existing supplies at the HSC as well as allowing the defendants to avoid engaging in more costly trading alternatives, such as buying and reselling practices. Finally, the defendants also employed a strategy of early and heavy fixed-price gas sales to affect the early market condition at the HSC creating pricing trends that induced other market traders to follow the pricing levels set by the defendants' early sales.[652]

FERC alleged that the defendants' trading of physical daily natural gas contracts was manipulative as their main motive was to affect the index prices which determined the profitability of the defendants' financial swap positions at the HSC and the Henry Hub.[653] The defendants' buying and selling activities could not be characterised as profit-maximising based on the forces of demand and supply. The defendants were eager to buy natural gas at the Katy hub, hitting every offer from natural gas suppliers irrespective of price. The trading activity aimed at acquiring large quantities of supplies even at the expense of paying high prices relative to the market prices. On the other side of the scheme, the defendants offered the supplies at low price levels to make sure that the offers were immediately lifted by other market participants moving down the market prices further. Such a trading activity was not economic and on a stand-alone basis could only be profitable when the profits derived from the swap spread positions held by the defendants were taken into account.[654] Accordingly FERC concluded that the defendants' trading activities engaging in uneconomic trades to affect prices exploiting the price relations between the physical and financial markets was fraudulent under the Section 1c.1 and therefore constituted a market manipulation.

[f] Barclays Bank PLC, Daniel Brin, Scott Connelly, et al.[655]

The defendants, Barclays Bank PLC, a major participant in the US electricity markets, plus its employees working in the trade department, were alleged to have manipulated the prices of several wholesale electricity products at four different locations, Mid-Columbia (MIDC), Palo Vere (PV), South Path 15 (SP), and North Path 15 (NP), between November 2006 and December 2008.[656] FERC asserted that the defendants engaged in a pattern of loss-incurring trading activities in daily electricity contracts traded on the ICE, a market platform for wholesale trading in a number of markets, to benefit from financial swap positions. The relevant trading activity involved several buy and sell orders in order to move the index prices up or down related to financial positions.

651. *Ibid.*, 27.
652. *Ibid.*, 31.
653. *Ibid.*, 68.
654. *Ibid.*, 41.
655. *Barclays Bank PLC, Daniel Brin, Scott Connelly, et al.*, 141 FERC ¶ 61,084 (2012).
656. *Ibid.*, 2.

The defendants acquired several financial swap positions in relation to daily,[657] monthly[658] and balance of month (BOM)[659] index prices, which were calculated by trade press entities on the basis of trading data reported by the market participants. According to the financial swap positions, when the defendants were buying the financial swaps, they would be paying a fixed price in return for a floating index price. On the other hand, selling the financial swaps, the defendants would be paying a floating index price in return for a fixed price. In order to suppress the monthly electricity prices during the bidweek, the defendants entered into large buy orders in daily markets throughout the relevant months. These large buy orders were loss-incurring on a stand-alone basis.[660] However, the defendants also engaged in financial swaps for daily and BOM index prices, which profited from high index prices compensating for the losses incurred during the daily trading. The large physical electricity position accumulated through daily trading activity was later offered in the bidweek at relatively low prices moving down the monthly index prices. Even though the defendants' activity in the bidweek was also loss incurring, the profits derived from financial swap positions in relation to low monthly index prices were more than enough to compensate for these losses. As a result, the defendants reaped significant profits from their trading in a combination of physical and financial products.

It is important to note that the relevant trading activities in *Barclays* were not of a fraudulent character as the trading activities at issue were mostly based on the defendants' transactions of buying and selling physical and financial electricity products at the wholesale level without engaging in a mechanism that operated as a deception or fraud over other market participants.[661] However, FERC developed an overarching concept of fraud within the meaning of its anti-manipulation prohibition as including any market activity, transaction, or conspiracy for the purpose of distorting or defeating the proper functioning of wholesale energy markets.[662] This concept is contested in the academic literature. Accordingly, FERC found that the trading of daily electricity products on the ICE with respect to the delivery of electricity at four different locations operated as fraud and therefore violated Section 1c.2, the anti-manipulation prohibition for electricity products.[663]

657. The daily index prices were calculated as the average price of all day-ahead transactions for a specific day on the ICE. *Ibid.*, 7.
658. The monthly index prices were calculated as the average price of all day-ahead transactions for a specific month on the ICE. *Ibid.*
659. The BOM contract 'means a strip of two or more Daily Contracts, tradeable on a Business Day ("the Trade Day") in a contract month, starting two Business Days forward from such Trade Day continuing through to the end of the contract month'. *See* Section UUU1 - Contract Rules: ICE Futures UK Natural Gas Daily Financial Futures Contract 2, https://www.theice.com/publicdocs/circulars/14101_attach_2.pdf (accessed 29 Jun. 2017).
660. *Barclays Bank PLC, Daniel Brin, Scott Connelly, et al.*, 141 FERC ¶ 61,084 (2012), 28.
661. *See* Matthew Evans, *Regulating Electricity-Market Manipulation: A Proposal for a New Regulatory Regime to Proscribe All Forms of Manipulation*, 113/4 Michigan Law Review (2015).
662. *Supra* note 497.
663. *Barclays Bank PLC, Daniel Brin, Scott Connelly, et al.*, 141 FERC ¶ 61,084 (2012), 37.

[g] *Evaluation*

[i] Overview

Market participants often engage in cross-market transactions for hedging and trading purposes. The energy firms operating at multi-market levels have a clear insight into the profitability of interrelated price movements among markets and generally incorporate specific trading desks in their organisational structure to design and monitor these cross-market transactions. Deriving profits through price arbitrage between different markets and prices, predictions of price movements based on market fundamentals,[664] or hedging risks arising out of deviations in price levels, are considered the essence of legitimate trading and crucial for increasing competition and liquidity in the markets as well as providing a means for convergence in prices between different delivery points. The legitimacy of these practices relies on the market principle that the traders operating in the energy markets and making predictions based on their perception of market fundamentals, act in a profit-maximising manner.[665] While the sellers' main objective is to receive the highest return from their transactions, buyers of energy products seek to pay the lowest price possible based on the demand and supply levels available in the market. Pricing of these energy products between sellers and buyers on the basis of the forces of supply and demand is fundamental for the functioning of the markets.

Cross-market manipulation occurs when the market participants intervene in the determination of market prices in a manner to profit from their related financial or physical positions. The revenues derived from these positions are no longer based on the perpetrators' perception of market fundamentals.[666] In fact, the relevant transactions involve no risk exposure to price changes as a result of deviations between supply and demand, which is present in the legitimate trading of price arbitrage. The perpetrators directly move prices at a level that they know will affect the value of their related positions and do not need at all the predictions of market fundamentals to profit from their trading activities. As the majority of the firms operating in the wholesale trading in energy products incorporates a specific trading department in their corporate

664. In *Total Gas & Power North America, Inc. et al.*, one of the defendants explained the type of fundamentals-based trading he was following in natural gas market as '*supply and demand balance sheet*' that forecasts '*what is going to happen to storage at the of a month, at the end of a season, the idea being that of storage is forecast to be full or more than full, it is bearish* [to sell] *[and if] storage is forecast to come in way under the working gas capacity, then that would be a bullish* [to buy] *indicator*'. *See In the matter of Total Gas & Power North America, Inc., and Therese Tran*, CFTC Docket No 16 -03 (CFTC 2015), 21.

665. '(T)*rading with the purpose of obtaining the best price (...) does not constitute, in itself, a violation of the Commodity Exchange Act.*' *In re Hohenberg Brothers*, [1975-1977 Transfer Binder] Comm. Fut. L. Rep. (CCH) ¶ 20,271 (CFTC 1977).

666. '(W)*hen a price is affected by a factor which is not legitimate, the resulting price is necessarily artificial.*' *In re Indiana Farm Bureau Cooperative Association*, [1982-1984 Transfer Binder] Comm. Fut. L. Rep. (CCH) ¶ 21,796 (CFTC 1982).

organisations monitoring price relations between multiple markets, the perpetrators are able to oversee and profit from these pricing relations.[667]

[ii] The Perpetration of Misconduct

In cross-market manipulation, the perpetrators profit from a portfolio of different physical and financial positions. First the perpetrators engage in trading of a specific physical natural gas or electricity product. These trades are regarded as price making, as they are fundamental in moving prices at a level that is profitable for the perpetrators' positions in other related markets. The trading of physical energy products is usually determined on the basis of their contractual terms with respect to the duration of their delivery obligation spanning from daily to yearly delivery periods. The perpetrators can engage in trading of these contracts to increase or decrease the price of the relevant contracts. For example, in order to decrease market prices for daily electricity contracts which involve an obligation to deliver a certain amount of electricity for the next day, a market participant can take part in a large-scale sale at prices lower than the prices at which other market players are trading. In contrast, a market participant seeking to move up prices for monthly natural gas contracts, which require the sellers to deliver a certain volume of natural gas in the next month, would engage in a large buy orders at higher prices. These trading practices at higher and lower prices will directly affect the perception of other market players of market conditions and the average market price for the trading of the relevant energy products is determined on the basis of the perpetrators' low or high selling and buying activity, rather than the forces of supply and demand available in the market. Therefore the markets in which the perpetrators employ their trading strategies to determine prices are identified as price-making positions.

Cross-market manipulation involving schemes that aim at distorting benchmark prices are also called 'benchmark manipulation'.[668] In this type of practice, the price-making activities that the perpetrators engage in aim at affecting benchmark prices such as settlement prices for exchanges[669] or the index prices the trade press publish on the basis of transaction reports they receive from traders operating in the markets.[670] These settlement and index prices are called price-taking positions as they are calculated based on the volume-weighted average price of all fixed-price or physical basis transactions executed in relevant markets and relevant trading periods.[671] The

667. Note that the majority of cross-market manipulative strategies discussed above were perpetrated by trading desks such as 'Texas Team' in *BP America Inc. et al.*, and 'West Desk' in *Total Gas & Power North America, Inc. et al.*, which are incorporated to manage and trade the parent companies' assets in energy markets, overseeing price movements and relations between multiple markets and contracts. *See BP America Inc., BP Corporation North America et al.*, 144 FERC ¶ 61,100 (2013); *In the matter of Total Gas & Power North America, Inc., and Therese Tran*, CFTC Docket No 16 -03 (CFTC 2015).

668. Article 12(1)(d), Regulation No 596/2014.

669. *See supra* note 601.

670. *Supra* note 600.

671. NYMEX Exchange Rulebook 220 Henry Hub Natural Gas Futures *see*: http://www.cmegroup.com/rulebook/NYMEX/2/220.pdf (accessed 29 Jun. 2017).

functioning of these price benchmarks is crucial for the functioning of the markets as they operate as indicators of the relevant price levels and forces of supply and demand. In that regard, these benchmarks also operate as price-making instruments and the majority of market participants trading in markets refer to these benchmarks in the pricing of their transactions. Any distortion in the determination of these benchmark prices gives rise to concerns on existing market conditions and true levels of supply and demand.

Benchmark prices also determine the profitability of several financial instruments such as swaps and options, which are regarded as benefiting positions. The perpetrators of cross-market manipulation hold substantial positions in financial instruments, either buying or selling them on the basis of deviations in benchmark prices. The perpetrators are generally eager to incur losses in their physical trading as long as their financial positions are large enough to compensate and further benefit from changes in prices. However, the profitability of financial positions in relation to price levels in the physical markets requires an extensive analysis of market information, including available demand and supply, as well as market liquidity and tendencies among other market participants. In order to execute a successful cross-market manipulation, the perpetrators are obliged to have a clear insight into the levels of volume and timing required for the trading activity to affect the average price of the underlying product being traded in the market. Accordingly, the perpetrators need to accumulate enough physical contracts prior to buying or selling activity during the trading period. Further, prices that the perpetrators are trading should be low or high enough to move the average prices traded in the relevant market, which in turn determines the settlement and index prices. The perpetrators also need to make sure that the settlement and index prices affected by their trades in physical markets are at levels that are profitable to the positions they hold in financial markets. The perpetration of cross-market manipulation requires an extensive market analysis involving the deviations between financial and physical positions. Otherwise the financial risks associated with the trading strategies pose a great economic threat to the perpetrators of cross-market manipulation.

[iii] Legitimate Trading Versus Manipulative Conduct

Separating legitimate price arbitrage or hedging practices from exploiting price relations between physical and financial positions is fundamental in the analysis of cross-market manipulation.[672] Within the context of legitimate trading, the financial instruments such as options and swaps are often used for hedging or profit-maximising purposes. Options are financial contracts that grant their buyer the right but not an obligation to make or receive delivery of an underlying product at a fixed price.[673] If a contract grants the right to receive a certain amount of delivery at a fixed price, this

672. *Supra* note 138.
673. Leonard R. Higgins, *The Put-and-Call* 6 (Effingham Wilson 1906).

contract is identified as a 'call option'.[674] If a contract grants the right to make a certain amount of delivery at a fixed price, this contract is identified as a 'put option'.[675] In either case, the buyer of option contracts makes a payment in return for the right to make or receive delivery, which is called a 'premium', negotiated between the parties of the option contract.[676] For the buyer of options contracts, the associated financial risks are limited to the amount of premium. For the seller, on the other hand, the financial risks with respect to the option contracts is unlimited, as they may be obliged to make or receive the delivery at a fixed rate irrespective of market prices. In order to show how options contracts operate as a hedging or trading strategy, hypothetical scenarios would be helpful.[677]

[iv] Legitimate Trading in Options Contracts

In the first scenario, consider an electricity producer who is concerned about market prices for electricity for next year delivery. According to its financial portfolio, the producer seeks to generate X amount of electricity for at least Y price. If the prices of electricity for next year delivery will be lower than Y, the producer will lose money from its generation business. In order to hedge this price risk, the producer enters into a put option contract buying the right but not an obligation to make delivery of X amount of electricity at Y price.[678] By buying the put option contract, the producer is no longer concerned about a decrease in electricity prices for next year delivery as it has the right to sell X amount of electricity at Y price.[679] If the prices increase in the next year, the producer can just let the option contract expire as it can sell its output at higher market prices. The only economic loss incurred by the producer is the premium it pays to the seller of the put option for the grant of the right. The seller, on the other hand, has the obligation to receive the delivery of X amount of electricity at Y price, if the producer exercises its right under the put option contract. The economic loss the seller incurs will depend on the decrease in market prices, as it could buy X amount of electricity at market prices lesser than Y price without the option contract. The seller's financial benefit is limited to the premium it receives from the buyer.

In the second scenario, consider an electricity distributor who buys electricity to resell in the retail market to the final costumers and is concerned about an increase in market prices for electricity to be delivered in next year. The distributor determines that the highest price it is willing to pay for X amount of electricity is Y. Any amount that is

674. *Ibid.*, 6.
675. *Ibid.*, 6.
676. *Ibid.*, 7.
677. For detailed understanding of strategies *see*: Australian Securities Exchange, 'Options Strategies: 26 Proven Options Strategies' (2011) http://www.asx.com.au/documents/resources/UnderstandingStrategies.pdf (accessed 10 Mar. 2016).
678. There are two types of put options traded in financial markets: the American option meaning that the right to sell can be exercised any time prior to expiration day and the European option the holder of which can exercise its right only on expiration day. *See* Australian Securities Exchange, 'Understanding Options Trading' (2015), 4, http://www.asx.com.au/documents/resources/UnderstandingOptions.pdf (accessed 10 Mar. 2016).
679. *Ibid.*, 5.

higher than Y will cause economic problems for the distributor. In order to hedge this economic risk associated with a possible price increase, the distributors enters into a call option contract which provides the right but not an obligation to receive the delivery of X amount of electricity at Y price for the next year.[680] By buying the call option contract, the distributor is no longer concerned about a prospective price increase in the electricity market as it can buy the necessary amount at a price level it is willing to pay, on the basis of the call option contract. The only economic loss the distributor incurs until the execution of the contract or the expiry date is the premium paid to the seller of the contract. The seller is obliged to make the delivery of X amount of electricity at Y price to the distributor, if the distributor exercises its right under the call option contract. The financial risk associated with the option contract depends on the difference between Y and prospective price increases in the next year. In return for this financial risk, the financial benefit the seller derives from the contract is limited to the premium paid by the buyer.

In the third scenario, consider a trader who seeks to derive profits from price changes in the electricity market. This scenario includes many facets as the profitability of each options contract differs based on the position of the trader as a buyer or seller. A trader can sell and buy call and put options. In order to profit from buying or selling options contracts, the trader will analyse the relevant market conditions, such as storage, transmission constraints and supply and demand levels available in the relevant market.[681] When the trader sells a call option contract, it has an obligation to sell X amount of electricity at Y price, when the buyer exercises its right to receive delivery. If the market prices for electricity decreases during the contractual period, the buyer of the contract will never invoke its right to receive delivery as it can access to cheaper supplies anytime at the market rates. The trader, in this scenario profits from premium it received from the buyers.[682] If the market prices for electricity increase, the buyer of the call option would have an incentive to exercise its right to receive delivery. If the trader is also an electricity generator, the trader will produce the X amount of energy to fulfil its obligation under the contract. If the trader does not have a generation facility, it will resort to other producers buying the X amount of energy at market rates higher than Y price to supply its customer. In either position, the trader incurs losses from the difference between Y and higher market rates. This scenario is illustrated in Figure 3.1.

680. *Ibid.*, 3.
681. FERC Enforcement Staff Report of the Division of Energy Market Oversight, *Energy Primer A Handbook of Energy Market Basics* 113 (Energy Primer July 2015).
682. Australian Securities Exchange, 5 (2015).

Figure 3.1 The Feasibility of Short Call Options[683]

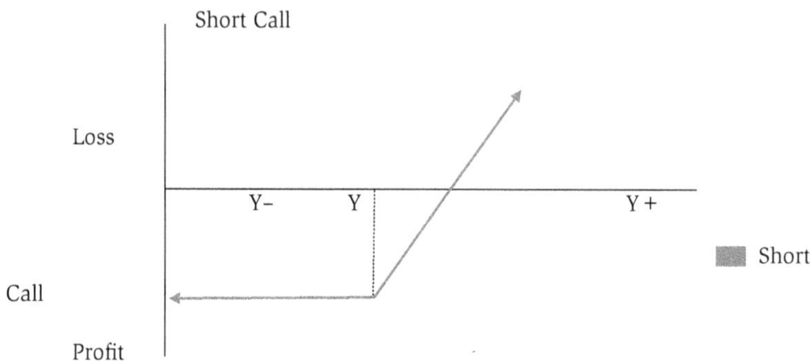

When the trader buys a call option, it will have a right but not an obligation to receive X amount of electricity at Y price.[684] In this position, the trader will look for price increases for the delivery of electricity to profit from the options contract. When electricity prices increase during the contractual period, the trader can sell the options contract that provides its holder the right to buy certain amount of electricity at lower than market prices. The financial benefits the trader derives from the options contract depends on the difference between Y and market prices. The economic risk the trader has taken with respect to the options contract is limited to the amount of premium it pays to the seller. If electricity prices drop, the options contract will have no or little value and the economic loss the trader incurs can be no more than the premium paid for the contractual period. The situation is reversed when the trader buys a put option meaning that it will have a right but not an obligation to take X amount of electricity at Y price.[685] In order to profit from this contract, the trader will seek price decreases for the delivery of electricity for the contractual period. Once the prices decrease, the value of the options contract which gives its holder the right to sell electricity at prices higher than market prices will increase and become more profitable. Again the financial benefits the trader will derive from the options contract depend on the difference between Y and market prices and the economic losses it can incur is limited to the premium it paid to the seller for the contractual period. This scenario is illustrated in Figure 3.2.

683. Australian Securities Exchange, 2 (2011).
684. Australian Securities Exchange, 11 (2015).
685. *Ibid.*

Figure 3.2 The Feasibility of Long Put Options[686]

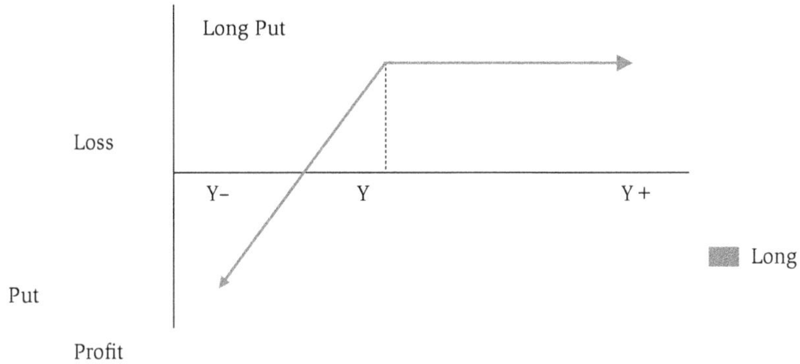

When the trader sells a put option, it has an obligation to buy X amount of electricity at Y price, when the buyer exercises its right to make delivery.[687] If the market price for electricity increases, the buyer of the options contract would never invoke this right as it can sell the same amount of energy at market prices higher than Y. The trader profits from the premium it receives from the buyer and can also trade this contract with other market participants, as the contract will continue to produce value for the contractual period. However, a decrease in market prices will lead the buyer to exercise its right to make delivery. In this position, the trader will have several options. It can first accept the delivery and use it for its own consumption. It can also find another electricity consumer who will accept the offer at market prices, which is lower than Y. The difference between market prices and Y will be the economic loss incurred by the trader. Finally, the trader can settle with the buyer of the put options contract financially paying a certain amount of compensation, which will be higher than Y. The trader again will incur financial losses.

The profitability of these options contracts depends on the trader's analysis of market fundamentals. If the trader decides that the market prices of electricity for next year delivery is too volatile and could incur financial losses as a result of the options contracts, it can also hedge this risk by entering into reverse options contracts with other traders or generators. These types of trades are called 'Box Spread'.[688] The trader can balance its losses with the profits it can derive from its reverse positions. For example, a trader who sells a put options contract, meaning that it is obliged to receive delivery once the buyer executes the contract, can hedge its risks by buying a call option contract to supply the same amount of electricity at the same price for a corresponding delivery period. In so doing the trader balances its put options contract with another call option contract and hedges the financial risk associated with the prospective price changes in the electricity market for next year delivery.

686. Australian Securities Exchange, 7 (2011).
687. *Ibid.*, 13.
688. *Ibid.*, 26.

[v] Legitimate Trading in Swaps

Swaps, another types of important financial instrument that perpetrators of cross-market manipulation use, involve an exchange of payments based on the value of energy products subject to the agreement between parties.[689] In general, swap agreements stipulate an exchange of a fixed and a floating price between buyers and sellers. Accordingly a buyer of a swap pays a fixed price and in return receives a floating price. The economic risk the buyer takes is limited, as it is not obliged to pay more than the fixed price. On the other hand, the seller's economic risk with respect to the swap agreement is unlimited since it pays the floating price which depends on changes in fundamentals of markets. In energy markets, the swap agreements include the exchange of different types of prices such as index prices and settlement prices. For example, a basis swap involves the exchange of a settlement price for a particular energy product such as the settlement price for NYMEX Natural Gas Futures Contracts (NG Futures Contract) for a particular month and an index price such as the price of natural gas to be delivered at HSC for a particular month.[690] In such a swap agreement, while the buyer pays the settlement price for NG Futures Contract which is a fixed price, the seller pays the floating index price.

Swaps can provide useful tools for traders to benefit from arbitraging price differences between different products and to hedge price risks associated with changes in market fundamentals.[691] As an instrument to earn profits, in swap agreements the parties generally enter into a bet involving a claim that the price of an underlying product will be higher or lower than the other product subject to exchange. The party who receives more than it pays profits from this swap agreement. Parties of swap agreements trade their positions to other market participants until an expiration day, and the value of the parties' positions change in accordance with market fundamentals directly or indirectly affecting the prices of underlying products.

Market participants also use swaps as a hedging mechanism against risks associated with price changes in physical markets.[692] For example a natural gas supplier who supplies natural gas to its customers based on the settlement price for NG Futures Contract as a benchmark price may seek protection from a potential plummet in NYMEX prices. In so doing, the gas supplier can enter into a swap agreement with another party, paying floating settlement prices in return for receiving a fixed price which is enough to compensate its operation costs. When the decrease in the settlement price occurs, the supplier's loss will be compensated from the price difference between the settlement price and the fixed price. If the unexpected happens and the settlement price increases, then the supplier benefits from its supply contracts fixing the NG Futures Contracts as the benchmark price, yet incurs losses from its swap agreement, paying a higher settlement price in return for receiving a lower fixed price.

689. There are various swap agreements based on the exchanged products. *See* CFTC Glossary, http://www.cftc.gov/opa/glossary/opaglossary_o.htm (accessed 29 Jun. 2017).
690. *Energy Transfer Partners, L.P. et. al.*, 120 FERC ¶ 61,086 (2007), 3.
691. Jerry Markham, 7 (2015).
692. *See* S. Stoft, et al., *Primer on Electricity Futures and Other Derivatives* 33-41 (Environmental Energy Technologies Division, University of California at Berkeley 1998).

Receiving neither profits nor losses, in both situations, the supplier hedges its price risks associated with the changes in market prices.

In a similar way, a distributor who acquires natural gas to supply retail markets to final consumers and a trader who engages in various trades and is exposed to several price risks can enter into swap agreements for hedging purposes. Accordingly a distributor who buys natural gas based on the settlement price for NG Futures Contracts can hedge the risk of a potential price increase in the NYMEX by entering into a swap agreement with another party paying the settlement price of NG Futures in exchange for receiving a fixed price. A trader finding that the prices of energy products for a particular market and particular period can also employ swap agreements with other traders to hedge risks related to its financial position. For example a trader who previously sold basis swaps meaning that it pays the index price, such as Platts' IFERC, and receives a settlement price for NG Futures Contract, can hedge its financial risk by buying an equal volume of basis swap, paying the settlement price and receiving the index price. Consequently, after the swap agreements, the distributor and the trader are no longer concerned as to whether the settlement price increases or decreases, as they have hedged their financial risks.

It is important to note that the scenarios provided above are not exclusive. The traders and market participants employ a diverse range of trading activities, buying and selling physical and financial products to create a financial portfolio that benefits from price movements as a result of manipulative trading. The majority of these energy products traded in the regulated markets such as NYMEX and the OTC markets such as ICE are standardised, meaning that they differ on the basis of their commodity, quantity, delivery date, and delivery point or cash settlement.[693] The only variable that is not standardised in the wholesale energy markets is the price of underlying products, as market participants are free to determine the price levels at which they want to trade their physical or futures contracts.[694] The overall price levels and movements calculated based upon the volume-weighted average price of all fixed-price or physical basis transactions executed in relevant markets and relevant trading periods, in turn determines the value of financial contracts such as swaps and options, which are identified as price-taking instruments, the value of which depends upon price movements in price-making positions. The scenarios provided above clearly indicate that the profitability of swaps and options that the traders and other market participants are trading are based upon market fundamentals, such as storage, transmission constraints and demand and supply levels available in the relevant markets.

[vi] Manipulative Trading

In cross-market manipulation, the perpetrators seek to exploit pricing relations between price-making and price-taking positions. In all the scenarios above, a legitimate trading or hedging activity involves an economic risk related to price changes in the

693. *Supra* note 17.
694. Energy Primer, 109 (2015).

relevant markets. The market participants either seek protection from economic losses or try to profit from price changes associated with market fundamentals. In cross-market manipulation, the perpetrators employ trading schemes that are specifically aimed at affecting the price-making positions in favour of the positions held at the price-taking level, creating a 'win-win' situation.[695] In these positions, the perpetrators, in fact, do not bet at all, based on their predictions on price movements. Instead, they directly intervene in the determination of prices moved up and down pursuant to the perpetrators' price-taking positions.

The perpetration of cross-market manipulation cannot be exclusively defined as a type of market activity, which directly results in artificial increases in market prices. It rather requires a combination of market activities that are specifically designed and utilised in furtherance of price movements directed pursuant to price-taking financial positions. As the case law on cross-market manipulation suggests, the perpetrators are often involved in large-scale trading activities, accumulating a market position, such as engaging in large buy or sell orders, that gives them the ability to move prices up or down pursuant to their price-taking swap and options contracts. Once these large positions are acquired, the perpetrators exercise a trading strategy designed to create a price movement that will be accepted and followed by other market participants trading in the same market. It is important to note that the accumulation and exercise of such market positions and trading strategies are not alone regarded to be manipulative.[696] Such practices can be held manipulative only if it is shown that it is the perpetrators' intent, in designing and exercising such trading strategies, to reap profits from their price-taking positions through exploiting their price relations with market activities in price-making instruments.

[vii] Behaviour That Affects Prices

Scale of Trading

In order to exert pressure on the settlement and index prices which are calculated based upon the volume-weighted average price of all fixed-price or physical basis transactions, the perpetrators have to engage in large-scale trading activities accounting for a significant proportion of all volumes transacted in the relevant pricing making market. While higher market shares can correlate with increases in prices on the buying side, they can also correlate with price decreases when transacted on the selling side.[697] For example, in *Energy Transfer Partners,* in which the defendants were found to be suppressing prices to benefit from their financial position, the defendants' sales of fixed-price gas contracts to delivered at HSC accounted for 80% of total sales transacted during the relevant period.[698] By dominating the trading of next month fixed-price natural gas on the selling side, the defendants were able to create a downward pressure

695. *Energy Transfer Partners, L.P. et. al.*, 120 FERC ¶ 61,086 (2007), 4.
696. *In re Indiana Farm Bureau Cooperative Association*, [1982-1984 Transfer Binder] Comm. Fut. L. Rep. (CCH) ¶ 21,796 (CFTC 1982).
697. *CFTC v. Amaranth Advisors, L.L.C., et. al.*, 523 F. Supp. 2d 328 (S.D.N.Y. 2007), 45.
698. *Energy Transfer Partners, L.P. et. al.*, 120 FERC ¶ 61,086 (2007), 3.

on market prices. Again in *Barclays,* the defendants' selling and buying activities designed to move daily fixed-price electricity prices up and down constituted 24% of the total daily fixed-price electricity trading during the relevant periods diverging from 10% to 58%.[699]

Even though the levels of market liquidity is an important factor for the perpetrators' accumulation of large market positions, market manipulation can happen in both illiquid and heavily traded markets. In *DiPlacido,* the NYMEX futures in the COB and PV were considered illiquid on the basis of low volume and open interest as well as a wide bid-ask spread demonstrated during the relevant trading period.[700] This was also supported by other experienced floor brokers and traders who noted that an order of twenty-five to thirty contracts was large enough to dictate prices. FERC found that the defendants' trading activity accounted for more than 50% of the total trading activity on the buying side of the market.[701] In *TGPNA,* however, the defendants manipulated the price of natural gas at four of the most heavily traded markets (SoCal, Waha, Permian, San Juan) in the south western US over a period of three years. In this case, the defendants' trading constituted 80% of total volume of fixed-price trading at SoCal, and even reached 100% market share in Waha, meaning that the defendants were part of every single contract to be delivered at Waha traded on the ICE.[702]

Even though the legal analysis developed through case law does not stipulate a demonstration of a traditional, antitrust concept of market power in furtherance of a manipulative activity, FERC included the calculation of market shares that the perpetrators held with respect to the total volume-based trading activity in relevant periods and trading locations. These concentrated trading activities create upward or downward price movements by conferring to defendants a transitory but substantial market power, signalling other market participants with respect to market trends boosting price effects,[703] and engaging in an explicit or tacit collusion with other traders recognising and participating in the manipulative scheme.[704] In *BP America Inc.* in which one of the defendants was a vertically integrated company, owning assets in both trading and transmission of natural gas markets, the perpetrators also allocated all capacity of their transmission pipelines, HPL, to boost their trading activity and market power.[705] The CFTC and FERC have consistently concluded that identifying market

699. *Barclays Bank PLC, Daniel Brin, Scott Connelly, et al.*, 141 FERC ¶ 61,084 (2012), 4.
700. *In re DiPlacido,* [2007-2009 Transfer Binder] Comm. Fut. L. Rep. (CCH) ¶ 30,970 (CFTC 2008), 5.
701. *In re Avista Energy, Inc. and Michael T. Griswold,* CFTC Docket No 01-21, 2001 WL 951736 (CFTC 2001), 5.
702. *In the matter of Total Gas & Power North America, Inc., and Therese Tran,* CFTC Docket No 16 -03 (CFTC 2015), 42.
703. '*Causation of artificial prices is established when it is demonstrated the artificial market prices resulted from the conduct of a trader, or group of traders acting in concert, rather than the legitimate forces of supply and demand.*' *See In re Avista Energy, Inc. and Michael T. Griswold,* CFTC Docket No 01-21, 2001 WL 951736 (CFTC 2001), 5, *citing Cargil v. Hardin,* 452 F.2d 1154 (8th Cir. 1971), *cert. denied,* 406 U.S. 932 (1972); *In re Indiana Farm Bureau Cooperative Association,* [1982-1984 Transfer Binder] Comm. Fut. L. Rep. (CCH) 21,796 (CFTC 1982).
704. *CFTC v. Amaranth Advisors, L.L.C., et. al.*, 523 F. Supp. 2d 328 (S.D.N.Y. 2007), 33.
705. *BP America Inc., BP Corporation North America et al.*, 144 FERC ¶ 61,100 (2013), 23.

power is not a requirement under the enforcement of anti-manipulation rules.[706] However the case law on cross-market manipulation clearly suggests that the perpetrators' acquisition of large buy and sell orders and engagement in concentrated trading activity constitute important elements in establishing the relation between the perpetrators' trading scheme and price movements in the relevant markets.

Timing of Trading

The case law provided above also illustrates that strategic timing of concentrated high trading activities engaged in by the perpetrators is another important factor to promote price movements in the relevant trading locations. For example, in *BP America Inc.*, the perpetrators specifically developed an early and heavy trading activity during the trading sessions[707] to induce other market participants to enact transactions in such a way to steer the market in their preferred direction. In *DiPlacido,* the defendants orchestrated their trading strategy to take place in 'the Close'; last two minutes of options expiration days in each month, which began at 3:23 pm and ended at 3:25 pm.[708] In *Energy Transfer Partners,* the perpetrators again concentrated their trading activity in the last-half hour of the closing day for monthly natural gas trading in the NYMEX to amplify their downward pressure on prices at HSC.[709] In the majority of regulated exchanges and the OTC markets, prices of energy products are determined during a specific balancing period such as closing sessions in daily and bidweeks in monthly markets and the perpetrators usually accumulate and exercise their large price-making positions in these narrow and concentrated trading periods. Therefore the timing of trading activities is important in cross-market manipulation.

[viii] Intent

FERC established that the acquisition of market power and early and heavy trading activities during certain trade periods are not enough to hold a market participant liable for violating anti-manipulation rules. Market participants can engage in these practices and cause upward or downward price movements without a clear manipulative intent. In certain market conditions, such as shortages, transmission constraints, or outages in production, market participants can acquire market power based on illiquidity and cause price increases in the relevant markets.[710] Accordingly, in order to assess

706. *Supra* note 558.
707. *'ICE next-day, fixed-price gas trading begins when the first trade is consummated. In 2008, physical gas trading at HSC typically began between 8:00 and 8:30 a.m. ET. On most days, there was consistent trading volume between 8:30 a.m. and 9:30 a.m. Trading would typically slow by 10:00 a.m. and was usually finished by 11:00 a.m.' See BP America Inc., BP Corporation North America et al.*, 144 FERC ¶ 61,100 (2013), footnote 107.
708. *In re DiPlacido,* [2007-2009 Transfer Binder] Comm. Fut. L. Rep. (CCH) ¶ 30,970 (CFTC 2008), 52.
709. *Energy Transfer Partners, L.P. et. al.,* 120 FERC ¶ 61,086 (2007), 5.
710. In *In re Indiana Farm Bureau,* aware of the tight supply in the grains market as a result of demand pressures from the Soviet Union, the defendants caused a dramatic price increase by standing for delivery. The CFTC concluded that the market conditions that caused the tight supply in the grains market were not a result of a market practice engaged in by the defendants

manipulative intent, the case law evaluates whether the market power or large positions in markets are created as a result of the perpetrators' intent to move prices artificially. In so doing, the regulatory agencies, the CFTC and FERC seek to identify the nature of the defendants' activity, analysing whether the defendant would engage in a similar price-making activity without holding financial positions and whether the market practices would be economic without the profits derived from financial positions. If the regulatory agencies find that the relevant market practices are uneconomic without financial benefits, then the defendants are considered to be in the sphere of anti-manipulation provisions and can be held liable for the violation of cross-market manipulation.

The case law provided above clearly promulgates that the uneconomic nature of the perpetrators' trading activities is a fundamental factor in establishing their manipulative intent. In *Energy Transfer Partners*, FERC identified that the defendants' transaction selling and buying back the similar volumes of fixed-price daily gas at Waha on December 23 and 28 were uneconomic as they had no legitimate reasons to transact such loss-making trades, but for an intent to suppress market prices.[711] In *DiPlacido*, the CFTC also found that the defendants' selling of electricity futures contracts was manipulative, since the instructions delivered to the brokers on the NYMEX floor, from the defendants were to sell the contracts at as low a price as possible to secure a certain settlement price.[712] In *Barclays*, the defendants were found to be eager to incur losses in relation to their fixed-price physical trading to move the index prices in a direction benefiting their related financial positions.[713] In *BP America Inc.* FERC again identified that the defendants preferred to lose money on their next day, fixed-price physical trading at HSC, even though more profitable alternatives were present.[714] In *Amaranth*, the defendants' trading activities in NG Futures Contracts are considered self-defeating without the benefits from opposing large financial and physical positions.[715]

It is important to note that the legal analysis developed under cross-market manipulation is not designed to punish any market participant that engages in trades that can be considered uneconomic compared to alternative trading practices. It is reasonable to expect market participants to incur losses from their trading activities and they can seek hedging mechanisms to eliminate or minimise such losses which are associated with the financial risks taken. In order to separate manipulative uneconomic trading activity from legitimate market practices that produce financial losses, the regulatory agencies seek a consistent pattern of trading activity[716] that proceeds for a certain period of time. Accordingly, taking into account the large positions held and

---

and thus there was no causation between price increases and the defendants' conduct. *In re Indiana Farm Bureau Cooperative Association*, [1982-1984 Transfer Binder] Comm. Fut. L. Rep. (CCH) ¶ 21,796 (CFTC 1982), 25.

711. *Energy Transfer Partners, L.P. et. al.*, 120 FERC ¶ 61,086 (2007), 4.
712. *In re DiPlacido*, [2007-2009 Transfer Binder] Comm. Fut. L. Rep. (CCH) ¶ 30,970 (CFTC 2008), 48.
713. *Barclays Bank PLC, Daniel Brin, Scott Connelly, et al.*, 141 FERC ¶ 61,084 (2012), 34.
714. *BP America Inc., BP Corporation North America et al.*, 144 FERC ¶ 61,100 (2013), 39.
715. *CFTC v. Amaranth Advisors, L.L.C., et. al.*, 523 F. Supp. 2d 328 (S.D.N.Y. 2007), 33.
716. *In the matter of Total Gas & Power North America, Inc., and Therese Tran*, CFTC Docket No 16 -03 (CFTC 2015), 68.

strategic trading activities employed, the CFTC and FERC will find the perpetrators liable for cross-market manipulation, once they engage in uneconomic trading activity in a consistent pattern and the losses incurred in price-making positions clearly correlates with the benefits derived from price-taking positions.

[4] Congestion-Related Manipulation

Electricity and natural gas markets are network-bound industries meaning that transmission of energy products from suppliers to consumers requires a capacity-restricted fixed infrastructure. The system of fixed infrastructure operates as nodes, which involve two points; a source, where energy is injected to the system and a sink where it is delivered to load. Each supplier of energy is also required to book the necessary capacity equivalent to its contractual obligations. Pricing of energy differs in each node due to changes at congestion levels, exposing the supplier to different price risks associated with the functioning of the transmission system. The market for supply and transmission of energy products is orchestrated and monitored by a transmission system operator, which is required to ensure that demand and supply levels available in the market are balanced.

In order to mitigate the financial risks arising from congestion occurring in the transmission system and balance the levels between supply and demand required for system integrity, transmission system operators issue 'Financial Transmission Rights' (the FTRs) which allow their holders to claim financial compensation when a difference occurs between prices in the source and the sink as a result of congestion in the transmission system.[717] Congestion occurs when the amount of energy demanded exceeds the capacity available in the transmission lines. Such a condition causes energy prices to decrease at source and increase at the sink, resulting in financial risks for traders required to book the capacity necessary to execute buying and selling orders. The FTRs are established to mitigate these financial risks and allow their holders to receive payments from transmission system operators, when congestion occurs at a specific node with which the FTRs are associated.

Transmission system operators mostly operate a dual market system consisting of DAMs designed to fulfil supply obligations and RTMs established to balance system conditions diverging from that of the DAMs. Demand for and supply of energy products in these markets differ. The majority of energy demand is supplied in the DAMs. In these markets, the transmission system operators collect and match bids and offers for energy products. Any divergence from these bids and offers scheduled in the DAMs is balanced with a separate auction market in the RTMs in which transmission system operators again collect and match bids and offers submitted by the market participants. The establishment of these two different supply markets with different demand and supply purposes creates two different pricing mechanisms for market participants.

717. William W. Hogan, *Electricity Market Design; Financial Transmission Rights, Up To Congestion Transactions and Multi-Settlement Systems* 3 (16 Jul. 2012). Retrieved from http://www.hks.harvard.edu/fs/whogan/Hogan_UTC_071612.pdf (accessed 18 Apr. 2018).

The dual pricing system also provides market participants mechanisms to balance their supply requirements and arbitrage price differences between the DAMs and the RTMs.[718] Accordingly a market participant who predicts that the price for an energy product for a specific hour in the DAMs will be higher than its price in RTMs, can place bids and offers to sell an amount of energy in the DAMs and buy the equivalent amount of energy in the RTMs, receiving payments in the former while paying in the latter. These types of market trading activities are called 'Virtual Trading' and are very common in energy markets. Through virtual trading, market participants make profits as their revenues in the DAMs are higher than the payments made in the RTMs. Market participants can place both virtual supply bids (incremental bids) meaning that they submit an offer to sell a certain amount of energy at a certain price and virtual demand bids (decremental bids) in which they submit an offer to buy a certain amount of energy at a certain price.[719]

Even though the physical volume traded in these virtual trading strategies is zero, each virtual trade creates effects on price and congestion levels. Economically, a virtual supply bid tends to decrease relevant energy prices, while a virtual demand bid does the opposite.[720] Transmission system operators require each market participant to book transmission capacity corresponding to the amount provided under the virtual trades for the integrity of transmission. Congestion-related manipulative practices involve market participants aiming at reaping profits from their positions in FTRs by engaging in virtual trading activities. Accordingly a perpetrator who wishes to make profits by artificially affecting congestion levels via virtual trading to increase the value of its FTRs engages in an illegitimate trading activity and violates anti-manipulation provisions. The chapter presents two cases in which the defendants were alleged to be in violation of anti-manipulation rules due to their activities in virtual and FTRs trading.

[a] Constellation Energy Commodities Group, Inc.[721]

In 2008, FERC's office of enforcement initiated an investigation into the Constellation Energy Commodities Group (CCG) which was active in physical power trading in and around the New York Independent System Operator's (NYISO) control area, on the grounds that from 1 October to 18 November 2008, the CCG's virtual bids departed significantly from legitimate trading activities creating an unwarranted difference between DAMs and RTMs for the benefits derived from its contract for difference (CFD) positions, which consisted of financial swaps, transmission congestion contracts and FTRs.[722] The profitability of the CFD positions depended on a price divergence between the NYISO's DAMs and RTMs. Accordingly, the CCG sought to decrease prices in the DAMs by engaging in virtual supply contracts to increase the value of its CFD

718. Energy Primer, 51 (2015).
719. Shaun Ledgerwood & Johannes P. Pfeifenberger, 7 (2012).
720. Energy Primer, 64 (2015).
721. *Coaltrain Energy, L.P., et al.*, 154 FERC ¶ 61,002 (2016).
722. *Ibid.*, 1.

positions.[723] Each virtual supply bid submitted by the CCG established a market assumption that the available electricity in the DAMs are more than enough to supply demand in the market, creating a downward pressure on prices. However, as the CCG was also required to book necessary capacity reservations corresponding to the amount of electricity contracted in the virtual supply bids, the congestion levels at the transmission system increased resulting in an increase in the value of FTRs associated with the congested transmission lines.[724] The supply bids submitted in the DAMs were later offset by the equivalent virtual demand bids in the RTMs.

The CCG also engaged in virtual demand bids in the DAMs market, where it was buying the CFD positions. The CCG's virtual demand bids created a market picture showing that there was a greater demand for electricity in the market to the extent that available production levels were not enough to meet it. The higher demand levels created by the virtual demand bids increased market prices in the DAMs and decreased the value of the CFD positions allowing the CCG to buy the CFD positions at depressed prices. By buying at low and selling at high prices, the CCG derived substantial profits from its CFD trading.[725]

FERC found that the perpetrator's trading of CFD was manipulative as it significantly departed from legitimate virtual trading activities.[726] Economically, a virtual trading activity is profitable as long as the price difference between the DAMs and the RTMs remains. The CCG, however, continued to place virtual supply and demand bids to the point that the relevant trading activity was no longer profitable and was in fact, loss incurring. FERC identified that in carrying out the virtual bidding strategies, the perpetrator was indifferent to the price levels in the DAMs and the RTMs and engaged in these loss-incurring practices in a consistent pattern. The CCG's trading of virtual bids were only profitable when the benefits from its trading of CFD positions were taken into account.

[b] Louis Dreyfus Energy Services L.P.[727]

As in *Constellation*, this case also involved a manipulation claim on the basis that Louis Dreyfus Energy Services L.P. (LDES) engaged in virtual supply (incremental) and virtual demand (decremental) bids for the benefit of the FTR positions held in one of the nodes, Velva in North Dakota, integrated in MISO's control area, from November 2009 to February 2010.[728] The LDES' virtual trading activities were uneconomic producing USD 390,353 financial losses at Velva during the relevant period.[729] However the benefits derived from FTR positions related to the price changes and congestion levels created by the virtual supply and demand trades exceeded USD

723. *Ibid.*, 3.
724. *Ibid.*, 4.
725. *Ibid.*
726. *Ibid.*, 5.
727. *MISO Virtual and FTR Trading*, 146 FERC ¶ 61,072 (2014).
728. *Ibid.*, 3.
729. *Ibid.*, 4.

3,344,000. FERC found that the LDES' trading pattern of virtual bids in DAMs and RTMs were manipulative and violated its anti-manipulation rule.[730]

[c] Evaluation

The fact that the virtual trades imposed no delivery obligations on parties did not result in a conclusion that these instruments were purely financial with no impact on physical markets. On the contrary, as long as they are large enough, they can directly affect price differences between DAMs and RTMs. The main reason why these types of market activities are allowed under energy market rules is that they play a central role in converging price differences between DAMs and RTMs.[731] While each virtual demand bidding in the DAMs creates an upwards price pressure, the corresponding virtual supply bidding in the RTMs pushes market prices down. In a heavily traded market these virtual trades result in similar prices for energy on both side of the markets and provide a single price. In other words, each virtual trading activity which is based on price differences between the DAMs and the RTMs undermines its further profitability by causing the convergence of these prices.

Price effects are not the only impact that virtual trades have on physical trading of energy products. These trading activities can also cause artificial congestion or aggregate existing congestion levels. In both *Constellation* and *Louis Dreyfus*, the perpetrators sought to create artificial congestion at specific nodes to benefit from their FTRs and other congestion-related financial positions. The price relations between virtual trades and the FTRs are analogous to the interplay between price-making and price-taking positions under cross-market manipulation. In both schemes, market participants seek to exploit price relations between two different but interlinked markets through engaging in uneconomic and large-scale trading. The FTRs and other financial products can be used as legitimate hedging or investment strategies that provide effective risk management and profit-maximising tools for market participants.

The chapter includes congestion-related market manipulation separately from cross-market manipulation, since the FTRs, the main financial positions the perpetrators seek to derive profit from, are different from other financial positions like swaps and options. They are peculiar to energy markets while swaps and options are heavily traded across several financial markets from securities to different types of commodities markets such as agriculture, metals and others. The number of the FTRs available in each node is limited to the node's physical constraints. The transmission system operators issue the FTRs on the basis of a simultaneous feasibility test and establish a certain threshold which limits the scale of positions market participants can acquire and hold. However such a threshold is not present in the trading of other financial contracts. Market participants can continue to enter into these financial instruments as long as a counterparty willing to transact is present. The availability of financial instruments provides the perpetrators a broader spectrum in establishing price-making

730. *Ibid.*
731. Shaun Ledgerwood & Johannes P. Pfeifenberger, 9–11 (2012).

and price-taking positions in cross-market manipulation. Therefore congestion-related manipulation which is peculiar to energy markets and limited to transmission constraints is addressed separately from cross-market manipulation.

[C] Outright Fraud

[1] Overview

The concept of outright fraud is different from other open market transactions such as market power and trade-based manipulation. As mentioned above, US federal courts, with respect to the application of the CFTC's rule Section 4(c), in *Sudheimer* and *Radley*, differentiated manipulative practices as open and closed market transactions.[732] While the former relates to manipulation through actual market transactions with actual parties and economic risks, such as market power and trade-based manipulation, the latter involves fictitious and wash trades that do not have any material effect on markets. The underlying factor in a market power manipulation is the perpetrators' accumulation of market power to trigger market manipulation. In trade-based manipulative schemes, the perpetrators can engage in various transactions that can either be fraudulent, triggering manipulation through distorting other market participants' perception of market fundamentals, or non-fraudulent, manipulating markets or prices without imposing a deception on market participants. In outright fraud, market participants can engage in market manipulation by either providing false information to the market or by the omission of material information.[733] In energy markets, the *Deutsche Bank* case illustrates a clear example of outright fraud as a market practice triggering market manipulation.

[2] **Deutsche Bank Energy Trading, LLC**[734]

FERC alleged that the defendant, Deutsche Bank Energy Trading LLC, violated its anti-manipulation rule Section 1c.2 by submitting false information with respect to its activities at 17 MW Silver Peak intertie in CAISO from January 2010 to March 2010 to profit from its positions in Congestion Revenue Rights (CRRs) which are FTRs issued and auctioned by the CAISO.[735] The defendant engaged in consecutive scheduling practices exporting electricity through Silver Peak intertie and importing the equivalent amount at Summit.[736] The defendant entered into this export and import scheduling as wheeling-through transactions, meaning that the defendant was using the CAISO's grid just for transit purposes and electricity flowing through Silver Peak and Summit was not injected into the transmission system to serve a load inside the CAISO.[737] The

732. *Supra* note 151.
733. Gary Taylor, et al. (2015).
734. *Deutsche Bank Energy Trading, L.L.C.*, 140 FERC ¶ 61,178 (2012).
735. *Ibid.*, 1.
736. *Ibid.*, 2.
737. *Ibid.*, 3.

defendant continued to schedule exports at Silver Peak and imports at Summit, conveying false information to the market that it used the CAISO's transmission grid to transport electricity that was produced and delivered outside the CAISO. However, it was revealed that the defendant also scheduled exports and imports on the Sierra Pacific Power Company (SPPC) system outside the CAISO corresponding to its schedules at Silver Peak and Summit.[738]

Capacity schedules between the CAISO and the SPPC created a circular scheduling mechanism between Silver Peak and Summit. FERC identified that the defendant's wheeling-through transactions, in fact, involved no physical flow of electricity across the transmission lines and created an artificial congestion that increased the value of CRRs related to the congestion levels at the Silver Peak intertie. In its scheduling practice across the Silver Peak and the Summit, the defendant incurred economic losses from capacity reservations, paying significant amount of transmission costs for electricity flow that had never occurred. The sole purpose of the defendant engaging in the circular scheduling was to render its CRRs profitable as the capacity reservations transacted for the purpose of electricity flow were uneconomic and self-defeating. Accordingly, FERC concluded that the defendant's circular scheduling activity was manipulative.

[3] Evaluation

Deutsche Bank provides a clear example of how a market participant can engage in manipulation without involving real parties and real economic risks. The defendant employed its strategy to profit from its CRRs which were based on the congestion levels at the Silver Peak intertie. The act of circular scheduling[739] between the CAISO and the SPPC operated as a fraud on market participants, disseminating false information that the defendant, through wheeling-though agreements, was transmitting electricity by using the Silver Peak and the Summit to supply a load outside the CAISO's transmission grid. In fact the defendant engaged in no buying or selling with respect to the amount of electricity scheduled to the CAISO and injected no power into these transmission lines. The transmission costs required for the scheduling were not deterrent as the revenues from its CRRs positions outweighed the financial losses.

The defendant's manipulative strategy in *Deutsche Bank* is very similar to the market practices discussed under the congestion-related market manipulation. Both types of market manipulation involve schemes that aim at creating artificial congestion levels at targeted transmission lines and collecting revenues from positions held in FTRs markets. However, it is important to note that congestion-related market manipulation is a trade-based manipulation and consists of virtual demand and supply bids which perpetrators place in order to affect congestion levels. These trades contain real trades and economic risks. Under congestion-related manipulation, a perpetrator can realise its manipulative scheme, only if its bids and offers are awarded by the system

738. *Ibid.*
739. For practices of circular scheduling in the 'Great Western Energy Crisis of 2001', *see* Gary Taylor, et al., 165 (2015).

operator in the DAMs or matched in the RTMs by other market participants. These manipulative strategies have physical effects on other market participants with whom the perpetrators transact as part of their manipulative strategy. The collective effects of virtual demand and supply bids were zero on the physical supply in the market as these bids balanced each other in the RTMs. In *Deutsche Bank*, the defendant engaged in no physical transactions that affected other market participants' physical position in the electricity supply. Therefore, they were addressed separately from other trade-based congestion-related manipulative practices.

§3.04 CONCLUSION

[A] Jurisdictional Dimensions

Traditionally, the SEC and the CFTC have been the major regulatory agencies that have intensively applied and enforced their anti-manipulation rules to securities and commodities markets under their jurisdiction. While the SEC adopts a fraud-based formulation of market manipulation, the CFTC, before the adoption of the Dodd-Frank, used an artificial price-based definition which stipulated the determination of price artificiality as a result of manipulative activity. Case law developed under the SEC's fraud-based provision and the SEC's experience in enforcing anti-manipulation rules against perpetrators resulted in other regulatory agencies, such as FERC[740] and the FTC,[741] to adopt identical anti-manipulation rules with a specific referral to the SEC's precedent on manipulative practices. The artificial price standard, however, has proved to be difficult for the CFTC to implement. It was not until *DiPlacido*, 2008 that the CFTC had successfully prosecuted a market participant for market manipulation.[742] Eventually, the CFTC followed in the footsteps of FERC and the FTC and adopted a fraud-based market manipulation provision after Dodd-Frank.

The CFTC developed several strategies to overcome the difficulties originating from its artificial price-based provision. Accordingly it started using the CEA's Section 4(c) that prohibits wash trades, accommodation trades and other fictitious trades in a manner to deal with all types of manipulative activities, similar to the SEC's application of its fraud-based formulation. This strategy failed in *US v. Radley*, et al. in which the CFTC tried to show the defendants' cornering of TET propane futures contracts as a type of fraud and therefore violating its anti-manipulation provisions.[743] The court noted that the CFTC had failed to show that the defendants engaged in activities that deceived other market participants' perception of legitimate forces of demand and supply and a mere concealment of buying large positions to corner markets was not

740. Energy Policy Act of 2005 §§ 314, 1284.
741. According to Section 811 of the Energy Independence and Security of 2007 which granted the FTC to impose penalties for the manipulation of crude oil, gasoline or petroleum distillates; '(i)*t is unlawful for any person, directly or indirectly, to use or employ* (...) *any manipulative or deceptive device or contrivance* (...)'. Energy Independence and Security of 2007, Pub. L. No 110-140 § 811, 121 Stat. 1723 (2007).
742. *Supra* note 513.
743. *Supra* note 341.

sufficient to find that the defendants' cornering activity was fraudulent.[744] In other words, a fraud-based market manipulation claim did not suffice to prosecute a market power manipulation or other activity that does not inherently operate as a deception or fraud over other market participants.

Such a differentiation between fraud and other types of market manipulation has not been present in the SEC's case law. This issue was specifically addressed in *SEC v. Masri*[745] in which the court identified the issue as whether the SEA's fraud-based rule Section 10b-5 which has traditionally been applied to fictitious trades with no rational purpose and specifically intended to create false impressions in markets was also applicable to open market transactions through which perpetrators can manipulate markets and prices by entering into aggressive short selling or large purchases rather than merely disseminating false information. Applying a legal standard known as 'sole intent' standard' the court found that the concept of fraud under the Section 10(b) was also applicable to open market transactions, as long as they are perpetrated with manipulative intent to affect prices of securities.[746] Accordingly, with respect to the manipulation of prices through open market transactions, the SEA's fraud-based rule §10b-5 does not require the SEC to establish that perpetrators' trading activity involves fictitious trades or disseminating false information to create false impression. Instead, the court concluded that proving that the defendant would not have conducted the transaction but for the manipulative intent is sufficient to impose liability for market manipulation.

[B] Fraud-Based Versus Artificial Price-Based Definitions

Traditionally, for a market activity to be in violation of SEA's rule Section 10b-5, the SEC was required to show that: (i) a fraudulent or deceptive device, scheme or statement was utilized; (ii) such a device, scheme, or statement was in relation to the sale or purchase of a product in the stock market; and (iii) the perpetrator of the device, scheme or statement acted with a requisite intent.[747] The court's ruling in *SEC v. Masri* changed this traditional legal framework, when it was applied to manipulative practices other than those amounting to fraud or deception within the meaning of the first element. Accordingly the establishment of manipulative intent on the basis of the '*but for*' test is enough for an open market transaction, such as market power and cross-market manipulation to be prosecuted under SEA's rule Section 10(b).

According to the artificial price based formulation of the CEA, in order to impose liability for market manipulation, the CFTC has to prove that: (i) the perpetrator had the ability to influence market prices; (ii) the perpetrator specifically intended to create or effect a price or price trend that does not reflect legitimate forces of supply and demand; (iii) artificial prices existed; and (iv) the perpetrator caused the artificial

744. *Ibid.*, 18.
745. *SEC v. Masri*, 523 F. Supp. 2d 361 (S.D.N.Y. 2007).
746. *Ibid. See also Markowski v. SEC*, 274 F.3d 525, 529 (D.C.Cir. 2001) ('"*manipulation" can be illegal solely because of the actor's purpose*').
747. 17 C.F.R. § 240.10b-5 (2011).

prices.[748] The legal framework developed under the artificial price test does not differentiate between fraud and non-fraud market practices. It is important to note that the CEA also adopted Section 4(c) prescribing wash trades, fictitious trades and accommodation trades and can be regarded as equivalent to the SEA's rule Section 10b-5. This results in the application of the artificial price test limited to the non-fraud, open market transactions, excluding frauds such as wash trade and fictitious trades which are dealt with under Section 4(c). However, the SEC's application of the rule Section 10(b) to an open market transaction on the basis of the sole intent standard gives rise to concerns on the conformity of legal standards adopted by these two regulatory agencies in prosecuting manipulative practices.

While the establishment of price artificiality and causation between the perpetrators' conduct and artificial prices have been the main obstacles to a successful prosecution of manipulative practices by the CFTC, the sole intent standard on the basis of the '*but for*' test applied in *SEC v. Masri* to a market power manipulation provides the SEC a regulatory flexibility in prosecuting open market transactions. The sole intent standard is not acknowledged by FERC. Even though its anti-manipulation rule is identical to the SEC's rule Section 10(b), FERC specifically noted in *TGPNA*, that it did not adopt a '*but for*' test in addressing open market transactions.[749] As previously mentioned, FERC's definition of fraud encompasses all types of market conduct that distort well-functioning of energy markets,[750] irrespective of whether they are open market transactions or fictitious trades with no actual economic risks or rational purpose.

After the enactment of Dodd-Frank, which conferred a fraud-based formulation of market manipulation on the CFTC based on the SEC's rule §10(b), the CFTC no longer referred to the '*but for*' test. Instead, in Regulation 180.2, it retained the traditional artificial price-based prohibition to deal with market practices that it deemed non-fraudulent in character, while referring to the new fraud-based formulation for fraudulent market practices. However, in *TGPNA*,[751] the CFTC applied its fraud-based prohibition, Regulation 180.1, to an open market transaction, to which it had previously applied its artificial price-based prohibition. It can be argued that rather than the SEC's '*but for*' test, the CFTC chose to apply FERC's approach identifying all types of market practices that distort the well-functioning of energy markets as fraudulent. This conclusion gives rise to questions of why the CFTC retained and on what occasions it can apply its artificial price-based rule, while it chose to prosecute all types of market manipulation under a single fraud-based prohibition. The inconformity in the formulation and the application of anti-manipulation rules along with the concurrent regulation of multiple authorities causes further ambiguities for energy

748. *Supra* note 361.
749. *Total Gas & Power North America Inc., et al.*, 155 FERC ¶ 61,105 (2016).
750. *Coaltrain Energy, L.P., et al.*, 154 FERC ¶ 61,002 (2016), 100.
751. *In the matter of Total Gas & Power North America, Inc., and Therese Tran*, CFTC Docket No 16 -03 (CFTC 2015).

markets, which require particular attention by the CFTC and FERC during the regulatory proceedings initiated in accordance with the MoU.

The definitions provided by the anti-manipulation rules adopted by the SEC, FERC and the CFTC give no guidance as to what types of market practices give rise to manipulation concerns or which factors can be regarded as relevant in identifying the illegitimacy of any market conduct. The absence of a clear legal framework that specifically separates manipulative conduct from legitimate trading practices has often been regarded as an approach called *'I know it when I see it'*[752] which implies adopting *ex-post* enforcement mechanisms rather than precautionary measures. Criticising this vague *'I know it when I see it'* approach,[753] the academic literature has developed several alternative definitions that seek to identify what market manipulation is.[754] Both the traditional approach developed under case law and the alternative frameworks offered in the academic literature focus on the nature of the price-making market activities, the activities that the perpetrators design to accomplish a certain market outcome that is valuable for their positions in markets. Therefore they constitute nothing more than a restatement or reconceptualisation of the legal analysis carried out by the courts in prosecuting manipulative practices throughout case law.

[C] Demarcation of Manipulative Practices

The chapter does not undertake to provide an alternative definition for market manipulation. Rather it seeks to identify the characteristics of practices in US energy markets that were deemed to be manipulative under US case law. The legal approach, focusing on the characteristics of price-making activities, provides only a differentiation between fraudulent and trade-based practices which has also proved to be problematic from a regulatory point of view as it fell victim to diverging definitions from different regulatory agencies. In this regard, the chapter also takes into account the price-taking positions that the perpetrators seek to exploit and substantially affect the nature and formulation of manipulative practices. In so doing, the chapter provides a demarcation of US case law on energy market manipulation by first, adopting the traditional differentiation between market power and trade-based manipulation as well as fraud and second, providing additional classifications based upon the positions that the perpetrators seek to profit from. Such an additional differentiation reveals the impact of price-taking positions on the perpetration of manipulative practices.

Accordingly, the chapter provides three different types of market manipulation in energy markets: (i) market power manipulation; (ii) trade-based manipulation; (iii) outright fraud. This differentiation is based on the traditional approach developed by

752. *Supra* note 327.
753. Shaun Ledgerwood, et al., *Defining Market Manipulation in a Post-REMIT World,* The Brattle Group Discussion Paper 2 (2011); Jerry Markham, 211 (2015).
754. Emilios E. Avgouleas, 114 (2005); Shaun D. Ledgerwood & Paul R. Carpenter (2012); Craig Pirrong, 14–15 (2010).

case law on market manipulation. While market power manipulation was a feature of commodity markets which had been under the jurisdiction of the CFTC,[755] fraudulent practices such as wash trades, matched orders,[756] and pump and dump[757] schemes were addressed by the SEC under its rule Section 10b-5.[758] It is important to note that the types of manipulation presented under this chapter's demarcation are not exclusive. Market participants may engage into a variety of practices that necessitates the development of new types of classification. Neither does it assert that each market practice represents only a single type of market manipulation. A perpetrator may devise a manipulative scheme that characterise one or more types of market manipulation. A cross-market manipulation may also include a gaming of market rules or directly exploit price relations through abusing congestion levels at transmission lines. The demarcation this chapter provides aims to illustrate and characterise market tools and conditions that perpetrators use in devising their manipulative schemes. Therefore, the classifications provided should not be read in an exclusive manner.

[1] Market Power Manipulation

The chapter identifies that the cases in which perpetrators engaged in market power manipulation involved petroleum products rather than electricity and natural gas. There are physical characteristics that render such products not susceptible to market power manipulation. It is not feasible for the perpetrators to hold substantial amounts of deliverable supply available in the market for these products. While electricity cannot be physically stored in great quantities, storage of natural gas generally functions for balancing purposes rather than for long-term usage. Therefore the cases in which the perpetrators manipulated prices through using market power involved petroleum products such as crude oil and heating oil, which require relatively low capital intensive investments for storage and transportation. For outright fraud, the chapter provides *Deutsche Bank* in which the defendant engaged in circular scheduling practice as an example of how market participants can manipulate energy markets through fictitious trades. There are numerous ways through which market participants can manipulate prices, such as disseminating false information in markets or false reporting to indexes, which operate as fraud and deception over other market players. The underlying factor that the chapter deems important for the determination of such practices as a different type of market manipulation is the fact that they involve no actual trades or real economic risks, in contrast to open market transactions.

755. Craig Pirrong, 947 (1994).
756. Manipulation is a 'term' that 'refers generally to practices, such as wash sales, matched orders, or rigged prices, that are intended to mislead investors by artificially affecting market activity'. *See Santa Fe Indus. Inc. v. Green*, 430 U.S. 462, 476 (1977). *See also Ernst & Ernst v. Hochfelder*, 425 U.S. 185, 199 (1976).
757. *See SEC v. Cavanagh, et al.*, 98 Civ. 1818 (DLC) (S.D.N.Y. 1999).
758. 17 C.F.R. § 240.10b-5 (2011).

[2] *Trade-Based Manipulation*

[a] *Overview*

The classification of trade-based market manipulation as a different type is relatively new due to the difficulties faced by the CFTC in bringing anti-manipulation claims against market participants without market power and has been contentious in the academic literature. While some commentators address trade-based manipulation under market power manipulation,[759] others consider it as a distinct market practice differentiating it from market power manipulation and outright fraud.[760] Some commentators even recommend the regulatory agencies to refrain from prohibiting trade-based manipulation due to the difficulties in separating legitimate market practices from manipulative conduct.[761] Trade-based market manipulation is generally identified as market behaviour that is not characterised as market power manipulation in which perpetrators corner markets accumulating large positions that amount to market power and outright fraud where prices are manipulated through fictitious trades, dissemination of false information or false reporting practices. However, the chapter reveals that perpetrators employ a diverse range of trading strategies for manipulating markets and prices. Each of these manipulative schemes devised by the perpetrators involves different underlying factors and physical and financial positions.

[b] *Gaming of Market Rules*

First, the chapter identifies that the perpetrators manipulate markets through gaming the market rules. Energy markets operate on the basis of several market rules, called tariffs, governing sale and purchase transactions, the transmission of energy products and establishing capacity and balancing mechanisms. In these markets, market operators establish numerous payment options to compensate financial losses incurred by market participants as a result of using transmission systems or provide incentives to direct market participants to behave in a certain way. In *Rumford Paper Company*, for example, the perpetrator sought to manipulate the DALRP system which was designed to steer market participants towards reducing their loads during peak hours.[762] In both *J.P. Morgan Ventures Energy Cooperation*[763] and *Coaltrain Energy L.P. et al.*,[764] the relevant manipulative schemes aimed at exploiting payment mechanisms, respectively make-whole and MLSA payments which were designed to compensate market participants' losses during the use of transmission grids. It is important to note that these manipulative practices involve a trading activity, that is, they are plausible

759. Craig Pirrong, 945 (1994).
760. Franklin Allen & Douglas Gale, 529 (1992).
761. *See*, e.g., Daniel R. Fischel & David J. Ross (1991); Albert S. Kyle & S. Viswanathan (2008); George A. Davidson, *Squeezes and Corners: A Structural Approach* 40 Business Law 1283 (1985).
762. *Rumford Paper Company*, 140 FERC ¶ 61,030 (2012).
763. *In Re Make-Whole Payments and Related Bidding Strategies*, 144 FERC ¶ 61,068 (2013).
764. *Coaltrain Energy, L.P., et al.*, 154 FERC ¶ 61,002 (2016).

only with a counterparty entering into a transaction with the perpetrators, distinguishing these types of market manipulation from certain outright fraud claims in which market participants do not need a counterparty for the perpetration of manipulative scheme. It is irrelevant whether counterparties also share or are aware of the perpetrators' manipulative intent.[765]

[c] *Cross-Market Manipulation*

Exploiting the price relations between different markets and products is identified as the second type of trade-based manipulation, cross-market manipulation. In these manipulative strategies, the market participants who often operate specific trading desks which oversee the trade of physical and financial energy products in wholesale energy markets, engage in price-making transactions mostly in physical markets that affect the profitability of their positions in other physical or financial markets. There are three important elements the regulatory agencies refer to in establishing the perpetrators' manipulative intent. First the regulatory agencies identify the uneconomic nature of the price-making transactions meaning that they are loss incurring and self-defeating on a stand-alone basis, without taking into account the positions the value of which is tied to price movements that occur as a result of uneconomic trading activities. The chapter provides several scenarios of trading activities that distinguish legitimate trading strategies from manipulative practices.

Second, the perpetrators strategically place their bids and offers so that they create a price trend followed by other market participants increasing the impact on prices. Finally, the perpetrators engaging in cross-market manipulation accumulate large trading positions which account for exceeding 50% and in some cases reaching 100% of the trading activity during the relevant periods to give effect to their price-making strategies. As mentioned above, it is established in case law that the holding of market power is not a prerequisite for the perpetration of market manipulation. However, case law also indicates that the accumulation of large positions and market power is important to obtain the derived price impact, even though such positions are on a temporary basis.

[d] *Congestion-Related Manipulation*

The final type of trade-based market manipulation the chapter identifies is congestion-related market manipulation in which the perpetrators engage in market practices to derive profits from FTRs in relation to congestion occurring in the transmission systems. These market practices seem identical to cross-market manipulative schemes as both involve market conduct in physical energy markets affecting profitability of positions in other financial and/or physical positions. In cross-market manipulation,

765. US anti-manipulation law does not distinguish manipulative practices on the basis on their unilateral or collusive nature. However such differentiation is of great importance in the legal analysis under antitrust rules. The issue of manipulative behaviour as a collusion or abuse of market power is discussed in Chapter 4.

the perpetrators engage in physical transactions that affect index or settlement prices for the underlying physical product and determine the profitability of financial and/or physical positions in relation to the price movements in index and settlement prices. In congestion-related manipulation, the perpetrators engage in transactions that affect congestion levels at the transmission system determining the profitability of their related FTRs.

An important feature that distinguishes congestion-related practices from cross-market manipulation is that in the former case, the FTRs that perpetrators can accumulate are limited to the amount that market operators issue for congestion purposes.[766] In cross-market manipulation, the perpetrators can engage in financial transactions as long as a counterparty is present. It is also important to note that congestion-related market manipulation is intrinsic to the energy markets as these markets are network-based industries meaning that the functioning of markets is dependent on the availability of fixed infrastructure and capacity. Cross-market manipulation, on the other hand, can be perpetrated in other commodity or securities markets. Therefore, the chapter identifies congestion–related manipulative practices as a different type of market manipulation specific to energy markets.

Market manipulation has several adverse consequences for competitive wholesale energy markets. These market practices undermine the credibility of certain mechanisms and price benchmarks that are necessary for the functioning of trading in energy products. Price signals in manipulated markets do not stimulate market forces on the basis of aggregated demand and supply levels. Market participants who engage in buying and selling in energy products are harmed due to manipulated prices. While producers are harmed selling at lower prices due to downwards pressure on prices by short selling practices, consumers suffer from higher prices as a result of buying at higher prices creating an artificial upward movement in prices. Prevention and mitigation of such adverse effects are the main objectives of anti-manipulation law. However, neither regulatory agencies nor academic literature have agreed upon a common approach in defining and prosecuting market manipulation.

[D] Convergence of Approaches

The current regulatory practice for the prosecution of market manipulation is based on the SEA's rule Section 10(b), as both FERC and the CFTC after Dodd-Frank adopted the SEC's precedence on market manipulation. The US Supreme Court has continuously noted that the concepts of fraud in common-law and Section 10(b) are different, which results in ambiguities as to the definition of fraud under anti-manipulation.[767] FERC identifies all types of market practices that distort the functioning of energy markets as fraud. Such a catch-all interpretation of fraud can be vulnerable to judicial rejection as where the CFTC fell victim in *US v. Radley*. Therefore an extensive economic analysis that takes into account not only price-making activities but also price-taking positions

766. Petri Mantysaari, 610 (2015).
767. Jerry Markham, 379 (2015).

that perpetrators derive their profits from, is vital in understanding the pricing relations the perpetrators exploit as well as the characteristics of manipulative practices that the perpetrators employ. The demarcation of market manipulation on the basis of such an economic analysis will facilitate the development of appropriate definitions for different types of manipulative practices and provide legal tools for the enforcement of anti-manipulation rules.

Despite controversies between artificial price-based and fraud-based anti-manipulation rules, US case law on energy market manipulation provides significant implications as to manipulative practices perpetrated in energy markets, which are fundamental in understanding the types of practices that are prohibited under REMIT's anti-manipulation rules. Undertakings can devise several plans that can circumvent loopholes in market rules, exploit pricing relations between different products, congest transmission lines to earn profits, and deceive other participants as to market conditions or the true value of certain products. Some types of manipulation, such as market power manipulation, that are common in other commodities, (e.g., oil) are not the case for electricity and natural gas markets, while other types of practices such as congestion-related manipulation constitute energy-specific manipulative schemes. The next chapter discusses the implications of US case law on the enforcement of REMIT's anti-manipulation regulations in EU wholesale energy markets. It also takes into account differences between US and EU energy markets, such as capacity withholding activities which was addressed as a major type of market manipulation in the EU, while, in the US, is considered a mere exercise of market power.

CHAPTER 4

Manipulation of EU Energy Markets: Experience and Prospects

§4.01 INTRODUCTION

Compared to the US, case law on market manipulation in the EU is far from being complete. The only case that has resulted in a penalty for finding of a breach under REMIT's anti-manipulation rule was brought against Iberdrola, a major electricity producer in Spain.[768] As will be discussed, herein below, in greater detail, the case involved a capacity withholding activity, through which the perpetrator sought to increase electricity prices in the wholesale markets. The SCA concluded that this type of market activity was in violation of REMIT's anti-manipulation rule and imposed a fine of EUR 25 million for the violation.[769]

Even though the case constituted the first instance in which the anti-manipulation regime set out under REMIT was enforced, capacity withholding activities have long been subject to investigations by national competent regulators and competition authorities as violations of competition law. There have been several cases and investigations at both national and EU levels that have involved alleged capacity withholding practices by one or multiple electricity generating companies in order to increase prices in wholesale electricity markets. In fact, the SCA itself has regularly dealt with this type of activity since the early 2000s, long before the adoption of REMIT.[770]

768. First Economic Sanctions for REMIT Breaches in Europe, (Lexology, 16 Feb. 2016), http://www.lexology.com/library/detail.aspx?g=66b554d0-514c-40b3-b4fb-67374a43b111 (accessed 29 Jun. 2017).

769. ACER, REMIT Quarterly Issue No 4, Q4 2015, Ljubljana, https://www.acer-remit.eu/portal/remit-quarterly-doc (accessed 29 Jun. 2017).

770. *Resolución del Tribunal de Defensa de la Competencia del Expediente 552/02 EMPRESAS ELÉCTRICAS, de 7 de julio de 2004.*

Prior to the adoption of REMIT, competition authorities at both national and EU levels investigated capacity withholding activities as violations of Articles 101 and 102 of TFEU. At national level, the investigations were generally carried out in close cooperation with national energy regulators providing significant market data in furtherance of the identification and the prosecution of these activities.[771] At EU level, the Commission also engaged in similar investigations and addressed concerns about their effects on the competitiveness of European wholesale energy markets.[772] The Commission's conclusions therein and its findings in the Energy Sector Inquiry of 2007[773] and subsequent consultation documents including the advice document by CESR and ERGEG[774] in 2008 and the impact assessment by the Commission in 2010,[775] together paved the way for the adoption of REMIT in 2011. Similar concerns were also included in merger cases in which the Commission addressed economic incentives that merging undertakings could hold as to capacity withholding practices.[776] These merger cases will not be included in the case law analysis below as they do not provide any allegations in relation to violations of Article 101 or 102 TFEU.

It is important to note that, even though capacity withholding practices constituted a major concern in the formulation of the new sector-specific regulations,[777] REMIT's market manipulation prohibition adopted a far-reaching definition for market manipulation prohibition which was designed to address a wide spectrum of market conduct.[778] This was confirmed later by ACER providing that certain types of market practices such as wash trades, marking the close and dissemination of false or misleading market information, are also regarded as violations subject to REMIT's anti-manipulation provision.[779] The case law on the application of REMIT's market manipulation prohibition to these market practices has not yet developed, as the extensive monitoring practices of wholesale energy markets by national competent authorities has only started as recently as 2016. In this regard, the analysis provided under US case law is fundamental in identifying the spectrum of market practices that anti-manipulation rules under REMIT are adopted to deal with.

This chapter first discusses the case law on capacity withholding practices by market participants at national and EU levels, involving both the pre- and post-REMIT eras. It initially evaluates case law on capacity withholding under competition law to provide an insight into how market participants increase their profits by reducing their output. Next, the study explores how a similar market practice was prosecuted as

771. John Ratliff & Roberto Grasso, *Unilateral Conduct in the Energy Sector: An Overview of EU and National Case Law* 44203 (E-Competitions 2012). http://www.oiguskantsler.ee/sites/default/files/IMCE/unilateral_conduct_in_the_energy_sector_-_an_overview_of_eu_and_national_case_law.pdf (accessed 29 Jun. 2017).
772. *German Electricity Wholesale Market* (COMP/39.388) Commission Decision [2008] OJ C36/8.
773. *Supra* note 20.
774. *Supra* note 21.
775. *Supra* note 22.
776. *EDF/British Energy* (COMP/M.5224) Commission Decision [2008] OJ C288/5; *EDF/Segebel* (COMP/M.5549) Commission Decision [2009] OJ C235/26.
777. CESR and ERGEG, 26 (2008).
778. Recitals 13 and 14, Regulation No 1227/2011.
779. ACER's Guidance, 36–40 (2016).

market manipulation under REMIT. The legal analysis this section provides is fundamental in identifying the implications of this new sector-specific framework on the prosecution of capacity withholding practices in European energy markets.

As discussed in Chapter 3, capacity withholding practices were also under legal and regulatory scrutiny in the US. Due to the approach FERC has taken to these practices, the book incorporates US case law on capacity withholding into this chapter to identify differences and similarities between the legal approaches taken by EU and US authorities. Finally, following the demarcation that US case law provides, this section discusses the implications of REMIT for manipulative practices other than capacity withholding.

§4.02 CAPACITY WITHHOLDING

[A] Overview

The Energy Sector Inquiry of 2007 specifically found that manipulation of wholesale electricity prices by electricity producers who withheld part of their generation capacity constituted a significant factor for high energy prices in the EU.[780] The findings of the Sector Inquiry were later cited by CESR and ERGEG in their consultation paper which provided a proposal for the establishment of a tailor-made market abuse framework for the European energy sector including contracts relating to supply and transmission of energy products.[781] In its impact assessment document,[782] the Commission stressed that the proposed tailor-made legal framework should establish effective mechanisms for the prevention and the prosecution of capacity withholding practices in wholesale energy markets. Therefore, it comes as no surprise to see that, the first case in which the anti-manipulation regime under REMIT was applied involved capacity withholding practices by electricity generators, rather than other types of market manipulation.

There are two types of capacity withholding practices.[783] First, electricity producers can withhold their capacity physically by reducing their output through, for example, scheduled or unscheduled maintenance periods for generating plants. In liberalised energy markets, the availability of generation facilities for short-term energy supply has a tremendous impact on energy prices for relevant wholesale markets.[784] Even though the liberalisation packages did not include a specific requirement for the structure of national wholesale markets, a continuous harmonisation process has resulted in the adoption of pool market models in all Member States, which are called energy-only markets.[785] In these markets, electricity is only procured for day-ahead or intraday supply through auctions in which electricity producers and other suppliers place bids and offers for either selling or buying electricity products. Transmission

780. The Inquiry, 150.
781. CESR and ERGEG, 26 (2008).
782. REMIT Impact Assessment, 4 (2010).
783. The Inquiry, 132–133.
784. *Ibid.*, 112–113.
785. *Supra* note 11.

system operators or market operators, depending on the level of market liberalisation and design, oversee demand and supply levels, procuring or removing capacity to keep the transmission system balanced. In so doing, transmission system operators and market operators determine price levels for electricity by identifying a single market price at which bids and offers for demand and supply during the auctions intersect, that is, paid for all energy produced and supplied for that particular hour.[786]

Each producer prices its output based on marginal operational costs of its generation plants.[787] The operational cost for each power plant differs on the basis of several factors such as the fuel type that is used for generation and the technology of the power plant. While low-margin power plants operate as a baseload generation producing electricity continuously, high-margin power plants operate only during the peak-demand periods when the demand for electricity reaches its highest levels. Therefore, during the peak-demand periods, electricity prices become more expensive. Knowing or correctly estimating demand and supply levels for peak-demand hours, producers have an incentive to physically withdraw their capacity especially in the baseload power plants, so that higher margin power plants can be called in to supply the necessary demand, which drives the price of electricity to higher levels where bids and offers for energy intersect.[788]

Second, electricity producers can withhold their capacity economically by simply raising the price of their energy over a competitive level.[789] Even though marginal operational costs of generation plants are low, producers bid in wholesale energy markets asking higher prices for their energy with the expectation that the market operator or transmission system operator would have to pick up their generation due to their pivotal position or the generation from other market players who have asked lower prices for their generation, which are still higher than the actual marginal cost of the former generation plants. In both physical and economic capacity withholding practices, bids and offers for electricity demand and supply intersect at higher price levels and thus increase the single marginal price that is determined by market operators or transmission system operators. Since the price where bids and offers intersect will be the market price for electricity and paid to all supplying market participants, every supplier whose generation is picked up by the market operator and transmission operator will benefit from higher prices, which gives rise to concerns about collusion and abuse of collective market power among electricity producers to fix wholesale electricity prices. These concerns are further elevated due to the characteristics of the European wholesale energy markets which still suffer high concentration,

786. David Newbery, *Missing Money and Missing Markets: Reliability, Capacity Auctions and Interconnectors* 5 (Cambridge University Energy Policy Research Group 2015).
787. David Newbery, et al., *A Review of the Monitoring of Market Power The Possible Roles of TSOs in Monitoring for Market Power Issues in Congested Transmission Systems* 30 (ENTSO 2004); Jens Perner & Christoph Riechmann, *Energy Market Design with Capacity Mechanisms*, in Leigh Hancher, Adrien De Hauteclocque & Malgorzata Sadowska (eds), *Capacity Mechanisms in the EU Energy Market: Law, Policy, and Economics* 59, 61–62 (OUP 2015).
788. David Newbery, et al., *A Review of the Monitoring of Market Power The Possible Roles of TSOs in Monitoring for Market Power Issues in Congested Transmission Systems* 11 (ENTSO 2004).
789. The Inquiry, 133.

low liquidity levels and vertical integration in the majority of national wholesale markets with very limited cross-border interconnection.

As mentioned above capacity withholding has been a major concern in European wholesale energy markets and was constantly cited by EU institutions in identifying the need for a tailor-made legal framework. Before the adoption of REMIT, such conduct was primarily subjected to proceedings under EU competition law. Even though the new market abuse regime under REMIT was provided by the Commission as complementary rather than an alternative to EU competition law, the legal literature and national competent authorities regarded the new market abuse regime and market manipulation prohibition, in particular, as necessary to effectively prosecute capacity withholding activities,[790] since the legal tools that EU competition law had to deal with such conduct were not efficient. An extensive analysis of EU case law involving both pre- and post-REMIT prosecution of capacity withholding activities is important in understanding the legal implications of the new market abuse regime under REMIT and its interplay with EU competition law.

[B] Case Law on Capacity Withholding Before REMIT

Prior to the adoption of REMIT, capacity withholding practices were investigated at both EU and national levels. At EU level, the Commission considered these practices as a violation of Article 102 of TFEU, the prohibition of abuse of dominance. *German Wholesale Energy Market*[791] constitutes the only case in which the Commission investigated a capacity withholding practice as a possible violation of Article 102 of TFEU. The case was resolved with a commitment decision[792] according to which the defendant agreed to relinquish its assets in a number of generation plants and to reduce its overall market share in wholesale energy markets. At national level, allegations of capacity withholding as violations of Articles 101 and 102 had been made in several Member States, such as Belgium, Denmark, Italy, and Spain. In this section, the chapter first discusses the Commission's prosecution of capacity withholding at EU level, followed by an analysis of enforcement activities by national competent authorities.

[1] EU Level

[a] German Wholesale Energy Market

This case involved the Commission's allegation that E.ON abused its dominant position in the wholesale energy market for electricity in Germany within the concept of Article 102 TFEU by withdrawing some of its available generation to raise prices to the

790. Adrien de Hauteclocque & Malgorzata Sadowska, *Antitrust Law; A Missing Piece in a Regulatory Puzzle?* in Leigh Hancher, Adrien De Hauteclocque & Malgorzata Sadowska (eds), *Capacity Mechanisms in the EU Energy Market: Law, Policy, and Economics* 193–196 (OUP 2015).
791. *German Electricity Wholesale Market* (COMP/39.388) Commission Decision [2008] OJ C36/8.
792. Article 9, Regulation 1/2003.

detriment of consumers. The Commission identified the relevant product market as the wholesale market for electricity including imports and generation of electricity for further sale.[793] The relevant market assessment did not differentiate between short-term and long-term supply or the contracts that are traded either bilaterally or at spot-trading markets. Accordingly, the analysis of relevant markets encompassed all electricity traded at the wholesale level, considering that each contract for sale of electricity such as day-ahead, intraday, weekly, monthly, and longer-term contracts were interchangeable from the demand side and thus substitutable. As to the geographic market, the Commission identified that it was limited to the territory of Germany due to low levels of interconnection between Germany and its neighbouring states.[794] Competitive pressure imposed by imports remained insignificant.

According to the Commission, the German electricity wholesale market was dominated by three companies; RWE, E.ON and Vattenfall, whose market share together reached 67% of total generation capacity.[795] Their control over cheap, baseload power generation was even more dominant, as their market share accounted for 77% of total cheap generation capacity in Germany.[796] Potential competitors were prevented due to the high entry costs intrinsic in the energy sector as introducing additional supplies requires capital intensive projects such as building new generation plants to produce electricity or new transmission lines to bring supplies from neighbouring countries. Along with their vertical integration operating both at supply and transmission levels, these companies enjoyed significant control over conditions and prices in the German wholesale market.

In the German spot market for wholesale supply of energy, each generation unit had different marginal costs determining the price levels of their bids in the market. The difference between cheap and expensive generation units sometimes reached sevenfold.[797] Accordingly, cheap production units operated as baseload suppliers that run twenty-four hours of a day, while expensive units were only picked up when demand for electricity increased, especially during peak hours. The alignment of generation plants on the basis of their marginal operational costs was called 'merit order'. The Commission referred to the 2007 Energy Sector Inquiry to illustrate the determination of market price on the basis of the interplay between the merit order of generation plants with the demand and supply curve, as shown in Figure 4.1.

793. *German Electricity Wholesale Market* (COMP/39.388) Commission Decision [2008] OJ C36/8, para. 11.
794. *Ibid.*, para. 12.
795. *Ibid.*, Table 1.
796. *Ibid.*, para. 15.
797. *Ibid.*, para. 35.

Figure 4.1 The Clearing Price for Electricity Before Withholding[798]

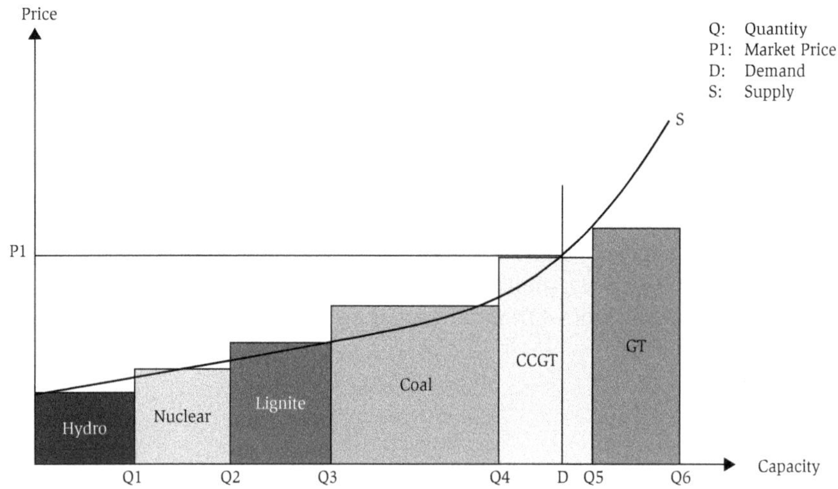

As mentioned, in short-term wholesale energy markets, the market operators or transmission system operators identify a single marginal price where the bids and offers intersect. This price corresponds to the marginal operational cost of the last generation plants picked up to supply demand. According to the illustration above, this price will be the marginal operational cost of the Combined Cycle Gas Turbine (CCGT), where demand for electricity intersects with available supply. This price is designated as the market clearing price which is paid to all electricity generators supplying power to the electricity grid for a specific supply period, which are, as the illustration above shows, hydro, nuclear, lignite, coal and CCGT power plants. Accordingly the Gas Turbines (the GTs) are not selected by transmission system operators or market operators and thus are outside the merit order. High electricity prices are not only a benefit to the last generation unit called by the market operator or transmission system operator. All electricity generators that stand at the left of the demand curve benefit from high electricity prices.

Identifying the shifts in the average marginal costs during January 2003, January 2004, January 2005 and December 2005, the Commission used a comparison between merit order curves of all plants greater than 25 MW operated by companies using a generation portfolio higher than 100 MW.[799] It was found that certain generation plants of E.ON did not operate at their full capacity and withdrew part of their generation capacity to increase electricity prices during the investigated time period between 2002 and 2007. Due to the withholding of cheaper generation plants, the German market operator sought more expensive generation units to supply demand for each hour.

798. The Inquiry, Figure 40, 123.
799. *German Electricity Wholesale Market* (COMP/39.388) Commission Decision [2008] OJ C36/8, para. 32.

The capacity withholding activity allegedly engaged in by E.ON can be simply illustrated through the Figures 4.2 and 4.3. As a dominant undertaking who owns a portfolio of generation assets, E.ON operates several generation plants including hydro, nuclear, coal, and CCGT. A certain amount of capacity withdrawal from any of these generation plants (say, coal) may result in the German market operator seeking additional supplies from more expensive generation plants such as gas turbines (GTs) which determine the market price for electricity for that particular hour as the last picked generation facility. All generation plants that remained to the left of the demand curve received this new price determined on the marginal operational cost of GT and thus would benefit from capacity withholding. E.ON lost profits it could have made, if it had operated the relevant plants. However, holding a dominant market position and assets from a portfolio of generation plants, E.ON compensated these losses through its remaining plants which profited from the higher electricity price.

Figure 4.2 The Effect of Withholding on Generation Portfolio

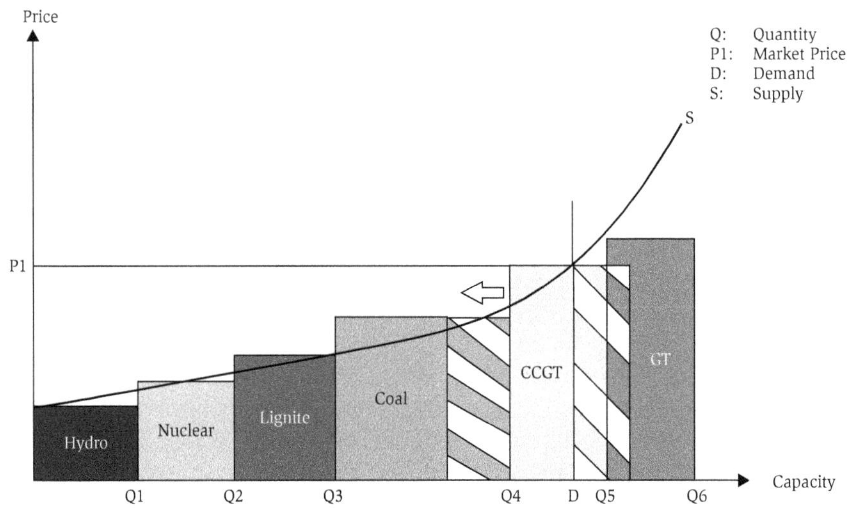

Figure 4.3 The Clearing Price for Electricity after Withholding[800]

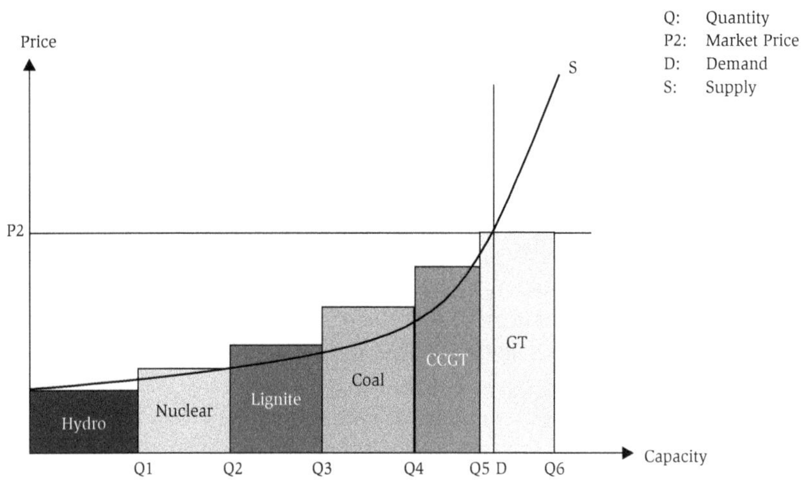

The Commission also noted that further profits could be derived from the long-term effects of artificially increased electricity prices.[801] A continuous practice of capacity withholding for a longer time period can be reflected by prices in long-term and forward contracts which generally follow the price trends in short-term wholesale electricity contracts. A seller in a long-term electricity contract may have a financial incentive to withhold its generation in short-term markets irrespective of whether its losses are subsidised by the profits derived from the remaining power plants. Conduct exploiting pricing relations between short-term and long-term electricity markets has more of the character of cross-market manipulation which will be discussed in greater detail later in the chapter. However, this two-pronged approach by the Commission to E.ON's allegedly manipulative conduct clearly demonstrates that an analysis of market manipulation requires monitoring of differing positions that can be exploited by market participants through a single manipulative conduct.

It is important to note the case did not result in an infringement decision by the Commission against E.ON. This is in line with the policy the Commission seeks in issuing Commitment Decisions under Article 9 of Regulation 1/2003[802] according to which, it avoids exercising extensive legal analyses of relevant markets, dominant positions and decisions of abuse. The Commission has refrained from holding E.ON liable in exchange for some commitments including divestiture of certain generation

800. *See* Malgorzata Sadowska, *Committed to Reform? Pragmatic Antitrust Enforcement in Electricity Markets* 146–149 (PhD Thesis, EDLE 2013).
801. *German Electricity Wholesale Market* (COMP/39.388) Commission Decision [2008] OJ C36/8, para. 38.
802. Recital 13, Council Regulation (EC) No 1/2003 of 16.12.2002 on the implementation of the rules on competition laid down in Articles 81 and 82 of the Treaty [2003] OJ L 1/1.

plants.[803] It did not provide a detailed legal and economic analysis on withholding activities in relation to price increases in the wholesale electricity prices. Instead, it preferred to reiterate the findings of the 2007 Energy Sector Inquiry without going into details of the market data. Even though alleging that E.ON was collectively dominant with RWE and Vattenfall, the Commission held only E.ON responsible for the conduct and left open the question of other companies' contribution.[804] Establishing a dominant position based on the calculation of a joint market share stemmed from the concern that the sole market share held by E.ON only accounted for 20%–30% of total capacity.[805] According to the Commission guidance on abuse of dominance, this does not suffice for the Commission to find it a dominant position.[806]

The Commission's analysis in this case does not provide clear guidance on the prosecution of capacity withholding practices in EU competition law. Several concerns were raised by some commentators[807] as to the effectiveness of divestiture measures, adopted as a remedy for the contested behaviour. It was asserted that the types of generation plants that the defendant was obliged to discard from its generation portfolio did not affect its ability to increase single marginal prices through capacity withholding.[808] Nevertheless, the case is of particular importance as it represents the first attempt by the Commission to deal with capacity withholding practices as an infringement of EU competition law.

[2] ***National Level***

[a] Electrabel *(Belgium)*

This case involved a 2014 decision by the Belgian Competition Authority (the BCA) which rejected claims that Electrabel, the largest electricity supplier in Belgium, abused its dominance in Belgian generation, wholesale and trading market by withholding its generation capacity and submitting purchase orders at very high prices on Belpex, the Belgian Electricity Spot Market.[809] The allegations originated from a report by the Belgian Energy Markets Regulator (the CREG) in 2009[810] which identified that the abnormal increase in electricity prices from EUR 50/MWh to EUR 2,500/MWh between

803. *German Electricity Wholesale Market* (COMP/39.388) Commission Decision [2008] OJ C36/8, paras 59–75.
804. *Ibid.*, para. 24.
805. *Ibid.*, Table 1.
806. Communication from the Commission, Guidance on the Commission's Enforcement Priorities in Applying Article 82 of the EC Treaty to Abusive Exclusionary Conduct by Dominant Undertakings [2009] OJ C45/2, para. 14.
807. Malgorzata Sadowska, *Committed to Reform? Pragmatic Antitrust Enforcement in Electricity Markets* (PhD Thesis, EDLE 2013).
808. *Ibid.*, 137.
809. Marc Martens & Peter Willis, *Electrabel Decision Outlines Application of Competition Rules to Withholding Capacity and Electricity Pricing* (Bird&Bird 29 Aug. 2014) https://www.twobirds.com/en/news/articles/2014/belgium/electrabel-decision-outlines-application-of-competition-rules-to-withholding (accessed 29 Jun. 2017).
810. CREG, *'Etude* 860 *relative aux comportements sur le marché de gros de l'électricité en Belgique durant* 2007 *et les six premiers mois de* 2008*', du 7 mai,* 2009.

2007 and 2008 might account for a possible manipulation of electricity prices by Electrabel.[811] In close cooperation with the CREG, the investigatory body of the BCA, provided an analysis of electricity prices in the relevant period concluding that Electrabel committed two types of conduct in violation of Article IV.2 of the Code of Economic Law and Article 102 of TFEU.[812] First, Electrabel was alleged to withhold part of its electricity generation from Belpex resulting in increases in electricity prices between 2007 and 2008. Second, the investigatory body asserted that Electrabel engaged in fictitious sales and double use of tertiary services which is a type of balancing service generators provide by reserving a part of their generation capacity for the grid operator to be called upon at short notice to relieve system imbalances.

The Competition College, the decision-making body of the BCA, rejected the investigatory body's allegation of capacity withholding, while approving the finding of abusive use of tertiary services.[813] Electrabel claimed that it did not hold a dominant position in the Belpex electricity spot market as it was a price-taking market participant which lacks a pivotal position in electricity generation in Belpex's DAM.[814] Rejecting Electrabel's claim, the College held that even though Electrabel was not in a pivotal position in the Belpex DAM, the liquidity levels in the market and the positions held in downstream markets were sufficient to conclude that Electrabel was a dominant market player in the Belgian wholesale electricity market.[815] The College found that Electrabel's withholding of generation capacity did not constitute an abuse of dominance, focusing first on the intent of Electrabel. Accordingly, during the contested period, withholding of generation capacity was not a clear-cut violation of competition law, as the case law lacked clear precedents on such conduct.[816] Furthermore, the College provided that Electrabel had a legitimate reason in withholding its capacity, keeping the withheld capacity as a reserve for the risk that it would have to pay penalties as a result of its balancing requirements.[817] The objective sought by Electrabel in withholding generation capacity was to secure its positions in the balancing market

811. Peter Willis, *Belgian Competition Authority Prosecutor Accuses Electrabel of Abuse of Dominance* (Bird&Bird 13 Feb. 2013) https://www.twobirds.com/en/news/articles/2013/belgian-competition-accuses-electrabel-abuse-dominance0213 (accessed 29 Jun. 2017).

812. *Projet de décision du 29 novembre* 2013, *affaire* CONC-I/O-09/0015: *Marché de gros de l'électricité; see* Cleary Gottlieb, '*EU Competition Law Quarterly Report, Belgium*' (Q3, July-September, 2014) https://www.clearygottlieb.com/-/media/organize-archive/cgsh/files/publication-pdfs/cleary-gottlieb-national-competition-report-q3-2014.pdf (accessed 29 Jun. 2017).

813. Belgian Competition Authority, Press Release No 11/2014 (12 Nov. 2014) https://www.belgiancompetition.be/sites/default/files/content/download/files/20141112_press_release_11_bca.pdf (accessed 29 Jun. 2017).

814. Marc Martens & Peter Willis (2014).

815. *Ibid.*

816. Stibbe, *Belgian Competition Authority fined Electrabel EUR 2 Million for Abuse of a Dominant Position* (Lexology 1 Sept. 2014) http://www.lexology.com/library/detail.aspx?g=177531a1-f5f7-40fc-bcad-7e9930d23933 (accessed 29 Jun. 2017).

817. The majority of spot markets require each market participant to sign a balancing market requirements contract which grants transmission system operators to require market participants to provide additional power to, or reduce power from the transmission grid when it is identified that the demand in the upcoming hour would be higher or lower than the expected levels projected under the spot markets. *See* Petri Mantysaari, 535–539 (2015).

rather than to increase electricity prices in the Belgian wholesale market. Finally, the College identified that the capacity withheld constituted only around 1.1% of total capacity in the spot market and thus did not suffice to cause the alleged price effects.[818]

The College's referral to the intent of Electrabel and the dearth of legal precedent on the prosecution of capacity withholding activity under competition law are illustrative as to the ambiguity at national level on the application of EU competition law rules to the European energy markets. The analysis of intent in establishing anti-competitive conduct under EU case law is not decisive. According to the European Union Court of Justice (the CJEU):

> The concept of abuse is an objective concept relating to the behaviour of an undertaking in a dominant position which is such as to influence the structure of a market where, as a result of the very presence of the undertaking in question, the degree of competition is weakened and which, through recourse to methods different from those which condition normal competition in products or services on the basis of the transactions of commercial operators, has the effect of hindering the maintenance of the degree of competition still existing in the market or the growth of that competition.[819]

The finding of the CJEU indicates that the perpetrator's intent is irrelevant in establishing whether the contested conduct is anti-competitive.[820] However, this is not an established case law principle that is followed in every antitrust analysis.[821] The case law also provides that the finding of an anti-competitive object with respect to a contested conduct is sufficient for a finding of an Article 102 violation. In *Michelin II*, the General Court (GC) stated that *'establishing the anti-competitive object and the anti-competitive effect are one and the same thing'*.[822] A market conduct without anti-competitive effects can be regarded as an abuse of dominance on the basis of its perpetrator's intent.[823]

The College considered the intent element of the market conduct along with its extent in and effects on the Belgian wholesale electricity market. The withheld capacity accounted for only 1.1% of total capacity and thus was regarded as unappreciable. Concluding that the conduct had very limited anti-competitive effects on the market, the College went on to decide whether the object of withholding capacity was anti-competitive. On the basis of lack of clear precedent on this type of conduct as well as the possible existence of a legitimate reason, namely securing positions under the balancing market, the College answered this question negatively and decided that Electrabel did not abuse its dominant position in the Belgian wholesale electricity market.

818. Marc Martens & Peter Willis (2014).
819. Case 85/76 *Hoffmann-La Roche & Co AG v. EC Commission* [1979] ECR 461, 91.
820. Pinar Akman, *The Role of Intent in the EU Case Law on Abuse of Dominance* 316 European Law Review (2014).
821. *Ibid.*, 333.
822. Case T-203/01 *Michelin v. Commission* (Michelin II) [2003] ECR II-4071, 239; *See also* Case T-219/99 *British Airways plc v. Commission* [2003] ECR II-5917, 293; *AstraZeneca* (Case COMP/A.37.507/F3) Commission Decision [2006] OJ L332/24.
823. Pinar Akman, 333 (2014).

As illustrated in the Figures 4.2 and 4.3, the ability of a withholding practice to influence price results does not depend on the extent of electricity withheld. The economics of capacity withholding does not require a certain threshold as to the needed electricity. As long as transmission system operators are required to call in more expensive plants to supply demand as a result of capacity withholding, the extent of the withholding activity is irrelevant. The College's decision admits Electrabel's evidence providing that Electrabel did not hold a pivotal position in Belpex. How the College calculated the pivotality of Electrabel is an open question, as the 861-page decision is not open to the public.[824] However an extensive analysis of supply and demand levels during the designation of generating plants to supply the transmission grids is substantial in identifying the pivotal positions. The pivotal supplier index (PSI) and other instruments, that are fundamental tools to identify pivotal positions in wholesale energy markets, will be discussed in greater detail.

[b] *Italian Cases*

[i] *Edipower/Enel*

In 2010, the Italian Competition Authority (the ICA) issued two decisions, on the basis of Articles 101 and 102 TFEU, against Edipower and Enel due to their activities in Sicily in which they held, respectively, 26% and 45% market share.[825] Enel produced electricity through CCGTs and Gas Turbo (GT) plants, while Edipower had one oil plant that was generally operational during peak hours and was thus important in setting electricity prices. The case originated from a notice[826] by the Italian Energy Regulator which provided that the findings of its investigation on electricity prices in Sicily between November 2008 and January 2009 indicated a possible withdrawal in electricity generation capacity in Sicily, since neither the availability levels at the generation system nor the fluctuations in fuel costs sufficed to explain extremely high zone-based prices[827] experienced in Sicily between 2008 and 2009.

---

824. Marc Martens & Peter Willis (2014).
825. Alessandro Noce, *Abuse of Dominant Position by Energy Incumbents: The Italian Experience* (Athens June 2013) https://www.energy-community.org/pls/portal/docs/2106181.PDF (accessed 29 Jun. 2017).
826. Autorità Garante della Concorrenza e del Mercato, 'Press Release: Electricity Market: Antitrust Authority Accepts and Enforces the Commitments of the Main Energy Companies Active in the Sicily Macro Area' (Rome, January 2011) http://www.agcm.it/en/newsroom/press-releases/1924-i721-a423-edipower-tolling-and-enel-dynamics-in-the-setting-of-electricity-market-prices-in-sicily-closure-of-investigation.html (accessed 29 Jun. 2017).
827. Due to transmission constraints and congestion levels, there are multiple zones where electricity is priced differently across Italy. Accordingly, there are seven physical national zones in Italy; Calabria, Northern-Italy, Central-Northern Italy, Central-Southern Italy, Southern Italy, Sardinia and Sicily. *See* Angelica Gianfreda & Luigi Grossi, *Zonal Price Analysis of the Italian Wholesale Electricity Market* (EEM 2009 June 2009).

The ICA initiated two distinct proceedings against Edipower and Enel. With respect to Edipower, the ICA found that tollers[828] of Edipower's oil plant adopted a common strategy in submitting their bids to increase prices in the DAM for peak hours. The investigation identified that the tollers of Edipower colluded in their bidding activity to give effect to their economic withholding and to fix higher prices during peak hours when Edipower's oil plant was price-setting for the merit order of Sicilian wholesale electricity market. Therefore, the ICA held that the bidding activity carried out by the tollers of the Edipower's oil plant constituted a violation of Article 101 TFEU.[829]

As to Enel, the investigation, first, focused on the available generation capacity in its CCGT and GT power plants offered by Enel in the Italian day-ahead electricity market. Analysing the generation capacity that was declared to be available and that were actually offered in the DAM, the ICA found no physical withholding of generation capacity by Enel.[830] The investigation highlighted the problems in measuring the available capacity that could have been offered in the Italian DAM and the difference between the capacity declared and the capacity offered seemed to be explained by technical constraints in generation. The ICA held that the findings of the investigation did not support the existence of an illegitimate activity as the main reason for the reduction in the available capacity offered in the DAM.

The investigation later focused on Enel's bidding activity with respect to its CCGT and GT generation plants. The ICA found that during a small part of peak hours, Enel submitted prices for its CCGT plants which were up to three times higher than their variable costs.[831] The prices Enel offered for electricity produced from its GT power plants were also higher than those offered by its competitors, even though difference between their variable costs were not substantial. The ICA identified that the bids submitted by Enel for its CCGT and GT power plants accounted for economic capacity withholding raising electricity prices in day-ahead electricity markets and thus were in violation of Article 102 of TFEU.

[ii] *EGL/Repower/Tirreno Power*

The case involved a cartel of three generating plants which allocated the market and fixed prices for ancillary services in Central-Southern Italy.[832] On 14 June 2012, the ICA imposed fines on EGL, Repower, and Tirreno Power (the generators, hereinafter) which operated power plants in the area of Naples for engaging in a concerted practice

828. Tolling agreements in electricity markets allow firms to use the generation service of power plants. In these agreements, firms buy fuels for the generation plants and sell the output. In exchange, plant operators receive a fee for their production service.
829. John Ratliff & Roberto Grasso, 133 (2012).
830. Alessandro Noce (2013).
831. *Ibid.*
832. *Autorità Garante della Concorrenza e del Mercato*, 'Press Release: Electricity Market: investigation launched into Egl, Repower and Tirreno power concerning a possible service dispatch agreement' (Rome, October 2010) http://www.agcm.it/en/newsroom/press-releases/1831-i736-electricity-market-investigation-launched-into-egl-repower-and-tirreno-power-concerning-a-possible-service-dispatch-agreement.html (accessed 29 Jun. 2017).

in breach of Article 2 of Law 287/1990 Italian Competition Act and Article 101 of TFEU.[833] The concerted practice involved the allocation of the markets for providing balancing services on Sundays and during holidays in Naples from April to August 2010.[834] The relevant balancing service was the procurement of reserve resources for local voltage support.[835] After the DAMs and intraday markets closed, the Italian TSO Terna evaluated positions in electricity supply and demand and opened these markets to secure system balancing. The contested conduct involved manipulation of electricity prices for ancillary services markets in Central-Southern Italy in relation to the capacity withholding practices in DAMs and intraday markets.

In order to secure that their output was pivotal for the balancing of the system, the generators engaged in a concerted act of physical and economic withholding of their capacity in the DAM. Due to the geographic location of generation plants, and technical constraints in grids that supply electricity from markets other than central-southern Italy, the generators knew that they were the only market players which could provide balancing services for voltage support in the area of Naples. If these generators were not picked up in DAMs or intraday markets on Sundays and holidays, the only way for Terna to secure the system balance was to procure electricity from these generators under ancillary markets.[836]

Accordingly, from April to August 2010, the generators, in collusion, physically and economically withheld their generation from DAMs and intraday markets to create a demand for balancing services in ancillary markets.[837] The strategy continued with each generator rigging the bids for voltage support to ensure higher returns from their balancing services. In order for the functioning of the cartel, each generator consecutively won the auctions for balancing services during holidays. During the relevant period, the price of electricity procured in the ancillary markets on Sundays and holidays was more than two and half times the price of that traded in DAMs. The scheme was brought to an end after the withdrawal of EGL whose generation plant had twice the size of two other generators and thus had an incentive to leave the cartel.[838]

Even though the ICA was unable to identify direct evidence of collusion, the allocation and timing of the bidding practices were sufficient to infer the agreement between the generators in the ancillary markets. While the prices the generators offered in ancillary markets reached EUR 140 MW/h during the relevant period, their margins

833. *Autorità Garante della Concorrenza e del Mercato*, 'Press Release: Electricity market: Repower Italia, EGL Italia and Tirreno Power penalised for agreement restricting competition' (Rome, June 2012) http://www.agcm.it/en/newsroom/press-releases/2000-electricity-market-repower-italia-egl-italia-and-tirreno-power-penalised-for-agreement-restricting-competition.html (accessed 29 Jun. 2017).
834. Javier Ruiz Calzado, et al., *Energy and Restrictive Practices: An Overview of EU and National Case Law* (e-Competition Bulletin, N° 70451 December 2014) https://www.lw.com/thoughtLeadership/energy-and-restrictive-practices-eu-case-law (accessed 29 Jun. 2017).
835. Peter Willis & Simone Cadeddu, *Italian Ancillary Services Cartel Highlights Risks of Electricity Market Transparency* (Bird&Bird 24 Jul. 2012) https://www.twobirds.com/en/news/articles/2012/italian-ancillary-services-cartel-highlights-risks-of-electricity-market-transparency (accessed 29 Jun. 2017).
836. *Ibid.*
837. *Autorità Garante della Concorrenza e del Mercato* (2012).
838. Peter Willis & Simone Cadeddu (2012).

in the DAMs were nearly zero, meaning that they provided no or very limited amount of electricity in DAMs.[839] The ICA refuted the generators' allegation that the practice was a competitive adaptation between market players rather than an anti-competitive concerted practice, providing that the bidding practices and the allocation of auctions were instantaneously adjusted without a transition period.[840] Moreover the generators' activity during the relevant period was in stark contrast with that in 2009 when they had regularly offered their generation in the DAM. Withholding their output in DAMs in 2010 provided greater opportunities for greater returns from the sales in ancillary markets. The symmetry in the bidding strategies and the allocation of auctions between these generators could only be explained via a concerted practice designed to exploit Terna's obligation to provide system security. Exploiting the linkage between DAMs and ancillary markets, the generators rigged their bids in these markets to allocate these returns.

[iii] *Enel/Sorgenia*

On 6 October 2016, ICA announced that two energy companies, Enel and Sorgenia, were being investigated for a suspected abuse of dominance under Article 102 of TFEU.[841] The case originated from a notification from the Italian Energy Regulator who also informed ACER and initiated proceedings under REMIT against two power producers.[842] The investigation related to strategies of withholding by four units of a coal-fired power station operated by Enel and Sorgenia's CCGT which together supply power to Southern Italy. As in *EGL/Repower/Tirreno Power*, the ICA, here, also alleged that Enel and Sorgenia engaged in capacity withholding practices in DAMs with the expectation that their generation would provide greater revenues in ancillary services markets. However, the ICA did not provide any allegations of collusion between Enel and Sorgenia as it did in *EGL/Repower/Tirreno Power*. Rather, it investigated the contested conduct on the basis of Article 102 and asked whether Enel and Sorgenia abused their dominant position in the relevant markets.[843]

The contested market behaviours involved physical capacity withholding practices by Sorgenia and economic capacity withholding practices by Enel. The ICA identified that during the relevant time period, Sorgenia refrained from offering its output in the DAMs. Enel, on the other hand, submitted bids at prices higher than those it submitted in previous years. This resulted in either exclusion of its output from DAMs or when the submitted bids were picked up by the Italian transmission system

839. *Ibid.*
840. *Ibid.*
841. *Autorità Garante della Concorrenza e del Mercato, 'A498A-A498B - Aumento costi in bolletta, istruttoria Antitrust su Enel e Sorgenia' (Roma, ottobre* 2016), http://www.agcm.it/stampa/comunicati/8411-a498a-a498b-aumento-costi-in-bolletta,-istruttoria-antitrust-su-enel-e-sorgenia.html *cited in;* Peter Willis, *Italian Competition Authority Investigates Suspected Abuses in Italian Electricity Balancing Markets* (Bird & Bird 18 Oct. 2016) https://www.twobirds.com/en/news/articles/2016/italy/italian-competition-authority-investigates-suspected-abuses-in-italian-electricity-balancing-markets (accessed 29 Jun. 2017).
842. Peter Willis (2016).
843. *Ibid.*

operator, Terna, at the DAM, buying back the relevant bids at the intraday market so that the generation plants would only operate under the ancillary market to supply voltage support services. Given the limited output from these generation plants, Terna would be required to seek balancing services under ancillary markets. These generators reap greater returns from selling their output in these markets at prices higher that those paid in DAMs.

Reviewing the relevant markets, the ICA noted that ancillary services markets are distinct from wholesale electricity markets which consist of bilateral contracts and spot markets and distinguished further that ancillary services markets are also divided into two markets on the basis of their timeframes, an *ex ante* balancing market and a real-time balancing market.[844] While the former utilises Terna to procure electricity to resolve network constraints in each zone and to ensure the consistency of voltage levels, the latter allows Terna to monitor balancing between electricity supply and demand and to sustain reserves. The ICA identified that voltage support in Southern Italy, in the area of Brindisi, in particular, can only be supplied by a limited number of plants.[845] Apart from those owned by Sorgenia and Enel, a plant owned by EniPower can be called in for voltage support services. However, the findings in the announcement show that the generation plants owned by Sorgenia and Enel would still be pivotal, irrespective of the level at which EniPower's plant operated. Enel and Sorgenia are obligatory trading partners for Italian transmission operator Terna and thus held to be dominant in the relevant electricity markets.

Two price comparisons were provided to show the excessiveness of prices offered by Enel and Sorgenia.[846] The first comparison involves the difference between the prices offered by Enel and Sorgenia during the relevant period and the prices offered in past years for the same time period. Second, the ICA compared the prices paid in ancillary markets with those of the DAMs. The findings of the price analysis showed that there were dramatic price differences between those charged in the contested period and those in the past years and DAMs. The ICA noted that this close correlation between capacity withholding practices and the corresponding price changes provided strong evidence of the abuse of a dominant position.[847] The ICA's investigation continues.

The Italian Energy Regulator which notified the ICA as to the relevant bidding activity has also initiated a separate investigation of the same activities as to whether they constitute market manipulation under REMIT.[848] The Regulator had already proscribed the firms to stop their bidding activity and submitted the details of bidding practices to ACER and the European Commission.[849] The legal implications under these enforcement proceedings are discussed later in greater detail. However, this case is of particular importance as it represents the first instance in which the same market practices are being investigated by both an energy regulator and a competition

844. *Ibid.*
845. *Ibid.*
846. *Ibid.*
847. *Ibid.*
848. *Ibid.*
849. *Ibid.*

authority under, respectively, REMIT and competition law and the number of similar cases is likely to rise as a result of data reporting obligations arising from REMIT and the new European financial regulations.

[iv] *Endesa/Iberdrola/Union Fenosa/Hidrocantabrico*

In November 2001, the Spanish energy regulator submitted a report to the SCA involving findings of unusually high prices in the electricity DAM for a three-day period.[850] On the basis of the report, SCA opened a competition law investigation into the bidding practices of four electricity generating firms, Endesa, Iberdrola, Union Fenosa, and Hidrocantabrico.[851] In 2004, SCA concluded that these firms abused their dominant positions by exploiting weaknesses in the Spanish electricity market design[852] and distorted electricity prices in the Spanish wholesale electricity market once they were picked up to produce in certain regions that suffered congestion in transmission grids. Accordingly, a fine of EUR 901,520 was imposed on each firm.[853]

According to the findings of SCA, the firms identified expected supply shortages in the relevant geographic regions and submitted bids at high prices on certain days to ensure that their generation would not be selected by the Spanish transmission system operator on the Spanish DAM and thus economically withheld their generation capacity. On the basis of the data of the last twelve months of peak hour electricity prices, SCA stated that the prices submitted by the firms for the relevant three-day period far exceeded their variable costs and were considerably higher than those offered in previous years. Due to the system restrictions and congestion levels at the transmission grids, the transmission system operator was forced to seek supplies from these firms at these unusually high prices to balance demand and supply on the markets for technical restrictions, '*restricciones técnicas*'.[854] SCA identified that the firms were pivotal suppliers in the market for technical restrictions and thus were considered dominant. Even though the contested abuse took place in the DAMs, where the firms were not dominant, dominance in technical restrictions markets where the anti-competitive effects of the conduct took effect was sufficient for SCA to hold the firms responsible for the abuse of market dominance.[855]

850. OECD, Directorate for Financial and Enterprise Affairs Competition Committee, 'Annual Report in Competition Policy Developments in Spain 2004' [2015] DAF/COMP(2005)32/06, para. 30.
851. *Resolución del Tribunal de Defensa de la Competencia del Expediente* 552/02 *EMPRESAS ELÉCTRICAS, de* 7 *de julio de* 2004.
852. When the contested bidding practices occurred, the Spanish wholesale electricity market consisted of just one spot market in which participants placed their bids and offers just once. A separate spot market for balancing mechanisms was missing. *See* John Ratliff & Roberto Grasso, 151 (2012).
853. *Ibid.*, para. 152.
854. The markets which the transmission system operators established for acquiring balancing services are called different names in different states. In terms of their functioning and purpose, the market for technical restrictions in Spain is very much the same as the ancillary services market in Italy.
855. John Ratliff & Roberto Grasso, 153 (2012).

The SCA also found that the specific weaknesses in the Spanish wholesale electricity market design were critical in the development of bidding schemes as the auction process allowed the market participants to submit only 'one bid' for electricity supply on the DAM.[856] The bids submitted at high prices and thus not selected on the DAM were called in later for the markets for technical restrictions. The 'one bid' auction design was an important factor that created the opportunity for the firms to foresee when their supplies would be pivotal and the transmission system operator would be forced to resort to their supplies despite the high prices. In the following years, the 'one bid' system was changed into a 'dual bids' system which involves two different auction procedures for DAMs and the market for technical constraints. While the former continues to function as the main wholesale market in which the general demand and supply levels are calculated, the latter involves a separate auction session in which electricity producers bid for balancing services. In other words, the transmission system operator no longer calls in generators based on their bids at DAMs, but rather opens a new auction in which generators compete with each other, and submit bids to supply the market for technical restrictions. In this new auction design, the generators are no longer able to derive profits from the market for technical restrictions on the basis on their economic withholding activity in the DAM.

On 27 January 2010, the Spanish Supreme Court annulled SCA's decision, after an appeal by Union Fenosa, finding that the generators at issue did not commit a violation of competition law by their activities during the relevant three-day period in 2001.[857] According to the Court, SCA erred in finding an abuse of dominance based on sporadic practices in very limited and temporary market conditions. The firms' temporary pivotal position for a period of three days did not suffice to find that these market players were dominant in the wholesale energy markets. SCA should have considered the economic risk of being excluded from the market for technical restrictions as well. The firms did not know whether their bids were finally awarded by the transmission system operator in the market for technical restrictions. There could be other market participants whose bids were also not selected in the DAM but were called in later to the market for technical restrictions since their bids were lower than those submitted by the firms. Moreover, the Court also found SCA's finding of high prices as unlawful, noting that the determination of high prices based solely on a comparison with historical prices did not show that the bids submitted by the firms exceeded their average variable costs and thus were anti-competitive. According to the court, rather than an analysis of historical prices in the DAM, SCA should have focused on usual costs incurred by the firms in the market for technical restraints in determining whether or not the prices submitted by the firms were excessive.

The Supreme Court's decision is an important turning point for the prosecution of capacity withholding practices in wholesale energy markets under competition law. SCA, based on its findings in 2004, adopted similar decisions against several market

856. *Ibid.*, para. 151.

857. International Competition Network, *Case Annex to IC Unilateral Conduct Working Group: Report on the Analysis of Refusal to Deal with a Rival Under Unilateral Conduct Laws* 56 (Istanbul April 2010).

participants, imposing fines that have amounted to EUR 56.5 million.[858] SCA abandoned its investigations in September 2011, after the Court's annulment. The reasoning underlying the Supreme Court's decision shows that traditional tools in identifying dominance were insufficient to address market power concerns in wholesale energy markets. Calculation of market shares and concentration levels with broadly defined relevant markets did not provide market data that was necessary to detect the exercise of market power in electricity markets. Some commentators and regulators argued that the findings of the Supreme Court against SCA's decisions of capacity withholding along with its decision in a later REMIT case involving similar capacity withholding claims clearly illustrate that competition law is not a suitable forum for dealing with market abuse in energy markets.[859] Nevertheless, whether or not the formalistic approach in competition law is sufficient to deal with capacity withholding and whether or not competition law is a suitable forum to address abuse in energy markets are two distinct questions. It is reasonable to conclude that traditional competition law methodologies are insufficient to address the complexities of energy markets. The suitability of competition law, on the other hand, requires an evaluation of the legal and economic tools available for the assessment of market power in energy markets. These questions are discussed later in greater detail.

[C] Case Law on Capacity Withholding after REMIT

Data collection based on REMIT began in October 2015 for standardised contracts and in April 2016 for non-standardised contracts. Until then, investigations into market conduct for possible breaches of REMIT provisions had been carried out on the basis of notifications from market participants, persons professionally arranging transactions in wholesale energy products (the PPATs), and information from public sources. ACER, in its 2015 annual report on its activities under REMIT, reports that there were seventy-eight cases reported between 2013 and 2015.[860] The report shows that forty-four of these cases involved allegations of market manipulation in relation to Article 5 of REMIT. In the majority of these cases, the national competent authorities and ACER either found insufficient evidence to support a manipulation claim or issued no sanctions against identified breaches, except for giving warnings as to possible

858. *See Resolución del Tribunal de Defensa de la Competencia del Expediente* 601/05 *IBERDROLA CASTELLÓN, de* 8 *de marzo de* 2007; *Resolución del Tribunal de Defensa de la Competencia del Expediente* 602/05 *VIESGO GENERACIÓN, de* 28 *de diciembre de* 2006; *Resolución del Consejo del Expediente* 624/07 *IBERDROLA, de* 14 *de febrero de* 2008; *Resolución del Consejo del Expediente* 625/07 *GAS NATURAL, de* 25 *de abril de* 2008.

859. The CREG, Belgian Energy Regulator, provides that it will use REMIT to deal with such market misconduct. *See* Marc Martens & Peter Willis (2014). *See also*, Leigh Hancher (2013); Christopher Jones (ed.), 311 (2016).

860. John Ratliff & Roberto Grasso, *REMIT – EU Legislation on Insider Trading and Market Manipulation in Wholesale Energy Markets Adopted* (WilmerHale 2011), https://www.wilmerhale.com/pages/publicationsandnewsdetail.aspx?NewsPubId=87107 (accessed 29 Jun. 2017).

repetitions. As of 2017, the only case that has resulted in a sanction on a firm for a breach of the prohibition of market manipulation is *Iberdrola* by SCA on 24 November 2015. There are also other ongoing cases in which the national competent authorities investigated for a breach of Article 5 of REMIT, such as the investigation against Enel and Sorgenia by the Italian energy regulator as discussed above. It is reasonable to expect that more investigations and decisions will follow as data reporting for standardised and non-standardised contracts as well as notifications as to possible breaches of anti-manipulation rules increase. However, as of January 2017, case law analysis on the prosecution of market manipulation under REMIT is limited to *Iberdrola*.

[1] Iberdrola *(Spain)*

On 24 November 2015, SCA established that Iberdrola, the second largest electricity generator after Endesa,[861] had committed market manipulation in Spanish wholesale electricity markets in violation of Article 5 of REMIT and fined the firm EUR 25 Million for the breach.[862] The finding stemmed from Iberdrola's activities during a time period between 30 November and 23 December 2013. According to SCA, Iberdrola engaged in physical capacity withholding during the relevant period to increase prices of electricity traded in the wholesale electricity market. The decision was contested by Iberdrola and the case is currently in appeal.

The alleged manipulative conduct involved a reduction of the electricity supply offered to the Spanish wholesale market by Iberdrola. SCA claimed that the firm deliberately withheld water at its Duero, Sil and Tajo hydroelectric power plants, which together constituted nearly half of the total hydroelectric capacity in Spain.[863] While the amount of electricity dispatched from these hydroelectric plants before the relevant period reached 45 GW/h with average daily prices at around EUR 45–55/MWh, electricity offered by Iberdrola reduced to 13 GW/h between 30 November and 23 December, despite the higher prices during the relevant period.[864] The withholding activity caused an increase of EUR 7 MWh in the wholesale electricity prices and 10% in retail prices as the relevant period intersected with a government tendering process which determined prices for domestic end users of the following period.[865]

861. Delloite (ND), European Energy Market Reform, 4, https://www2.deloitte.com/content/dam/Deloitte/global/Documents/Energy-and-Resources/gx-er-marketreform-spain.pdf (accessed 29 Jun. 2017).
862. Peter Willis & Hermenegildo Altozano, *Spanish Authority Fines Iberdrola €25m in First REMIT Market Manipulation Infringement Decision* (Bird & Bird 4 Feb. 2014), https://www.twobirds.com/en/news/articles/2016/spain/spanish-authority-fines-iberdrola-25m-in-first-remit-infringement-decision (accessed 29 Jun. 2017).
863. *Supra* note 769.
864. Peter Willis & Hermenegildo Altozano (2014).
865. First Economic Sanctions for REMIT Breaches in Europe, (Lexology, 16 Feb. 2016), http://www.lexology.com/library/detail.aspx?g=66b554d0-514c-40b3-b4fb-67374a43b111 (accessed 29 Jun. 2017).

SCA identified that reservoirs held in the hydroelectric capacity of these three power plants during the relevant period were higher than those in past years. Historical analysis revealed that Iberdrola's production figures from these plants were considerably larger in previous years, despite the lower water levels at their reservoirs. Economically, Iberdrola should have had an incentive to increase its output as the financial profits it could have derived from per MWh, increased due to high electricity prices during the relevant period and its water reservoirs were available for further production. Nor could the withholding be justified on the basis of forward prices. Iberdrola could not claim that it had held withheld its capacity with the expectation of higher electricity prices in upcoming months, as forward contracts prices were at levels lower than those in the DAM. According to SCA, the main motive behind Iberdrola's withholding of capacity in its three hydroelectric units was to render operational its more expensive CCGT plants which would move the merit order in the Spanish wholesale electricity market to more expensive generation plants and set electricity at higher prices so that it could derive more profits from its overall output. SCA estimated that the financial benefit accrued by Iberdrola from increased electricity prices reached EUR 21.5 million for the relevant period.[866]

Iberdrola objected to SCA's allegations, claiming that the contested practice was carried out for legitimate reasons. On 16 December 2015, the firm's Chief Executive Officer, Jose Ignacio Sanchez Galan said that:

> Those days, we were buying, not selling, we are a producer of wind and hydro. There was a tremendous drop, no wind. If we do not have enough energy to supply our customers, we are forced to buy. So if we are forced to buy, we have no interest to increase the price.[867]

Galan's comment on the *'tremendous drop'*, in the firm's hydroelectric capacity contradicts SCA's finding of water reservoirs held available during the relevant period. Whether Iberdrola was forced to buy and in fact did buy electricity from other producers to supply its consumers or whether the available reservoirs held in its hydroelectric capacity were sufficient remains to be seen during the judicial review.

This case is of great importance for the future of the regulation of European wholesale energy markets. It is the first time that a national competent authority has applied the prohibition of market manipulation to an energy supplier. The legal analysis carried out by SCA did not include an identification of relevant markets in the Spanish wholesale markets. Nor did it discuss whether Iberdrola held market dominance or a pivotal position for electricity supply. The findings of SCA provide significant legal implications as to the differences in enforcement procedures under REMIT and competition law.

866. Peter Willis & Hermenegildo Altozano (2014).
867. Jim Polson, *Iberdrola Appealing Fine for Manipulating Market, CEO Says* (Bloomberg December 2015), https://www.bloomberg.com/news/articles/2015-12-16/iberdrola-appealing-fine-for-manipulating-market-ceo-says (accessed 29 Jun. 2017).

[D] Evaluation

[1] Types of Capacity Withholding

As mentioned above, the EU authorities continuously argued that a specific, tailor-made legal framework was required to deal with certain types of market abuse such as capacity withholding activities, in wholesale energy markets.[868] Economic literature and case law also suggested that parties would withhold their capacity either physically or economically.[869] While the former indicates a reduction in output deliberately perpetrated to move merit curves to expensive power plants, the latter involves a strategic bidding activity that is designed to be not selected, yet again to ensure demand and supply for energy is settled at expensive power plants. In physical withholding, perpetrators may allege that the contested practices stem from expected or unexpected maintenance measures in generation facilities. In fact, electricity producers may present various reasons for not continuing electricity production. The legitimacy of withholding practices were widely discussed, during the consultation period, prior to the publication of the CESR-ERGEG's advice document in 2008, and it was accepted that in certain conditions, a capacity withholding activity could be justified on the basis of legitimate reasons. Consequently, REMIT adopted the concept of 'Accepted Market Practices' to provide a safe harbour for market participants in engaging in certain practices.[870] The legitimacy of these reasons will be evaluated on case-by-case basis.

In economic withholding, generators submit bids at high prices during capacity auctions in wholesale markets. Whether or not a bid submitted to a wholesale market is high depends on the marginal operational costs of generation plants.[871] An energy producer is expected to price its output on the basis of operational costs of its generation plants and a mark-up price including certain fixed and variable expenses. Each generation capacity has different operational costs depending on fuel types, and generation technology. An analysis of price levels should include any external or internal factors that affect operational costs. When such factors do not correspond to price levels at which bids are submitted, generators can be presumed to be engaged in a targeted bidding strategy to achieve a certain market outcome. Therefore, while the legal analysis in economic withholding practices focuses on price relations between submitted bids and operational costs, the issue in physical withholding activities is based on the legitimacy of reductions in generation output. In either case, the price of wholesale electricity would be lower but for the withholding activities.

868. CESR and ERGEG (2008); REMIT Impact (2010).
869. The Inquiry, 132–133. *See also* David Newbery, et al., 17 (2004); Shaun D. McRae & Frank A. Wolak, *How Do Firms Exercise Unilateral Market Power? Evidence from a Bid-Based Wholesale Electricity Market* EUI Working Papers (2009).
870. Article 2(2)(a)(ii), Regulation No 1227/2011. *See also* ACER's Guidance, 73–76 (2016).
871. David Newbery, et al., 30 (2004).

[2] *Feasibility*

[a] *Generation Portfolio*

Both physical and economic withholding practices are loss incurring, that is, generators which engage in withholding practices forego financial profits that could have been derived from the withheld generation.[872] Therefore the sustainability and profitability of such practices requires perpetrators to hold other positions that render them profitable.[873] There are different ways that an electricity producer can benefit from withholding. The existence of a portfolio of generation facilities, for example, may provide financial incentives for generators to engage in capacity withholding. As mentioned above, while less expensive generation plants operate as baseload power, more expensive plants become operational only when there is a peak demand when baseload power plants do not suffice to supply. Producers which have a generation portfolio and generate electricity from different types of generation facilities and resources such as renewables, nuclear power, coal, lignite, gas turbines or combined combustion gas turbines may seek to reduce operation of their less expensive generation facilities such as renewables or nuclear power to have more expensive gas turbines or CCGTs included in merit curves. As the last selected plants determine the market price for electricity produced in this particular hour, the price that a withholding generator would receive from its overall production increases. Market participants profit more from their output, despite the lower levels of production.

[b] *Sales in Balancing Markets*

EU case law also provides that generators may engage in withholding activities to profit from higher prices in balancing markets.[874] Wholesale electricity markets consist of wholesale spot[875] and balancing markets.[876] While the former operates as the main markets in which market operators determine demand for and supply of electricity on the basis of expected use, the latter is designed to ensure that demand for and supply of electricity is balanced. Differences between electricity produced and electricity consumed pose significant threats to the integrity of transmission systems to the extent that slight deviations between demand and supply may result in the collapse or malfunctioning of transmission grids.[877] In order to ensure that demand for and supply of electricity matches all the time, transmission system operators or market operators open a separate balancing market in which electricity is procured on the basis of actual

872. Catherine D. Wolfram, *Strategic Bidding in a Multiunit Auction: An Empirical Analysis of Bids to Supply Electricity in England and Wales* 29/4 The RAND Journal of Economics 703 (1998).
873. Paul Joskow & Edward Kahn (2002).
874. *See Endesa/Iberdrola/Union Fenosa/Hidrocantabrico; EGL/Repower/Tirreno Power; Enel/Sorgenia.*
875. For more information on wholesale spot markets, *see* Petri Mantysaari, 198–225 (2015).
876. REMIT considers balancing markets as part of wholesale energy markets. Article 2(4), Regulation No 1227/2011.
877. Petri Mantysaari, 313 (2015).

demand. The generators which have flexible generation facilities with lower start-up costs and better transmission connections have a comparative advantage and thus can be pivotal in supplying these markets. Through withholding supply in wholesale markets, generators make sure that more electricity is needed in balancing markets and their output is pivotal for demand. As the price of electricity in balancing markets is more expensive than that in wholesale markets, perpetrators derive more profits from withheld capacity.

[c] Cross-Product Positions

Producers of electricity may also have incentives to engage in capacity withholding due to their positions in long-term contracts or other contracts such as financial derivatives. Continuous high prices in wholesale markets may affect prices in long-term supply contracts. A producer which bilaterally contracted with consumers or other suppliers to sell large amounts of electricity for a long supply period may have an incentive to increase prices in DAMs or intraday markets, if these prices directly or indirectly affect the price of electricity determined under long-term supply contract. This was the Commission's main concern in *German Electricity Wholesale Market*,[878] in which E.ON, selling electricity through both wholesale markets and long-term contracts, allegedly withheld its capacity to increase prices. The losses incurred due to non-operated facilities were compensated via profits gained in the overall sale of electricity at higher prices. A similar pricing relationship may also be relevant for financial contracts which derive their value based on fluctuations in wholesale electricity markets. Nevertheless, this type of market practice should be regarded as cross-market manipulation, despite involving capacity withholding.

[3] Perpetration

Case law indicates that there are a number of factors required to ensure the profitability of withholding practices. Accordingly, a market participant seeking to profit from withholding its capacity should have a market power in comparison with the total generation capacity available for the particular geographic region and time period. The analysis of market power is not limited to the mere calculation of market shares. In certain market conditions, such as periods of high demand (e.g., *Edipower/Enel*), or the unavailability of transmission capacity (e.g., *Enel/Sorgenia*), generators may acquire a pivotal position in supplying electricity for the relevant period or the relevant location. Furthermore, the generation portfolio held by the withholding producers (e.g., *German Electricity Wholesale Market*) should have cheaper generation facilities to the extent that withholding these facilities creates sufficient capacity shortages that more expensive generation facilities are called in. The profits from operating units must surpass the losses from the withheld capacity. While the analysis of market power focuses on the ability of a generator or generators to affect prices in wholesale electricity markets, the

878. *German Electricity Wholesale Market* (COMP/39.388) Commission Decision [2008] OJ C36/8.

analysis of a generation portfolio evaluates whether one or more generators have an incentive to withhold capacity from wholesale electricity markets.

An electricity producer who seeks to raise profits through capacity withholding will do so, only if it knows when the planned withholding activity will result in expected price increases. Other factors, such as the ability and the incentive to withhold capacity, are closely related to market information, such as when to exercise the relevant bidding activity. In all of the cases discussed above, the generation companies exploited specific time periods such as peak hours and specific locations where only a limited number of suppliers could participate in balancing services. This was strikingly clear in *EGL/Repower/Tirreno Power,* in which the companies knew that they could exercise their collective market power in the Italian ancillary services market only if none of them was picked by the Italian transmission operator, Terna, to generate power in the DAM.[879] The pivotality of each firm led them to cooperate to give effect to withholding practices. Without the information on the periods of higher demand and pivotality, these generation companies would have incurred substantial financial risks, as the withheld capacity can always be supplied by other competing, low-cost generation companies.

[4] Legal Analysis under Competition Law

[a] Prohibitions

Withholding their capacity, electricity producers either alone or collaboratively seek to move market prices at higher levels to earn more profits from their output.[880] Under EU competition law, these types of activities are prohibited as violations of competition law under Articles 101 and 102 of TFEU. Article 101 directly provides that all agreements, decisions or concerted practices which constitute price fixing and output limitation may account for a distortion of competition,[881] as they cause consumers to pay higher prices and not receive the desired quantities.[882] These types of agreements are generally considered as *'hardcore restraints'*[883] and *'restrictions by object'*,[884] meaning that the Commission and national competition authorities are not required to

879. Peter Willis & Simone Cadeddu (2012).
880. Economic analysis shows that the perpetration of capacity withholding does not require a collusive conduct by multiple undertakings. *See* Carolyn A. Berry, et al., *Analysing Strategic Bidding Behaviour in Transmission Networks* in Harry Singh (ed.), *Game Theory Applications in Electric Power Markets* (IEEE Power Engineering Society Winter Meeting 1999).
881. Article 101(1)(a), (b) of TFEU.
882. Christopher Jones (ed.), 166 (2016).
883. Commission, 'Guidelines on the application of Article 101(3) TFEU (formerly Article 81(3) TEC)' (Communication) OJ 2004 C101/97: Vol II App C13, para. 23.
884. In *European Night Service v. Commission*, the General Court found that agreements containing certain provisions fixing prices or sharing markets will automatically be held to restrict competition under Articles 101, T-374, 375, 384 and 388/94 *European Night Service v. Commission* [1998] ECR II-3141 198, para. 136. *See also Competition Authority v. Beef Industry Development Society Ltd*, the CJEU held that agreements between competitors to reduce capacity had as their object the restriction of competition. Case C-209/07 *Competition Authority v. Beef Industry Development Society Ltd* [2008] ECR I-8637 643.

show negative effects on trade to prove that these agreement are anti-competitive and a distortion to competition.[885] These agreements are presumed to have negative effects on competition and are thus prohibited.

Article 102 of TFEU, on the other hand, prohibits the abuse of dominance by undertakings through imposing, *inter alia,* unfair prices and limiting production.[886] In *Sirena v. Eda*, the CJEU noted that particularly high price levels of products can reveal an abuse of dominance, unless there is a justification by any objective criteria.[887] In *General Motors,* the Commission adopted the concept of excessive pricing to illustrate unfair pricing practices.[888] The concept was further elaborated in *United Brands* in which the Court explained that a price would be deemed '*excessive*', if it unreasonably deviated from the *economic value* of the product.[889] In order to identify whether a price is based on its economic value, the Court introduced a two-stage test providing that excessive prices '*could, inter alia, be determined objectively if it were possible for it to be calculated by making a comparison between the selling price of the product in question and its cost of production, which would disclose the amount of the profit margin. The questions therefore to be determined are whether the difference between the costs actually incurred and the price actually charged is excessive, and, if the answer to this question is affirmative, whether a price has been imposed which is either unfair in itself or when compared to competing products. Other ways may be devised of selecting the rules for determining whether the price of a product is unfair*'.[890] Accordingly, in order to determine whether a price is excessive, the court first evaluates actual costs and prices. This is followed by a comparison of the price with those of the company's competitors. Since the holding in *United Brands,* the CJEU has engaged in several price comparisons, such as price-cost margin analysis, price comparisons between markets or rivals, price comparisons across geographic areas, and comparisons over different time periods.[891]

[b] Capacity Withholding as Excessive Pricing

[i] General

The concept of excessive pricing is highly contested in economic and legal literature as well as case law. In *Trinko,*[892] the US Supreme Court noted that '*(t)he mere possession of monopoly power, and the concomitant charging of monopoly prices – at least for a*

885. Case C-49/92 P – *Commission v. Anic Partecipazioni* [1999] ECR I-4125, para. 99; Case C-209/07 *Competition Authority v. Beef Industry Development Society Ltd* [2008] ECR I-8637 643, para. 16.
886. Article 102 (a), (b) of TFEU.
887. Case 40/70 *Sirena S.R.L. v. Eda S.R.L. and others* [1979] ECR-03169 236, para. 17.
888. Case C-26/75 *General Motors Continental NV v. Commission of the European Communities,* [1975] ECR I-01367 150, paras 12, 22.
889. Case C-27/76 *United Brands Company and United Brands Continentaal BV v. Commission of the European Communities* [1978] ECR-I00207 22, para. 235.
890. *Ibid.*, paras 251–252.
891. Christopher Jones (ed.), 365 (2016).
892. *Verizon Communications Inc v. Law Offices of Curtis V Trinko LLP,* 3540 US 398, 407 (2004).

short period – is what attracts "business acumen" in the first place; it induces risk taking that produces innovation and economic growth. To safeguard the incentive to innovate, the possession of monopoly power will not be found unless it is accompanied by an element of anti-competitive conduct'. The term *'anti-competitive conduct'* in the decision refers to Section 1 of the Sherman Act which is equivalent to Article 101 of TFEU and Section 2 of the Sherman Act which mirrors the concept of exclusionary abuse of dominance under EU competition law. Accordingly, US antitrust law does not proscribe exploitative practices by monopolists, unless it coincides with an anti-competitive agreement or an exclusionary abuse of market power such as margin squeeze, tying and bundling, or predatory pricing practices.[893]

This is similar to the Commission's approach[894] which holds that price regulation is in contrast to the concept of a free market economy and should not be applied without finding that the market in question suffers a natural or legal monopoly and thus did not enforce Article 102 against pricing practices. The complexity of excessive pricing cases stems from the difficulties in identifying the correct benchmark price that competition authorities regard as the price that would have been in place but for the anti-competitive conduct.[895] The two-pronged analysis developed under *United Brands* is not regarded as illustrative as a cost/price analysis, and the concept of economic value does not indicate the extent of value and types of costs to be included in final prices. The Commission, in *Scandlines Sverige AB v. Port of Helsingborg*, concluded that the test developed by the CJEU in *United Brands*, is very difficult to apply, providing very little guidance on how to determine unfair prices.[896]

[ii] Enforcement at EU Level

The limited case law on capacity withholding at EU level can be explained by the EU's reluctance to enforce competition law against excessive and unfair pricing practices.[897] Even though capacity withholding practices by energy producers were considered a major problem for the competitiveness of European energy markets in the 2007 Energy

---

893. Donal F. Turner, *The Definition of Agreement under the Sherman Act: Conscious Parallelism and Refusals to Deal* 75/4 Harvard Law Review 655, 669 (1962).
894. Philip Lowe, *Consumer Welfare and Efficiency – New Guiding Principles of Competition Policy?* (13th International Conference on Competition and 14th European Competition Day, Munich March 2007) http://ec.europa.eu/competition/speeches/text/sp2007_02_en.pdf (accessed 29 Jun. 2017).
895. Christopher Jones (ed.), 366–367 (2016).
896. *Scandlines Sverige AB v. Port of Helsingborg* (Case COMP/A.36.568/D3) Commission Decision [2004], para. 217.
897. *'The existence of a dominant position is not itself against the rules of competition. Consumers can suffer from a dominant company exploiting this position, the most likely way being through prices higher than would be found if the market were subject to effective competition. However, the Commission in its decision-making practice does not normally control or condemn the high level of prices as such. Rather it examines the behaviour of the dominant company designed to preserve its dominance, usually directly against competitors or new entrants who would normally bring about effective competition and the price level associated with it.'* XXIVth Report on Competition Policy, (Commission, 1994), para. 207. *See also* Alison Jones and Brenda Sufrin, 579 (2014).

Sector Inquiry, the first and only enforcement action by the Commission on this issue came only in 2008, against E.ON in *German Wholesale Energy Market.*[898] The evidence used by the Commission in its holding of capacity withholding by E.ON was based on the findings of the Sector Inquiry which had calculated the load factors of major electricity producers in Germany to identify generation facilities which are not optimally operated.[899] The Commission broadly described its finding of capacity withholding in *German Wholesale Energy Market,* without providing details on when the German electricity producers engaged in withholding practices and how they colluded to give effect to price increases. Even though E.ON, RWE and Vattenfall are together held collusively dominant in the broadly defined German wholesale electricity market, the Commission alleged that E.ON alone accounted for capacity withholding and thus was in violation of Article 102 of TFEU. As the case was settled under the 'Commitment Decisions' procedure under Article 9 of Regulation 1/2003,[900] the decision did not provide an in-depth analysis on how the generators' activities infringed EU competition law.[901] Instead, the investigation concluded with poorly evaluated divestiture obligations on E.ON's generation assets.[902]

[iii] Enforcement at National Level

At national level, more insight is given into how competition law rules are applied to capacity withholding practices. National competent authorities from Belgium, Italy and Spain initiated several proceedings against electricity producers for withholding practices. The proceedings included allegations of violation of both Articles 101 and 102 of TFEU. The cases clearly established that capacity withholding activity was a form of exercise of market power. The perpetrators could engage in such practices by either abusing their own market power (e.g., *Enel/Sorgenia, Endesa/Iberdrola/Union Fenosa/Hidrocantabrico*) or colluding with other market participants (e.g., *EGL/Repower/Tirreno Power*) to give effect to the desired price increases. Moreover, it was also implied that the analysis of the application of competition law to electricity markets required innovation in the legal approaches taken by competition authorities and courts. For example, in the Italian cases, the ICA defined relevant markets

898. *German Electricity Wholesale Market* (COMP/39.388) Commission Decision [2008] OJ C36/8.
899. The Sector Inquiry did not seek to analyse whether relevant market participants, in deed, committed excessive pricing or capacity withholding practices.
900. *Supra* note 259.
901. Regulation 1/2003 provides two procedural regimes for the investigation of anti-competitive practices to the European Commission. While Article 7 serves as the standard infringement procedure when the Commission believes that there is sufficient evidence to hold a market participant liable for a violation of competition law rule, Article 9 establishes 'the Commitment Decisions' procedure through which the Commission engages in negotiations with market participants and concludes binding decisions that the market participants undertook to comply with. Article 9 has been effectively used by the Commission in pursuing its energy liberalization agenda, as it has enjoyed a wider margin of appreciation in designing commitments. However, it is also provided that concerns arise as to the uncertainties in the application of competition law due to excessive use of the Commitment Decisions. Alison Jones & Brenda Sufrin, 983 (2014).
902. Malgorzata Sadowska, 88 (2013).

narrowly on the basis of market characteristics and transmission constraints. The ICA established a zone-based pricing mechanism that involved pricing of electricity based on the transmission constraints between different geographic locations, so-called zones, rather than a single Italian transmission market,[903] contradicting the Commission's practice which defined markets for transmission of electricity in a broader manner.[904] Another example is SCA's finding of temporary dominance in *Endesa/Iberdrola/Union Fenosa/Hidrocantabrico*, concluding that market power on electricity prices by producers was exercised for only a three-day period.

Even though the national competent authorities played an active role in fighting capacity withholding practices in electricity markets, their approaches to the enforcement and prosecution of such activities were far from being consistent. The ICA can be considered more successful in prosecuting capacity withholding as a violation of competition law. The Italian wholesale electricity market has been segmented into multiple sub-markets on the basis of transmission constraints. The determination of market power in these markets was carried out via an evaluation of pivotal positions held by electricity producers rather than through a calculation of market shares in electricity generation.[905] In *Electrabel*, the Competition College, the decision-making body of the Belgian Competition Authority, the BCA concluded that there had been no violation of abuse of dominant position, pointing out the defendant generator's lack of anti-competitive intent in withholding its capacity from the Belgian wholesale electricity market. The reason behind this evaluation stemmed from the finding that the withheld capacity accounted for only 1.1% of total capacity available in the Belgian wholesale electricity market, which, as the Competition College considered, was insufficient to affect electricity prices in the respective market.[906] The College also remarked that whether or not capacity withholding practices constituted violations of competition law was not clear according to EU case law. The SCA's approach was different. It specifically identified temporary markets that arose due to exceptional congestion problems and held that the positions held by the Spanish electricity producers in these markets could be considered dominant as they could act independently of their competitors to set prices at higher levels. Nevertheless, SCA's decision was later quashed by the Spanish Supreme Court which rejected the ability to affect prices temporarily as a factor in determining dominance.[907]

The legal analysis carried out in *Iberdrola* highlights legal implications of the differences between EU competition law and REMIT in prosecuting capacity withholding practices. As mentioned above, in order to hold an undertaking liable for an Article 102 violation, the competition authorities are required to show that this undertaking holds dominance in relevant markets. Iberdrola's market share in the Spanish wholesale electricity market was 20%,[908] not sufficient to establish dominance under EU

903. Angelica Gianfreda & Luigi Grossi (2009).
904. *Sydkraft/Graninge* (Case COMP/M.3268) Commission Decision [2003] OJ L2985, paras 74, 75.
905. Peter Willis & Simone Cadeddu (2012).
906. *Supra* note 816.
907. Malgorzata Sadowska, 153 (2013).
908. *Supra* note 861.

competition law. The concept of wholesale electricity markets is defined very broadly under EU case law which encompasses:

(1) the production of electricity in power plants;
(2) import or export of electricity via interconnectors; and
(3) the sale on the wholesale market to:
  - traders;
  - regional distribution companies; and
  - occasionally large industrial final users, only if they are directly connected to the transmission grid and able to be directly supplied on the wholesale market.[909]

Moreover, competition authorities are obliged to establish that electricity producers hold at least 40% of the market share in these broadly described relevant markets. In paragraph 12 of the Guidance Paper, the Commission explains that the calculation of market shares is not the sole indicator of dominance, as barriers to entry or expansion and countervailing buyer power are also important factors in demarcating the market power undertakings can exert in relevant markets.[910] However, the Commission's approach to market shares was not welcomed by EU courts. In *Telefonica,* the General Court held that it was the calculation of market shares indispensable for the assessment of market dominance rather than the existence of the ability to increase prices.[911] In *United Brands* the CJEU suggested that market shares below 40% would be unlikely to raise concerns about market power.[912] Accordingly, capacity withholding practices would be prosecutable under EU competition law, only if they were perpetrated by major electricity companies with large incumbent powers. The companies with less market presence can easily withhold their capacity with impunity, which raises concerns about 'Type 2 errors' in competition law meaning that courts or competition authorities fail to proscribe agreements, conduct or mergers where there is actual or likely anti-competitive harm.[913] This was, in fact, the case after the Spanish Supreme

909. *Sydkraft/Graninge* (Case COMP/M.3268) Commission Decision 2003/297/EC OJ C 297/22; *EDP/ENI/GDP* (Case COMP/M.3440) Commission Decision 2005/801/EC, [2005] OJ L302/69; *E.ON/MOL* (Case COMP/M.3696) Commission Decision 2006/622/EC OJ L253/20; *RWE/Essent* (Case COMP/M.5467) Commission Decision 23/06/2009 OJ C222/1; *EDF/British Energy* (Case COMP/M.5225) Commission Decision 22/12/2008 OJ C38/8.
910. Guidance on the Commission's Enforcement Priorities in Applying Article 82 of the EC Treaty to Abusive Exclusionary Conduct by Dominant Undertakings [2009] OJ C45/2, para. 12.
911. Case T-336/07 *Telefonica SA and Telefonica de Espana v. European Commission* [2012], paras 166, 148–150, 2008 OJ C83/6, the appeal from *Wanadoo Espana/Telefonica* (COMP/38.784) Commission Decision of 4 Jul. 2007.
912. In fact, the CJEU examined lower market shares and did not directly dismiss the possibility of undertakings with lower market shares holding dominance in several cases. *See* Case C-250/92, *Gottrup Klim v. KLG* [1994] ECR I-5641, in which the Court evaluated as to whether a company with 36% and 32% of share in two different markets held dominance, which it responded as negative. The lowest market share, the Court deemed dominant under its case law is 39.7%. *See British Airways plc v. Commission* Case C-95/04 [2006] ECR I-2331.
913. Alison Jones & Brenda Sufrin, 57–58 (2014).

Court's annulment of SCA's decisions on capacity withholding practices under competition law.

[5] Legal Analysis under REMIT

[a] Identification of Prima Facie Case

SCA, in *Iberdrola*, applied REMIT's anti-manipulation rules to the defendant generator and did not engage in a legal analysis of the dominant position to hold that the defendant generator violated Article 102 of TFEU. ACER's guidance on the application of REMIT specifically identifies capacity withholding as a type of price manipulation[914] and Article 2(2)(a)(ii) of REMIT defines pricing manipulation as:

> entering into any transaction or issuing any order to trade in wholesale energy products which: (...) secures or attempts to secure, by a person or persons acting in collaboration, the price of one or several wholesale energy products at an artificial level, unless the person who entered into the transaction or issued the order to trade establishes that his reasons for doing so are legitimate and that that transaction or order to trade conforms to accepted market practices on the wholesale energy market concerned (...).

This article lists five elements for a market behaviour to be prohibited as market manipulation. First, there must be any transaction or order to trade in wholesale energy products.[915] Second, this transaction or order to trade must secure or attempt to secure the price of wholesale energy products at a specific level. Third, this new price level must be artificial. Fourth, the artificial prices are caused by the relevant transaction or order to trade. Fifth, reasons presented by perpetrators for engaging in such transactions or orders to trade are not legitimate or regarded as accepted market practices by other regulatory frameworks.

[i] Securing the Price of a Wholesale Energy Product

The second, third and fourth elements are of particular importance in finding a capacity withholding activity is a violation of REMIT's anti-manipulation rules. The second element requires a capacity withholding practice to affect or attempt to affect the price of a wholesale electricity product. This element is related to the ability of each market participant in affecting wholesale electricity prices. The determination of merit curves by transmission system operators or market operators is fundamental for the assessment of power generators' abilities to increase prices of wholesale electricity markets. This ability does not require large market shares. The analysis of market shares does not provide sufficient tools to measure how dominant electricity producers can increase prices by withholding their capacity.[916] In fact, a producer with a high market

914. *Supra* note 163.
915. Article 2(4), Regulation No 1227/2011.
916. Gary Taylor, et al., 38 (2015).

share may not be able to increase prices through withholding its capacity, if other market players have enough capacity to offer the same amount of electricity at the same prices. On the other hand, a producer with a relatively small market share can easily increase the price of wholesale electricity product, if it knows when its capacity is pivotal for the supply of a certain amount of electricity at a certain price. This is incorporated in REMIT which specifically refrains from using the term 'dominant position' and instead, describes the ability to secure prices as *'decisive position'*.[917]

The legal analysis under the second element is very similar to those carried out by the national competition authorities before REMIT. The assessment of a dominant position for the electricity producers in these cases was based on the pivotality of their generation facilities in given merit curves. In describing dominant positions held by the relevant electricity producers, BCA, ICA and SCA put particular focus on the supply levels at respective merit curves. The establishment of the ability to affect electricity prices was a fundamental factor for the national competition authorities in identifying dominant positions held by the electricity producers. This was in compliance with the General Court's approach in *AstraZeneca*, in which market power was defined as *'(...) the ability of an undertaking to behave to an appreciable extent independently of its competitors, its customers and, ultimately, consumers, in the sense that it is in particular able to maintain prices at a higher level while retaining a much higher market share than those of its competitors (...)'*.[918] The producers which ensured that their capacity was necessary for the supply of electricity at certain price levels and at certain periods were able to act independently of their competitors and operated as price-setting rather than price-taking market participants. Accordingly the assessment of dominance by the national competition authorities in capacity withholding cases is similar to that of the ability to affect prices in wholesale energy products under REMIT's anti-manipulation rule.

[ii] Artificial Price

The third element focuses on the analysis of price artificiality in wholesale electricity markets. REMIT describes artificiality as price levels that are *'not justified by market forces of supply and demand, including actual availability of production, storage or transmission capacity and demand'*.[919] The formulation of a legal approach to the application of the concept of artificiality is important for the enforcement of REMIT against market manipulation. Two different approaches can be taken for the establishment of artificiality. First, national competent authorities may identify that prices in wholesale electricity markets are artificial, once it is found that one or multiple electricity producers active in the relevant wholesale markets withheld their capacity. Given the reference to the availability of production facilities as a factor that impacts market forces of supply and demand, the definition in REMIT may indicate the adoption of such an approach. This analysis may provide legal advantages with respect

917. Recital 14, Regulation No 1227/2011.
918. Case T-321/05 *AstraZeneca v. Commission* [2010] ECR II-2805, para. 267.
919. Recital 13, Regulation No 1227/2011.

to relieving competent authorities from identifying competitive benchmark prices and engaging in complex price evaluations including price-cost margin analysis, price comparisons between markets or rivals, price comparisons across geographic areas and comparisons over different time periods.

This is, in fact, the approach adopted by the CFTC in *DiPlacido*[920] on the enforcement of an anti-manipulation law under the artificial price-based definition of the CEA.[921] As discussed above, under US case law, the identification of price artificiality by the CFTC had proved to be very difficult to satisfy until *DiPlacido* as it had required the CFTC to establish artificiality on the basis of prices rather than a manipulative conduct. The complexity of the context was further elevated due to the stance of US law on pricing behaviours which is stricter than that of EU law in forbidding competent authorities to act in the manner of price regulators.[922] In order to avoid burdensome price evaluations, in *DiPlacido*, the CFTC changed its approach to price artificiality and held that once it was established that perpetrators engaged in a conduct that was uneconomic and did not represent true forces of supply and demand, prices would be presumed artificial.[923]

Nevertheless, the applicability of this approach to capacity withholding practices is problematic. The economics of merit curves under wholesale electricity markets does not lead to the conclusion that any withholding activity would directly result in price increases in wholesale electricity products. It can affect prices, only if withheld capacity is pivotal, meaning that the relevant generation capacity is needed to supply a certain amount of electricity at a certain price for a certain period of time. As long as wholesale electricity markets include other electricity producers which can produce a similar amount of electricity at similar price levels, price changes that are required to establish artificiality will not arise. In other words, a withholding activity may create no price change that can be presumed artificial under this approach. The identification of price change is a requirement for national competent authorities to identify a withholding activity manipulation, and they can do so only after engaging in extensive pricing evaluations including cost/price analysis and comparisons between markets products and time periods.

The second approach is similar to those taken by the CFTC before *DiPlacido*[924] and the national competition authorities in the aforementioned cases under EU

920. *In re DiPlacido*, [2007-2009 Transfer Binder] Comm. Fut. L. Rep. (CCH) ¶ 30,970 (CFTC 2008).
921. Section 6(c) of 7 U.S.C. § 13b (2010).
922. Diana Moss & Sandeep Vaheesan, *Antitrust Tools for Challenging Capacity Withholding in Wholesale Electricity Markets*, AAI The American Antitrust Institute, 3–4 (2014).
923. *In re DiPlacido*, [2007-2009 Transfer Binder] Comm. Fut. L. Rep. (CCH) ¶ 30,970 (CFTC 2008), 18.
924. '[T]*o determine whether an artificial price has occurred one must look at the aggregate forces of supply and demand and search for those factors which are extraneous to the pricing system, are not a legitimate part of the economic pricing system, are not a legitimate part of the economic pricing of the commodity, or are extrinsic to that commodity market.' In re Indiana Farm Bureau Cooperative Association, [1982-1984 Transfer Binder] Comm. Fut. L. Rep. (CCH) ¶ 21,796 (CFTC 1982)*. For further information on approaches taken by the Commodity Futures Trading Commission to the prosecution of artificial price-based market manipulation *see* Jerry Markham (2015).

competition law. Accordingly, competent authorities establishing that capacity withheld by perpetrators in furtherance of their scheme were pivotal in wholesale electricity markets, to engage in pricing evaluations to establish price artificiality. Even though the CFTC's experience with these pricing evaluations was problematic under US case law, the EU, despite the existence of limited case law, has been more successful in prosecuting pricing abuses under competition law. SCA included price evaluations also in *Iberdrola* under REMIT to determine whether the withholding activity had artificially increased pricing in the Spanish wholesale electricity market. The second approach is more suitable for the determination of withholding activities as a market manipulation under REMIT.

It is important to note that the concept of market manipulation under REMIT is not limited to capacity withholding practices. EU case law on market manipulation is limited and does not suffice to provide a more detailed legal analysis as to how anti-manipulation rules could be applied in European wholesale energy markets. The chapter's consideration of a second approach as appropriate for the prosecution of capacity withholding practices may not be true for that of other manipulative practices under REMIT. In order to identify the scope of REMIT's market manipulation prohibition, the chapter discusses possible scenarios in relation to the examples provided under EU soft law and the enforcement activities under US case law. The latter clearly illustrates that the second approach which would be suitable for the prosecution of capacity withholding practices may lead to significant problems for that of other manipulative practices. As discussed under US case law, the CFTC's experience in market manipulation under artificial price-based definitions which required extensive pricing evaluations for the determination of price artificiality, clearly showed the difficulties inherent in the adoption of this approach to prosecuting other types of pricing manipulation such as cross-market manipulation.[925] The identification of different legal standards for different types of market manipulation, on the other hand, undermines the adoption of a single coherent legal methodology applying to all types of market manipulation.

[iii] Causation

Reading Article 2(2) of REMIT indicates a causation element for a finding of market manipulation. It prohibits market conduct that secures or attempts to secure prices of wholesale energy products at an artificial level. Price results in a market may hinge upon several factors that are not manipulative or anti-competitive. In wholesale energy markets, for example, price increases may be a result of constraints in transmission networks or shortages in supply of several resources such as, oil, natural gas, or low levels of rainfall.[926] Changes in wholesale electricity prices due to such factors may not

925. Shaun Ledgerwood & Dan Harris, 4 (2012).
926. Petri Mantysaari, 398–399 (2015).

be deemed artificial and manipulative. In order to establish price artificiality, competent authorities should provide evidence showing that price changes in wholesale electricity markets stem from capacity withholding activities, rather than from these external factors.

The approaches provided above for the establishment of price artificiality are fundamental for the role played by the causation element in the finding of capacity withholding as market manipulation. Under the first approach which the CFTC adopted in *DiPlacido*, the causation does not constitute a major element for the establishment of market manipulation. As mentioned in *DiPlacido* the mere identification of conduct that is uneconomic and does not reflect the true forces of demand and supply would suffice to establish that prices were artificial.[927] Under this approach competent authorities may establish the causation element by simply proving that electricity producers withheld their capacity for a certain period of time. Whether or not the perpetrators' withholding caused price changes or whether there were price changes at all is irrelevant to the legal analysis.

Under the second approach, the causation element represents a major part in pricing evaluations. In determining manipulation at wholesale electricity markets, competent authorities identify capacity withholding practices and corresponding price changes.[928] This analysis also includes the impact of factors other than capacity withholding on prices such as shortages in resources and transmission constraints. The causation element does not require competent authorities to precisely prove that capacity withholding is the sole reason for price changes in wholesale electricity markets. Instead, a proof of the proximate cause of the artificial price suffices to sustain a charge of manipulation.[929] This does not mean that a mere finding of capacity withholding is sufficient to find market manipulation. The investigation should include a cost/price analysis and comparisons in relation to price fluctuations corresponding to withholding activities. This is in line with the analysis carried out by SCA in *Iberdrola* where the electricity producer was found to cause price increases between 30 November and 23 December 2013 by withholding its capacity from three of its hydroelectric plants.[930]

The identification of the causation element was a major problem in the prosecution of market manipulation under the CEA's artificial price-based rule, and the CFTC faced difficulties in identifying what a competitive price level would be for a particular product before the Dodd-Frank which introduced SEC's and FERC's fraud-based anti-manipulation rule into the CEA.[931] Nevertheless, the finding of price effects is an

927. *In re DiPlacido*, [2007-2009 Transfer Binder] Comm. Fut. L. Rep. (CCH) ¶ 30,970 (CFTC 2008), 18.
928. *In re Indiana Farm Bureau Cooperative Association*, [1982-1984 Transfer Binder] Comm. Fut. L. Rep. (CCH) ¶ 21,796 (CFTC 1982).
929. *CFTC v. Parnon Energy Inc.*, 11 Civ. 3543 (S.D.N.Y. 2014), 23. *See* further Rosa M. Abrantes-Metz, et al., *Revolution in Manipulation Law: The New CFTC Rules and the Urgent Need for Economic and Empirical Analyses* 15/2 University of Pennsylvania Journal of Business Law 357, 370 (2013).
930. Peter Willis & Hermenegildo Altozano (2014).
931. For example, in *in re Indiana Farm Bureau*, the CFTC found no violation of its anti-manipulation rule on the ground that market conditions that caused tight supply in US grains

important element for establishing capacity withholding as market manipulation. If it is shown that despite the withdrawal, wholesale electricity prices do not change or reflect the forces of demand and supply, the producer cannot be held liable for market manipulation. This case can be subject to further investigation on the basis of the prohibition on attempting to manipulate or competition law as an abuse of dominance by object. Therefore, the elements of artificiality and causation are important factors for the analysis of capacity withholding practices under REMIT's anti-manipulation rules.

It is important to note that capacity withholding practices were outside the scope of the CFTC's anti-manipulation jurisdiction. The CFTC has exclusive jurisdiction over futures trading and enforces its anti-manipulation rules against mostly cross-market manipulations through which perpetrators exploit price relations between futures and other markets.[932] The regulatory history on the application of artificial price based definitions to these types of market manipulation provides legal implications as to the application of REMIT's anti-manipulation rules. The artificiality and the causation elements are fundamental for establishing capacity withholding as market manipulation. However, the CFTC's experience of these elements clearly shows that they create problems in the prosecution of other types of pricing manipulation.

The competent authorities in the EU may adopt two different approaches to deal with capacity withholding practices and other types of pricing manipulation. While the first approach taken by the CFTC in *DiPlacido* may apply market manipulation other than capacity withholding practices, the second approach, which is based on artificial price analysis, may be adopted to deal with the latter. However, REMIT does not provide two different definitions for pricing manipulation. The adoption of two different approaches to the application of the same market manipulation provision gives rise to concerns on the integrity and consistency of the anti-manipulation regime under REMIT. If the competent authorities adopt the first approach to prosecute pricing manipulation, capacity withholding practices would be deemed manipulative even if they do not have any impact on wholesale electricity prices, which both raises concerns about 'type 2 errors'[933] and renders inapplicable the prohibition on attempted market manipulation. If the competent authorities adopt artificial price based analysis as the sole approach to enforce pricing manipulation, they may end up having similar difficulties to the ones the CFTC faced in its regulatory history. In sum, REMIT's anti-manipulation rule is not designed to be applicable to both capacity withholding practices and other types of pricing manipulation.

market had not been a result of a market practice engaged in by the defendants but rather due to external factors. The perpetrators, aware of the tight supply due to high demand from the Soviet Union, exploited these market conditions, which was acceptable under the US law. *In re Indiana Farm Bureau Cooperative Association*, [1982-1984 Transfer Binder] Comm. Fut. L. Rep. (CCH) ¶ 21,796 (CFTC 1982). *See* section 3.02[C].

932. Section 2(a)(1)(A) of 7 U.S.C. (2010).

933. Alison Jones & Brenda Sufrin, 57–58 (2014).

[E] Capacity Withholding in the US

[1] General

The identification of how capacity withholding practices have been dealt with in US case law is a prerequisite in explaining the differences between legal approaches taken by the US and EU authorities to the enforcement of anti-manipulation rules. As mentioned above, this chapter follows the demarcation of US case law in providing a legal analysis of other types of market manipulation in the EU context. However, the chapter on US case law does not address the practice of capacity withholding as a type of market manipulation. Soft law and consultation instruments in the EU clearly point out that capacity withholding practices were a major concern in devising anti-manipulation rules under REMIT. This is not the case in US case law. During the Western Energy Crisis in the early 2000s, the FERC published a report on price manipulation in California energy markets which regarded economic and physical withholding practices as efforts to manipulate market prices, finding that the inflated bidding strategies of Enron and physical withholding of supply by Reliant Energy and BP energy Traders in California electricity markets might be potentially manipulative.[934] In these investigations, FERC relied on tariffs of the California Power Exchange,[935] due to the absence of a specific prohibition applied to market manipulation in energy markets which was given later in 2005 with the adoption of EPAct.[936] Therefore, FERC did not provide a legal analysis on how physical withholding practices by Reliant Energy and BP Energy Traders constituted a violation of anti-manipulation rules.

The first and only case that the FERC analysed was whether a withholding activity by an electricity generator violated an anti-manipulation rule namely FERC's anti-manipulation Rule 18 C.F.R. § 1c.2 is *KeySpan.*[937] Establishing that the defendant had withheld capacity from markets the FERC found that the relevant withholding practices did not add up to market manipulation under its Rule 18 C.F.R. § 1c.2. The finding of capacity withholding later gave rise to an antitrust investigation by the US Department of Justice (the DoJ) under the Sherman Act.[938] The findings of FERC and the DoJ on KeySpan's conduct are illustrative as to the differences in the prosecution of capacity withholding practices under anti-manipulation rules and competition law.

---

934. *Supra* note 479.
935. Section 2.1.1. of the California Independent System Operator's (ISO) and California Power Exchange's (PX) Market Monitoring and Information Protocol (MMIP). https://www.sec.gov/Archives/edgar/data/894253/000095013402007966/d97931a1exv99w435.txt (accessed 29 Jun. 2017).
936. Energy Policy Act of 2005, Public Law 109–58, *see* https://www.congress.gov/109/plaws/publ58/PLAW-109publ58.pdf (accessed 29 Jun. 2017).
937. FERC Enforcement Staff Report, 'Findings of a Non-Public Investigation of Potential Market Manipulation by Suppliers in the New York City Capacity Market', Docket No IN08-2-000 & EL07-39-000 (February 2008) https://www.ferc.gov/enforcement/market-manipulation/nyiso-icap.pdf (accessed 29 Jun. 2017).
938. *U.S. v. KeySpan Corportation*, Memorandum & Order, Case 1:10-cv-014115 (S.D.N.Y., 2 Feb. 2011).

[2] KeySpan

The case involved a capacity withholding practice by KeySpan, a major electricity generator in New York State supplying electricity in the NYISO capacity markets. Separate from wholesale electricity markets, capacity markets are established for system reliability purposes, ensuring the supply of electricity during peak hours or when planned or unplanned generation outages occur.[939] In New York State, generators also submit bids to supply electricity in the capacity market, separate from their bids in wholesale DAMs and RTMs. NYISO established a bid cap representing the highest bid a generator can submit in supplying electricity in the capacity market. Until 2006 when an additional 1,000 MW electricity capacity became operational, KeySpan had been in a position of indispensable supplier of electricity in the New York capacity markets as NYISO had to procure electricity from KeySpan to maintain system reliability in peak hours or supply shortages. This pivotal position allowed KeySpan to bid at price caps without the incentive to compete with other generators on electricity supply. According to the NYISO, this position would no longer exist and electricity prices would drop as a result of the new capacity introduced in 2006.

Nevertheless, electricity prices in the New York capacity market remained unchanged despite the additional 1,000 MW/h capacity installed in 2006. Monitoring the bids and offers in the capacity markets, NYISO found that KeySpan had reduced its output by approximately the same amount as the new capacity and continued to place bids at price caps.[940] Further investigation into KeySpan's activities in the New York electricity market revealed that KeySpan had also entered into swap agreements directly with Morgan Stanley and indirectly with Astoria, its major competitor in the electricity generation market, mostly operating generation units at low marginal costs.[941] These swap agreements allowed KeySpan to receive payments on the condition that electricity prices in the NYISO area remained higher than a certain price level. Accordingly, the issue FERC and the DoJ sought to resolve in their investigation was whether the relevant capacity withholding activity along with the swap agreements between KeySpan, Morgan Stanley, and Astoria constituted a violation of anti-manipulation rules and antitrust law. The findings of FERC and the DoJ in their investigation differed significantly.

[3] *FERC's Findings*

FERC found that KeySpan's capacity withholding practice and swap agreement did not constitute a market manipulation under its anti-manipulation law.[942] First, it held that KeySpan's bidding activity did not violate the market rules as it did not exceed the price caps designated by the NYISO. Having capability and incentive to offer capacity at price caps did not necessarily account for a manipulation of electricity prices as these caps

939. Energy Primer, 59 (2015).
940. FERC Enforcement Staff Report, 9 (2008).
941. *Ibid.*, 2.
942. *Ibid.*, 24.

were anticipated as market clearing prices until market conditions dictated that offering capacity at price caps was no longer feasible on the basis of demand and supply levels. FERC concluded that such conditions did not exist even after the instalment of new capacity in 2006. Given its large market share, KeySpan still profited from its bidding activity at price caps despite the reduction in its output. The profits from operating power plants were sufficient to cover the losses incurred from the withheld capacity. This business model was rational on economic terms and thus constituted a legitimate business reason. The fact that this type of activity constituted an exercise of market power was irrelevant for the evaluation of market manipulation.[943] FERC decided that capacity withholding was not a per se violation of its anti-manipulation rules. KeySpan exercised its market power by reducing its output and bidding at the price caps. The exercise of market power might be considered as a factor in the evaluation of market manipulation. Nevertheless it was not alone sufficient to hold that KeySpan had violated FERC's anti-manipulation rules by withholding its capacity to continue bidding at price caps.

Second, FERC also found that swap agreements between KeySpan, Morgan Stanley and Astoria were designed to serve legitimate business purposes and thus were not manipulative. According to the swap agreements KeySpan profited from high electricity prices. The company's bidding activity was aimed at keeping electricity prices at or near the price caps. In other words, KeySpan's bidding in the capacity market directly affected the profits it derived from these swap agreements which made KeySpan's capacity withholding activity even more profitable. However, this did not mean that the capacity withholding activity was only profitable due to the benefits derived from swap agreements. FERC found that despite the decreases in revenues as a result of new capacity installed in 2006, KeySpan's capacity withholding and bidding behaviour was still economically profitable, and there was no economic evidence that the company would have discontinued its practice in the absence of its swap agreement.[944] KeySpan's swap agreement served a legitimate business purpose which was to offset the decreases in revenues derived from electricity generation. Therefore, FERC concluded that KeySpan's swap agreement was not in violation of its anti-manipulation rule, Section 1c.2.

[4] The DoJ's Findings

According to the DoJ, KeySpan's swap agreement with Morgan Stanley and Astoria, along with its capacity withholding activities, constituted a violation of Section 1 of the Sherman Act.[945] While withholding a small amount of capacity had been sufficient to ensure that electricity prices in the capacity market were set at price cap due to tight demand and supply conditions, with the instalment of new capacity in 2006, KeySpan was forced to withhold more of its capacity which meant a decrease in its revenues

943. *Ibid.*, 17.
944. *Ibid.*, 20.
945. *U.S. v. KeySpan Corporation*, Complaint, Case 1:10-cv-01415 (S.D.N.Y., 22 Feb. 2010), para. 37.

from its electricity generation business by as much as USD 90 million a year.[946] The DoJ identified that KeySpan alternatively could have competed with other generators for sales through submitting more capacity at lower prices. This would also have resulted in drops in electricity prices benefitting the customers of NYISO.

Instead of competing for sales, KeySpan continued its withholding practice. In order to mitigate its losses from its withheld capacity, KeySpan considered buying Astoria, which owned generation units with low marginal costs, to adapt to the new market conditions. However, this option was later discarded; as such a merger would give rise to concerns on competition in New York's wholesale electricity markets. Instead, KeySpan entered into an indirect swap agreement with Astoria, using a common counterparty, Morgan Stanley, which would enter into two corresponding swap agreements with KeySpan and Astoria. According to this scheme, Morgan Stanley paid KeySpan the difference between the specified price level and existing electricity prices, while receiving the same amount from Astoria.[947] In fact, Morgan Stanley functioned only as an intermediary, as the actual parties to the swap agreement were KeySpan and Astoria. Subsidising the losses incurred from the withheld capacity, the swap agreement allowed KeySpan to continue to bid at price caps which would also benefit Astoria acquiring more revenues from its low-cost generation units.

The case concluded with a settlement between the DoJ and KeySpan, according to which the latter was obliged to pay USD 12 million as a disgorgement of profits from its swap agreement. This was the first time that the DoJ applied for a remedy in a civil antitrust action for a violation of the Sherman Act.[948] Even though the DoJ asserted that the *'disgorgement of Keyspan's revenues will best remedy its anti-competitive conduct'*, establishing the collusion between KeySpan and its counterparties proved to be very difficult. Furthermore, the availability of legitimate business reasons that could have explained why the defendants entered into the swap agreements presented further challenges for the DoJ to prove the defendants' anti-competitive intent. The consent judgment published after the settlement required KeySpan to pay USD 12 million, and the DoJ guaranteed that no further action would be brought against KeySpan with respect to this case. The settlement would not constitute 'any evidence against or an admission by KeySpan with respect to any allegation'.[949]

[5] Evaluation

KeySpan clearly illustrates how the same market conduct may lead to different conclusions from regulatory and competition authorities. FERC, which exercises

946. *Ibid.*, para. 3.
947. *Ibid.*, para. 28.
948. *U.S. v. KeySpan Corportation*, Memorandum & Order, Case 1:10-cv-014115 (S.D.N.Y., 2 Feb. 2011), 15.
949. *U.S. v. KeySpan Corportation*, Final Judgment, Case 1:10-cv-01415.

regulatory oversight over the US energy market,[950] found that KeySpan's bidding activity was not in violation of its market manipulation prohibition as the company's withholding activity and swap agreement served a legitimate business purpose. The withholding practice was still economically profitable after the introduction of new capacity in 2006 and offsetting decreases in revenues as a result of capacity withholding provided a legitimate reason for entering into swap agreements. Whether or not KeySpan exercised its market power to inflate electricity prices was irrelevant for the evaluation of market manipulation. Identifying that the company would have continued to withhold its capacity, if it had not entered into swap agreements with its counterparties, FERC concluded that the company's capacity withholding could not be regarded as manipulative under the Section 1c.2.

The DoJ, on the other hand, was of the view that KeySpan, in violation of Section 1 of the Sherman Act, colluded with other parties through swap agreements to ensure that electricity prices in New York's capacity markets remained at price caps, despite the instalment of new capacity. KeySpan's withholding activity was not as profitable as it had been before 2006, and it would have had to consider competing for sales of electricity to increase profits from its operating generation units. Instead, KeySpan entered into swap agreements that would profit from high electricity prices which provided incentives to continue capacity withholding and bidding at price caps. According to the DoJ, these swap agreements would have reduced the generators' incentive to compete for electricity sales as well as harm consumers who would have benefitted from lower electricity prices if it were not for these agreements.

Economic and physical withholding practices are clear examples of how generators and suppliers can exercise their market power in energy markets to inflate prices and to exploit their dominant position.[951] Nevertheless, neither FERC nor the DoJ considered such practices as per se violations of anti-manipulation and antitrust rules. FERC explained that such an activity would be manipulative only if it were uneconomic meaning that the perpetrator had no legitimate, economic reason to engage in such conduct, but for the manipulative intent. This is not compatible with the approach taken in REMIT which prohibits capacity withholding without investigating whether it is economic or not. REMIT deems capacity withholding manipulative, since it is an exercise of market power. The generators who wish to withhold their capacity can do so only if they can show legitimate reasons such as maintenance that make the withholding activity necessary for the functioning of power plants.

It is important to note that the DoJ did not approach KeySpan's capacity withholding activity as a violation of Section 2 of the Sherman Act, equivalent to Article 102 of TFEU. This stems from the legal approach taken by the US to the prosecution of abuse of dominance through pricing behaviours. As noted in *Trinko*,[952] US authorities have been more reluctant to prosecute exploitative abuse of dominance such as

950. FERC's jurisdiction encompasses '*the transmission of electric energy in interstate commerce and to the sale of electric energy at wholesale in interstate commerce* (...)' and it has authority and responsibility '(...) *over all facilities for such transmission or sale of electric energy* (...)'. 16 U.S.C § 824(b)(1) (2006).
951. David Newbery, et al., 17 (2004).
952. *Verizon Communications Inc v. Law Offices of Curtis V Trinko LLP*, 3540 US 398, 407 (2004).

excessive or unfair pricing activities. Accordingly, capacity withholding can be considered a violation of US antitrust law on two different grounds, either as a violation of Section 1 of the Sherman Act, if it is found to be part of a collusion between two or more undertakings to enable price fixing purposes or as a violation of Section 2 of the Sherman Act if it also involves exclusionary abusive practices such as a margin squeeze, tying or bundling, so-called bad act. As to the analysis of market manipulation, FERC considers that capacity withholding, as a mere exercise of market power to change price levels, is a legitimate business practice and thus does not constitute market manipulation.

Read with EU case law, *KeySpan* clearly shows the differences in approach taken by the US and the EU authorities in prosecuting capacity withholding practices. The approach taken in EU competition law as to the prosecution of pricing abuses differs from that of the US authorities. As discussed above, the national European competition authorities have been active in prosecuting excessive and unfair pricing practices which are called exploitative abuse under EU competition law, while such practices are considered legitimate under US antitrust law. In EU case law, capacity withholding practices are considered a violation of Article 102 of TFEU as they are a form of exercise of market power and establishing that perpetrators withhold their capacity in order to increase energy prices is sufficient to find a violation of EU competition law. Nevertheless, difficulties in establishing market dominance under EU competition law caused EU institutions to seek alternative ways to prosecute these practices. *Iberdrola* shows that capacity withholding constitutes a clear example of market manipulation. This is also supported by soft law instruments[953] which had considered that a tailor-made legal framework was necessary to deal with such misconduct and paved the way for the adoption of REMIT. In sum, capacity withholding practices which are held in violation of both REMIT's anti-manipulation rules and EU competition law are considered legitimate business activities under relevant US anti-manipulation and antitrust rules.

§4.03 OTHER TYPES OF MARKET MANIPULATION

[A] Overview

EU case law on energy market manipulation is not as rich as US case law. Other than capacity withholding cases, EU case law does not provide sufficient details on other types of market manipulation that would be prohibited under REMIT. Some examples of manipulative conduct such as wash trades, improper matched orders, pump and dump schemes, etc. that are anticipated to be under the jurisdiction of REMIT are given in certain soft law instruments and in ACER's guidance document. The majority of these examples are derived from practices in the US securities markets under the jurisdiction of SEC.[954] The chapter does not discuss these practices in greater detail as

953. CESR and ERGEG (2008); REMIT Impact Assessment (2010).
954. Gary Taylor, et al., 194 (2015).

legal documents and case law on energy market manipulation provide limited guidance on how such manipulative practices might be perpetrated in European wholesale energy markets. Instead, the chapter follows the demarcation identified under US case law and discusses the legal implications of this demarcation for European wholesale energy markets.

[B] Market Power Manipulation

[1] ACER's Definition

ACER's guidance document identifies market power manipulation, called 'market cornering', as a type of price positioning which is defined under Article 2(2)(a)(ii) as follows, market conduct which '*involves a party or parties with a significant influence over the supply of, or demand for, or delivery mechanisms for a wholesale energy product and/or the underlying product of a derivative contract exploiting a decisive position in order to materially distort the price at which others have to deliver, take delivery or defer delivery of the instrument/product in order to satisfy their obligations*'.[955] Similarly to that given under US case law,[956] the definition does not provide details on perpetrators' motives in accumulating control over the deliverable product. In US case law, whether or not perpetrators accumulate such control to artificially move prices is fundamental in establishing market power manipulation and so distinguish these types of practices from mere exercise of market power. For example, in *Indiana Farm Bureau,* the CFTC concluded that the defendants' control over the deliverable product was not a result of a prior scheme but was because of a shortage in supplies due to external market conditions and thus the exploitation of this control would not be regarded as market manipulation.[957] Accordingly, in order to hold a market participant liable for market power manipulation, it must be established that the market participant's intent in accumulating its control over deliverable products is to move prices.

ACER acknowledges that having a decisive control over the supply of, demand for, or delivery mechanisms for wholesale energy products is not sufficient for a finding of market manipulation.[958] Nevertheless, REMIT's market manipulation prohibition does not entail an intent element, meaning that a market participant's motive in engaging in a conduct is irrelevant for the analysis of market manipulation under REMIT. This blurs the distinction between the concepts of market manipulation and the exercise of market power. A participant may acquire a dominant position due to a myriad of reasons, such as tightness in demand and supply, economies of scale, natural monopoly, mergers and acquisitions, etc. Under EU competition law, Article 102 of TFEU applies when dominant undertakings exercise their market power through

955. ACER's Guidance, 37 (2016).
956. *Cargill v. Hardin,* 452 F.2d 1154, 1163 (8th Cir. 1971), *cert. denied,* 406 U.S. 932 (1972), paras 37–39.
957. *In re Indiana Farm Bureau Cooperative Association,* [1982-1984 Transfer Binder] Comm. Fut. L. Rep. (CCH) ¶ 21,796 (CFTC 1982). For the economics of market power manipulation *see* Emilios E. Avgouleas, 147–154 (2005).
958. ACER's Guidance, 37 (2016).

abusive practices such as excessive pricing and does not include an *a priori* intent requirement for the establishment of abuse.[959] The omission of intent element from anti-manipulation provisions results in complexities in identifying applicable jurisdictions. The current legal framework does not distinguish market power manipulation from an exercise of market power which results in jurisdictional overlap between EU competition law and REMIT.

[2] Relevance for REMIT

Despite these inconsistencies in the legal framework, the concept of market power manipulation does not pose serious risks for the enforcement of REMIT in wholesale energy markets, especially in electricity markets. US case law requires that in order to perpetrate a market power manipulation:

(i) a market participant must hold a large buy (long) or sell (short) position in contracts for the delivery of a particular product;
(ii) this market participant must hold the possession of a large portion of the relevant product in its reserves or storages; and
(iii) the portion held by the market participant must be to the extent that available supplies other than the market participant's possession are not sufficient for the counterparties of the contracts to fulfil their obligation.

The perpetration of this scheme is not possible in European wholesale electricity markets. As discussed above, electricity is a product that cannot be stored in economically feasible high quantities. As generation and consumption have to take place simultaneously, imbalances between demand and supply levels directly affect the functioning of transmission grids. It is the transmission system operators' task to ensure this system balancing. In so doing, transmission system operators monitor and/or operate wholesale electricity markets in which electricity in large quantities is bought and sold in advance, prior to the generation and consumption of the traded electricity taking place. It is impossible to hold control over electricity supplies before they are generated. Even though a market participant can place large buy or sell orders in wholesale electricity markets, demand and supply levels are always balanced and settled in balancing markets in which excess and missing quantities are compensated at market rates. At this stage, electricity is produced only if a simultaneous demand arises. It is impossible for a market participant to force generators to make delivery or to force consumers to receive delivery which is not simultaneously consumed.

Wholesale natural gas markets are more prone to market power manipulation than wholesale electricity markets. Natural gas, as a deliverable product, can be stored in high quantities and its extraction and consumption can take place in different time periods. It can also be in a liquefied form, called LNG, and transported across long distances without the necessity of an established network connecting production and consumption centres. Accordingly, a market participant can commit a market power

959. *Supra* note 822.

manipulation in wholesale natural gas markets by holding large long (buy) positions, meaning that it enters into contracts as a buyer of natural gas that is to be delivered in the future, in the meantime stocking large quantities of natural gas in its storage, to the extent that supplies other than those stocked by the market participant are not sufficient for counterparties to fulfil their contractual obligations. Having no access to economically feasible substitutes, sellers of natural gas have no option other than negotiating a financial settlement which could be exploited by the market participant.

This does not mean that every market participant can corner markets. There are multiple factors that render the perpetration of market power manipulation unlikely in European wholesale natural gas markets by merely relying on storage facilities. Storage capacity constitutes only a limited portion of general natural gas consumption across the EU,[960] and in most Member States, market participants do not have enough storage capacity to hold a substantial sway over natural gas supplies. The construction of storage facilities requires capital intensive projects which are undertaken by multiple parties including gas suppliers, banks, insurance companies, governments, etc. The related costs inherent in the conclusion and realisation of these projects vary due to several factors, such as geographic location, corresponding design and equipment requirements, the proximity to pipelines, and environmental concerns.[961] Of the EU Member States, only the Czech Republic, Hungary and Austria have storage capacity that can meet more than 50% of their natural gas consumption, while the rest suffer a lack of enough storage capacity and rely on other flexibility measures.[962]

Access conditions and the allocation of storage facilities are regulated under 2009/73/EC, The Natural Gas Directive.[963] Storage facilities are operated by storage system operators which are required to establish compliance and monitoring mechanisms ensuring that storage capacity is allocated on a non-discriminatory manner.[964] A special regime for capacity allocation is also established, stipulating the effective use of existing capacities through firm and interruptible allocation mechanisms and the relief of long-term reserve contracts that date back to the pre-liberalisation era.[965] Even though the regulatory framework sets out an exemption regime for newly constructed storage facilities,[966] storage system operators are still required to refrain from discriminating between system users. Accordingly a natural gas supplier which also operates a

---

960. European Commission, *The Role of Gas Storage in Internal Market and in Ensuring Security of Supply* 23 (Luxembourg 2014), https://ec.europa.eu/energy/sites/ener/files/documents/REPORT-Gas%20Storage-20150728.pdf (accessed 29 Jun. 2017).
961. Barry Stevens, *Natural Gas Storage is Vital for Future Industry Growth* (OilPrice 11 Jun. 2012), http://oilprice.com/Energy/Natural-Gas/Natural-Gas-Storage-is-Vital-for-Future-Industry-Growth.html (accessed 29 Jun. 2017).
962. European Commission, *The Role of Gas Storage in Internal Market and in Ensuring Security of Supply* 10–11 (Luxembourg 2014).
963. The operation and management of storage facilities are dealt with in Article 13 and the third-party access rights to the storage facilities are included in Article 33 of Directive 2009/73/EC of the European Parliament and of the Council of 13 Jul. 2009 concerning common rules for the internal market in natural gas.
964. Article 15, Directive 2009/73/EC.
965. Article 33(3) of Article 6(3), Directive 2009/73/EC.
966. Article 36, Directive 2009/73/EC.

newly built storage facility cannot reserve all capacity for its supply business excluding other suppliers in a discriminatory manner.[967]

A market participant, on the other hand, can engage in market power manipulation without the necessity of access to storage facilities under certain market conditions. A dominant undertaking which has access to natural gas supplies through its activities in upstream markets and operates as a pivotal supplier for other market participants active in wholesale natural gas markets may engage in supply contracts in which it holds long positions. When contracts mature and the contracted quantities must be delivered, the dominant undertaking can use its pivotal role to corner its counterparties which have no substitutes to fulfil their contractual obligation. Even though the perpetration of this scheme requires substantial market dominance involving very large market shares and vertical integration, the characteristics of European natural gas markets are sufficient to allow market power manipulation. Almost all European national markets are dominated by state-owned energy supply undertakings active in upstream, midstream and downstream segments of the natural gas sector and the majority of trading activities is carried out in OTC markets under bilateral contracts through which dominant suppliers can exploit their market power.[968]

It is important to note that the market manipulation prohibition under REMIT is not the sole remedy that national competent authorities can resort to in prosecuting these market activities in European wholesale natural gas markets. EU competition law can also play a major role through antitrust proceedings[969] and commitment decisions[970] under Article 102 of TFEU. How this type of market behaviour is prosecuted without giving rise to concerns on the *ne bis in idem* principle (double jeopardy) and overlapping jurisdictions remains to be seen.

[C] Trade-Based Manipulation

[1] Concept

US case law defines these types of manipulation as 'open market transactions' providing that they involve actual market transactions in which perpetrators engage in actual buy and sell orders with actual parties with economic risks and consequences.[971] These practices differ from fraud-based transactions and outright fraud, as the perpetrators of trade-based manipulation do not directly employ fraudulent schemes such as wash trades, matched orders or dissemination of false information to mislead other

967. Article 13 (1)(b), Directive 2009/73/EC.
968. Even though, as of 2015, the OTC trading accounts for 67% of all natural gas traded in the EU, the share of hub trading in which natural gas contracts are cleared through an established clearinghouse is increasing. *Supra* note 24.
969. Article 7, Council Regulation (EC) No 1/2003 of 16 Dec. 2002 on the implementation of the rules on competition laid down in Articles 81 and 82 of the Treaty [2003] OJ L 1/1.
970. Article 9, Council Regulation (EC) No 1/2003.
971. *Sundheimer v. CFTC*, 688 F.2d 150 (2d Cir. 1982), *cert. denied*, 460 U.S. 112 (1983); *United States v. Radley*, 659 F. Supp. 2d 803 (S.D. Tex. 2009); *United States v. Mulheren*, 938 F.3d 364 (2d Cir. 1991).

traders into believing that certain demand and supply levels other than those that represent actual conditions in markets are present. Perpetrators rely on their trading activities and their effects on market prices, rather than providing false information to markets to deceive other market participants. A trade-based manipulation can also operate as a deceit upon markets and other traders. Nevertheless, whether or not a trade-based manipulation is of a fraudulent character does not lead to the conclusion that such a manipulation is regarded as outright fraud. A transaction can be considered as outright fraud, only if it is established that it has no actual effects on markets and involves no economic risk and net change in beneficial ownership.[972]

As discussed above, market power manipulation such as corners and squeezes can also be considered a trade-based manipulation, as perpetrators of these practices engage in actual trades with actual counterparties to give effect to and profit from consequent price changes. In fact the prosecution of these practices under US law even predates the identification of trade-based manipulation as a separate type. The traditional classification demarcated market manipulation into two types as artificial price-based and fraud-based practices did not provide a further classification under artificial price-based manipulation. This is because market power manipulation constituted the only type of market manipulation through which a market participant could move prices at artificial level without resorting to fraudulent or fictitious practices.[973] This has changed since the advent of derivatives and new market platforms which have made it possible for market participants to devise a wide spectrum of strategies without resorting to fraudulent behaviour and the concept of market manipulation has evolved with market innovation in the preparation and the execution of contracts.[974] These new strategies are of a character different from that identified under market power manipulation and, as US case law clearly illustrates, they have been effectively used in energy markets. In pursuant to the approach adopted in the previous chapter, this chapter examines market power manipulation and trade-based manipulation as two distinct forms to evaluate the legal implications of these new strategies in European wholesale energy markets.

[2] Demarcation of Trade-Based Manipulation

In analysing the examples of trade-based market manipulation and their implications in the EU, the chapter follows the demarcation provided under US case law. As

972. *See Markowski v. SEC*, 274 F.3d 525 (D.D.Cir. 2011), *cert. denied*, 537 U.S. 813 (2002). The District of Columbia Court of Appeals stressed that transactions that involved real customers, real transactions and real money could not be considered as market manipulation that use fraudulent devices.

973. Marking the close and successive bidding practices can also be considered as examples of traditional trade-based market manipulation as these types of activities were frequent in 'Wall Street Pools' later in nineteenth century. However, the effectiveness of these strategies proved to be very difficult and risky without supporting cross-market positions or fraudulent behaviour. *See* Daniel R. Fishel & David J. Ross, 520 (1991).

974. Maxwell K. Multer, *Open-Market Manipulation under SEC Rule 10b-5 and Its Analogies: Inappropriate Distinctions, Judicial Disagreement and Case Study: FERC's Anti-Manipulation Rule* 97 Securities Regulation Law Journal (2011).

discussed in detail, the legal literature, so far, has failed to provide a definition and a classification of market manipulation. This is partly because of the difficulties in establishing taxonomy of factors that render market behaviour manipulative. It is not the aim of this book to construct an alternative definition for market manipulation which requires extensive econometric calculations, evaluating price relations between multiple markets and effects of market practices thereon. Instead of providing an alternative definition or choosing one proposed in the legal literature, the book engages in case law analysis to evaluate on what grounds market practices are regarded as manipulative and how they mirror or differ from each other. Following the demarcation under US case law, this chapter analyses trade-based market manipulation in European wholesale energy markets in relation to REMIT and discussions provided in EU soft law.

[a] Gaming of Market Rules

US case law clearly illustrates that energy markets are prone to gaming practices by market participants who seek to exploit loopholes in market rules to reap financial benefits from their activities in wholesale energy markets.[975] The feasibility of these market practices does not rely on trading in wholesale energy products. Sell and buy orders submitted by perpetrators are either uneconomic or of little value. The trading activities are profitable only after payments meaning that the perpetrators' conduct is not profitable but for the related payments, due under market rules are received. FERC concluded that these market practices constitute the gaming of market rules and thus are in violation of its anti-manipulation rule.

[i] In Electricity Markets

The establishment of a competitive energy market design has been a crucial policy objective under the liberalisation of European energy markets seeking to ensure a secure and affordable energy supply to all European consumers.[976] In electricity, continuing integration of national markets since the adoption of early liberalisation packages has led all Member States to adopt a pool market model, called 'energy-only markets' meaning that all suppliers of electricity submit bids at which they want to sell their output in a market which is operated by transmission system operators or designated market operators.[977] These markets consist of sub-markets such as DAMs, RTMs and balancing markets in which suppliers submit bids on the basis of marginal costs at which their generation facilities operate. This process results in the

975. *Rumford Paper Company*, 140 FERC ¶ 61,030 (2012); *In Re Make-Whole Payments and Related Bidding Strategies*, 144 FERC ¶ 61,068 (2013); *Coaltrain Energy, L.P., et al.*, 154 FERC ¶ 61,002 (2016).
976. Communication from the Commission to the European Parliament, the Council, the European Economic and Social Committee, the Committee of the Regions and the European Investment Bank, A Framework Strategy for a Resilient Energy Union with a Forward-Looking Climate Change Policy (COM/2015/080) final.
977. *Supra* note 11.

establishment of a 'merit order' where market operators align suppliers based on their bids from cheap to expensive for further dispatch. Market operators select generating units from cheaper plants until they satisfy the projected electricity demand. The highest bid that is selected by market operators determines market prices that would be paid to all generating units. While plants with lower marginal costs are mostly selected, those with higher marginal costs are often left outside the merit order.

While selecting the cheaper generation units for merit order is useful for the objective of providing electricity at affordable prices, this market mechanism gives rise to concerns on the reliability of electricity supply as the functioning of these low-margin generation units depends on several factors such as weather conditions. The volume of electricity produced from these units fluctuates considerably over seasons and market operators are obliged to look for other supplies from more reliable generators which can be very expensive to operate. Nevertheless, these expensive generators are generally left out of money in energy-only markets and face decommissioning, since they are not feasible to operate. This endangers the market operators' access to reliable and uninterrupted access to electricity and threatens the functioning of European wholesale markets when additional demand arises or a malfunction or interruption takes place in low-margin generation plants. In order to balance demand and supply throughout the year and to ensure uninterrupted and reliable access to electricity at affordable rates, market operators are required to establish a market model that effectively utilises generation units with low and high marginal costs. This model often takes the form of 'Capacity Mechanisms' through which market operators guarantee that a substantial volume is available for use as a reserve capacity.[978] Accordingly, generation units which are generally not included in merit orders are paid a premium which is higher than usual market prices determined under wholesale markets, to ensure that they stay operational when related market conditions arise.

Even though the availability of such mechanisms is fundamental for security of supply, they are also vulnerable to market manipulation by market participants seeking to receive additional payments, called capacity payments, outside the prices paid under wholesale electricity markets. Market participants either alone or in collaboration may engage in certain schemes that lead market operators to make these capacity payments. The objective of these schemes does not involve supplying electricity to transmission grids for system balancing and security of supply. Rather, market participants transact to create market conditions that lead transmission or market operators to make payments on the basis of capacity mechanism. The legal analysis must show that the perpetrators' scheme is profitable only after the capacity payments were received due to related market conditions and that the perpetrators engaged in such conduct in order to exploit these payments rather than profiting from their output or price differential.

978. There is a wide range of capacity mechanism designs such as 'Strategic Reserve', 'Capacity Obligation', 'Capacity Auction', 'Reliability Option', 'Strategic Reserve'. *See* ACER, 'Reports on Capacity Remuneration Mechanisms and The Internal Market for Electricity' (30 Jul. 2013). For a detailed information, *see also* L. Hancher, et al., *Capacity Mechanisms in the EU Energy Market: Law, Policy and Economics* (OUP 2015).

US case law clearly illustrates how payments under capacity mechanisms can be exploited by suppliers in electricity markets. In *Rumford Paper Company*,[979] for example, the DALRP was a capacity mechanism, the market operator in New England (ISO-NE) adopted to ensure system balancing. Accordingly, market participants buying electricity from wholesale markets were paid when they reduced their electricity demand during peak hours. The scheme devised in *Rumford Paper Company* allowed the perpetrator to receive the capacity payments without reducing its electricity demand in the wholesale market. Even though the scheme was uneconomical on a stand-alone basis, the payments received through the DALRP were more than enough to compensate the losses incurred by the perpetrator. Therefore FERC found that the relevant conduct was in violation of its anti-manipulation rule, 18 C.F.R. § 1c.2. The market conduct in *Rumford Paper Company* constitutes a clear example of 'gaming' practices in wholesale electricity markets and is relevant to the establishment of capacity mechanisms across the EU.[980]

[ii] In Natural Gas Markets

In natural gas, the EU adopted several measures establishing entry-exit zones across Member States, along with the hub-based pricing mechanism in which quantities of natural gas are traded in liquid spot markets through forward and futures contracts.[981] A gas trading hub is a liquidity instrument in which exchanges between the buyers and sellers in the market take place. They may have a physical geographical location and can be linked to a physical installation, e.g., the Henry Hub in the US and the Zeebrugge gas hub in Belgium. On the other hand, a gas hub can also be virtual without physical installations, such as the NBP in the UK or the TTF in the Netherlands. These hubs provide great flexibility to market participants[982] and help them anticipate the correlations between supply and demand before booking the infrastructure capacities, which in turn ensures the effective flow of natural gas and effective allocation of existing capacities and also operate as a market-based pricing benchmark which is used in the greater geographic region as an indicator of natural gas prices.

979. *Rumford Paper Company*, 140 FERC ¶ 61,030 (2012).
980. Charles River Associates, *Capacity Market Gaming and Consistency Assessment – Final Report* 41–42 CRA Project No D18985-00 (September 2013).
981. The restructuring of wholesale markets is still in progress. Despite the considerable success in the northwestern natural gas hubs, 'National Balancing Point' (the NBP) in the UK and 'Title Transfer Facility' in the Netherlands which together host 88% of all hub-traded natural gas in the EU, the majority of natural gas in the EU is still traded through OTC trading. The hub-based trading only constitutes around 30% of all natural gas traded. See *supra* note 24.
982. Natural gas markets generally consist of three different classes of market participants. *Producers* are market participants who engage in exploration and extraction business to produce natural gas from on-shore or offshore natural gas reserves. *Suppliers* are those which buy natural gas to supply to small/medium sized enterprises and households. *Shippers* are the main market participants that participate in trading in hubs and use transmission systems to transport natural gas from producers to suppliers.

Hubs are operated by transmission system operators or independent market operators and the reliability of transmission systems requires certain capacity mechanisms through which market operators seek to balance between demand/supply levels and ensure security of supply. To a limited extent, natural gas injected into pipelines can be compressed or expanded when the volume of natural gas injected does not match that withdrawn from the transmission system. When this flexibility does not suffice to maintain the system integrity, market operators can apply measures and charges that provide financial incentives to market participants to inject to or withdraw from transmission systems. These measures are called imbalance charges and are adopted to ensure system balancing by market participants themselves.[983] Complexities in a transmission system may also require market operators to engage in trading and act as a Residual Balancer.[984] Accordingly market operators can buy or sell natural gas to balance pressure exerted by supply of or demand for energy.

Existing case law in the US and the EU does not suffice to provide an insight into how certain rules in natural gas markets can become subject to proceedings under anti-manipulation provisions. Nevertheless, the measures adopted for transmission system balancing constitute clear examples of financial positions that market participants can seek to exploit and to derive profits from their activities in wholesale natural gas markets. A market participant may find it profitable to receive payments on the basis of imbalance charges or a market operator's participation in wholesale markets as a residual balancer. In these situations, case law on gaming of market rules provides that the legal analysis should assess whether the trading practice by the market participant is uneconomic or of little economic value but for the payment received via balancing measures. A competent regulatory or competition authority may find a violation of the anti-manipulation rule, if it is established that the practice at issue aims at receiving payments or benefits under balancing measures rather than profiting from output or price differentials.

The perpetration of these types of market manipulation is closely related to inefficiencies in market design and monitoring measures which together render European wholesale energy markets vulnerable to manipulative practices. Certain measures, such as capacity mechanisms or imbalance charges, necessary for the reliability of transmission system operators and security of supply, can be used by market participants in perpetration of their manipulative schemes. The establishment

983. There are two types of imbalance charges. First, transmission system operators may pay a certain price to market participants who inject natural gas more than had been contracted. As the price paid by the transmission system operators is less than market-based rates, market participants incur losses and have an incentive to withdraw the excess volume. Second, transmission system operators may charge a certain price which is higher than market rates, when it is established that market participants required to inject certain volume of natural gas to transmission systems are short of delivery. In order to prevent paying charges higher than market rates, market participants inject more natural gas to transmission systems. National Grid, *End-to-end Balancing Guide*, 13 (March 2016). *See also* EFET Gas Committee, *Framework Guidelines for Gas Balancing*, (June 2010), http://www.efet.org/Files/Documents/Gas%20Market/Gas%20balancing%20market/EFET%20FG%20on%20Gas%20Balancing.pdf (accessed 18 Apr. 2018).

984. National Grid, 6 (2016).

of a market design which provides a level playing field along with the security of supply is the key for dealing with market manipulation in energy markets. In order to increase regulatory oversight and prevent market abuse, the European Commission and ACER proposed several market models.[985] To what extent the proposed market designs may be effective in preventing market manipulation remains to be seen.

[b] Cross-Market Manipulation

Given the advent of derivatives which enabled energy suppliers and traders to exploit pricing relations between different contracts and markets, cross-market manipulation has become a major concern in wholesale energy products. US case law clearly illustrates that perpetrators holding physical and/or financial positions in different, yet closely related markets have incentives to exploit the links between these positions. Profit maximisation is achieved through a portfolio of positions rather than profiting from output or trading in price differentials. Price levels artificially determined by these manipulative trades do not represent actual market conditions and send misleading signals to other suppliers and traders not justified by the existing forces of demand and supply levels.

Despite providing several examples that are regarded as in-scope for the prohibition of market manipulation, REMIT does not directly address and define cross-market manipulation. Instead, it holds that effects of manipulation may not be confined to markets where perpetration takes place.[986] It is ACER which provides a definition of cross-market manipulation and identifies it as a form of price positioning under Article 2(2)(a)(ii). ACER defines cross-market manipulation as '(t)*rading on one market to improperly position the price of a wholesale energy product on a related market*'.[987] The scope of this definition is wide and is not limited solely to price effects which occur across physical and financial markets. Various positions such as those across borders or between natural gas and electricity can be subject to manipulative schemes by market participants who seek to exploit through practices in related markets.

[i] Perpetration

The perpetration of a cross-market manipulation involves two different but related positions: price-making and price-taking markets.[988] While the former represents

985. *See* Gas Target Model and Proposal for a Regulation of the European Parliament and of the Council on the Internal Market for Electricity, COM(2016) 861 final/2.
986. '*Manipulation and its effects may occur across borders, between electricity and gas markets and across financial and commodity markets, including the emission allowances markets.*' Recital 13, Regulation No 1227/2011.
987. ACER's Guidance on the application of Regulation (EU) No 1227/2011 of the European Parliament and of the Council of 25 Oct. 2011 on wholesale energy market integrity and transparency, (4th edn., 2016), 38.
988. Some authors argue that the perpetration of market manipulation also requires a nexus element that connects price-making and price-taking positions. This is particularly true in benchmark cases in which perpetrators transact to change index prices which in turn affect the profitability

markets and products where perpetrators engage in transactions, the latter consists of positions whose value depends on prices and conditions in the former. Price-making positions are usually held in physical markets or physical products as changes in these positions directly affect the forces of demand and supply. Since perpetrators aim at moving prices at artificial levels rather than profiting from output or price differentials, manipulative transactions often involve selling and buying orders at respectively low and high prices.[989] Therefore, these transactions are often loss incurring or uneconomic on a stand-alone basis. Price-taking positions, on the other hand, may be held in both physical and financial markets and products. For example, as in *Energy Trading Partners,* a market participant which is a net purchaser in an energy product or market may engage in short selling at lower prices so that it can buy larger volumes at these artificially decreased prices. Accordingly, both the price-making and price-taking positions are in physical markets and products. The perpetrator's activity of short selling is uneconomic as it could have sold the relevant volume at higher market prices. However, its net buyer position in the forward market benefits from lower energy prices which more than compensates the losses incurred due to short selling.

Examples of price-making and price-taking positions are provided by several EU soft law instruments, prior to the adoption of REMIT, to stress the necessity of a tailor-made legal framework to deal with anti-competitive practices in wholesale energy markets. The CESR and ERGEG, in their advice to the European Commission in the context of market abuse in energy markets, pointed out that there are crucial interdependencies between electricity and natural gas markets.[990] Natural gas is a major product that is used for electricity generation and price changes occurring in natural gas affect prices in wholesale electricity markets. Market participants active in both electricity and natural gas supply markets are better positioned to explore and exploit these interdependencies.

Another significant factor that gives rise to concerns on cross-market manipulation is increasing price correlations between different national wholesale energy markets. The current developments in the structure of wholesale energy markets, such as the establishment of power exchanges and hubs where spot electricity and natural gas products are traded, results in transactions in energy products having more of a cross-border character. Providing the example of the price correlations in France and Germany to illustrate how they create possibilities for cross-border market manipulation, the Commission's impact assessment points out that the correlation between prices of neighbouring countries is increasing to the extent that market participants active in neighbouring Member States may easily foresee how changes in market conditions in a national or regional energy market may affect prices in neighbouring

of related financial and physical positions and index prices serve as a nexus for these price-making and price-taking positions. Nevertheless, the chapter does not prefer to address a nexus position as a requirement for defining market manipulation as the methods that market participants perpetrate market manipulation evolve based on market innovation and a nexus position may not be available for all types of market manipulation. *See* Shaun D. Ledgerwood & Paul R. Carpenter (2012).

989. Gary Taylor, et al., 194 (2015).
990. CESR and ERGEG, 6 (2008).

markets.[991] Any shortages in energy supply or outages in electricity generation in one Member State, the triggering Member State, may directly affect market prices in neighbouring Member States, targeted Member States and market participants which are net buyers of energy products in one or more targeted Member States have financial incentives to engage in short selling in the triggering Member State. Detection and prosecution of these manipulative schemes require monitoring measures at supranational level and close collaboration between national and community competent authorities.

Finally, the pricing relations between physical and financial markets or products constitute a major concern in wholesale energy markets as to cross-market manipulation. US case law clearly illustrates that the linkages between physical and derivatives contracts are vulnerable to market manipulation by undertakings trading in both physical and financial markets.[992] Market participants have significant incentives to gain profits from derivatives contracts through trading in underlying products. Identifying the scope of REMIT's anti-manipulation provision, ACER addresses this type of market conduct as a major example of cross-market manipulation.[993] The impact assessment further refers to *Amaranth* as a case study to demonstrate the adverse effects that the exploitation of price relations between physical and financial products could have on energy markets and the necessity of a legal framework that specifically deals with this type of market misconduct.[994]

[ii] Applicable Frameworks

It is important to note that the nature of positions that are subject to cross-market manipulation is important in determining jurisdictions under which anti-manipulation rules are applied. As mentioned above, MAR also includes anti-manipulation rules which differ from those adopted under REMIT.[995] The scope of MAR is far-reaching, including commodity products that affect in-scope financial instruments, which are not limited to and extend beyond those provided under Annex I, Section C of MiFID/MiFIR 2014.[996] The only carve-out provision that MAR incorporates is wholesale spot energy products which MAR does not apply to, even if they have price impacts on in-scope financial instruments.[997] Wholesale energy derivatives which can be settled financially and physically are under MAR's jurisdiction and are thus outside the scope of REMIT.[998]

991. REMIT Impact Assessment, 9 (2010).
992. *See Barclays Bank PLC, Daniel Brin, Scott Connelly, et al.*, 141 FERC ¶ 61,084 (2012); *Amaranth Advisors L.L.C. et. al.*, 120 FERC ¶ 61,085 (2007); *Total Gas & Power North America Inc., et al.*, 155 FERC ¶61,105 (2016); *BP America Inc., BP Corporation North America et al.*, 144 FERC ¶ 61,100 (2013); *Barclays Bank PLC, Daniel Brin, Scott Connelly, et al.*, 141 FERC ¶ 61,084 (2012).
993. ACER's Guidance, 38 (2016).
994. REMIT Impact Assessment, 14 (2010).
995. Article 12(1)(d), Regulation No 596/2014.
996. Article 2(1), Regulation No 596/2014.
997. Article 2(2)(a), Regulation No 596/2014.
998. Article 1(2), Regulation No 1227/2011.

The exclusion of derivatives from REMIT's jurisdiction is important as it directly affects the prosecution of market manipulation in wholesale energy markets. First, as MAR is the applicable jurisdiction for market misconduct which includes trading in energy derivatives, the competent authorities that oversee and enforce the anti-manipulation rule would be financial regulators. This requires extensive collaboration between energy and financial regulators at both national and EU levels in monitoring trading in energy derivatives and detecting market manipulation. Second, these types of market misconduct are subject to the enforcement regime under MAR which provides that practices violating its anti-manipulation rules would be punishable by a term of imprisonment of at least four years. Despite requiring Member States to adopt the necessary enforcement mechanisms for the prosecution and the punishment of market manipulation, REMIT does not adopt a sanction regime that requires harmonisation of penalties for the breaches in its anti-manipulation rules. Enforcement powers conferred on competent authorities by Member States at national level with respect to the prosecution of market manipulation under REMIT are very diverse.[999] Finally, this type of market misconduct is not identified as price positioning under MAR. As discussed, ACER stipulates that cross-market manipulation in wholesale energy markets constitutes a form of price positioning and thus is prosecuted under Article 2(2)(a)(ii) of REMIT. MAR, on the other hand, puts forward a new type of market manipulation definition, called *Benchmark manipulation*, to identify and prosecute these types of market misconduct.

MAR introduces a separate definition for benchmark manipulation which proscribes any type of market behaviour, such as transmitting false information or submitting transactions seeking to move prices of a particular financial instrument at artificial level.[1000] This demarcation is particularly important for the establishment of cross-market manipulation in wholesale energy markets, as the majority of cross-market practices involve market participants seeking to distort benchmark prices through transactions in physical markets to derive profits from financial positions. As mentioned above, prior to the adoption of REMIT, EU soft law specifically cited *Amaranth Advisors L.L.C. et al.* to stress the necessity of a tailor-made legal framework to deal with market manipulation in wholesale energy markets.[1001] ACER also notes the abuse of price relations between financial and physical products as an example of market misconduct and price positioning and thus prosecutable under Article 5. Nevertheless, the consequent sector-specific regulation does not apply to these types of market manipulation since wholesale energy derivatives are excluded from the scope of REMIT. In other words, although market misconduct which is similar to that perpetrated in *Amaranth Advisors L.L.C. et al.* paved way for the adoption of REMIT, it is not prosecutable and punishable under REMIT.

999. ACER, *ACER's Annual Report on Its Activities under REMIT in 2014* 63 (September 2015), https://www.acer.europa.eu/Official_documents/Acts_of_the_Agency/Publication/REMIT%20Annual%20Report%202015.pdf (accessed 18 Apr. 2018).
1000. Article 12(1)(d), Regulation No 596/2014.
1001. REMIT Impact Assessment, 14 (2010).

The majority of cases of market manipulation in the US involve the abuse of price relations between physical and financial markets through manipulating index prices.[1002] These cases clearly show that index prices constitute a nexus between physical and financial positions, that is, perpetrators submit their manipulative transactions to indices to affect index prices which determine the profitability of related financial positions. Energy derivatives contracts such as options and swaps often involve reference to index prices published by trade press entities, such as Platts and NGI in the US or Argus and ICIS Heren in the EU which collect transactions and information as to particular markets and products to publish index prices. The profitability of these derivatives contracts depends on changes in index prices. Given that transactions are collected by or reported to indices for index publishing, perpetrators engage in manipulative trades in physical markets to move index prices at levels profitable to their related financial positions. Despite the jurisdictional discussions between financial and sector-specific regulators in the US, FERC effectively exercises its authority over these types of market conduct under its anti-manipulation rules. The legal framework in the EU, on the other hand designates only financial regulators as appropriate authorities under MAR, which considerably limits the scope of REMIT's market manipulation prohibition.

[iii] Commission's Role

It is important to note that the Commission is more active than energy and financial regulatory authorities in prosecuting cross-market manipulation. How anti-manipulation rules under REMIT and MAR are enforced remains to be seen, since the existing regulatory framework is rather new and case law on cross-market manipulation has not yet developed. Nevertheless, the Commission has continuously opened proceedings under EU competition law against several market practices that can be identified as cross-market manipulation.[1003] *EURIBOR*[1004] is an important example in which the Commission found that the defendants' fixing of several interest rates such as the London Interbank Offered Rate (LIBOR) and the Euro Interbank Offered Rate, (EURIBOR) constituted collusion and thus was a violation of Article 101 of TFEU.[1005] EURIBOR is a benchmark interest rate reflecting the cost of interbank lending in euros and determining the profitability of several financial contracts such as swaps, options and futures, which derive their value on the basis of fluctuations in interest rates. The Commission concluded that the defendants, eight of the biggest international financial

1002. *See Energy Transfer Partners, L.P. et. al.*, 120 FERC ¶ 61,086 (2007); *Amaranth Advisors L.L.C. et. al.*, 120 FERC ¶ 61,085 (2007); *Total Gas & Power North America Inc., et al.*, 155 FERC ¶61,105 (2016); *BP America Inc., BP Corporation North America et al.*, 144 FERC 61,100 (2013); *Barclays Bank PLC, Daniel Brin, Scott Connelly, et al.*, 141 FERC ¶ 61,084 (2012).
1003. *Euro Interest Rate Derivatives* (Case AT.39914) Commission Decision of 4 Dec. 2013; *Yen Interest Rate Derivatives* (Case AT. 39861) Commission Decision of 4 Dec. 2013; *Ethanol Benchmarks* (Case AT.40054).
1004. *Euro Interest Rate Derivatives* (Case AT.39914) Commission Decision of 4 Dec. 2013.
1005. European Commission, *Press Release, Antitrust: Commission Fines Banks € 1.49 Billion for Participating in Cartels in the Interest Rate Derivatives Industry* (Brussels, 4 Dec. 2013) http://europa.eu/rapid/press-release_IP-13-1208_en.htm (accessed 29 Jun. 2017).

institutions which held significant financial positions, engaged in information sharing practices as to their submissions to the European Banking Federation which calculated and published EURIBOR. In so doing, the defendants derived significant profits from their related financial positions.

The establishment of price fixing cartels among competitors is considered a hardcore restriction to trade meaning that given that their objective is to restrict competition, these market practices are in violation of EU competition law per se, and it is very difficult for defendants to establish that their conduct, in fact, increases competition across the EU or serves a legitimate business purpose.[1006] In *EURIBOR*, the Commission considered that the defendants' conduct aiming at distorting benchmark prices constituted hardcore restrictions to trade, when they were perpetrated by multiple market participants in collaboration and thus in violation of Article 101 of TFEU. Imposing fines exceeding USD 2 million on the banks, the Commission has shown that it has no compunction in enforcing Article 101 in unconventional situations, beyond the usual price fixing cartels.[1007]

The Commission's findings under *EURIBOR* raise important questions as to the legal implications underlying wholesale energy markets. It is reasonable to expect that misconduct perpetrated by multiple market participants to collaboratively manipulate benchmark prices for wholesale electricity and natural gas products would result in antitrust proceedings at EU level. However, whether or not the Commission's practice would be the same, if it is established that the relevant benchmark manipulation is perpetrated by one dominant trader, rather than multiple market participants, is an open question. As mentioned, the Commission has been reluctant to enforce Article 102 of TFEU against excessive pricing practices by dominant undertakings. In *EURIBOR*, acknowledging that the reliability of benchmarks is crucial for the proper functioning of financial markets, the Commission specifically stressed that it was the collusion between banks that was targeted under its antitrust enforcement. Therefore, benchmark manipulation by a single market participant may not result in an intervention by the Commission under Article 102.

At national level, such misconduct can be subject to investigations under MAR and competition law. National competition authorities are more active in prosecuting excessive pricing practices under Article 102 and can exercise their authority over market participants who manipulate benchmarks by using their market power. In *EURIBOR*, the defendants' conduct was also subject to proceedings at national level under financial regulation. In the UK, the Financial Services Authority imposed the largest fines in its history on the defendants for their manipulation of LIBOR and EURIBOR.[1008] The defendants have been fined under different jurisdictions and

1006. *See* Commission, *Guidelines on the application of Article 101(3) TFEU (formerly Article 81(3) TEC)* (Communication) OJ 2004 C101/97: Vol II App C13, paras 20, 46.
1007. *Supra* note 1005.
1008. *See* Financial Conduct Authority, Press Release, *UBS fined £160 million for significant failings in relation to LIBOR and EURIBOR* (19 Dec. 2012), https://www.fca.org.uk/news/press-releases/ubs-fined-%C2%A3160-million-significant-failings-relation-libor-and-euribor (accessed 29 Jun. 2017).

different legal frameworks.[1009] This may result in overlapping jurisdictions between national competition authorities and financial regulators, as the latter can also open proceedings under Article 12 of MAR giving rise to concerns about the *ne bis in idem* principle. Even though EU case law provides that the existence of sector-specific regulation at national or EU level cannot preclude competition authorities exercising their authority under EU competition law,[1010] the collaboration between competition and financial regulators is fundamental for the effective prosecution of market manipulation.

The Commission's intervention in *EURIBOR*, also raises questions as to the enforcement of competition law to cross-market manipulation which does not involve manipulation of benchmark prices. As discussed, physical wholesale products are subject to market manipulation prohibition under REMIT. A cross-market manipulation can involve physical wholesale markets in different wholesale energy markets. For example market participants can engage in continuous short sales in physical electricity or natural gas markets to reduce prices with the expectation that achieved low price levels can enable market participants access to energy supplies at low prices. The findings in *EURIBOR* show that such cross-market practices can also give effect to proceedings by the Commission under EU competition law, if they are perpetrated by multiple parties through collusive conduct.

Furthermore, *EURIBOR* clearly shows that a misconduct prosecuted by the Commission under EU competition law can also be investigated and sanctioned by financial regulators at national level. Even though the application of multiple jurisdictions to the same market misconduct may be regarded as problematic for the establishment of a consistent single rulebook that governs European energy markets, it has not given rise to concerns on the *ne bis in idem* principle. It can be reasonable to assert that the Commission may exercise its jurisdiction at EU level under EU competition law against a conduct, due to its effects on trade between Member States, though the same conduct may also prosecuted and sanctioned at national level under national regulation. However, concerns can arise when the same misconduct is prosecuted under both national competition law and REMIT or corresponding national sector-specific regulation.

[c] Congestion-Related Manipulation

This type of market manipulation involves market participants engaging in practices to benefit from alterations in congestion levels in national or regional transmission systems, rather than trading in output or price differences. Energy markets are

---

1009. Banks' rate fixing activities have also become subject to investigations in the US Also Libor case in the US. *See* U.S. Commodity Futures Trading Commission, *CFTC Orders Barclays to pay $200 Million Penalty for Attempted Manipulation of and False Reporting concerning LIBOR and Euribor Benchmark Interest Rates*, pr6239-12 (27 Jun. 2012), http://www.cftc.gov/PressRoom/PressReleases/pr6289-12 (accessed 29 Jun. 2017).

1010. Case T-336/07 *Telefonica SA and Telefonica de Espana v. European Commission* [2012] 2008 OJ C83/6, the appeal from *Wanadoo Espana/Telefonica* (COMP/38.784) Commission Decision of 04 July, 2007; Case T-271/03, *Deutsche Telekom v. Commission* [2008] ECR II-477.

network-based and pipelines and grids that serve the purpose of transmitting natural gas and electricity from producers or generators to other suppliers and consumers are capacity-restricted, that is, the amount of natural gas and electricity to be transported for a certain time period depends on the capacity of pipelines and grids used for transportation. When the amount of energy to be transported exceeds the capacity of transmission lines to be used, congestion occurs.[1011] Generally, the majority of baseload power plants such as nuclear and hydropower generators are located in rural areas far from major consumption centres and where demand for energy is low. Congestion generally takes place from geographic regions where demand for energy is low to those where it is high. When demand for electricity exceeds available transmission capacity, flow from these rural areas to the consumption centres is congested. This results in changes in energy prices across transmission systems and the division of national or regional markets into different pricing zones where energy products are traded.

[i] Perpetration

Exploiting Congestion Management Mechanism

In order to alleviate congestion levels, transmission system operators have developed several CACM mechanisms. The methods that transmission system operators use in relieving congestion involve both financial and physical instruments. Financial congestion management mechanisms include FTRs and contracts for difference (CfDs). Congestion in a particular transmission line results in price differences between the point energy is injected into the system (source) and the point where it is withdrawn from the system (sink). While the price for energy decreases at source, it increases at sink. The price difference between the source and sink is called the congestion price.[1012] Suppliers who wish to transport energy at congested lines indirectly pay this congestion price by selling their energy output at source at decreased prices. FTRs entitle their holders to receive price differences between source and sink.[1013] CfDs, on the other hand, operate as swap agreements through which market participants hedge their financial risks arising from congestion levels and price differences.[1014]

Even though being financially settled, FTRs are not one of the financial instruments listed under the MiFID 2014 Annex I, Section C.[1015] Unlike other energy

1011. Petri Mantysaari, 45 (2015).
1012. Paul Joskow & Jean Tirole, *Transmission Rights and Market Power on Electric Power Networks I: Financial Rights* 2 Centre for Economic Policy Research, Discussion Paper No 2093 (1998).
1013. ENTSO-E, *Transmission Risk Hedging Products*, An ENTSO-E Educational Paper, 8 (ENTSO-E Education Paper 2012), https://www.entsoe.eu/fileadmin/user_upload/_library/consultations/Network_Code_CACM/20120619_Educational_Paper_on_Risk_Hedging_Instruments_review5.pdf (accessed 29 Jun. 2017).
1014. *Ibid.*, 11.
1015. Whether or not FTRs constitute financial instruments under financial regulation has been discussed in the EU, since such rights have been first introduced in energy markets. Transmission system operators argue that even though such rights can be considered as financial instruments, they should benefit from the incidental activity exemption under

derivatives which can be issued by market participants without any limitations on quantity, FTRs can only be issued by transmission system operators and have to reflect the physical capacity available in relevant transmission lines. Market participants cannot acquire as many FTRs as they want and they can receive these rights only for hedging price risks arising from capacity congestion and not for speculation purposes. The CfDs also constitute an effective hedging mechanism, as market participants who are trading energy products via highly congested transmission lines are exposed to serious price risks. These contracts involve two different reference prices at which market participants value their positions. Generally, but not necessarily, these reference prices consist of one fluctuating and one fixed price. If the difference between the fluctuating price and the fixed price is positive, the buyer of CfDs receives payment on the basis of this positive price difference. If it is negative, however, the buyer of CfDs pays the difference between the fixed price and the negative price to the seller.

In US case law, the availability of FTRs and CfDs has been a major factor for the perpetration of congestion-related manipulation. In both *Constellation*[1016] and *Louis Dreyfus Energy Services L.P.*,[1017] market participants trading to increase congestion levels had significant positions in related FTRs and CfDs which became profitable with the changes in congestion levels. In these cases, the perpetrators' trading of wholesale electricity products was uneconomic, leading to limited financial returns or even losses. The trading practices were profitable, only after the profits derived from related FTRs and CfDs were included. Placing bids and offers for purchase and sale of energy products, the perpetrators did not aim at profit maximisation from their output or price differences. Rather they sought to increase congestion levels at transmission lines which directly affected the profitability of their FTRs and CfDs.

Even though the use of FTRs[1018] and CfDs[1019] for congestion management purposes is increasing, the development of financial mechanisms is still under development as the majority of Member States implement physical measures to deal with congestion.[1020] Physical instruments that transmission system operators designate to alleviate congestion levels include market-based and non-market-based methods.

Article 2(1)(c) of MiFID 2014. *See ibid.*, 29; *See also* Eurelectric, *Eurelectric's concerns on the negative impact of Financial Transmission Rights being classified as financial instruments under MiFID 2014 on the completion of the internal energy market,* (Eurelectric letter to the DG FISMA of 19 Nov. 2015), http://www.eurelectric.org/media/247826/20151119_eurelectric_ftr_letter_to_dg_fisma_final-2015-2220-0014-01-e.pdf (accessed 29 Jun. 2017).

1016. *Constellation Energy Commodities Group Inc.*, 138 FERC ¶ 61,168 (2012).

1017. *MISO Virtual and FTR Trading,* 146 FERC ¶ 61,072 (2014).

1018. FTRs have been used in Italy and Spain-Portugal border. *See* Economic Consulting Associates, *European Electricity Forward Markets and Hedging Products – State of Play and Elements for Monitoring,* VIII (Final Report, September 2015), http://www.acer.europa.eu/en/electricity/market%20monitoring/documents_public/eca%20report%20on%20european%20electricity%20forward%20markets.pdf (accessed 29 Jun. 2017). Belgium and the Netherlands also introduced FTRs in their congestion management mechanism. *See* EFET, *Introduction of Financial Transmission Rights* (Market ESC, Brussels 3 Dec. 2015).

1019. Since 2000, CfDs have been traded in Nordic electricity markets including Sweden, Denmark, Norway, Finland as well as in Spanish-Portuguese cross-border transmission networks. *See* ENTSO-E Education Paper, 20.

1020. *See* Christof Duthaler & Matthias Finger, *Financial Transmission Rights in Europe's Electricity Market* (2008).

Redispatching and countertrading are market-based methods through which transmission system operators seek to alter the flow pattern that causes congestion at transmission lines. Redispatching involves increasing energy production and injecting it at points where energy is withdrawn from congested transmission lines, resulting in the counter flow of energy and relieving congestion. In countertrading, transmission system operators engage in energy buying from suppliers and producers closer to the point where congested energy is withdrawn and sell on other side of the congested transmission line, again resulting in counter-flowing of energy and relieving congestion. Transmission system operators also apply curtailment to deal with congestion as a non-market-based method. In so doing, transmission system operators may require the limitation of energy production from certain energy producers or suppliers contributing to congestion in transmission lines. In natural gas markets, Article 16 of Regulation 715/2009 limits the congestion management measures only for market-based methods. In electricity markets, on the other hand, Article 16 of Regulation 714/2009 provides that transmission system operators may curtail certain power plants to relieve congestion levels. Nevertheless, the use of curtailment is limited to emergency situations and considered only as a secondary option after the application of redispatching and countertrading measures.

Exploiting Price Differences

The Commission's decision in *Svenska Kraftnät*[1021] provides a clear example of how congestion levels impact on prices and the scope of wholesale markets in the EU. The case involved an abuse of the dominant position by the Swedish transmission system operator (Svenska Kraftnät) on the grounds that by imposing a single price zone and limiting electricity exports from Sweden to Denmark to relieve congestion, Svenska Kraftnät engaged in discrimination between Danish and Swedish electricity markets and thus abused its dominant position in violation of Article 102 of TFEU.[1022] Sweden's electricity market has been mostly dependent on hydroelectric power produced in the northern region of the country, while the major consumption centres where the bulk of electricity produced is needed is in the South. This led to congestion in electricity flow from the north to the south and resulted in Svenska Kraftnät engaging in countertrading measures to relieve the congestion. Sweden had a single pricing zone where a single market clearing price determined in the national wholesale electricity market was applicable over the country. In order to keep this uniform price, Svenska Kraftnät limited electricity exports to Denmark, even though the relevant congestion did not take place in the interconnectors that connect the Swedish and Danish transmission grids. The Commission found that Svenska Kraftnät had violated Article 102 of TFEU by seeking to keep a uniform price in exchange for cross-border trade and competition. As a result, Svenska Kraftnät was required to divide Sweden into several price zones on

1021. *Swedish Interconnectors* (Case COMP/39.351) OJ C 239/4.
1022. *Ibid.*, para. 42.

the basis of transmission capacity and allow Danish customers access to cheap electricity generated in the north.[1023]

Despite being an antitrust case, *Svenska Kraftnät* shows how congestion levels at transmission lines can affect prices and render wholesale energy markets vulnerable to market manipulation. Market participants that have information on available transmission capacity and the congestion levels thereof can manipulate wholesale energy markets, if such misconduct is also profitable. Consider an electricity producer which has high-margin generation units producing electricity at expensive prices and operates in a country like Sweden, where low-margin cheaper electricity production facilities are concentrated in certain regions for geographic reasons. It is reasonable to expect that transmission lines which convey electricity from cheap electricity generators to places with high energy demand would be congested. Accordingly, an electricity producer may find itself out of the relevant merit order in the wholesale market due to competition from the cheaper power plants. Foreseeing when and how transmission lines are congested, this market participant can buy a purchase order in the DAM to increase electricity demand and congestion. The market participant can offset this purchase order with an equivalent sell order in the real-time or balancing market. When congestion at the transmission lines takes place, the transmission system operator can apply countertrading measures and call electricity production from the market participant's high-margin generation units to alleviate congestion levels at the relevant lines. The market participant's purchase and sell orders can be uneconomic or even loss incurring. Nevertheless, the profits derived from electricity produced for countertrading would be more than enough to compensate the losses incurred in the wholesale electricity market.

[ii] Applicable Frameworks

Congestion-related market manipulation can also account for violations of Articles 101 and/or 102 of TFEU. Market participants can engage in agreements or concerted practices to increase congestion levels at given transmission lines. Such schemes can account for said violation, if competent competition authorities find that perpetrators are collectively dominant.[1024] The identification of relevant markets and dominant positions constitute key factors in abuse of dominance cases. Whether or not the relevant geographic and product markets are determined on the basis of pricing zones rather than the scope of national transmission networks, or whether or not the analysis of market power should also take into account the identification of pivotal positions, substituting or supplementing the calculation of market shares is important for the legal analysis carried out under Article 102. Nevertheless, the application of Articles 101 and 102 to such market practices also give rise to concerns about the *ne bis in idem* principle.

1023. *Ibid.*, para. 47.
1024. For 'Collective Dominance', *see* Vivien Rose & David Bailey (eds), *Bellamy & Child – European Union Law of Competition* 779–783 (OUP 7th ed. 2013).

The prevention of congestion-related market manipulation requires effective CACM mechanisms as well as strong monitoring of markets by competent regulatory authorities. The determination of pricing zones and splitting of energy markets on the basis of capacity constraints are fundamental in identifying positions that can be exploited and abused by market participants. The EU adopted rules on CACM along with several other network codes pursuant to the regulations and directives under the Third Energy Package[1025] which provides legal rules for transparency, transit and market structure for both natural gas and electricity. Despite significant progress in the integration of transmission lines between Member States, EU wholesale energy markets are still mostly national in scope and there are significant price differences among national energy markets. To what extent the existing regulatory framework ensures the functioning of wholesale energy markets and how EU case law on market manipulation under EU competition law and REMIT develop remains to be seen.

[D] Outright Fraud

[1] Concept

Outright fraud involves market practices that operate as a deceit upon other market participants. The major factor distinguishing transactions that constitute outright fraud from those identified as market power and trade-based manipulation is that these transactions are aimed at deceiving other market participants as to the conditions in markets or value of particular products. As mentioned, US case law distinguishes fictitious transactions from real transactions.[1026] Transactions with actual parties with actual economic risks and material effects on markets are defined as open market transactions.[1027] Market power manipulation and trade-based manipulative practices are regarded as open market transactions. When transactions do not involve actual trades with actual parties on the basis of economic risks, yet still aim at manipulating markets and prices, they are identified as closed market transactions and considered to be outright fraud. Wash trades, matched orders, pump and dump schemes, pre-arranged and circular trading are all examples of closed market transactions.[1028]

Market participants can also engage in unilateral acts to deceive other market participants and seek financial profits therefrom. These types of practices often take the form of distorting information in markets through dissemination or publication of false statements to markets. The dissemination can be perpetrated via media organisations,

1025. Third Energy Package involves Directive 2009/73/EC of the European Parliament and of the Council of 13 Jul. 2009 concerning common rules for the internal market in natural gas, Directive 2009/72/EC of the European Parliament and of the Council of 13 Jul. 2009 concerning common rules for the internal market in electricity, Regulation (EC) 2009/715 on conditions for access to natural gas transmission networks, Regulation (EC) 2009/714 on conditions for access to the network for cross-border exchanges in electricity.

1026. *Sundheimer v. CFTC*, 688 F.2d 150 (2d Cir. 1982), *cert. denied*, 460 U.S. 112 (1983).

1027. *United States v. Mulheren*, 938 F.3d 364, 368 (2d Cir. 1991).

1028. *Sundheimer v. CFTC*, 688 F.2d 150 (2d Cir. 1982), *cert. denied*, 460 U.S. 112 (1983); *See Markowski v. SEC*, 274 F.3d 525 (D.D.Cir. 2011), *cert. denied*, 537 U.S. 813 (2002); *United States v. Radley*, 659 F. Supp. 2d 803 (S.D. Tex. 2009).

internet or other platforms where market participants communicate or seek access to necessary market data. Whether or not the relevant false information is published under transparency or data reporting obligations under energy or financial regulation is irrelevant for a finding of market manipulation. Information that is disseminated voluntarily or made public under regulatory obligations must be false or not completely accurate and must be in a position that has a significant effect on prices. ACER refers to the concept of inside information[1029] as a benchmark in identifying what type of information is significant enough to affect market prices. Such a reference does not provide much clarification in market manipulation cases as EU case law on inside information has not yet developed.

REMIT does not offer a specific definition of outright fraud. Instead it provides two different definitions that can be considered as indicating market manipulation as outright fraud. Article 2(2)(b)[1030] proscribes dissemination of false information through the media or other means. This article does not necessarily relate to the existence of a transaction which is required under Article 2(2)(a). Market participants who render public false information without engaging in a transaction that gives effect to that publication is in violation of Article 2(2)(b). Article 2(2)(a)(iii), on the other hand, refers to transactions that employ a fictitious device or any other form of deception which gives false or misleading signals as to wholesale energy products. This definition mirrors the fraud-based definition given under SEA's Section 10(b)[1031] and follows the demarcation of US case law which identifies such transactions as closed market transactions meaning that they do not involve actual parties and economic risks with material effects on markets.

[2] ACER's Examples

In its guidance document, ACER provides a list of examples of outright fraud under Article 2(2)(b) and Article 2(2)(a)(iii). Accordingly, pump and dump schemes, circular and pre-arranged trading activities and spreading false information through media are market misconduct characterised as outright fraud under REMIT's anti-manipulation rules. The list does not include wash trades and matched orders. ACER specifies that these market practices are prohibited under Article 2(2)(a)(i) which proscribes transactions that give false or misleading signals as to wholesale energy products. As discussed above, these market practices have been regarded as major examples of market manipulation under fraud-based prohibitions.[1032] However the reading of

1029. ACER's Guidance, 39 (2016).
1030. Article 2(2)(b) of REMIT identifies market manipulation as '*disseminating information through the media, including the internet, or by any other means, which gives, or is likely to give, false or misleading signals as to the supply of, demand for, or price of wholesale energy products, including the dissemination of rumours and false or misleading news, where the disseminating person knew, or ought to have known, that the information was false or misleading*'.
1031. Securities Exchange Act § 10(b), 15 U.S.C.A. § 78l; 17 C.F.R. § 240.10b-5.
1032. Securities Exchange Act § 10(b), 15 U.S.C.A. § 78l; Commodity Exchange Act § 4(c), 7 U.S.C. §6c.

Article 2(2)(a)(i) suggests that it identifies trade-based transactions other than those involving price positioning, which is defined under Article 2(2)(a)(ii).

ACER's perception of Article (1)(a)(i) and its inclusion of wash trades and matched orders as examples of this article creates uncertainty as to the distinction between Article 2(2)(a)(i) and 2(2)(a)(iii). While it is sufficient for the former to show that signals given by the transactions at issue do not represent actual conditions as to the supply of, demand for, or price of wholesale energy products, for the latter, the national competent authorities are required to establish that transactions have employed a fictitious device or any other form of deception which gives false or misleading signals as to wholesale energy products. The phrase that a transaction which *gives, or is likely to give, false or misleading signals as to the supply of, demand for, or price of wholesale energy products* under Article 2(2)(a)(i) does not necessarily indicate that relevant transactions must operate as fraud to result in market manipulation. In fact, all types of trade-based market manipulation including both market power and cross-market manipulation give false or misleading signals as to demand and supply levels existing in market places. Their impact on market information does not suffice to classify all types of manipulative practices as outright fraud. Trade-based market manipulation constitutes open market transactions which materially affect markets and/or prices through actual trades with actual counterparties. Accordingly Article 2(2)(a)(i) aims at defining trade-based market manipulation which do not constitute price positioning which is defined under Article 2(2)(a)(ii). Article 2(2)(a)(iii), on the other hand, directly refers to a transaction that '*employs or attempts to employ a fictitious device or any other form of deception or contrivance*' to stress that these transactions must operate as a fraud upon markets. Therefore, ACER's reference to wash trades and matched orders as examples of market manipulation under the definition provided in Article 2(2)(a)(i) is erroneous.

[3] Applicable Frameworks

While the prohibitions on dissemination of false information are included in several regulations at national[1033] and EU levels,[1034] EU competition law, as established under Articles 101 and 102, does not specifically deal with such market misconduct. As mentioned above, while Article 101 deals with agreements and concerted practices

1033. For example, the Trade Descriptions Act 1968, The Consumer Protection from Unfair Trading Regulations of 2008 in the UK and *Gesetz gegen den unlauteren Wettbewerb vom*, 3 Jul. 2004 (BGBl. I 2004 32/1414) in Germany prohibit dissemination of false information., *See* Jan Peter Heidenreich, *The New German Act Against Unfair Competition*, http://germanlawarchive.iuscomp.org/?p=349#sdfootnote2sym (accessed 29 Jun. 2017).

1034. For transactions between consumers and undertakings, Directive 2005/29/EC of the European Parliament and of the Council of 11 May 2005 concerning unfair business-to-consumer commercial practices in the internal market and amending Council Directive 84/450/EEC, Directives 97/7/EC, 98/27/EC and 2002/65/EC of the European Parliament and of the Council and Regulation (EC) No 2006/2004 of the European Parliament and of the Council ('Unfair Commercial Practices Directive'); for transactions between undertakings, Directive 2006/114/EC of the European Parliament and of the Council of 12 Dec. 2006 concerning misleading and comparative advertising ('Comparative Advertising Directive').

between multiple market participants, Article 102 prohibits abuse of dominance by dominant undertakings through exclusionary and/or exploitative conduct. It is reasonable to expect that EU competition law applies to the dissemination of false information when it is perpetrated in a way that also violates one or more prohibitions under Articles 101 and 102. For example, if relevant dissemination practices are perpetrated by two or more market participants in a collusive way, competition authorities may interfere and open proceedings as to a probable violation of Article 101. However, if such a relationship cannot be established, relevant dissemination practices would be left outside the scope of EU competition law.

Closed market transactions constitute violations of EU competition law, Article 101 of TFEU in particular, as they involve agreements or collusion between market participants aiming at distorting markets and/or prices. Whether or not they involve actual trades that materially affect conditions in markets is irrelevant for a finding of a violation of Article 101. In fact, the perpetrators' practices that employ a fictitious device, deception or contrivance can account for *restriction by object* within the meaning of Article 101. Wash trades, matched orders, pre-arranged and circular trading practices involve multiple parties that seek certain market outcomes such as achieving certain price or output levels, and can even account for cartels which are regarded by the European Commission as restrictions by object as well as per se violations of EU competition law.[1035] For example multiple suppliers and traders carrying out wash trades, matched orders or pre-arranged and circular trading practices and submitting these trades to indices to affect index prices can be held to be engaging in cartels and thus in violation of Article 101 per se. Consequently the concurrent application of competition law and REMIT results in application of multiple jurisdictions to the same market conduct and gives rise to concerns about the *ne bis in idem* principle.

[E] Concurrency of Anti-manipulation and Antitrust Rules and *Ne Bis In Idem*

The legal analysis of the *ne bis in idem* principle involves market misconduct that is deemed to be manipulative and therefore prohibited under REMIT or MAR. This market misconduct can also lead to proceedings under EU competition law as a distortion of competition in wholesale energy markets. In this situation, the jurisdiction of two authorities can intersect each other and lead to concurrent application of regulatory prohibitions and antitrust rules. Perpetrators who are troubled due to multiple proceedings opened by two different authorities for the same market misconduct can raise a double jeopardy claim to escape from the duplicative proceedings. In

1035. *'It is not necessary that the agreement expressly or directly fixes the selling or purchasing price: it is sufficient if the parties agree on certain parameters of the price composition, such as the amount of rebates given to customers.'* Commission Staff Working Document, 'Guidance on restrictions of competition "by object" for the purpose of defining which agreements may benefit from the De Minimis Notice (COM(2014) 4136 final).

this regard, the Courts and/or the Commission can assess whether the facts of the cases at issue meet the threefold criteria established under EU case law.[1036]

In order to invoke the *ne bis in idem* principle, defendants are required to show that persons, facts, and legal interests protected in the concurrent proceedings must be the same. While anti-manipulation rules under REMIT[1037] and MAR[1038] apply to any legal or natural person engaging in or attempting to engage in market manipulation on wholesale energy markets,[1039] Articles 101 and 102 can be enforced against only undertakings or associations of undertakings.[1040] A national competent regulator can sanction both legal and natural persons for the violation of the relevant market manipulation prohibition. For example, a proceeding under REMIT for a violation of a market manipulation prohibition can be brought against both undertakings and people working in these undertakings and responsible for the relevant manipulative conduct. Remedies issued by the national competent regulators on undertakings and natural persons can differ. National competition authorities or the Commission, on the other hand, can hold only undertakings or association of undertakings liable for antitrust violations. People, working in these undertakings and responsible for anti-competitive conduct, cannot be subject to antitrust proceedings. Therefore, double jeopardy defence cannot be invoked, if it is shown that the persons that are subject to concurrent proceedings are different, even if other requirements of threefold criteria are met.

As to the facts that are investigated by concurrent proceedings, defendants must show that market practices prosecuted by regulatory and competition authorities are the same. If regulatory and competition authorities investigate different practices, defendants cannot raise a *ne bis in idem* claim to avoid concurrent proceedings. For example, an electricity generator engaging in a capacity withholding practice to raise electricity prices can also have financial positions that profit from higher electricity prices. This market conduct can provoke both competition and regulatory authorities to exercise their jurisdictions. The Commission may find the existence of physical or financial positions benefitting from capacity withholding practices irrelevant for applying competition law as its main focus is the evaluation of capacity withholding practice as an abuse of dominance. For an anti-manipulation investigation, on the other hand, perpetrators' exploitation of price relations between physical and financial positions through capacity withholding is prerequisite for a finding of manipulation. Even though the proceedings opened by competition and regulatory authorities are closely related, the facts of these cases are not the same and thus do not suffice for the generator to invoke the principle of *ne bis in idem.*

1036. Case C-204/00 *P Aalborg Portland A/S et al., v. Commission* [2004] ECR I-123; Telekomunikacja Polska (Case COMP/39.525) Commission Decision [2011] OJ C327/7. *See* section 1.04[C].
1037. Article 5, Regulation No 1227/2011.
1038. Article 12, Regulation No 596/2014.
1039. Regine Feltkamp & Cecile Musialski, 26 (2013).
1040. The concepts of undertaking and association of undertakings have the same meanings for both Articles 101 and 102. *See* Cases T-68, 77 and 78/89, *Societa Italiana Vetro SpA v. Commission* [1992] ECR II-1403, para. 358. Every entity, which, regardless of their legal status, engages in economic activity can constitute undertaking. *See* Case C-309/99, *Wouters v. Algemene Raad van de Nederlandse Orde van Advocaten* [2002] ECR I-1577.

The Commission, in *Telekomunikacja Polska*, identified that the aim of EU competition law was to ensure the functioning of undistorted competition in the EU, without stipulating any distinction between Articles 101 and 102. The legal interests protected by market manipulation prohibitions, as included in REMIT and MAR, are to ensure integrity of energy and financial markets in which prices reflect fair and competitive interplay between supply and demand,[1041] to foster open and fair competition[1042] and to prevent significant distortions of competition arising from the differences between national law.[1043] Despite the specific emphasis on the purpose of ensuring fair competition in REMIT and MAR, the Commission will probably consider that the legal interests protected by REMIT and MAR are not the same and thus do not suffice to raise a *ne bis in idem* claim. *EURIBOR*[1044] is illustrative of the approach taken by the Commission, involving an Article 101 proceeding initiated against a market practice which had already been prosecuted as market manipulation by a national financial market regulator under national financial regulation. This case clearly shows that the Commission will apply competition law, if it is shown that the relevant market practice distorts competition across Member States. Whether or not the same market practice is also prosecuted under REMIT or MAR is irrelevant for the purposes of an antitrust investigation. Nevertheless, it is important to note that *EURIBOR* involved an antitrust enforcement at EU level. The same conclusion may not be the case if both antitrust and anti-manipulation proceedings are opened at national level. In this case, the analysis of legal interests protected and the applicability of *ne bis in idem* principle are determined on case-by-case basis.

§4.04 CONCLUSION

[A] Capacity Withholding

Even though *Iberdrola* represents the first and only market manipulation case carried out under REMIT, the relevant market misconduct has been subject to several investigations and legal proceedings at national level under competition law. These cases involved capacity withholding practices by market participants who sought profits from artificially inflated electricity prices as a result of reducing their output. The national competition authorities investigated these market practices on the basis of Articles 101 and 102 which respectively prohibit anti-competitive agreements or concerted practices and abuse of dominance.

Establishing the violation of EU competition law in these cases proved to be difficult for national authorities. In Article 101 cases, a high concentration in the energy supply provided significant opportunities for market participants to engage in collusive behaviour without material contact or agreements between competitors. Market structures, regulations on transparency and data reporting obligations and bidding

1041. Recital 1, Regulation No 1227/2011.
1042. Recital 2, Regulation No 1227/2011.
1043. Recital 5, Regulation No 596/2014.
1044. *Euro Interest Rate Derivatives* (Case AT.39914) Commission Decision of 4 Dec. 2013.

activities further increased transparency levels and allowed market participants to predict applicable merit orders more accurately which, in turn, enabled market participants to foresee when their energy output might become pivotal for the supply of energy products at certain price levels.[1045] Due to the difficulties in acquiring direct evidence such as agreements or meetings between colluding parties, national competition authorities mostly relied on allocation and timing of bidding practices such as identifying symmetries in instantaneous dealings to prove that market participants engaged in a collusion or concerted practice to fix prices and share energy markets.

In Article 102 cases, on the other hand, the identification of dominant positions constituted the major obstacle to the finding of violations. EU case law clearly illustrates that the national competition authorities have been eager to apply new methodologies in measuring and establishing market power and dominant positions such as the PSI and the Residual Supplier Index (RSI). Nevertheless, such recalibrations in competition law methodologies in accordance with the characteristics of energy markets was hardly accepted by the national courts which still relies on conventional methods such as measuring market shares for the determination of market power and dominance.

In *Iberdrola,* the SCA:

(i) defined the relevant time periods in which it found the defendant withheld its capacity;
(ii) established that the defendant, in deed, committed capacity withholding;
(iii) established that prices moved as a result of withheld capacity; and
(iv) concluded that the defendant's withholding did not serve a legitimate business reason, as it was uneconomic and loss incurring but for the profits derived from withheld capacity.

Even though the SCA did not specifically establish that the defendant used its market power and abused their dominant position by withholding its generation capacity from the Spanish wholesale electricity market, its legal analysis was similar to that it had done under competition law cases as it applied an evaluation of pivotal positions held by the perpetrators in establishing the causation between capacity withholding and price changes. In *Endesa/Iberdrola/Union Fenosa/Hidrocantabrico,* SCA similarly identified the relevant time periods in which the defendants withheld their capacity and established how these capacity withholding strategies influenced electricity prices in the Spanish balancing markets. The factor that distinguishes SCA's legal analysis in *Iberdrola* from that in *Endesa/Iberdrola/Union Fenosa/Hidrocantabrico,* is that, in the former, SCA did not need to establish that the defendant's pivotal position in the relevant time period constituted a dominant position, as the prohibition of market manipulation under REMIT does not require undertakings to have dominance. In the latter, on the other hand, the identification of

1045. Adrien de Hauteclocque & Malgorzata Sadowska, 191 (2015). *See also*: David Newbery, *Electricity Liberalisation in Britain: The Quest for a Satisfactory Wholesale Market Design* 26 The Energy Journal Special Issue 43-70, 57 (2005).

the defendants' pivotal position as dominance was fundamental in establishing that the relevant capacity withholding strategy constituted an abuse of a dominant position.

[1] Incompatibility of Conventional Antitrust Methodologies

Despite the willingness of national competition authorities to use pivotal positions held by market participants to identify market power and dominant position in national wholesale energy markets, *Endesa/Iberdrola/Union Fenosa/Hidrocantabrico* clearly showed that this approach was not accepted by national courts which preferred the conventional methodologies such as market share and the Herfindahl-Hirschman Index (HHI), in these decisions. The Commission also followed a similar approach in *German Wholesale Energy Market* and rested its market power analysis solely upon the calculation of market shares held by the relevant market participants. This resulted in the Energy Sector Inquiry of 2007 and subsequent soft law instruments arguing that since EU competition law does not suffice to deal with such practices, a tailor-made legal framework was necessary to address anti-competitive conduct peculiar to wholesale energy markets. Nevertheless, the development of new indices such as the PSI and the RSI clearly shows that it is the conventional methodologies rather than EU competition law itself that give rise to concerns about competition in wholesale energy markets.

Traditional methods for the identification of market power such as the calculation of market shares[1046] and the HHI[1047] that are commonly used in the economics of EU competition law,[1048] do not suffice to obtain optimal results for detecting market power in energy markets.[1049] Demand for energy supply changes on an hourly basis and transmission of energy products from suppliers to consumers is capacity-restricted, that is, the capacity available for supply determines the amount and suppliers of energy for a certain period of time. Undertakings with relatively small market shares can assess these market and capacity conditions and exercise significant market power to affect prices. This was clearly illustrated in the Western Energy Crisis of 2001 in which suppliers with less than a 10% market share in relatively deconcentrated California electricity with market participants, none of whom exceeded 20% market share, could significantly influence market clearing prices.[1050]

1046. Market share indices involve calculation of the percentage of market shares that are held by the largest companies in a specifically defined relevant product and geographic markets.
1047. The Herfindahl-Hirschman Index provides a concentration ratio in relevant markets. The level of concentration is important in the assessment of markets power. For example, the market power exercised by an undertaking with 20% market share in a highly concentrated market may not be equivalent to that of the same undertaking in a deconcentrated market. The HHI evaluates market power on the basis of concentration levels at markets.
1048. Damien Geradin, Anne Layne-Farrar & Nicolas Petit, *EU Competition Law and Economics* 87–88 (OUP 2012).
1049. David Newbery, et al., 23 (2004).
1050. Anjali Sheffrin, *Critical Actions Necessary for Effective Market Monitoring* 5 Draft Comments Department of Market Analysis, California ISO, FERC RTO Workshop (19 Oct. 2001).

[2] Adoption of Sector-Specific Methodologies

The PSI and the RSI are indices developed to address the peculiarities of the energy markets. The PSI involves an assessment of necessity of a relevant generator to supply load for a given time period. The assessment first calculates the difference between total supply and demand levels in wholesale energy markets for a given period of time to identify the extent of supply surplus. If the difference is positive, the assessment then compares this supply surplus with capacity of given generators. Here the calculation uses a binary variable which takes two values: either 0 or 1. If supply surplus is higher than the capacity of given electricity generation plants, the assessment concludes that the value is 0, and generators are not pivotal in serving demand for the given time period. If the assessment finds otherwise, the value is 1, and the generators are held pivotal and can exercise market power to change clearing prices in energy markets. The PSI has been used by FERC since 2004 as an important instrument in determining market power in energy markets[1051] and is regarded as one of the most reliable indicators of market power in wholesale energy markets.[1052]

Similar to the PSI, the RSI is also based on the calculation of the necessity of generation plants in serving energy demand. The motivation behind the development of the RSI is that the PSI, which identifies the necessity of a given generation capacity on the basis of supply surplus, does not focus on the extent of market power exercised by generation capacity which is less than supply surplus. The PSI finds market power only if the capacity of a given generator is higher than supply surplus available in the market. However, the economic literature suggests that generation capacity that is near to, yet not totally pivotal for, supplying demand can also exercise market power and influence the market clearing price.[1053] In other words, even if the value of a given generation capacity in the PSI is 0, this generation capacity can still influence the market and exercise market power. The RSI provides a ratio of residual supply which is the difference between total available supply and the capacity of a given generator over demand.

RSI = (Total Supply - Supply by the Given Generator) / (Total Demand)

If the ratio is more than 100% of total demand, the RSI concludes that the given generator is not pivotal. If the ratio is less than 100%, the given generation capacity is necessary to meet demand and thus pivotal. The RSI has been successfully used by the CAISO in identifying market power in energy markets.[1054]

1051. FERC, 'Order on rehearing and modifying interim generation market power analysis and mitigation policy' (2004) Docket No ER96-2495-016, et al., 15.
1052. Gary Taylor, et al., 39 (2015).
1053. David Newbery, et al., 27 (2004).
1054. *Ibid.*, 28.

[3] *Effectiveness of Competition Law*

Even though the establishment of the exercise of market power through the PSI or the RSI is sufficient to hold that suppliers abused their dominant position through capacity withholding and the legal analysis under Article 102 does not require competition authorities to show that suppliers benefit from capacity withholding, economically these market practices would not be profitable in competitive markets as they would lead to lesser market shares and revenue losses incurred from unused generation units.[1055] By reducing its output, suppliers forego the revenues that could have been derived from withheld capacity. Accordingly a generator would withdraw its capacity and increase electricity prices, only if such a withdrawal is economically profitable.

The profitability of these market practices depends on the availability of certain factors, such as market concentration, transparency, market designs and generation portfolios. Electricity can be produced from several resources, such as natural gas, nuclear, renewables and coal, which is called an energy mix. The operational costs of power plants are mainly dependant on the type of energy source with which the electricity is produced. While renewables and nuclear constitute low-cost energy sources, natural gas and coal power plants operate at high marginal costs. In order to supply electricity at low prices, market operators use low-cost power plants as baseload, that is, these plants remain operational during all hours, while those with high marginal costs are called in only when demand for electricity is at its peak, called peak hours. The price of electricity that is to be paid to all supplying plants is determined on the basis of the highest cost generation unit that supplied electricity to the electricity grid for the relevant time period, the market clearing price.

Suppliers who own a portfolio of generation assets involving high cost and low-cost power plants have substantial financial incentives to withhold the capacity in lower cost power plants to earn more profits from higher cost power plants. As market operators are obliged to call in higher cost generation plants as a result of capacity withholding to supply electricity demand, perpetrators can reap more revenues from their operating power plants and selling electricity at high prices, even though their overall electricity production is reduced. A successful perpetration of these strategies is generally pertinent in concentrated and transparent markets in which a market participant can easily anticipate when their withholding practices would result in higher electricity prices. In these hours, even market participants with a small market share in electricity production can result in higher electricity prices and become pivotal. The availability of these positions and the evidence that market participants acquire benefits in relation to their capacity withholding can also allow competition authorities to refute any objective justification claims put forward by the perpetrators.[1056]

1055. *Ibid.*, 18.

1056. Even though Article 102 does not include an exception regime for exercise of market power, the CJEU, in *Post Denmark*, set out two particular grounds of justification: (i) Objective necessity, meaning that market conduct was necessary due to external factors; (ii) Efficiency, that is, undertakings must show that:

In *KeySpan*, FERC followed a similar approach concluding that capacity withholding practices which aimed at profiting from an overall portfolio of generation assets constituted exercise of market power rather than market manipulation. FERC found that the defendant's activity to withhold capacity to increase electricity prices and derive more revenues from its other generation assets was an economic and legitimate business practice, as it accounted for a mere example of exercise of market power. For a capacity withholding activity to be held in violation of FERC's anti-manipulation rules, it must be shown that despite the revenues from other generation assets or balancing markets, the market conduct is still loss incurring and uneconomic. The withholding activity must be economic only after the profits from other financial or physical positions, such as swaps, options, futures, etc. are included. Since the defendant's market conduct was an exercise of market power and economic, FERC found that it did not constitute a violation of its anti-manipulation rules.

The market conduct in *KeySpan* would be a clear example of the abuse of a dominant position under EU competition law and Article 102. It is important to note that the defendant's withholding would also remain unpunished under Section 2 of the Sherman Act which corresponds to Article 102. This is mainly because of the difference between the approaches taken by US antitrust law and EU competition law to the concept of exploitative abuse such as excessive pricing or monopoly pricing practices. These types of market conduct are not identified as abusive under US antitrust law. Section 2 only proscribes exclusionary abuses such as predatory pricing, margin squeeze, exclusive purchasing, tying and bundling. Nevertheless, exploitative abuse and excessive pricing practices have long been regarded as an abuse of dominance under EU competition law. The difficulties pertinent to the prosecution of capacity withholding practices in EU case law stem from the adoption of conventional methodologies in measuring market power in energy markets and they can be mitigated with the introduction of more suitable methodologies, such as the PSI and the RSI. Therefore, the argument that EU competition law is not efficient in dealing with capacity withholding practices in energy markets is unfounded.

[B] Other Types of Market Manipulation

The interplay between EU competition law and REMIT is not limited to the prosecution of capacity withholding practices in wholesale energy markets. There are significant questions remaining as to the applicability of REMIT and EU competition law to similar market practices. EU case law on market manipulation is limited and does not provide detailed guidance on the concurrent application of REMIT and EU competition law to

'the efficiency gains likely to result from the conduct under consideration counteract any likely negative effects on competition and consumer welfare in the affected markets, that those gains have been, or are likely to be, brought about as a result of that conduct, that such conduct is necessary for the achievement of those gains in efficiency and that it does not eliminate effective competition, by removing all or most existing sources of actual or potential competition'. *Case C-209/10 Post Denmark A/S v. Konkurrenceradet*, [2012] ECR I-000, para. 42.

wholesale energy markets. ACER provides examples of market manipulation to give an insight into what type of market practices are considered within the scope of REMIT's anti-manipulation rules. However, these examples are mostly derived from legal experience under US regulations on commodities and securities markets, and they provide little guidance on their application to wholesale energy markets. In order to discover what types of activities would be subject to the anti-manipulation rules under REMIT, and how they would relate to the prohibitions under Articles 101 and 102 of TFEU, the chapter follows the demarcation under US case law on energy market manipulation.

Incorporating the structure of electricity and natural gas markets in the EU, the chapter provides an extensive legal analysis on how such practices would be relevant in EU wholesale energy markets. Market power manipulation and cross-market manipulation constitute examples of price positioning under Article 2(2)(a)(ii), since these market practices seek to achieve certain price levels in the wholesale energy market. Other types of trade-based market manipulation, gaming of market rules and congestion-related manipulation are defined under Article 2(2)(a)(i), as they aim at exploiting market rules or creating congestion to earn profits. Market practices that can be regarded as outright fraud are set out in Article 2(2)(a)(iii) and 2(2)(b). While the former addresses fictitious transactions and other transactional frauds, the latter proscribes dissemination of false information through media and other means. This chapter shows that market participants may devise a wide spectrum of strategies in perpetrating the forms of manipulation defined under Article 2(2) of REMIT.

The chapter identifies that the majority of market practices that can account for market manipulation under Article 2(2) can also constitute violations of Articles 101 and/or 102 of TFEU. The concept of excessive pricing as an abuse of a dominant position under Article 102 is particularly applicable to price positioning strategies through which perpetrators seek to alter prices of wholesale energy products. The arguments raised above with respect to the introduction of new market-specific methodologies such as the PSI and the RSI play a major role in the identification of a dominant position. Competition authorities may find infringements of Article 102, when they establish that market participants who engage in price positioning strategies hold dominance or pivotal positions in wholesale energy markets. The chapter also shows that manipulative practices as defined under Article 2(2) of REMIT can also become subject to antitrust investigations under Article 101. This is particularly important for strategies where market participants engage in pre-arranged trades, matched orders, or collusive pricing practices in perpetrating market manipulation. Competition authorities can consider these practices as collusion and even hardcore cartels when it is established that through these practices, perpetrators sought to achieve a certain price level.

In sum, the legal analysis the chapter provides on the interplay between REMIT and EU competition law shows that in most cases, these two jurisdictions will likely intersect each other. The same market practices can easily give rise to investigations from multiple jurisdictions. The Commission's proceedings under *EURIBOR* in which perpetrators engaged in benchmark manipulation provide a clear example of the concurrent application of EU competition law and sector-specific regulation. REMIT does not offer an indication that it has a priority jurisdiction over EU competition law, when its anti-manipulation rules are breached. On the contrary, Article 1(2) specifically notes that it applies without prejudice to the application of EU competition law. The concurrent application of REMIT and EU competition law to the same market practices will give rise to concerns on the *ne bis in idem* principle.

Even though REMIT entered into force on 28 December 2011, Member States were not required to confer necessary powers on their national regulators or other competent authorities for the enforcement of the Regulation until 29 June 2013.[1057] Moreover, data reporting obligations only became operational on 7 October 2015 for standardised contracts and 7 April 2016 for non-standardised contracts.[1058] In its annual report, ACER noted that thirty-three cases were reported in 2015, twenty-six of which involved breaches of Article 5, REMIT's anti-manipulation provision, and it was expected that reporting by market participants about possible breaches of REMIT obligations to the Agency would increase, with growing awareness as to the implementation of REMIT in the wholesale energy markets.[1059] The investigations on these reported practices are ongoing and have not given rise to a formal enforcement procedure under REMIT. Nevertheless, this also means that as more market data becomes public, more investigations of potential market manipulation by competent authorities will follow. The jurisdictional interference by competition authorities into these investigations is very likely, according to the existing legal framework. Therefore the establishment of a mitigation process for the application of multiple jurisdictions is of utmost importance for a coherent and effective regulation of EU wholesale energy markets.

1057. Article 13, Regulation No 1227/2011.
1058. Article 12, Regulation No 1348/2014.
1059. *Supra* note 860.

CHAPTER 5

General Conclusions

Despite providing a general understanding of the legal framework established after the adoption of REMIT, this book mainly focuses on the prohibition of market manipulation and its interplay with EU competition law rules. It provides an extensive legal analysis of case law and discusses the features of practices regarded as manipulative in greater detail. Nevertheless, legal implications of REMIT with respect to EU wholesale energy markets are not limited to the concept of market manipulation. In fact, the prohibition of market manipulation constitutes only a part of the legal regime REMIT introduced.

This book provided an extensive legal analysis of the enforcement of anti-manipulation rules in EU wholesale energy markets. The exploration of the legal regime that REMIT established led the book to identifying three interrelated questions:

(1) What is the concept of market manipulation?
(2) What types of practices constitute market manipulation?
(3) What is the interplay between market manipulation and EU competition law?

The legal analysis concluded that the concept of market manipulation is far from being precise. Academic literature produced several definitions to determine and prosecute manipulative conduct.[1060] Nevertheless, to what extent these definitions were sufficient to identify manipulative behaviour has been a matter of discussion. Case law was also divided between two definitions which adopted different formulations and legal methodologies for the determination of market manipulation. While each addressed a certain type of manipulative practice, neither was applicable to all. The uncertainty as to the definition of market manipulation led this book to exploring practices considered to be manipulative, rather than the definitions.

As prohibition of market manipulation has been newly incorporated into EU law and related case law has yet to develop, a comparative approach was needed to

1060. *See* Ch. 3.

evaluate what type of practices in energy markets has been subject to enforcement procedures under anti-manipulation rules. US case law on energy market manipulation has been considered suitable for this comparative study, given the myriad of proceedings that have resulted in findings of manipulation. This book engaged in a demarcation of manipulative practices on the basis of legal and financial instruments perpetrators have utilised. Accordingly, undertakings in energy markets have perpetrated manipulation through corners, gaming market rules, exploiting price relations between different, yet linked, physical and financial products, congesting transmission lines or deceiving other undertakings. After the evaluation of US case law on energy market manipulation, the book explored its implications for EU wholesale energy markets.

The analysis of EU case law identified that there were significant differences between energy markets in the EU and the US. The first and only case in which a market participant was found in violation of REMIT's anti-manipulation rule involved a capacity withholding practice which was considered as a mere example of exercise of market power and thus legitimate in the US. Several EU soft law instruments which paved the way for the adoption of REMIT also stressed the necessity of a tailor-made legal framework that can efficiently establish and prosecute capacity withholding practices. The book identified that such practices have been previously addressed under antitrust rules at both national and EU level and resulted in remedies in relation to Articles 101 and 102 of TFEU. Accordingly, an EU case law study on capacity withholding revealed that certain aspects of the legal methodology, such as relevant market and dominance analyses, which were developed under EU competition law, did not suffice to establish these practices as violations of antitrust rules.

This book did not agree with the proposition that EU competition law was not a suitable tool to deal with capacity withholding by electricity generators. Several sector-specific methodologies identified in legal and economic literature, such as the identification of relevant markets in relation to time periods, the PSI and RSI as indicators of dominance, and the concept of temporary dominance, can offer effective means to enforce antitrust rules on these practices. The importance of this approach is twofold. First, the idea that competent authorities should be flexible in adopting legal approaches to the enforcement of EU competition law enables these authorities to follow innovation and development in markets and apply antitrust rules to a wide range of sectors. Second, the identification of capacity withholding as an illegitimate conduct requires the establishment of, on the one hand, price changes which are favourable to perpetrators and, on the other, the causation between price changes and relevant withholding practices. The establishment of these elements can be achieved through close monitoring of merit orders in electricity markets. Nevertheless, this is not the case for other types of market manipulation such as cross-market, congestion-related manipulation, etc. This book concluded that there were significant differences between capacity withholding practices and other types of market manipulation with respect to legal methodologies necessary for effective enforcement procedures.

The EU case law analysis also included several scenarios with respect to manipulative practices other than capacity withholding. This book illustrated that several practices addressed in these scenarios could also give effect to antitrust proceedings, if certain conditions were met. Even though a direct reference to such an overlap in energy markets could not be possible, this book addressed cases from other sectors in which both sector-specific regulators and the European Commission prosecuted market manipulation on the basis of, respectively, sector-specific regulation and EU competition law. This directed the book to explore the concept of concurrency in EU law and its implications as to the overlap between anti-manipulation and antitrust rules.

The concurrent application of sector-specific rules with EU competition law was not a new phenomenon in the EU. Telecommunications sector, in particular, has involved several cases in which the same market practices were sanctioned concurrently by both competition and regulatory authorities. Finding that concurrency was allowed by EU courts, this book engaged in an analysis assessing the concurrent application of anti-manipulation and antitrust rules in EU wholesale energy markets, in relation to the concept of *ne bis in idem*, which is the EU equivalent of the double jeopardy doctrine. The analysis indicated that it was unlikely for the *ne bis in idem* principle to constitute a barrier to the concurrent application of multiple jurisdictions to these market practices.

In sum, this book concluded several uncertainties with respect to the application of anti-manipulation rules and REMIT, and the existing legal framework does not provide effective mechanisms to mitigate these uncertainties. Apart from that on capacity withholding, whose identification as market manipulation is questionable, EU case law on market manipulation is very limited and far from providing an insight into what types of activities would be subject to proceedings under anti-manipulation rules. The uncertainties are further elevated due to the concurrency of EU competition law which gives rise to concerns about over-regulation and additional regulatory costs, which, in turn, cause detriments to investments and liquidity in EU wholesale energy markets. In this regard, the availability of effective mitigation measures is of great importance for an effective application of the new legal framework.

Based on its findings, this book deems it necessary for EU institutions to establish necessary mechanisms that can mitigate concerns about the uncertainties, pertinent to the adoption and the enforcement of obligations and prohibitions under REMIT. Strong cooperation and coordination between regulatory and competition authorities are prerequisite for an effective enforcement regime. These mechanisms should ensure that the obligations and prohibitions under REMIT are comprehended and prosecuted at national level in a harmonised way. Uniformity in legal approaches and enforcement procedures is fundamental for a coherent application of the regulatory framework REMIT established. The divergences thereof would result in further uncertainties as to the operation of energy markets across the EU and regulatory arbitrage, that is, market participants would abuse the differences in the regulatory regimes between Member States, which would undermine the functioning of EU wholesale energy markets.

This book proposes a two-pronged mitigation mechanism that addresses legal procedures and the uncertainties with respect to the prosecution of market manipulation in the EU. First, it suggests the adoption of a non-binding guidance paper by ACER on the application of Article 5 of REMIT to EU wholesale energy markets. The proposed guidance should include legal methodologies that give competent authorities insight into how to establish abuse of Article 5 and distinguish manipulative practices from other legitimate trading practices. Second, the book proposes that ACER and the European Commission should conclude a MOU concerning the prosecution of market manipulation under REMIT and EU competition law. As the book clearly put it, the majority of market practices that constitute market manipulation under anti-manipulation rules can also account for proceedings under EU competition law as violations of Articles 101 and 102, and this gives rise to concerns about the multiplicity of jurisdictions that can exercise authority over the same market practices. The proposed 'Memorandum of Understanding' should provide guidance on how overlapping proceedings are carried out or, if deemed suitable, avoided.

This book suggests that in designing guidance and a MOU, particular consideration must be given to the operation of wholesale energy markets and market practices therein. ACER should address the elements of legal methodology that national competent authorities can follow in enforcing anti-manipulation rules. The proposed guidance should include details about the concepts incorporated in REMIT's anti-manipulation rules, such as false and misleading signals, artificial prices, and forces of supply and demand which, as the case law on market manipulation suggests, are of great importance in the determination of manipulation. As mentioned, defining market manipulation has proved to be a very difficult task not only for the courts but also for academic literature which has produced a myriad of alternative definitions each of which criticises the other. In that guidance, ACER should discuss direct examples of market manipulation, rather than simply giving vague definitions which no matter how complicated they are designed, always fall short of addressing all types of market manipulation due to continuous market development and innovation. This would allow national competent authorities to assess established legal methodologies on case-by-case basis and effectively enforce their anti-manipulation rules.

The proposed MOU should encompass details on how the coordination and cooperation between national regulatory and competition authorities function in enforcing anti-manipulation rules. National regulatory authorities should not be limited only to energy regulators. Financial regulators who can open proceedings against in-scope manipulative practices on the basis of MAR should also be included in the conclusion of this memorandum. The document should address how notices of manipulative practices should be made between competition and regulatory authorities and which authority should be granted to open proceedings against relevant violations. Particular focus should be given to the elimination of the duplicative proceedings by regulators and competition authorities with respect to the same market practice.

Of course, the multiplicity of proceedings can still be the case on the grounds that the proceedings opened by one authority may not be considered sufficient to serve the remedy sought by the other due to the effects of relevant misconduct. For example, a regulatory authority can open proceedings against a market participant, while a national competition authority considers that relevant misconduct is of a collusive behaviour, rather than unilateral. Again a market practice which had been found to be a legitimate trading activity under anti-manipulation litigation can still be subject to antitrust proceedings. Facts and the identity of interested parties are of great importance in determining whether a market conduct may account for duplicative actions by regulatory and competition authorities. The availability of efficient tools with respect to the cooperation and coordination between regulatory and competition authorities is fundamental in identifying facts and undertakings concerned and evaluating whether concurrent proceedings by regulatory and competition authorities are necessary to achieve a sufficient remedy for disputed market practices. The proposed memorandum should set effective mechanisms through which regulatory and competition authorities evaluate the details of disputes and determine, if facts and parties concerned are the same, the appropriate jurisdiction that provides the best remedy for relevant market misconduct. This would eliminate the concerns about the application of multiple jurisdictions to the same market practices.

This book proposes that particular focus should also be paid to the characteristics of certain market practices in determining the authority who exercises jurisdiction. US case law on energy market manipulation provides significant implications as to the practices that have been prosecuted as violations of the relevant anti-manipulation rules, Section 1c.1 and 1c.2 for FERC[1061] and Rule 180.1 and 180.2 for the CFTC.[1062] It is reasonable to expect that these types of practices would be dealt with more effectively under anti-manipulation rules. Even though the consultation documents by EU institutions suggest otherwise, the book considers that capacity withholding practices can be prosecuted more effectively under antitrust rules. This is supported by some commentators[1063] and also in compliance with FERC's findings in *KeySpan*, in which the Commission concluded that the defendant's activity of generation withholding constituted a basic example of exercise of market power rather than that of market manipulation.[1064] As discussed in detail, the complexities with respect to the prosecution of capacity withholding practices under EU competition law stem from conventional legal methodologies that proved to be insufficient in identifying relevant markets and dominant positions in energy markets which would be established more appropriately with the adoption of new, energy-specific methodologies. This approach would clarify the concept of market manipulation and its difference from antitrust rules.

While EU competition law rule can be applied by national regulators in certain Member States, if they also possess powers to do so, in others, the jurisdictional authority to open proceedings under anti-manipulation rules can be conferred upon national competition authorities.[1065] As mentioned, this is why this book prefers to use the term 'competent authorities' rather than directly mentioning regulatory or competition authorities. It can be argued that the divergence between Member States in designating relevant authorities may raise questions as to the conclusion of the

1061. 18 C.F.R. §§ 1c.1, 2.
1062. 17 C.F.R. Part 180, §§ 180.1, 2.
1063. Gary Taylor, et al., 193 (2015).
1064. '*There is a difference between engaging in (1) market manipulation in violation of section 1c.2, which includes fraud or deceit as discussed above and (2) a party exercising market power. Of course, an exercise of market power may be a factor to consider in examining whether Part 1c was violated. However, it is not the only relevant factor.*' *See* FERC Enforcement Staff Report, 17 (2008).
1065. *Supra* note 274.

proposed memorandum. This book considers that such a differentiation does not pose risks to the development and implementation of the proposed memorandum which aims at identifying whether anti-manipulation or antitrust rules should be applied, rather than whether regulatory or competition authorities should exercise jurisdiction over certain market misconduct. A national regulator may exercise competition law against capacity withholding practices, while a competition authority can find a market practice that exploits price relations between two different yet linked products or markets in violation of anti-manipulation rules under REMIT or MAR.

This book considers that this two-pronged approach would sufficiently eliminate concerns about legal uncertainties and duplicative jurisdictions related to the application of anti-manipulation rules. As non-binding documents, the contexts of the proposed guidance and MOU are explanatory and thus do not give rise to concerns about over-regulation and additional regulatory costs. Furthermore, even though the main focus of this mechanism is on the enforcement of anti-manipulation rules under REMIT, other obligations and prohibitions can also be incorporated into the mechanism which would promote the development of a single rulebook that is relied upon by, and applicable to all, market participants operating in wholesale energy markets across the EU.

This book substantially contributes to the understanding of the new regulatory framework under REMIT. It explores the concept of market manipulation and its legal implications in EU wholesale energy markets. Nevertheless, the unveiling of the Regulation in its entirety requires an atmosphere of intensive discussion in academic literature which is currently missing. The concepts of inside information and insider trading as well as the development of electricity and natural gas markets are relatively new in the EU and thus legal studies that explore these issues are needed. In this respect, this book also constitutes a 'call' for academic attention to these issues.

Bibliography

Abrantes-Metz, Rosa M., et al., 'Revolution in Manipulation Law: the New CFTC Rules and the Urgent Need for Economic and Empirical Analyses' (2013) 15/2 *University of Pennsylvania Journal of Business Law* 357.

Akman, Pinar, 'The Role of Intent in the EU Case Law on Abuse of Dominance' (2014) *European Law Review* 316.

Allen, Franklin & Gale, Douglas, 'Stock-Price Manipulation' (1992) 5/3 *The Review of Financial Studies* 503.

Avgouleas, Emilios E., *The Mechanics and Regulation of Market Abuse: A Legal and Economic Analysis* (OUP 2005).

Baer, William J. & Ramirez, Edith, 'Antitrust Tools for Challenging Capacity Withholding in Wholesale Electricity Markets' (2014) *AAI The American Antitrust Institute* 3.

Borenstein, Severin & Bushnell, James, 'An Empirical Analysis of the Potential for Market Power in California's Electricity Industry' (1999) *Journal of Industrial Economics* 47.

Borenstein, Severin, 'The Trouble with Electricity Markets: Understanding California's Restructuring Disaster' (2002) 16/1 *Journal of Economic Perspectives* 191.

Cameron, Peter D., *Competition in Energy Market: Law and Regulation in the European Union* (2nd ed., OUP 2007).

Christie, Edward, 'Energy Vulnerability and EU-Russia Energy Relations' (2009) 5/2 *Journal of Contemporary European Research* 225.

Davidson, George A., 'Squeezes and Corners: A Structural Approach' (1985) 40 *Business Law* 1283.

Delvaux, Bram, et al., (eds), *EU Energy Law and Policy Issues* (Intersentia 2013).

Dune, Niamh, *Competition Law and Economic Regulation: Making and Managing Markets* (CUP 2015).

Easterbrook, Frank H., 'Monopoly, Manipulation, and the Regulation of Futures Markets' (1986) 59/2 *The Journal of Business* 103.

Evans, Matthew, 'Regulating Electricity-Market Manipulation: A Proposal for a New Regulatory Regime to Proscribe All Forms of Manipulation' (2015) 113/4 *Michigan Law Review.*

Faull, Jonathan & Nikpay, Ali (eds), *The EC Law of Competition* (OUP 2007).

Feltkamp, Regine & Musialski, Cecile, 'Integrity and Transparency in the EU Wholesale Electricity Market: New Rules for a Better Functioning Market?' (2013) *Oil, Gas & Energy Law* 1.

Fischel, Daniel R. & Ross, David J., 'Should the Law Prohibit Manipulation in Financial Markets?' (1991) 105 *Harvard Law Review* 503.

Geradin D. & O'Donoghue, R., 'The Concurrent Application of Competition Law and Regulation: The Case of Margin Squeeze Abuses in the Telecommunications Sector (2005) 1/2 *Journal of Competition Law & Economics* 355.

Geradin, Damien, et al., *EU Competition Law and Economics* (OUP 2012).

Gianfreda, Angelica & Grossi, Luigi, *Zonal Price Analysis of the Italian Wholesale Electricity Market* (EEM 2009 June 2009).

Gonzales-Diaz, Francisco Enrique, 'EU Policy on Capacity Mechanisms' in Leigh Hancher, Adrien De Hauteclocque & Malgorzata Sadowska (eds), *Capacity Mechanisms in the EU Energy Market: Law, Policy, and Economics* (OUP 2015).

Graham, Cosmo, 'UK: The Concurrent Enforcement by Regulators of Competition Law and Sector-Specific Regulation' (2016) 7/6 *Journal of European Competition Law & Practice* 407.

Hancher, Leigh, 'Capacity Mechanisms and State Aid Control A European Solution to the Missing Money Problem?' in Leigh Hancher, Adrien De Hauteclocque & Malgorzata Sadowska (eds), *Capacity Mechanisms in the EU Energy Market: Law, Policy, and Economics* (OUP 2015).

Hancher, Leigh, et al., (eds), *Capacity Mechanisms in the EU Energy Market: Law, Policy, and Economics* (OUP 2015).

Harvey, Scott M. & Hogan, William W., *Further Analysis of the Exercise of Market Power in the California Electricity Market* (2001). Derived from https://sites.hks.harvard.edu/m-rcbg/research/w.hogan_ksg_further.analysis.pdf (accessed 18 Apr. 2018).

Hauteclocque, Adrien de & Glachant, Jean-Michel, 'Long-Term Energy Supply Contracts in European Competition Policy: Fuzzy not Crazy' (2009) 37 *Energy Policy* 5399.

Hauteclocque, Adrien de & Sadowska, Malgorzata, 'Antitrust Law; A Missing Piece in a Regulatory Puzzle?' in Leigh Hancher, Adrien De Hauteclocque & Malgorzata Sadowska (eds), *Capacity Mechanisms in the EU Energy Market: Law, Policy, and Economics* (OUP 2015).

Hauteclocque, Adrien de & Talus, Kim, 'Third Party Access: A Comparative Study on Access Regimes in EU Electricity Grids and Natural Gas Pipelines' (2011) 9/3 *OGEL* 1.

Heather, Patrick, 'The Evolution and Functioning of the Traded Gas Market in Britain' (2010) *OIES Paper*: NG 44.

Heather, Patrick, 'The Evolution of European Traded Gas Hubs' (2015) *OIES Paper*: NG 104.

Hieronymus, Thomas A., 'Manipulation in Commodity Futures Trading: Toward a Definition' (1977) 6/1 *Hofstra Law Review* 41.

Higgins, Leonard R., *The Put-and-Call* (Effingham Wilson, 1906).

Hogan, William W., *Electricity Market Design; Financial Transmission Rights, Up To Congestion Transactions and Multi-Settlement Systems* (16 July 2012). Retrieved from http://www.hks.harvard.edu/fs/whogan/Hogan_UTC_071612.pdf (accessed 18 Apr. 2018).

Horwich, Allan, 'Warnings to the Unwary: Multi-Jurisdictional Federal Enforcement of Manipulation and Deception in the Energy Markets after the Energy Policy Act of 2005' (2006) 27/2 *Energy Law Journal* 364.

Johnston, Angus & Block, Guy, *EU Energy Law* (OUP 2012).

Jones, Alison & Sufrin, Brenda, *EU Competition Law; Text, Cases, and Materials* (5th ed., Oxford 2014).

Jones, Christopher (ed.), *EU Energy Law, Volume II, EU Competition Law and Energy Markets* (Claeys & Casteels 2016).

Jones, Christopher (ed.), *The Internal Energy Market: The Third Liberalisation Package* (3rd ed., Claeys & Casteels 2014).

Joskow, Paul & Kahn, Edward, 'A Quantitative Analysis of Pricing Behavior in California's Wholesale Electricity Market During Summer 2000' (2002) 23/4 *Energy Journal* 1.

Joskow, Paul & Tirole, Jean, 'Transmission Rights and Market Power on Electric Power Networks I: Financial Rights' (1998) *Centre for Economic Policy Research*, Discussion Paper No 2093.

Joskow, Paul L., 'California's Electricity Crisis' (2001) 17/3 *Oxford Review of Economic Policy* 365.

Kozinn, Benjamin E., 'The Great Copper Caper: Is Market Manipulation Really a Problem in the Wake of the Sumitomo Debacle' (2000) 69 *Fordham Law Review* 243.

Kumar, Praveen & Seppi, Duane J., 'Futures Manipulation with Cash Settlement' (1992) 47/4 *The Journal of Finance* 1485.

Kyle, Albert S. & Viswanathan, S., 'How to Define Illegal Price Manipulation' (2008) 98/2 *American Economic Review: Papers & Proceedings* 278.

Ledgerwood, Shaun & Harris, Dan, 'A Comparison of Anti-Manipulation Rules in US and EU Electricity and Natural Gas Markets: A Proposal for a Common Standard' (2012) 33/1 *Energy Law Journal.*

Ledgerwood, Shaun D. & Carpenter, Paul R., 'A Framework for the Analysis of Market Manipulation' (2012) 8/1 *Review of Law and Economics* 253.

Ledgerwood, Shaun D. & Pfeifenberger, Johannes P., 'Using Virtual Bids to Manipulate the Value of Financial Transmission Rights (2012) *Brattle Group.* Derived from https://pdfs.semanticscholar.org/5e4f/f9e0770dc157975f2f4ad3c67517da505b44.pdf (accessed 18 Apr. 2018).

Ledgerwood, Shaun, et. al., 'Defining Market Manipulation in a Post-REMIT World' (2011) *The Brattle Group Discussion Paper.*

Leveque, Francois, 'Antitrust Enforcement in the Electricity and Gas Industries: Problems and Solutions for the EU' (2006) 19/5 *The Electricity Journal* 27.

Lowe, Philip, 'Effective Unbundling of Energy Transmission Networks: Lessons learned from the Energy Sector Inquiry' (2007) 1 *Competition Policy Newsletter* 23.

Mantysaari, Petri, *EU Electricity Trade Law: The Legal Tools of Electricity Producers in the Internal Electricity Market* (Springer 2015).

Markham, Jerry W., 'Manipulation of Commodity Futures Prices-The Unprosecutable Crime' (1991) 8 *Yale Journal on Regulation.*

Markham, Jerry, *Law Enforcement and the History of Financial Market Manipulation* (M.E. Sharpe Inc., 2015).

McDermott, Edward T., 'Defining Manipulation in Commodity Futures Trading: The Futures Squeeze' (1979) 74/2 *Northwestern University Law Review* 202.

McRae, Shaun D. & Wolak, Frank A., 'How Do Firms Exercise Unilateral Market Power? Evidence from A Bid-Based Wholesale Electricity Market' (2009) *EUI Working Papers.*

Moloney, Niamh, *EU Securities and Financial Markets Regulation* (3rd edn, OUP 2014).

Multer, Maxwell K., 'Open-Market Manipulation under SEC Rule 10b-5 and Its Analogies: Inappropriate Distinctions, Judicial Disagreement and Case Study: FERC's Anti-Manipulation Rule' (2011) *Securities Regulation Law Journal* 97.

Nazzini, Renato, *Concurrent Proceedings in Competition Law: Procedure, Evidence and Remedies* (OUP 2004).

Newbery, David, 'Electricity Liberalisation in Britain: The Quest for a Satisfactory Wholesale Market Design' (2005) 26 *The Energy Journal,* Special Issue 43–70.

Newbery, David, 'Missing Money and Missing Markets: Reliability, Capacity Auctions and Interconnectors' (2015) *Cambridge University Energy Policy Research Group,* EPRG Working Paper 1508.

Newbery, David, et al., 'A Review of the Monitoring of Market Power The Possible Roles of TSOs in Monitoring for Market Power Issues in Congested Transmission Systems' (2005). 11/2 *Journal of Energy Literature* 3.

Perner, Jens & Riechmann, Christoph, 'Energy Market Design with Capacity Mechanisms' in Leigh Hancher, Adrien De Hauteclocque & Malgorzata Sadowska (eds), *Capacity Mechanisms in the EU Energy Market: Law, Policy, and Economics* (OUP 2015).

Pirrong, Craig, 'Commodity Market Manipulation Law: A (Very) Critical Analysis and a Proposed Alternative' (1994) 51/3 *Washington and Lee Law Review* 945.

Pirrong, Craig, 'Energy Market Manipulation: Definition, Diagnosis, and Deterrence' (2010) 31/1 *Energy Law Journal* 1.

Purdue, Wendy C., 'Manipulation of Futures Markets: Redefining the Offense' (1987) 56 *Fordham Law Review* 345.

Ratliff, John & Grasso, Roberto, *Insider Trading and Market Manipulation in the European Wholesale Energy Markets – REMIT* (Claeys & Casteels 2017) (forthcoming).

Ratliff, John, 'Transparency under REMIT and EU Competition Law' (2015) 1/2 *Competition Law and Policy Debate.*

Roggenkamp, Martha, et al., (eds), *Energy Law in Europe* (OUP 2016).

Rose, Vivien & Bailey, David (eds), *Bellamy & Child – European Union Law of Competition,* (7th ed., OUP 2013).

Sadowska, Malgorzata, *Committed to Reform? Pragmatic Antitrust Enforcement in Electricity Markets* (PhD Thesis, EDLE 2013).

Schaub, Alexander, *Competition Policy and Liberalisation of Energy Markets* (Speech At European Utilities Circle, 2000).

Scholz, Ulrich & Purps, Stephan, 'Application of EU Competition Law in the Energy Sector' (2015) 6/3 *Journal of European Competition Law & Practice* 200.

Stern, Jonathan P, & Howard V Rogers, 'The Transition to Hub-Based Gas Pricing in Continental Europe' (2011) NG 49 *Oxford Institute for Energy Studies.*

Stern, Jonathan P., 'Continental European Long-Term Gas Contracts: Is a Transition Away from Oil Product-Linked Pricing Inevitable and Imminent?' (2009) NG 34 *Oxford Institute for Energy Studies.*

Talus, Kim, *Introduction to EU Energy Law* (OUP 2016).

Taylor, Gary, et al., *Market Power and Market Manipulation in Energy Markets; From the California Crisis to the Present* (Public Utilities Report Inc., 2015).

Thel, Steve, 'The Original Conception of Section 10(b) of the Securities Exchange Act' (1990) 42 *Stanford Law Review* 385.

Torre, Fernando Castillo De La, 'State Action Defence in EC Competition Law' (2005) 28/4 *World Competition* 407.

Turner, Donal F., 'The Definition of Agreement under the Sherman Act: Conscious Parallelism and Refusals to Deal' (1962) 75/4 *Harvard Law Review* 655.

Wagner, Dr. Albrecht, *Functioning of European Gas Wholesale Markets* (Wagner, Elbling & Company Management Advisors, Quantitative Study 15 May 2014).

Walde, Thomas W. & Gunst, Andreas J., 'International Energy Trade and Access to Energy Networks' (2002) 36/2 *Journal of World Trade* 191.

Weare, Christopher, *The California Electricity Crisis Causes and Policy Options* (Public Policy Institute of California 2003).

Wolak, Frank A. & Patrick, Robert H., *The Impact of Market Rules and Market Structure on the Price Determination Process in the England and Wales Electricity Market* (1997) PWP-047 *Working Papers Series of the Program on Workable Energy Regulation (POWER).*

Wolfram, Catherine D., 'Strategic Bidding in a Multiunit Auction: An Empirical Analysis of Bids to Supply Electricity in England and Wales' (1998) 29/4 *The RAND Journal of Economics* 703.

Wood, David A., 'Natural Gas Imports to Europe: The Frontline of Competition between LNG and Pipeline Supplies' (2016) 36 *Journal of Natural Gas Science and Engineering* A1–A4.

Xunpeng, Shi, 'Development of Europe's gas hubs: Implications for East Asia' (2016) *Natural Gas Industry* 357.

Yafimava, Katja, 'The EU Third Package for Gas and the Gas Target Model: Major Contentious Issues Inside and Outside the EU' (2013) *OIES Paper*: NG 75.

Other Resources

Alessandro Noce, *Abuse of Dominant Position by Energy Incumbents: the Italian Experience* (Athens June 2013) https://www.energy-community.org/pls/portal/docs/2106181.PDF.

Anjali Sheffrin, *Critical Actions Necessary for Effective Market Monitoring* (Draft Comments Dept of Market Analysis, California ISO, FERC RTO Workshop 19 October 2001).

Association of Energy Producers, *AEP Response to CESR/ERGEG Consultation on Market Abuse* (2008), http://www.ceer.eu/portal/page/portal/EER_HOME/EER_CONSULT/CLOSED%20PUBLIC%20CONSULTATIONS/CROSSSECTORAL/Financial%20Services/Market%20abuse%20framework/RR/AEP.pdf.

Australian Securities Exchange, *Options Strategies: 26 Proven Options Strategies* (2011) http://www.asx.com.au/documents/resources/UnderstandingStrategies.pdf (accessed on 10 March 2016).

Australian Securities Exchange, *Understanding Options Trading* (2015), http://www.asx.com.au/documents/resources/UnderstandingOptions.pdf (accessed on 10 March 2016).

Autorità Garante della Concorrenza e del Mercato, 'Press Release: Electricity Market: investigation launched into Egl, Repower and Tirreno power concerning a possible service dispatch agreement' (Rome, October 2010) http://www.agcm.it/en/newsroom/press-releases/1831-i736-electricity-market-investigation-launched-into-egl-repower-and-tirreno-power-concerning-a-possible-service-dispatch-agreement.html.

Autorità Garante della Concorrenza e del Mercato, 'Press Release: Electricity Market: Antitrust Authority Accepts and Enforces the Commitments of the Main Energy Companies Active in the Sicily Macro Area' (Rome, January 2011) http://www.agcm.it/en/newsroom/press-releases/1924-i721-a423-edipower-tolling-and-enel-dynamics-in-the-setting-of-electricity-market-prices-in-sicily-closure-of-investigation.html.

Autorità Garante della Concorrenza e del Mercato, 'Press Release: Electricity market: Repower Italia, EGL Italia and Tirreno Power penalised for agreement restricting competition' (Rome, June 2012) http://www.agcm.it/en/newsroom/press-releases/2000-electricity-market-repower-italia-egl-italia-and-tirreno-power-penalised-for-agreement-restricting-competition.html.

Autorità Garante della Concorrenza e del Mercato, 'A498A-A498B - Aumento costi in bolletta, istruttoria Antitrust su Enel e Sorgenia' (Roma, ottobre 2016), http://www.agcm.it/stampa/comunicati/8411-a498a-a498b-aumento-costi-in-bolletta,-istruttoria-antitrust-su-enel-e-sorgenia.html.

Barry Stevens, *Natural Gas Storage is Vital for Future Industry Growth* (*OilPrice* 11 June 2012) http://oilprice.com/Energy/Natural-Gas/Natural-Gas-Storage-is-Vital-for-Future-Industry-Growth.html.

British Energy, *CESR / ERGEG Consultation Paper on Draft Advice to the European Commission Proposing an EU Market Abuse Framework for Energy Markets* (2008), http://www.ceer.eu/portal/page/portal/EER_HOME/EER_CONSULT/CLOSED%20PUBLIC%20CONSULTATIONS/CROSSSECTORAL/Financial%20Services/Market%20abuse%20framework/RR/E08-PC-30%20-%2004.

BP, *Statistical Review of World Energy* (65th edn, June 2016).

Carolyn A. Berry, et al., 'Analysing Strategic Bidding Behaviour in Transmission Networks' in Harry Singh (ed.), *Game Theory Applications in Electric Power Markets* (IEEE Power Engineering Society Winter Meeting 1999).

Charles River Associates, *Capacity Market Gaming and Consistency Assessment – Final Report* (CRA Project No D18985-00, September 2013) 41–42.

Cleary Gottlieb, *EU Competition Law Quarterly Report, Belgium* (Q3 July–September 2014) https://www.clearygottlieb.com/-/media/organize-archive/cgsh/files/publication-pdfs/cleary-gottlieb-national-competition-report-q3-2014.pdf.

Comments of The Electricity Consumers Resource Council (ELCON), Fact-Finding Investigation Into Possible Manipulation of Electric and Natural Gas Prices, DOCKET NO. PA02-2-003 3 http://www.elcon.org/Documents/FERCFilings/CAISOgamingcomments.pdf.

CFTC Glossary, http://www.cftc.gov/opa/glossary/opaglossary_o.htm.

Delloite (ND), European Energy Market Reform, 4 https://www2.deloitte.com/content/dam/Deloitte/global/Documents/Energy-and-Resources/gx-er-marketreform-spain.pdf.

Economic Consulting Associates, *European Electricity Forward Markets and Hedging Products – State of Play and Elements for Monitoring* (Final Report September 2015), VIII http://www.acer.europa.eu/en/electricity/market%20monitoring/documents_public/eca%20report%20on%20european%20electricity%20forward%20markets.pdf.

EFET Gas Committee, *Framework Guidelines for Gas Balancing* (June 2010) http://www.efet.org/Files/Documents/Gas%20Market/Gas%20balancing%20market/EFET%20FG%20on%20Gas%20Balancing.pdf.

EnBW, *Response by EnBW on the CESR and ERGEG Advice to the European Commission in the Context of the Third Energy Package* (2008), http://www.ceer.eu/portal/page/portal/EER_HOME/EER_CONSULT/CLOSED%20PUBLIC%20CONSULTATIONS/CROSSSECTORAL/Financial%20Services/Market%20abuse%20framework/RR/EnBW%20Consultation%20on%20Market%20Abuse%20Response.2008.08.22.pdf.

ENTSO-E, 'Transmission Risk Hedging Products' (2012) An ENTSO-E Educational Paper, 8 https://www.entsoe.eu/fileadmin/user_upload/_library/consultations/Network_Code_CACM/20120619_Educational_Paper_on_Risk_Hedging_Instruments_review5.pdf.

Eurelectric, Eurelectric's Concerns on the Negative Impact of Financial Transmission Rights Being Classified as Financial Instruments under MiFID II on the Completion of the Internal Energy Market (Eurelectric letter to the DG FISMA of 19 November 2015) http://www.eurelectric.org/media/247826/20151119_eurelectric_ftr_letter_to_dg_fisma_final-2015-2220-0014-01-e.pdf.

Federal Energy Regulatory Commission, '18 C.F.R. Part 1c' (19 January 2006) Docket No RM06-3-000; Order No 670.

FERC Enforcement Staff Report, 'Findings of a Non-Public Investigation of Potential Market Manipulation by Suppliers in the New York City Capacity Market', Docket No IN08-2-000 & EL07-39-000 (February 2008) https://www.ferc.gov/enforcement/market-manipulation/nyiso-icap.pdf.

FERC Enforcement Staff Report of the Division of Energy Market Oversight, *Energy Primer A Handbook of Energy Market Basics* (July 2015).

FERC, 'Order on rehearing and modifying interim generation market power analysis and mitigation policy' (2004) Docket No ER96-2495-016, et al.

FERC Staff Report, Final Report on Price Manipulation in Western Markets Fact-Finding Investigation of Potential Manipulation of Electric and Natural Gas Prices Docket No PA02-2-000. (March 2003) http://www.ferc.gov/legal/maj-ord-reg/land-docs/PART-I-3-26-03.pdf.

Financial Conduct Authority, Press Release, *UBS fined £160 million for significant failings in relation to LIBOR and EURIBOR* (19 December, 2012) https://www.fca.org.uk/news/press-releases/ubs-fined-%C2%A3160-million-significant-failings-relation-libor-and-euribor.

First Economic Sanctions for REMIT Breaches in Europe, (Lexology 16 February 2016), http://www.lexology.com/library/detail.aspx?g=66b554d0-514c-40b3-b4fb-67374a43b111.

http://www.acer.europa.eu/Electricity/Regional_initiatives/Cross_Regional_Roadmaps/Pages/1.-Market-Coupling.aspx.

http://www.cmegroup.com/trading/energy/natural-gas/natural-gas.html.

http://www.cmegroup.com/rulebook/NYMEX/2/220.pdf.

https://www.esma.europa.eu/press-news/consultations/joint-consultation-cesr-and-ergeg-advice-european-commission-in-context.

http://www.forbes.com/sites/shahgilani/2013/06/28/marc-rich-the-legend-behind-the-legend/#7e544b495feb.

https://www.ferc.gov/market-oversight/mkt-electric/new-england.asp.

http://www.pjm.com/about-pjm/who-we-are/territory-served.aspx.

https://www.platts.com/IM.Platts.Content/ProductsServices/Products/gasmarketreport.pdf.

International Competition Network, *Case Annex to IC Unilateral Conduct Working Group: Report on the Analysis of Refusal to Deal with a Rival under Unilateral Conduct Laws* (Istanbul April 2010).

Investigation of Terms and Conditions of Public Utility Market-Based Rate Authorisations, 105 F.E.R.C. ¶ 61,218 (2003), *reh'g denied*, 107 FERC ¶ 61,175 (2004) at Appendix A (Market Behavior Rules Order).

Javier Ruiz Calzado, et al., 'Energy and restrictive practices: an overview of EU and national case law' (e-Competition Bulletin, N° 70451, December 2014) https://www.lw.com/thoughtLeadership/energy-and-restrictive-practices-eu-case-law.

Jim Polson, *Iberdrola Appealing Fine for Manipulating Market, CEO Says* (Bloomberg December 2015) https://www.bloomberg.com/news/articles/2015-12-16/iberdrola-appealing-fine-for-manipulating-market-ceo-says.

John Ratliff & Roberto Grasso, 'REMIT – EU Legislation on Insider Trading and Market Manipulation in Wholesale Energy Markets Adopted' (2011) WilmerHale https://www.wilmerhale.com/pages/publicationsandnewsdetail.aspx?NewsPubId=87107.

John Ratliff and Roberto Grasso (2012), 'Unilateral conduct in the energy sector: An overview of EU and national case law', E-Competitions 44203, http://www.

oiguskantsler.ee/sites/default/files/IMCE/unilateral_conduct_in_the_energy_sector_-_an_overview_of_eu_and_national_case_law.pdf.

John Ratliff & Roberto Grasso, 'REMIT – Implementing Measures Clarifying Data Reporting Obligations' (2015) WilmerHale https://www.wilmerhale.com/pages/publicationsandnewsdetail.aspx?NewsPubId = 17179876224.

J-M Glachant, 'Understanding the REMIT: Aims and Limits' (GME Annual Conference 11 July 2012) https://www.mercatoelettrico.org/en/MenuBiblioteca/Documenti/20120711RelazioneAnnuale2011Glachant.pdf.

Kenneth M. Morris, *Standard & Poor's Dictionary of Financial Terms* (McGraw-Hill Professional; Rev Ed edition 2007).

Leigh Hancher, 'Energy Markets: A legal Perspective on Market Abuse (REMIT)' (Florence, April 2013), https://www.youtube.com/watch?v = 3tSmdPtTG1k.

Marc Martens & Peter Willis, 'Electrabel decision outlines application of competition rules to withholding capacity and electricity pricing' (Bird&Bird, 29 August, 2014) https://www.twobirds.com/en/news/articles/2014/belgium/electrabel-decision-outlines-application-of-competition-rules-to-withholding.

Mark Jickling, 'The Enron Loophole' (7 July 2008) CRS Report for Congress.

Memorandum of Understanding Between The Federal Energy Regulatory Commission and The Commodity Futures Trading Commission Regarding Information Sharing and Treatment of Propriety Trading and Other Information (2 January 2014).

National Commission for Energy Control and Prices, (NCC), 'Annual Report on Electricity and Natural Gas Markets of the Republic of Lithuania to the European Commission' [2014].

National Grid, 'End-to-end Balancing Guide' (March 2016).

OECD, Directorate for Financial and Enterprise Affairs Competition Committee, 'Annual Report in Competition Policy Developments in Spain 2004' [2015] DAF/COMP(2005)32/06.

Ofgem, Pricing Benchmarks in Gas and Electricity Markets – A Call for Evidence, (6 June 2013) https://www.ofgem.gov.uk/ofgem-publications/40363/pricing-benchmarks-gas-and-electricity-markets.pdf.

Ofgem, Wholesale Energy Markets in 2015, (9 September 2015) 35 https://www.ofgem.gov.uk/sites/default/files/docs/2015/09/wholesale_energy_markets_in_2015_final_0.pdf.

Peter Willis & Simone Cadeddu, 'Italian ancillary services cartel highlights risks of electricity market transparency' (Bird&Bird, 24 July, 2012) https://www.twobirds.com/en/news/articles/2012/italian-ancillary-services-cartel-highlights-risks-of-electricity-market-transparency.

Peter Willis & Hermenegildo Altozano, 'Spanish authority fines Iberdrola €25m in first REMIT market manipulation infringement decision' (Bird&Bird, 4 February, 2014) https://www.twobirds.com/en/news/articles/2016/spain/spanish-authority-fines-iberdrola-25m-in-first-remit-infringement-decision.

Peter Willis, 'Italian competition authority investigates suspected abuses in Italian electricity balancing markets' (Bird&Bird, 18 October 2016) https://www.twobirds.com/en/news/articles/2016/italy/italian-competition-authority-investigates-suspected-abuses-in-italian-electricity-balancing-markets.

Philip Lowe, 'Consumer Welfare and Efficiency – New Guiding Principles of Competition Policy?' (13th International Conference on Competition and 14th European Competition Day, Munich, March 2007) http://ec.europa.eu/competition/speeches/text/sp2007_02_en.pdf.

Pittsburgh G20 Summit, September 2009, Leaders' Statement, Strengthening the International Financial Regulatory System, https://www.oecd.org/g20/summits/pittsburgh/G20-Pittsburgh-Leaders-Declaration.pdf.

S. Stoft, et al., 'Primer on Electricity Futures and Other Derivatives' (Environmental Energy Technologies Division, University of California at Berkeley 1998).

Section UUU1 - Contract Rules: ICE Futures UK Natural Gas Daily Financial Futures Contract 2, https://www.theice.com/publicdocs/circulars/14101_attach_2.pdf.

Shaun D. Ledgerwood, 'Screens for the Detection of Manipulative Intent', (2010) p. 41 *available at* http://papers.ssrn.com/sol3/papers.cfm?abstract_id = 1728473 accessed at 10 May 2016.

Shaun D. Ledgerwood, ' Market Manipulation Without Market Power' (*Law360*, 23 June 2011) http://www.law360.com/articles/252314/market-manipulation-without-market-power accessed 10 May 2016.

Stibbe, 'Belgian Competition Authority fined Electrabel EUR 2 million for abuse of a dominant position' (Lexology, 1 September 2014, Belgium) http://www.lexology.com/library/detail.aspx?g = 177531a1-f5f7-40fc-bcad-7e9930d23933.

Sonja van Renssen, 'Capacity Mechanisms: DG Competition and DG Energy Clash over Future of EU Energy Market' (energypost, 11 May 2016) http://energypost.eu/capacity-mechanisms-dg-competition-dg-energy-clash-future-eu-energy-market/.

Technical Committee of the International Organisation of Securities Commissions (IOSCO), 'Investigating and Prosecuting Market Manipulation' (May 2000).

The California Independent System Operator's (ISO) and California Power Exchange's (PX) Market Monitoring and Information Protocol (MMIP). https://www.sec.gov/Archives/edgar/data/894253/000095013402007966/d97931a1exv99w435.txt.

US Commodity Futures Trading Commission, 'CFTC Orders Barclays to pay $200 Million Penalty for Attempted Manipulation of and False Reporting concerning LIBOR and Euribor Benchmark Interest Rates' (27 June 2012) pr6239-12 http://www.cftc.gov/PressRoom/PressReleases/pr6289-12.

Table of Cases

Case Law from the EU

Commission Decisions

Swedish Interconnectors (Case COMP/39.351) Commission Decision [2010] OJ C239/4, 18, 230
Sydkraft/Graninge (Case COMP/M.3268) Commission Decision 2003/297/EC OJ C297/22, 18, 23, 60, 199
Telekomunikacja Polska (Case COMP/39.525) Commission Decision [2011] OJ C327/7, 66, 67, 236, 237
Wanadoo Espana/Telefonica (COMP/38.784) Commission Decision of 4 July 2007, 199, 227
Yen Interest Rate Derivatives (Case AT. 39861) Commission Decision of 4 December 2013, 225

The CJEU and GC Decisions

Case 120/78 *Rewe-Zentral AG v. Bundesmonopolverwaltung fur Branntwein* (Casis de Dijon) [1979] ECR 649, 44
Case 14/68 *Walt Wilhelm and Others v. Bundeskartellamt* [1969] ECR 1, 67
Case 40/70 *Sirena S.R.L. v. Eda S.R.L. and others* [1979] ECR-03169 236, 195
Case 6/64 *Costa v. ENEL* [1964] ECR 585, 59, 67
Case 85/76 *Hoffmann-La Roche & Co AG v. EC Commission* [1979] ECR 461, 180
Case C-204/00 P *Aalborg Portland A/S et al. v. Commission* [2004] ECR I-123, 67, 236
Case C-209/07 *Competition Authority v. Beef Industry Development Society Ltd* [2008] ECR I-8637 643, 194, 195
Case C-209/10 *Post Denmark A/S v. Konkurrenceradet*, [2012] ECR I-000, 242
Case C-250/92, *Gottrup Klim v. KLG* [1994] ECR I-5641, 199
Case C-26/75 *General Motors Continental NV v. Commission of the European Communities*, [1975] ECR I-01367 150, 195
Case C-27/76 *United Brands Company and United Brands Continentaal BV v. Commission of the European Communities* [1978] ECR-I00207 22, 195
Case C-280/08 P *Deutsche Telekom AG v. Commission* (2010) ECR I-9555, 66
Case C-309/99, *Wouters v. Algemene Raad van de Nederlandse Orde van Advocaten* [2002] ECR I-1577, 236
Case C-375/09, *Prezes Urzedu Ochrony Konkurencji i Konsumentow v. Tele2 Polska sp. Z o.o., now Netia SA* [2011] ECR I-3055, 61
Case C-45/08 *Spector Photo Group NV, Chris Van Raemdonck v. Commissie voor het Bank-, Financie- en Assurantiewezen (CBFA)* [2009], ECR I-12073, 31
Case C-49/92 P - *Commission v. Anic Partecipazioni* [1999] ECR I-4125, 195
Case C-62/86 *AKZO Chemie BV v. Commission of the European Communities* [1991] ECR I-03359, 97
Case C-95/04 *British Airways plc v. Commission* Case [2006] ECR I-2331, 199
Case T-203/01 *Michelin v. Commission* (Michelin II) [2003] ECR II-4071, 239, 180
Case T-219/99 *British Airways plc v. Commission* [2003] ECR II-5917, 293, 180
Case T-271/03, *Deutsche Telekom v. Commission* [2008] ECR II-477, 227
Case T-336/07 *Telefonica SA and Telefonica de Espana v. European Commission* [2012], 199, 227

Cases from National Jurisdictions

Case Law from the US

Table of Legislation

Primary Resources

EU Primary Legislation

Charter of Fundamental Rights of the European Union [2000] OJ C364/1, 67
Commission Implementing Regulation (EU) No 1348/2014 of 17 December 2014 on data reporting implementing Article 8(2) and Article 8(6) of Regulation (EU) No 1227/2011 of the European Parliament and of the Council on wholesale energy market integrity and transparency, OJ L363/121, 28, 52, 53, 244
Commission Regulation (EU) 2015/1222 of 24 July 2015 establishing a guideline on capacity allocation and congestion management [2015] OJ L197/24, 3, 26
Commission Regulation (EU) 2015/703 of 30 April 2015 establishing a network code on interoperability and data exchange rules [2015] OJ L113/13, 3
Commission Regulation (EU) 2016/631 of 14 April 2016 establishing a network code on requirements for grid connection of generators [2016] OJ L112/1, 3
Commission Regulation (EU) No 312/2014 of 26 March 2014 establishing a Network Code on Gas Balancing of Transmission Networks [2014] OJ L91/15, 3, 4
Commission Regulation (EU) No 984/2013 of 14 October 2013 establishing a Network Code on Capacity Allocation Mechanisms in Gas Transmission Systems and supplementing Regulation (EC) No 715/2009 of the European Parliament and of the Council [2013] OJ L273/5, 3
Consolidated Version of the Treaty on the Functioning of the European Union, Articles 107, 108, and 109, [2012] OJ C326/47, 17
Convention for the Protection of Human Rights and Fundamental Freedoms (the European Human Rights Convention) (Rome, 4 November 1950), Protocol No 7, 67
Council Directive 1990/377/EEC of 29 June 1990 concerning a Community procedure to improve the transparency of gas and electricity prices charged to industrial end-users, OJ L185, 17.7.1990, 1, 59
Council Directive 1990/547/EEC of 29 October 1990 on the transit of electricity through transmission grids, OJ L313, 13.11.1990, 59
Council Directive 1991/296/EEC of 31 May 1991 on the transit of natural gas through grids OJ L147, 12.6.1991, 59

EU Instruments

European Commission, Press Release, 'Antitrust: Commission fines banks € 1.49 billion for participating in cartels in the interest rate derivatives industry' (Brussels, 4 December 2013) http://europa.eu/rapid/press-release_IP-13-1208_en.htm, 225

US Legislation

Other Primary Resources

Index

E

F

L

M

N

S

T

U

V

W

Z

ENERGY AND ENVIRONMENTAL LAW & POLICY SERIES

1. Stephen J. Turner, *A Substantive Environmental Right: An Examination of the Legal Obligations of Decision-makers towards the Environment*, 2009 (ISBN 978-90-411-2815-7).
2. Helle Tegner Anker, Birgitte Egelund Olsen & Anita Rønne (eds), *Legal Systems and Wind Energy: A Comparative Perspective*, 2009 (ISBN 978-90-411-2831-7).
3. David Langlet, *Prior Informed Consent and Hazardous Trade: Regulating Trade in Hazardous Goods at the Intersection of Sovereignty, Free Trade and Environmental Protection*, 2009 (ISBN 978-90-411-2821-8).
4. Louis J. Kotzé and Alexander R. Paterson (eds), *The Role of the Judiciary in Environmental Governance: Comparative Perspectives*, 2009 (ISBN 978-90-411-2708-2).
5. Tuula Honkonen, *The Common but Differentiated Responsibility Principle in Multilateral Environmental Agreement's: Regulatory and Policy Aspects*, 2009 (ISBN 978-90-411-3153-9).
6. Barbara Pozzo (ed.), *The Implementation of the Seveso Directives in an Enlarged Europe: A Look into the Past and a challenge for the Future*, 2009 (ISBN 978-90-411-2854-6).
7. Henrik M. Inadomi, *Independent Power Projects in Developing Countries: Legal Investment Protection and Consequences for Development*, 2010 (ISBN 978-90-411-3178-2).
8. Nahid Islam, *The Law of Non-Navigational Uses of International Watercourses: Options for Regional Regime-Building in Asia*, 2010 (ISBN 978-90-411-3196-6).
9. Yasuhiro Shigeta, *International Judicial Control of Environmental Protection: Standard Setting, Compliance Control and the Development of International Environmental Law by the International Judiciary*, 2010 (ISBN 978-90-411-3151-5).
10. Katleen Janssen, *The Availability of Spatial and Environmental Data in the European Union: At the Crossroads between Public and Economic Interests*, 2010 (ISBN 978-90-411-3287-1).
11. Henrik Bjørnebye, *Investing in EU Energy Security: Exploring the Regulatory Approach to Tomorrow's Electricity Production*, 2010 (ISBN 978-90-411-3118-8).
12. Véronique Bruggeman, *Compensating catastrophe victims: A Comparative Law and Economics Approach*, 2010 (ISBN 978-90-411-3263-5).
13. Michael G. Faure, Han Lixin & Shan Hongjun, *Maritime Pollution Liability and Policy: China, Europe and the US*, 2010 (ISBN 978-90-411-2869-0).

14. Anton Ming-Zhi Gao, *Regulating Gas Liberalization: A Comparative Study on Unbundling and Open Access Regimes in the US, Europe, Japan, South Korea and Taiwan*, 2010 (ISBN 978-90-411-3347-2).
15. Mustafa Erkan, *International Energy Investment Law: Stability through Contractual Clauses*, 2011 (ISBN 978-90-411-3411-0).
16. Levente Borzsa´k, *The Impact of Environmental Concerns on the Public Enforcement Mechanism under EU law: Environmental protection in the 25th hour*, 2011 (ISBN 978-90-411-3408-0).
17. Tarcísio Hardman Reis, *Compensation for Environmental Damages under International Law: The Role of the International Judge*, 2011 (ISBN 978-90-411-3437-0).
18. Kim Talus, *Vertical Natural Gas Transportation Capacity, Upstream Commodity Contracts and EU Competition Law*, 2011 (ISBN 978-90-411-3407-3).
19. WangHui, *Civil Liability for Marine Oil Pollution Damage: A Comparative and Economic Study of the International, US and Chinese Compensation Regime*, 2011 (ISBN 978-90-411-3672-5).
20. Chowdhury Ishrak Ahmed Siddiky, *Cross-Border Pipeline Arrangements: What Would a Single Regulatory Framework Look Like?*, 2012 (ISBN 978-90-411-3844-6).
21. Rozeta Karova, *Liberalization of Electricity Markets and Public Service Obligations in the Energy Community*, 2012 (ISBN 978-90-411-3849-1).
22. Sandra Cassotta, *Environmental Damage and Liability Problems in a Multilevel Context: The Case of the Environmental Liability Directive*, 2012 (ISBN 978-90-411-3830-9).
23. Mark Wilde, *Civil Liability for Environmental Damage: Comparative Analysis of Law and Policy in Europe and US*, 2013 (ISBN 978-90-411-3233-8).
24. Bernard Taverne, *Petroleum, Industry and Governments: A Study of the Involvement of Industry and Governments in Exploring for and Producing Petroleum*, 2013 (ISBN 978-90-411-4563-5).
25. Anton Ming-Zhi Gao & Chien Te Fan (eds), *Legal Issues of Renewable Energy in the Asia Region: Recent Developments in a Post-Fukushima and Post-Kyoto Protocol Era*, 2014 (ISBN 978-90-411-4856-8).
26. Sabina Manea, *The Instrumentalization of Property: Legal Interests in the EU Emissions Trading System*, 2014 (ISBN 978-90-411-5420-0).
27. Joseph A. Tolorunse, *Protection of Property Rights in Discovered Petroleum Reservoirs*, 2014 (ISBN 978-90-411-5604-4).
28. Katelijn Van Hende, *Offshore Wind in the European Union: Towards Integrated Management of Our Marine Waters*, 2015 (ISBN 978-90-411-5613-6).
29. Ken'ichi Matsumoto & Anton Ming-Zhi Gao (eds), *Economic Instruments to Combat Climate Change in Asian Countries*, 2015 (ISBN 978-90-411-5408-8).

30. Eduardo Pereira (ed.), *Joint Operating Agreements: Challenges and Concerns from Civil Law Jurisdictions*, 2015 (ISBN 978-90-411-5934-2).
31. Ying Shen, *China's Way to Carbon Emissions Reduction: The Choice of Regulatory Instruments and Its Legal Challenges*, 2015 (ISBN 978-90-411-6049-2).
32. Roy Andrew Partain, *Environmental Hazards from Offshore Methane Hydrate Operations: Civil Liability and Regulations for Efficient Governance*, 2017 (ISBN 978-90-411-8730-7).
33. Anton Ming-Zhi Gao & Chien-Te Fan (eds), *The Development of a Comprehensive Legal Framework for the Promotion of Offshore Wind Power: The Lessons from Europe and Pacific Asia*, 2017 (ISBN 978-90-411-8397-2).
34. Tade Oyewunmi, *Regulating Gas Supply to Power Markets: Transnational Approaches to Competitiveness and Security of Supply*, 2018 (ISBN 978-90-411-9869-3).
35. Huseyin Cagri Corlu, *Application of Anti-manipulation Law to EU Wholesale Energy Markets and Its Interplay with EU Competition Law*, 2018 (ISBN 978-90-411-9603-3).

www.ingramcontent.com/pod-product-compliance
Ingram Content Group UK Ltd.
Pitfield, Milton Keynes, MK11 3LW, UK
UKHW020242290926
15470UKWH00002B/693

9 789041 196033